The Talibanization of Southeast Asia

THE TALIBANIZATION OF SOUTHEAST ASIA

Losing the War on Terror to Islamist Extremists

Bilveer Singh

PRAEGER SECURITY INTERNATIONAL

Westport, Connecticut · London

Library of Congress Cataloging-in-Publication Data

Singh, Bilveer, 1956–
    The Talibanization of Southeast Asia : losing the war on terror to Islamist extremists / Bilveer Singh.
        p. cm.
    Includes bibliographical references and index.
    ISBN: 978–0–275–99995–7 (alk. paper)
1. Terrorism—Southeast Asia. 2. Terrorism—Religious aspects—Islam. 3. Jemaah Islamiyah
(Organization) 4. Political violence—Southeast Asia. I. Title.
HV6433.S644S56 2007
363.3250959–dc22   2007026124

British Library Cataloguing in Publication Data is available.

Library of Congress Catalog Card Number: 2007026124
ISBN: 978–0–275–99995–7

First published in 2007

Praeger Security International, 88 Post Road West, Westport, CT 06881
An imprint of Greenwood Publishing Group, Inc.
www.praeger.com

Printed in the United States of America

The paper used in this book complies with the
Permanent Paper Standard issued by the National
Information Standards Organization (Z39.48–1984).

10 9 8 7 6 5 4 3 2 1

To Gurdial Kaur,
my beloved wife who has
been the pillar of strength
and inspiration in my life.

Contents

Preface

Southeast Asia had been afflicted with the danger of terrorism, long before the United States and the Western world became aware of the threat in the wake of September 11, 2001 (hereafter referred to as the 9/11 Incident), attacks on New York and Washington. Various enduring factors such as historical developments, nature of geography, ethnic-religious makeup, accessibility to external forces, the role of extraneous actors in dominating the politics and economy of the region, and the nature of regimes in the region have entrenched terrorism, particularly associated with religious extremism in the region. This was evident in Indonesia, Thailand, Myanmar, and the Philippines since the end of the Second World War in 1945.

The terrorist challenge was essentially national in character, with groups attempting to either secede from the central government to form a new state or to force the central government to adopt policies that would support the *raison d'être* of these extremist groups. Essentially, this involved the establishment of a political system that was more Islamic in character, either nationally or within a specific territory of a national state. This changed fundamentally with the emergence of new terrorist threats in the region in the post–Cold War period. This study analyzes the increasing *Talibanization* of Southeast Asia, a relatively new phenomenon. It involves the adoption of Islamist doctrines, ideologies, and values that are largely militant in character, which for some groups includes the adoption of violence to achieve their goals. The emergence of organizations that are prepared to adopt terrorism as a means to achieve their goals is particularly pertinent, especially since it is rationalized in the name of Islam. While there were groups that adhered to these principles and mode of operations in the past, what is new is the expanse of the network, their extranational goals and linkages. However, religious-oriented terrorism is not a stand-alone phenomenon. It is largely a function of the introduction and adoption of radical and extremist religious ideologies, in this case, the radicalization of Islam in Southeast Asia, hitherto one of the few oases of moderate Islam in the world. Understanding this process, referred to in this study as *Talibanization,* is the key to unraveling the increased radicalization in Southeast Asia.

What has made the challenge of this new terrorism distinct, especially with regard to the emergence of the *Al-Jama'ah Al-Islamiyyah* (AJAI), is that while it aims to establish an Islamic state, its goals, organizational structures, and operations are far more wide-ranging. Unlike the terrorism and challenges of past religious extremists in the region, the AJAI represents the birth of the first regional terrorist organization in Southeast Asia. It is a transnational terrorist organization along the lines of the *Al Qaeda,* even though on a much smaller scale in terms of objectives and goals. It aims to establish a regional Islamic state (*Dauliah Islamiyah Nusantara,* or DIN) covering most of southern Southeast Asia that would ultimately form a new Islamic epicenter in the Asia-Pacific region. Additionally, what has made the AJAI a potent force has been its ability to synergize with various existing religious extremist groups in the region and beyond, including the *Al Qaeda* and other like-minded groups based in Afghanistan and Pakistan. This has succeeded in posing one of the most serious security challenges to the region since the end of the Cold War.

This study is an attempt to understand and unravel the growing nexus between extremist Islamists and terrorism as evident in the operation of various terrorist groups in Southeast Asia, particularly AJAI. The term "Islamist" is deliberately chosen to distinguish it from the common term "Islamic." In this study, "Islamic" refers to what is written in the *Koran* and *Hadith,* whereas "Islamist" is the use of "Islam" for specific purposes. Many political actors have often tried to justify their actions on grounds that these are "Islamic," when indeed they are not. To that extent, "Islamists" usually manipulate and distort what is "Islamic" to achieve political goals. While "radical piety" is fast becoming a fact of life in the region, what is most dangerous is its abuse and manipulation to achieve the political goals of Islamists. The rise of the Islamist agenda is a key cause of extremism and terrorism. This study examines the problems and challenges facing Islam, the rise of Islamic radicalism, and the emergence of various Islamist extremist groups that are threatening secular regimes in Southeast Asia.

The emergence of Islamist radicalism will mainly focus on the AJAI, especially in Indonesia. What the AJAI is, how it emerged, what threat it poses, and the measures adopted to manage it will be examined. Whether there is a future for Islamist extremism and how Southeast Asian states have responded to the phenomenon will also be studied. A key theme throughout this study is the resilience of Islamist extremism and the apparent inability of governments in the region to annihilate the menace, especially at its roots. This study argues that due to inappropriate measures and approaches, and a lack of understanding of the key challenge at hand, governments in the region are "barking up the wrong tree," as they have largely missed the nexus between religion and terrorism, leading in reality to the rapid *Talibanization* of Southeast Asia. Despite various counterterrorism measures since 2001, the region has failed to prevent terrorist organizations such as the AJAI and its affiliates from regenerating and mounting attacks. If anything, the threat of Islamist extremism and terrorism has worsened even though the region has launched a "war on terror" since 2001.

The rising *Talibanization* of Southeast Asia is a function of the spread of radical Islam into the region. This has spread from the epicenter of Islamic radicalism, namely, the Middle East. While Southeast Asian Muslims had long-standing historical ties with the Middle East, the spread of radical Islam to the region is a recent phenomenon, especially since the 1980s. Southeast Asia had in the past experienced spurts of radicalism, such as the *Padri* movement in Sumatra in the nineteenth century and Moro challenge in southern Philippines. However, due to various factors, the intensity of radicalization has heightened tremendously. While radicalism has colored Middle East Islamic politics since the 1960s and 1970s, and aims to overthrow the outwardly secular regimes, in Southeast Asia, the initial goals have been somewhat different, aimed largely at the adoption of the *Sharia*. Many groups and agencies have facilitated the spread of radical Islam into Southeast Asia. What is pertinent in this regard is the growing propensity to adopt radical Islamist ideology, almost akin to Liberation Theology, and this largely accounts for Islamist activism in the region. In terms of Islamic outlook, what was essentially regarded as a "moderate" region, Southeast Asian Islam increasingly has shifted to that of an Arabized and radical strain. This has made it increasingly amenable for militancy and extremism, accounting primarily for the march of *Talibanization* in Southeast Asia.

While Southeast Asian counterterrorism measures have primarily focused on a policy of "search and destroy," in reality, and for the long term, this is not where the real danger lies. Just as Saddam Hussein and Osama bin Laden are no longer critical for the rise and sustenance of Iraqi insurgency and the *Al Qaeda,* respectively, likewise, leaders such as Abdullah Sungkar, Abu Bakar Ba'syir, and Hambali are not vital for the continuation of Islamist extremism in Southeast Asia. The rise of Islamist extremism and *Jihadism* lies in the proliferation of extremist Islamist ideology that has sunk deep roots in Southeast Asia. Dismantling the AJAI or other terrorist groups will only make a small dent in the struggle. This is because the process of radicalization, due to both internal and external imperatives, has spread widely and is intensifying through the Internet. What is worrisome is not only its ability to spread rapidly but even more dangerous is the anonymous manner this is being undertaken. *Jihadists* are operating diffusively in small and localized cells, even though the broad goals remain the same—to spread *Sharia,* establish an Islamic state, and bring down secular regimes—and are largely anti-Western, especially anti–United States. As most governments do not have the credibility or expertise to diminish the threat posed by Islamist extremism, *Wahhabism* and *Salafism,* Southeast Asia is in danger of being *Talibanized* in the near future.

Acknowledgments

I wish to express my heartfelt thanks to the many people who assisted me in completing this study. The research has been ongoing since 2002 and the final stage of the writing was undertaken during my sabbatical at the Department of Political Science, School of Behavioral Science, Leiden University. I wish to thank the Department of Political Science, Faculty of Arts and Social Sciences and the National University of Singapore for granting me leave and financial support for the entirety of my stay in Leiden from January to June 2006.

I am also greatly indebted to many close friends who have helped me in one way or another with regard to the study. In Singapore, the following deserve special mention: Dr. Rohan Kumar Gunaratna, Dr. Kumar Ramakrishna, Associate Professor Farid Alatas, Mr. Haniff Hassan and Mr. Mohamed Bin Ali. In Thailand, the following friends were extremely helpful: Dr. Panitan Wattanayagorn, Professor Perayot Rahimulla, Ms. Chidchanok Rahimulla, Dr. Ismail Lutfie, and General (Rtd.) Kitti Ratanachaya. In Malaysia, Dr. Kamarulzaman Askandar and Dr. Kamarulnizam Abdullah proved particularly helpful. In Indonesia, I received help and assistance from the following: Dr. Sidney Jones, Sri Yunanto, Dr. Sukardi Rinakit, Rear Admiral (Rtd.) R. M. Sunardi, Major-General Bambang Sutedjo, Colonel Petrus Reinhard Golose, Major-General Made Pastika, Lieutenant-General (Rtd.) Agus Widjoyo, Mr. Lambang Trijono, Mr. Muhammad Najib Azca, Mr. Thaha Moh. Alhamid, Professor Munir Mulkhan, Mr. Abdi Supriyanto, Uztad Irfan Suryahardi Awwas, and Uztad Abu Bakar Ba'asyir. From India, I owe a special debt to Mr. B. Raman for his insights and understanding on *jihadi*-oriented terrorism.

Throughout the research of the book, I was assisted by a number of research assistants. I would like to thank Mr. Andy Mickey, Jasminder Singh, Mr. Mohamad

Rizuan Bin Pathie, Ms. Sharifa Aminah, and Mr. Terenjit Singh. All of them worked meticulously in collecting and collating materials from the Central Library of National University of Singapore as well as providing inputs to the various chapters. I am most grateful to them for the patience and assisted that was provided that ensured the completion of this study.

I would also like to thank Praeger Security International, a member of the Greenwood Publishing Group, for publishing the book. In particular, Ms. Hilary Claggett, the senior editor, deserves special mention, for the highly professional manner she went about in advising on how the manuscript should be submitted for publication.

Finally, I am most grateful for all the blessings and support I received from my family members. They remained my primary source of strength and inspiration. The love, affection and understanding of my wife, Gurdial Kaur, and my sons, Jasminder Singh and Prabhinder Singh, sustained me in the travails of this study.

I, however, take full responsibility for the views put forth and for any error that may occur in the book.

Bilveer Singh

Abbreviations

ADJACT	ASEAN Declaration on Joint Action to Counter-Terrorism
AJAI	*Al-Jama'ah Al-Islamiyyah* (The Congregation of Muslims. It also stands for *Jemaah Islamiyyah*.)
AMMTC	Annual Ministerial Meeting on Transnational Crime, ASEAN
ARF	ASEAN Regional Forum
ASEAN	Association of Southeast Asian Nations
ASIO	Australian Security Intelligence Organization
ASNLF	Aceh/Sumatra National Liberation Front
BAKIN	*Badan Koordinasi Intelijen Negara* (State Intelligence Coordinating Agency)
BMIAF	*Bangsa Moro* Islamic Armed Forces
BNPP	*Barisan Nasional Pembebasan Pattani* (National Front for the Liberation of Pattani)
BRN	*Barisan Revolusi Nasional* (National Revolutionary Front)
CIA	Central Intelligence Agency, U.S.
DDII	*Dewan Dakwah Islamiyah Indonesia* Indonesian Council for Islamic Mission
DI	*Darul Islam* House or Abode of Islam

DIN *Daulah Islamiyah Nusantara*
(Archipelagic Islamic State or Southeast Asian Islamic State)

DOM *Daerah Operasi Militer*
(Military Operations Region)

GAM *Gerakan Aceh Merdeka*
(Free Aceh Movement)

GAMPAR *Gabungan Melayu Pattani Raya*
Association of Malays of Greater Pattani

HMI *Himpunan Mahasiswa Islam*
Islamic Students' Association

HTI *Hizbut Tahrir* Indonesia
(Indonesian Party of Liberation)

ISD Internal Security Department, Singapore

KAMMI *Kesatuan Aksi Mahasiswa Muslim Indonesia*
(Muslim Students' Action Union)

KMM *Kumpulan Mujahidin/Militant Malaysia*
(Malaysian Mujahidin/Militant Group)

MASYUMI *Majelis Syuro Muslimin Indonesia*

MILF Moro Islamic Liberation Front

MIM Mindanao Independence Movement

MMI *Majlis Mujahidin Indonesia*
(Indonesian *Mujahidin* Council)

MNLF Moro National Liberation Front

MP–GAM *Majlis Pemerintahan–Gerakan Aceh Merdeka*

NAD *Nanggroë Aceh Darusalam*

NII *Negara Islam Indonesia*
(Indonesian Islamic State)

PARNAS *Partai Revolusi Nasional*
(National Revolutionary Party)

PKS *Partai Keadilan Sejatera*
(Prosperous Justice Party)

PPP Unity Development Party

PSII *Partai Syarikat Islam Indonesia*
Indonesian Islamic Association Party

PULA	Pattani United Liberation Army
PULO	Pattani United Liberation Organization
RO(s)	Restriction Order(s)
SAJAIW	Singapore AJAI *Wakalah*
SAS	Special Air Service Regiment, Australia
SOMTC	Senior Officials Meeting on Transnational Crime, ASEAN
STA	Singapore Technologies Aerospace
TII	*Tentara Islam Indonesia* (Indonesian Islamic Army)
UIFO	Union of Islamic Forces and Organizations
UN	United Nations
U.S.	United States of America

Glossary of Key Islamic Terms

Alim   A learned person in Islam.

Allahu Akbar   The Arabic expression meaning "*Allah* is great."

Al-Masjid al-Haram   The most sacred mosque in Mecca. The *ka'bah* is situated in it.

Al Masjid al-Aqsa   The most sacred mosque in Jerusalem.

Al Qur'an   The holy book of the Islamic faith. It was revealed to Prophet Muhammad from *Allah* through angel Gabriel (*Jibril*) over a period of 23 years. There is only one Quran (*Koranic*) in the world and it is in Arabic language.

Da'awah   Missionary work for the Propagation of Islam; inviting others to Islam.

Duniawi   Worldly, mortal life.

Fai'   War bounty gained without fighting.

Fatwa   Legal opinion with regards to Islamic laws. *Fatwa* varies according to the various schools of jurisprudence.

Hadith   The sayings, deeds, and approvals accurately narrated from the Prophet.

Halal   Permitted in Islam.

Haj   *Haj* is one of the five pillars of Islam. It is the act of pilgrimage to the holy land of Mecca. *Haj* is a duty one must perform during one's lifetime if one has the financial resources for it.

Haram   Forbidden, unlawful, and punishable in Islam.

Imam   The person who leads others in prayers or the Muslim Caliph.

Iman   Trust, faith, and acceptance in *Allah* and the *Quran* (i.e., Islam).

Islam   Arabic word that comes from the root words of *Silm* and *Salam*. It means, among others, peace, obedience, loyalty, allegiance, and submission to the will of *Allah*. The religion of the Muslims.

Jannah   Paradise.

Jihad   Holy fighting in the Cause of *Allah* or any effort to make *Allah's* words (Islam) superior.

Jizyah   Head tax imposed by Islam on all non-Muslims living under the protection of an Islamic government.

Ka'bah   A cubed-shaped structure based in the city of Mecca to which all Muslims turn to in their five daily prayers.

Kafir   One who disbelieves in *Allah,* his messengers, all the angels, the holy book, the day of resurrection, and divine preordainments. Also referred to as infidels or unbelievers.

Khalifah   Caliph, a successor. An Islamic term for the first four rulers after the death of the Prophet.

Khutbah   Religious sermon.

Masjid   Mosque

Mujahid   A Muslim fighter in *Jihad.*

Mu'min   Refers to a Muslim who has deep faith in *Allah* and is a righteous and obedient servant.

Mushrikin   Polytheists, pagans, idolaters, and disbelievers of *Allah,* Islam, and the Prophet.

Muttaqun   Pious and righteous persons who love *Allah,* abide by his commandments, and refrain from misdeeds and sins.

Nabi   Prophet of *Allah.*

Ramadan   The holy month of prescribed fasting for the Muslims. It was also during Ramadan that the *Koranic* revelations began to be conveyed to Prophet Muhammad.

Shaheed   A martyr. Someone who dies in the Cause of *Allah* or Islam.

Shaikh   A title or a nickname for a wise, elderly person or a religious leader in a community.

Ukhwari   Otherworldly, heavenly.

Ulama   The learned, knowledgeable persons in Islam.

Ummah   A religious community.

Chronology: The *Al-Jama'ah Al-Islamiyyah* in Southeast Asia

1940s	Origins of AJAI in *Darul Islam* (DI), an organization that fought for Indonesian independence as well as the creation of an Islamic state.
1949	Embryo of AJAI (DI's *Tentara Islam Indonesia*, TII) was formed along with the proclamation of the *Islamic State of Indonesia* (NII).
1963	Abdullah Sungkar and Abu Bakar Ba'asyir met in Solo (Java, Indonesia).
1965	*Gestapu* (*Gerakan September Tigapuluh* or the 30 September Movement) coup and the subsequent displacement of Sukarno; rise of Suharto and the repression of militant Islamic groups under the New Order regime
1967	Sungkar and Ba'asyir set up a radio station called *Radio Dakwah Islamiyah Surakarta*, the Islamic Proselytization Radio of Surakarta (Solo).
1971	Sungkar and Ba'asyir founded *Pesantren Al-Mu'min*, which moved to the village of Ngruki, outside Solo, in 1973 and became known as *Pondok Ngruki*.
1976	Alleged induction of Sungkar and Ba'asyir into DI.
1978	Arrest of Sungkar and Ba'asyir. Trial in 1982 sentenced the pair to nine years in prison for involvement in *Komando Jihad;* sentences were reduced on appeal to three years and 10 months.
1979	Series of crimes tied to people from *Pondok Ngruki* and referred to as *Terror Warman*.
1980s	Movement in disarray following arrest of leading members for involvement in *Terror Warman* activities; AJAI regrouped into a network called *Usroh*.

1982	Pakistan's Inter-Service Intelligence (ISI) began to recruit radical Muslims from around the world to fight with the *Mujahidin* in the Soviet-Afghan War (1979–1989).
1985	Indonesian Supreme Court summoned Sungkar and Ba'asyir, and the pair fled to Malaysia. *Usroh* movement collapsed. AJAI's name resurfaced in *Usroh* trials; AJAI began to take its current form.
Mid-1990s	Movement was already becoming international; most members in Indonesia had gone underground, fled to Malaysia, joined the international network in Afghanistan, or were arrested.
Jan 1993	AJAI is formally established in Malaysia.
1996	AJAI movement extended to Perth, Melbourne, and Sydney, Australia, as *Mantiqi* (District) 4 and led by Abdul Rahim Ayub.
May 1998	Suharto's resignation ended 32 years of rule; subsequent return of Sungkar, Ba'asyir, and other exiles to Indonesia.
April 1999	Bombing of *Istiqal* Mosque, Jakarta.
November 1999	Death of Sungkar; Ba'asyir took over the leadership (*Amir*) after Sungkar's death; as head of AJAI, Ba'asyir called a meeting at the International Islamic University (*Universiti Islam Antarabangsa*) in Malaysia to set up the International *Mujahidin* Association (*Rabitatul Mujahidin* or RM).
August 2000	*Majlis Mujahidin Indonesia* (MMI) is established and Ba'asyir elected as its first *Amir;* bombing of the residence of the Philippines Ambassador, Jakarta.
December 2000	Christmas Eve Bombings in 11 cities in Indonesia.
June 2001	Arrest of Abu Jibril in Malaysia.
July 2001	Bombings of *Gereja HKBP* and *Gereja Santa Ana,* Jakarta.
August 2001	Arrest of Nik Adli Nik Aziz in Malaysia; Atrium Mall bombing, Jakarta.
September 2001	*Al Qaeda* terrorists hijacked four U.S. airlines, which they used to crash into the Twin Towers of the World Trade Center in New York, the Pentagon in Washington, and an unintended target in Pennsylvania.
November 2001	*2001 ASEAN Declaration on Joint Action to Counter Terrorism;* AJAI's bombing of *Gereja Petra,* North Jakarta.
December 2001	Singapore's Internal Security Department (ISD) arrested Ibrahim Maidin, Faiz Abu Bakar Bafana, and 13 others connected to the AJAI branch in Singapore; another 21 were arrested in August 2002 in Singapore.

January 2002	Arrest of Fathur Rahman Al-Ghozi (alias "Mike") in Philippines. Joint U.S.-Filipino military exercise known as "Operation Balikatan," in southern Philippines.
February 2002	Meeting of key AJAI leaders takes place in Bangkok to plan bombing of soft targets in Southeast Asia.
March 2002	Arrest of Agus Dwikarna in Philippines.
May 2002	Joint Communiqué of the Special ASEAN Ministerial Meeting on Terrorism, Kuala Lumpur. Work Programme to Implement the ASEAN Plan of Action to Combat Transnational Crime, Kuala Lumpur. Indonesia, Malaysia, and the Philippines' trilateral *Agreement on Information Exchange and Establishment of Communication Procedures* sealed in Putrajaya, Malaysia, to combat the spread of terrorism and transnational crime.
July 2002	The U.S. government charges five leaders of the *Abu Sayyaf* for the murder of American missionary Martin Burnham. The five leaders were: Khadafi Abubaker Janjalani, Isnilon Totoni Hapilon, Aldam Tilao, Jainal Antel Sali, and Hamsiraji Marusi Sali.
August 2002	*ASEAN–United States of America Joint Declaration for Cooperation to Combat International Terrorism,* Bandar Seri Begawan, Brunei.
September 2002	Grenade explosion near U.S. Embassy warehouse; Jakarta. Wan Min arrested in Malaysia.
October 2002	Bombings of Sari Club and Paddy's Café, Bali. Bombing of the U.S. consulate in Denpasar, Bali, and the Philippine consulate in Menado, North Sulawesi. Series of bombings in Zamboanga and the southern city of Kidapawan, the Philippines. Inclusion of AJAI into United Nations (UN) List of Terrorists; arrest of Ba'asyir in Indonesia. UN lists AJAI as a terrorist organization.
November 2002	Arrest of Amrozi and Imam Samudra in Indonesia. Suicide bomber in Bali bombings identified as Iqbal; Malaysia's AJAI/ *Kumpulan Militant Malaysia* (KMM) murdered a Christian Member of Parliament (MP), Dr. Joe Fernandez in Malaysia; subsequent arrest of Zulkifi Abdul Hir. *Declaration on Terrorism by the 8th ASEAN Summit,* Phnom Penh, Cambodia.
December 2002	Arrest of Mukhlas in Indonesia. Indonesian police captures PUPJI, key AJAI document.

January 2003   Arrest of Ali Imron in Indonesia.
                  Joint Declaration on Co-operation to Combat Terrorism, 14th ASEAN-EU Ministerial Meeting, Brussels.
                  Indonesian police officially link AJAI with Bali bombing.

February 2003   Arrest of Mas Selamat Kastari in Indonesia
                  Car bomb attack at the Cotabato airport, the Philippines.

March 2003   Bombing of Davao Airport, the Philippines.

April 2003   Arrests of Abu Rusdan and Nasir Abbas in Indonesia; Ba'asyir's trial for treason; Bombing of United Nations building, Jakarta; Bombing of Soeharto-Hatta International Airport, Jakarta; Bombing of Sasa Wharf Terminal, Davao City, the Philippines.

May 2003   Arrest of Arifin Ali in Thailand.
                  Arrests of an Egyptian, Esam Mohamid Khid Ali, and two Thais, Haji Ichiming Abdul Azi and Muhammadyalludin Mading, after Cambodian police raided a mosque north of the capital, Phnom Penh.
                  Amrozi's trial for terrorism.
                  Ba'asyir's trial for treason and terrorism.
                  Grenade explosion in Cubao, Quezon City, the Philippines.

June 2003   Arrest of Idris in Indonesia.
                  Arrests of Maisuri Haji Abdulloh, Muyahi Haji Boloh, and Waemahadi Wae-dao in southern Thailand.
                  Imam Samudra's trial for terrorism.
                  Mas Selamat Kastari testified at Ba'asyir's trial; Videoconferencing testimonies of Faiz Abu Bakar Bafana, Jaafar Mistooki, and Hashim Aba at Ba'asyir's trial.

July 2003   Mas Selamat Kastari sentenced to 18 months jail in Indonesia for immigration violations.
                  Videoconferencing testimonies of Ahmad Sajuli, Agung Diyadi, Ferial Muchlis, and Fariq Hafid at Ba'asyir's trial.
                  Arrests of Ichwanudin, Pranata Yuda (alias "Mustofa"), Suyono and six others in Indonesia; Ichwanudin committed suicide in police custody.
                  Bombing of Indonesia's Parliament compound, Jakarta.
                  Fathur Rahman Al-Ghozi and two Filipino *Abu Sayyaf* members, Abdul Mukim Edris and Merang Abante, escaped from jail in Camp Crame, Manila.

August 2003   Bombing of J.W. Marriott Hotel, Jakarta.
                  Suicide bomber of J.W. Marriott Hotel bombing identified as Asmar.
                  Amrozi sentenced to death after being found guilty for involvement in the Bali bombings by the Denpasar District Court, Bali.
                  Bomb explosion outside Thai courthouse, Thailand.
                  Arrest of Hambali in Thailand.

Five suspected terrorists, including three from Pakistan and two from Myanmar, were arrested for violations of immigration laws in Chiang Mai, Thailand. A sixth man—a Thai national who was also arrested—was reported to have given shelter to the five suspected terrorists.

September 2003   Ba'asyir sentenced to four years' imprisonment for subversion with the aim of overthrowing the government by a Jakarta court. He was, however, found not guilty on terrorism charges due to a lack of evidence to prove that he was the leader of AJAI.
Imam Samudra sentenced to death after being found guilty of involvement in the Bali bombings by the Denpasar District Court, Bali.
Ali Imron sentenced to life imprisonment after being found guilty for involvement in the Bali bombings by the Denpasar District Court, Bali.
Arifin Ali and four others charged in Bangkok for planning to bomb foreign embassies and tourist spots in Thailand.
Fifteen linked to Abu Rusdan, including a Malaysian national, Syamsul Bahri, alias Farhan, and a Universitas Semarang professor, Bambang Tutuko, alias Abu Umar, were captured in separate arrests in Jakarta, Central Java, and Lampung that began in the middle of August 2003. They had plotted to blow up the Indonesian police headquarters.

September 2004   Kuningan bombing outside the Australian High Commission in Indonesia, claiming the lives of 11 people and injuring 185 people. Indonesia and Australian forensic experts said the explosives used were similar to those used on the city's 2003 Marriott Hotel and Bali nightclubs in 2002, hence linking Islamists' AJAI to the attack. AJAI formally claims responsibility for the Kuningan bombing. Thailand claims AJAI behind attacks in its troubled southern provinces.

October 2004   Abu Bakar Ba'asyir is put to trial on charges of leading a terrorists' network which is responsible for a string of suicide bombings. The U.S. Department of State redesignates AJAI as a "foreign terrorist" organization.

November 2004   Indonesia's South Jakarta district court rules that Abu Bakar Ba'asyir's trial must continue after dismissing defense arguments that the case was full of short comings and contradicted laws that prevents suspects from being tried twice for a similar offense.

December 2004   Malaysian Nasir Abbas, a key prosecution witness in Abu Bakar Ba'asyir's trial, testified that Abu Bakar headed the AJAI. Nasir alleges that Abu Bakar Ba'asyir had personally sworn him in the group in the cleric's hometown of Solo.
Thirteen cell phones were seized from 12 AJAI detainees in a detention camp in Malaysia after a fracas (December 8).
Five Muslims—two Thai, one Cambodian, one Malaysian, and one Egyptian—were sentenced to life imprisonment by a Cambodian court for collaborating with Hambali in a plot to bomb American and British

embassies in Cambodia. Hambali was also sentenced to life imprisonment in absentia.

Allan Bulagnatan, an alleged Filipino member of AJAI, was shot by a policeman in an attempt to escape from jail.

January 2005   The Singapore government announced the release of AJAI member Othman Bin Mohammed from detention (first arrested in December 2001); extends the detention of Mohd Aslam bin Ahmad Selani for a further two years (first arrested in January 2003); and detains for two years Mohd Agus bin Ahmad Selani and Anis bin Mohammed Mansor.

A Thai police officer testified against four people suspected to be AJAI members and planning to attack five foreign embassies in Bangkok. The suspects were Maisuri Haji Abdulloh, Muyahid, Dr. Waemahadi Waedao, and Samarn Wae-kaji. The officer said that Arifin bin Ali, an alleged key member of AJAI, revealed during an interrogation in Singapore that he had met the four suspects twice to plan sabotages.

Bangladeshi S. S. Hoque Sindik was arrested in Bangkok for making a fake passport for Hambali, one of the AJAI key leaders.

AJAI member Mohamed Agus bin Ahmad Selani, was rearrested in Singapore under the Internal Security Act after he frequently violated restrictions imposed on him after his release in January 2002.

Indonesian police claimed to have found a copy of AJAI's constitution after a bomb explosion in Kalimantan Island. It consisted of 15 chapters and 34 articles.

Singapore government arrested 48-year-old carpenter Anis Mohamed Mansor for his alleged participation in AJAI activities since the 1990s. He allegedly supported AJAI's aim in creating an Islamic state through violence, traveled to Thailand and Yemen to obtain weapons, and suggested water pipelines and embassies as terrorist targets. He was detained for two years.

Singapore released AJAI member Othman bin Mohamed, more than three years after his arrest. A press statement claimed than he had been cooperative in investigations and also responded positively to counseling.

Syafii Ma'arif, general chairman of *Muhammadiyah,* testified in the South Jakarta District Court that the United States had intervened in the case of Abu Bakar Ba'asyir, an Islamic cleric accused of being linked to AJAI and the 2002 Bali bombings. Syafii revealed that former U.S. ambassador Ralph Boyce had visited him on March 28, 2004, requesting that Ba'asyir not be released before the 2004 general elections.

Fred Burks, a former U.S. State Department interpreter, testified that one month before the 2002 Bali bombings, the United States had asked Indonesia to arrest Abu Bakar Ba'asyir and send him to America. Former Indonesian President Megawati Sukarnoputri turned down the request.

The Philippine military claimed that there were 33 AJAI members on Mindanao Island. They were suspected to be training rebel groups on bombs.

Ali Imron, a convicted Bali bomber, testified in court and denied that Abu Bakar Ba'asyir had any involvement in the 2002 Bali bombings in any way.

Convicted Bali bomber and key witness Mubarok refused to testify in court during the trial of Abu Bakar Ba'asyir. Mubarok's police statement was forced to be read out, stating that Mubarok together with others Bali bombers had asked for permission to "hold an event in Bali," to which he gave an answer, "It is up to all of you since you are the ones who know the situation in the field."

Forty Islamic militants, including two suspected members of the AJAI, were killed in a military air strike on their hideout in Maguindanao, Philippines.

Twenty-three AJAI members were reported to be stranded in Lanao del Sur, southern Philippines, after the Maguindanao air raid, as they have no money to return to Indonesia. They are reported not to be receiving anymore funds from Indonesia.

February 2005   Abu Bakar Ba'asyir testified in court that he did not agree with the 2002 Bali bombings and that religious extremists were wrong to carry out the attack. He also reinforced that he was not involved in the 2002 Bali bombings.

Dr. Waemahadi Wae-dao, accused of planning failed attacks on five foreign embassies in Bangkok, denied in court any involvement with AJAI. He also denied knowing AJAI member Arifin bin Ali.

The Malaysian Federal Court dismissed an appeal for *habeas corpus* by nine suspected AJAI members who were detained under the Internal Security Act three years ago. The appellants were Ahmad Yani Ismail, Abdul Samad Shukri Mohamad, Mat Sah Mohd Satray, Mohd Sha Sarijan, Abdullah Mohamed Noor, Nordin Ahmad, Abdul Murad Sudin, Abdullah Minyak Silam, and Shamsuddin Sulaiman.

Prosecutors demanded that Abu Bakar Ba'asyir be sentenced to eight years' imprisonment for his alleged role in the 2002 Bali bombings.

Munfiatun, wife of AJAI key suspect Noordin Mohammad Top, had her application for temporary release denied. She was detained for protecting her husband and hiding information.

Three bomb blasts shook three Philippine cities—Makati, Davao, and General Santos City—on Valentine's Day, killing 17 people. Although militant group *Abu Sayyaf* claimed responsibility for the attacks, AJAI was also suspected to have some involvement in the coordination and finance of the event.

Abu Bakar Ba'asyir told the court that he was innocent and that U.S. President George W. Bush had framed him for supporting Islam.

The Philippines announced the arrest of two Indonesians, Mohammad Nasir Hamid and Mohammed Usop Karim Faiz, and a Malaysian, Ted

Yolanda, who were all suspected members of AJAI. They had planned to carry out car bomb attacks on U.S. and local targets in the Philippines during Christmas Day, but were interrupted by the arrest. Ted Yolanda was also involved in the 2004 Australian Embassy bombing.

March 2005   Alleged spiritual leader of AJAI, Abu Bakar Ba'asyir, was convicted and sentenced to jail for 30 months for instigating the 2002 Bali bombings. Ba'asyir filed an appeal against his conviction to overturn the 30-month jail sentence.

Indonesia opened the trial of Irun Hidayat, suspected to be involved in the 2004 Australian Embassy bombing.

Rohmat, an alleged AJAI member, was arrested in Maguindanao after being found with a .45 caliber pistol. He was also an alleged bomb specialist involved in the Valentine's Day bombings.

Prosecutors sought five- to 10-year jail sentences for three suspects in the Marriot Hotel bombing—Sunarto, Rahmat Uji Prabowo, and Sabturani.

Indonesia opened trial of Agus Ahmad bin Engkos Kosasih, suspected to be involved in the 2004 Australian Embassy bombing.

Malaysian authorities released a former university lecture, Wan Min Wan Mat, who allegedly gave $30,500 to AJAI members for the Bali bombings, after showing remorse. Although fearing that he might get kidnapped by the AJAI for betraying them, he was still willing to help the Indonesian police.

Detained bomb specialist Rohmat revealed that the southern Philippines has been a AJAI training ground since the 1990s and that 23 Indonesians had just "graduated" from an explosives and combat training.

April 2005   The *Straits Times* reported that AJAI would be carrying out more deadly bomb attacks this year, similar to those in the 2002 Bali bombings. The information was based on an intercepted letter obtained, dated November 26, 2004, and written by Akhmad Mulkhani, a AJAI operative in Sumatra, to Azahari Husin, a bomb specialist.

Khadaffi Janjalani, head of *Abu Sayyaf,* admitted that he was chosen to lead AJAI in Philippines in 2003.

Self-confessed AJAI member Rohmat denied having any involvement in the Valentine's Day bombings. However, he admitted to have trained three other suspects—Gamal Baharan, Abu Khalil Trinidad, and Gappal Bannah, all of whom pleaded guilty.

Sunarto bin Kartadiharja was sentenced to seven years imprisonment for protecting Noordin Mohammad Top, a prime suspect wanted for the Bali and Marriot Hotel bombings.

Singapore released AJAI member Abdul Majid Niaz Mohamed, after detaining him since September 2002. He cooperated with the Internal Security Department and responded well to counseling.

Singapore government arrested a suspected AJAI member, 35-year old Jahpar bin Osman. He had been a AJAI member since mid-1990s and

had gone for training on weapons and bombs in the Philippines.
The Philippine government handed a list of 53 names, 32 of which were
of suspected AJAI members, to the Moro Islamic Liberation Front
(MILF) in a joint attempt to eradicate them.

May 2005   Three unnamed men were arrested in central Sulawesi. Two homemade
guns, 15 bullets, and explosive powder were seized. They were suspected
to be members of AJAI and involved in the Marriot Hotel bombing.
Ismail, alias Muhammad Ikhwan, was sentenced to three years
imprisonment for sheltering Noordin Mohammad Top and Azahari bin
Husin, both prime suspects wanted for the Bali and Marriot Hotel
bombings.
Four more suspects were charged by the Indonesian authorities for the
2004 Australian Embassy bombing.
Indonesian prosecutors asked for a four-year sentence for Munfiatun,
wife of wanted AJAI member Noordin Mohamed Top. She allegedly
withheld information about the whereabouts of her husband.
As ordered by the U.S. government, U.S. banks blocked financial assets
to three suspected AJAI members—Zulkarnaen, Abu Rusdan, and Joko
Pitono.
Neri Anshori, 23, went on trial for allegedly transporting explosives dur-
ing the AJAI-planned 2004 Australian Embassy bombing. Danu
Mohammad Hasan went on trial for allegedly helping to make the
bomb during the AJAI-planned 2004 Australian Embassy bombing.
Abu Bakar Ba'asyir's appeal to overturn his 30-month sentence was
rejected by Indonesia's High court.
Two men, Agus Budi Pranoto and Lutfi Haidaroh, were sentenced to 42
months in jail for sheltering two wanted Malaysian terrorist suspects,
Noordin Mohammad Top and Azahari Husin.
Syaiful Bahri, 29, went on trial for allegedly helping to make the bomb
during the AJAI-planned 2004 Australian Embassy bombing.
Two bombs exploded in a busy marketplace in the town of Tentena,
central Sulawesi, killing 22 people. Police suspected that wanted AJAI-
linked bomb maker Azahari Husin was behind the blast.

June 2005   The four suspects, namely Maisuri Haji Abdulloh, Muyahid, Dr.
Waemahadi Wae-dao and Samarn Wae-kaji, accused of planning to
attack five foreign embassies in Bangkok, were finally set free as there
was insufficient evidence linking them to AJAI.
Abu Bakar Ba'asyir's lawyers sued Indonesian Justice and Human Rights
Minister Hamid Awaluddin and head of Jakarta's Cipinang prison Dedi
Sutard, insisting the release of the Muslim cleric from his 30-month
sentence.
A small bomb exploded outside the house of suspected senior member
of AJAI and Indonesian cleric Abu Jibril. No one was hurt.
Abu Bakar Ba'asyir appealed to Indonesia's Supreme Court to overturn

his conviction and 30-month jail term for involvement in the 2002 Bali bombings.

Munfiatun was sentenced to 3 years in jail for concealing information on the whereabouts of her fugitive husband, Noordin Mohammad Top, the brains behind the AJAI-planned Bali and Australian Embassy attacks.

Abu Bakar Ba'asyir withdrew his lawsuit against Indonesian Justice and Human Rights Minister Hamid Awaluddin and head of Jakarta's Cipinang prison Dedi Sutard.

Philippines National Security Adviser Norberto Gonzales received an intelligence report that 10 AJAI suicide bombers from Indonesia managed to enter Philippines, including its leader, Dulmatin. They are suspected to be collaborating with Philippine terror group, *Abu Sayyaf.*

Abu Bakar Ba'asyir appealed to Indonesia's Supreme Court in a second bid to overturn his conviction and 30-month jail term for involvement in the 2002 Bali bombings.

Philippines military mounted a hunt for 18 suspected top AJAI members seeking refuge in Mindanao, Philippines. Among them are Dulmatin, Umar Patek, Usman, Ahmad al-Ghozi, Marwan and brothers Abdul Rahman Ayob and Abdul Rahim Ayob.

Seventeen suspects in planning terrorist attacks were arrested in the Central Java towns of Solo and Wonogiri. Some of them were involved in the AJAI-planned 2004 Australian Embassy bombing in Jakarta or in the hiding of two most-wanted AJAI terrorists Azhari Husin and Noordin Mohammad Top.

Philippine police arrested three suspected Filipino AJAI members on the southern island of Mindanao for their involvement in the 2004 bombing of a marketplace in General Santos City in southern Philippines. The suspects were identified as Ustadz Norodin Mangelen, Pedro Guiamat and Ali Salipada.

Al Qaeda's number three man, Abu Faraj al-Libbi, was claimed to have revealed during interrogation, AJAI's plans to carry out bomb attacks targeting especially American, British, and Australian embassies, as well as hotels in Jakarta, Manila, and Mindanao, with the help of local militant groups to destabilize the region.

July 2005   Indonesia police arrested at least 24 people allegedly associated with AJAI, as well as for their connection to the 2002 Bali bombings and the 2003 Marriot Hotel blast, both of which are linked to AJAI.

Indonesia officially announced the names of 11 suspects who were involved in the AJAI-planned 2004 Australian Embassy bombing in Jakarta.

A man with the initial "SS," alias MD, AI, AM, and JP, was arrested in Jakarta for allegedly hiding two most-wanted AJAI terrorists Azhari Husin and Noordin Mohammad Top. He was also charged for illegal possession of weapons, ammunition and explosive material.

Irun Hidayat was sentenced to 3 years in jail by the South Jakarta

District Court for being involved in the AJAI-planned 2004 Australian Embassy bombing in Jakarta.

Agus Ahmad, was sentenced to four years in jail by the South Jakarta District Court for being involved in the AJAI-planned 2004 Australian Embassy bombing in Jakarta.

London suicide bombings take place on one double-decker bus and three London Underground trains, killing 55 people and injuring over 700.

August 2005	Abu Bakar Ba'asyir's appeal to overturn his 30-month sentence was rejected by Indonesia's Supreme Court.

Two bombs exploded in Zamboanga City, southern Philippines, destroying a passenger vehicle and a fast-food restaurant. The blast injured 26 people. Authorities suspected that AJAI, working with *Abu Sayyaf,* could be behind the attacks.

The Philippines announced that they had found the remains of senior AJAI member Umar Patek, one of the suspects for the 2002 Bali bombings, in Mindanao island together with an *Abu Sayyaf* militant.

Indonesian prosecutors demanded the death sentenced be placed upon Iwan Darmawan for helping AJAI to plan the 2004 Australian Embassy bombing in Jakarta.

Four suspects in connection with the two bombings at Zamboanga City were detained for questioning.

Abu Bakar Ba'asyir was given a sentence reduction by 4 months in celebration of Indonesia's 60th Independence Day. Eighteen others who were involved in the 2002 Bali bombings also had their sentences reduced by between one and seven months.

French investigating magistrate Jean-Louis Bruguière singles out Singapore along with Tokyo and Sydney as potential terrorism targets of the *Al-Qaeda.*

October 2005 The second Bali bombing occurs, with three suicide bombers exploding devices in areas frequented by tourists. A series of explosions kills at least 23 in resort areas of Jimbaran Beach and Kuta in Bali, Indonesia. However, unlike the first bombings, the casualties are minimal.

The U.S. government offers a reward of US$10 million and US$1 million for the capture of Dulmatin and Umar Patek, respectively. Surprisingly, Umar Patek, who is senior to Dulmatin, is given a smaller reward compared to Dulmatin.

November 2005 Singapore hosts the Regional Special Forces Counter-Terrorism Conference.

May 2006 Malaysia arrests 12 Islamist militants in Sabah, belonging to *Darul Islam,* 10 Indonesians and 2 Malaysians, who were planning terrorist attacks.

June 2006	Ba'asyir is released from prison.
August 2006	*Al Qaeda*'s Al Zawahiri appears on a recorded video, claiming that the AJAI and *Al Qaeda* had joined forces and that the two groups will form "one line" to fight its "enemies." Australia re-lists AJAI as a terrorist organization according to its laws.
September 2006	Singapore releases two AJAI detainees, Sarid Bin Ismail and Munain Bin Turron.
October 2006	It was revealed that Australia's telecommunications corporation Telstra and the Defense Signals Directorate helped to track the Bali bombers, especially Imam Samudra and Ali Gufron. A survey by an Indonesian pollster, *Lembaga Survei Indonesia* found that 10 percent of Indonesians supported *Jihad* and AJAI's suicide bombing in Bali. Malaysia releases 17 KMM and AJAI detainees including Nik Adli Nik Aziz, the alleged KMM leader, who is also the son of the PAS leader.
December 2006	The Indonesian Supreme Court acquitted Abu Bakar Ba'asyir of all charges linking him to the 2002 Bali bombing that also sent him to more than two years jail. The court also ordered that the authorities rehabilitate the cleric's reputation. The firebrand cleric also announced that he would be suing the Indonesian police for wrongfully building a case against him.
January 2007	Two high-ranking AJAI leaders, Ustad Riansyah and are killed in police raids in Poso, Sulawesi. Abu Bakar Ba'asyir called for a *Jihad* against the Police for their operations in Poso. Indonesian police arrest two AJAI militants, Abu Sayap and Subur Sugiarto, who were reportedly close aides of Nordin Top. A leading *Abu Sayyaf* leader, Jainal Antel Sali, aka Abu Sulaiman, is killed on the island of Jolo, Philippines, in a gun battle with the Philippines military. In the same clash, a leading AJAI militant, Dulmatin, is reported to have been injured. The Philippines Government confirms the death of Khadafi Janajlani. He was killed in a shootout with the Philippines military on September 4, 2006, and buried in a makeshift grave. The body was recovered in December 2006, and following DNA tests, his death was confirmed, leaving the *Abu Sayyaf* in disarray, with two of Khadafi's deputies, Radullah Sahiron and Isnilon Hapilon, fighting for its leadership.
February 2007	Basri and Adrin, two leading militants operating in Poso with links to the AJAI are arrested. Indonesia's top counterterrorism official, Major-General Ansyaad Mbai, maintained that Abu Bakar Ba'asyir remains the spiritual mentor to the AJAI militants operating in Poso, Sulawesi.

June 2007   A number of key AJAI leaders, including the interim *Amir,* Zarkasih, and Commander of its Military Wing, Abu Dujana, are arrested, along with a number of their followers in Central Java.

Introduction ――――――――――――――

Behind the Veil of Successful Counterterrorism

Prior to the September 11, 2001 (hereafter the 9/11 Incident), attacks on the United States, governments and security planners in Southeast Asia had already been preoccupied with the threat posed by religious extremism and terrorism. There is a long history of both secular and religious-oriented terrorism in the region. In particular, the region has long been threatened by *Jihadists,* armed Islamist groups who declared war against various central governments with the goal of either gaining greater political autonomy, as was the case in southern Thailand and the Philippines, or outright secession, as was the case in Aceh, Indonesia.

In this connection, the emergence of the *Al-Jamaah Al-Islamiyyah* (AJAI), or "The Congregation of Muslims," has increasingly focused attention on the role of religious-oriented terrorist organizations in Southeast Asia. The Southeast Asian region is particularly prone to Islamist-oriented violence for a number of reasons. Firstly, there is a sizeable presence of Muslims in the region, one of the largest in the world, amounting to a total of more than 230 million.[1] Even more important, there are three Muslim-majority countries and others with sizeable Muslim minorities. The percentage of Muslim population in Southeast Asia is as follows: 90 percent in Indonesia, 67 percent in Brunei, 65 percent in Malaysia, 16 percent in Singapore, 6 percent in Thailand, 5 percent in Cambodia and the Philippines, and 4 percent in Myanmar. While mere Muslims' presence does not translate into a threat due to the emergence of extremist Islamist concepts and ideology, it has made the region particularly vulnerable. Secondly, historically the region has been closely linked with the Muslim world, especially to the Middle East, South Asia, and even China.[2] This has meant that there has been transmission of all kinds of influences, and with the Middle East being radicalized since the 1960s, extremist ideas and ideologies have also found its way into the region. Thirdly, the region is fairly accessible to outsiders, and this has also contributed to close interactions with Islamists elsewhere. Fourthly, the largely secular governments of the region are often alleged to have failed to effectively manage their Islamic constituencies, due either to pressures from external great powers or to anti-Islamic authoritarian national regimes that have persecuted Muslims in the region. Fifthly, the long-standing Islamic insurgencies in the region, some decades old, have also provided opportunities for all kinds of transnational influences to penetrate the region. Many extraneous extremist groups have supported and abetted these organizations, with the synergy aggravating the security situation in the region. Sixthly, the region has also been experiencing a rise of religious revivalism and fundamentalism, a phenomenon that has afflicted all religions everywhere in the world. Seventhly, due to the demographic expanse of Muslims, in particular against the backdrop of a glorious Islamic past in Southeast Asia, evident from the various indigenous Islamic powers in Southeast Asia such as the Malacca, Mataram, and Pattani empires, there has been a tendency among some groups to look back to the past for inspiration to address the problems and challenges of the present and future. Finally, due to concerted efforts by various external groups and particularly due to developments elsewhere, there has been a general revivalism of things Islamic, even in Southeast Asia.[3] Some of these events include the successful Islamic revolution in Iran; Israel's continued repression of the Palestinians; the United States' aggressive policies towards Islamic countries, best evident in the invasion and occupation of Afghanistan and Iraq; and the general perception that the "war on terror" is actually a "war on Islam" by the West, as seen from the American support for Israel's invasion of Lebanon in August 2006.

The AJAI is, however, not the first organization to use religion to mobilize support and construct its cause and ideology on the basis of a particular religion, albeit along hard-line interpretations that justified the use of violence to achieve political objectives. What distinguished the pre-AJAI religious-based terrorist organizations in the region was essentially their national character. This was evident from the *modus operandi* of various Islamist groups in Indonesia, southern Thailand, Myanmar and southern Philippines.

Prior to the 9/11 incident, governments in the Southeast Asian region managed the threat of "Islamist extremism and terrorism" nationally. Since the United States launched its war on terror, Southeast Asia likewise commenced its "war on AJAI," even though with a different degree of intensity. Since Singapore detained what were described as AJAI "foot soldiers" in the republic, the terrorist organization has been described as the most dangerous to emerge in the region. Many of the counterterrorism policies were undertaken in concert with external support, especially from the United States and Australia, as well as through multilateral support of various groupings such as the United Nations, Association of Southeast Asian Nations (ASEAN), and ASEAN Regional Forum (ARF). As a consequence, many AJAI leaders were either killed or arrested and the organization crippled, especially in Indonesia, Malaysia, Singapore, and to some extent the Philippines. This led many governments in the region and their allies abroad to roost the idea that the war on terror in Southeast Asia, often dubbed the "second front," was or has been won. A testimony before the House International Relations Subcommittee on International Terrorism and Non-proliferation on September 29, 2005, manifested part of this triumphalism:

> The most dangerous *Al Qaeda*–linked terrorist group in Southeast Asia was *Jemaah Islamiyah* (JI), responsible for the Bali bombing in 2002, the Marriot bombing in 2004 and suspected of a host of other bombings across Southeast Asia. But in September 2005 Gareth Evans, President of the International Crisis Group, declared that JI was "effectively smashed" and "no longer constituted a serious threat." This remarkable change of fortune for JI came about because of good police work and the democratic transition in Indonesia. The United States, Australia and the international community invested heavily in training and equipping Southeast Asia's police, prosecutors and judiciaries...Additionally, while the police have arrested and convicted active JI members, the democratic transition has apparently dried up the recruit pool. Jemaah Islamiyah was founded to oppose Indonesia's authoritarian government. With former dictator Suharto out and a democratically elected President and legislature in, the armed struggle had lost its point to many of its supporters.[4]

While Southeast Asian officials and their counterparts in the West have echoed the notion of "success against AJAI and Islamist extremism," the reality is far from this. This is mainly due to two main factors. First, unlike the Cold War against communism, Islamist extremism and terrorism are anchored on one of the most important religions, philosophies, and ideologies in the world, namely Islam. As long as Islam is used to mobilize support for causes of extremism and terrorism, this "war" is unlikely to be won. Also, if many continue to perceive that the war on terror is a war on Islam, there is every possibility that adherents of Islam, the second-largest religion in the world, will intensify their defense of their religion at any cost.

When President George W. Bush used the expression, "this crusade—the war on terrorism," it has unnecessarily evoked the historical ideological clash between Christianity and Islam, with Muslims being viewed as "fifth columnists" in the West, and hence targeted for persecution.[5] The U.S.-led attacks on Afghanistan and Iraq, and the threat to do likewise in Iran and Syria, has strengthened the perception that the White House, under the influence of anti-Islam fundamentalists, were waging a war against Islam and not against terrorism. Islamist ideologues, having found convenient evidence of "Christian fanaticism," have been able to grow and nurture dangerous bands of Islamist fundamentalists and extremists in response, thereby exacerbating the security situation worldwide and endangering both Muslims and non-Muslims.

Second, the governments in Southeast Asia and their allies have been concentrating on physically destroying the extremists and terrorists. While this is an important strategy, they have failed to address a whole array of other factors that have succeeded in ensuring the continuous swelling in the ranks of extremists and terrorists. If anything, killing alleged AJAI leaders and publicly demonizing the organization have had the reverse effect of enhancing AJAI's image and strengthening its mass appeal. There is no better person to confirm the worsening of the radicalization and terrorist threat in Southeast Asia than Rohan Gunaratna, who has widely researched on this subject. Rohan argued, "We have seen that extremist groups that were modest in size have grown significantly. The number of regional 'jihad' groups has grown from around 30 to 47 in the past five years. They have recruited, raised funds and become more influential."[6]

In this regard, Southeast Asia deserves to be labeled as the "second front" in the war on terror. This is justifiable on a number of grounds. First, it is an important part of the Muslim world and where radical Islam is fast gaining ground. Despite being a Sunni-dominant region due to various influences, extremist Islamist ideology from the Middle East has become a major part of the religious discourse. Second, there is the presence of many radical groups, not just in Indonesia, the largest Muslim country in the world, but also in Malaysia, Thailand, and the Philippines. Third, the most dangerous Islamist terrorist group, the AJAI, continues to operate in the region. Fourth, since the 9/11 Incident, the region has witnessed a number of violent attacks against what has been dubbed as anti-Islamic "Western targets." Fifth, the region continues to host many training camps that are churning out violent *Jihadists,* especially in southern Philippines. Sixth, in addition to various suicide bombings, there are nearly 300 Islamist radicals in jail in the region.[7] There are probably many more that are operating clandestinely and whose existence is not even known by the security apparatus,best evident from the so-called "ghost bombers" that operate in southern Thailand.

THE DEFINITIONAL ABYSS

While scholars and practitioners have debated on the term "terrorism," there is an underlying consensus between them.[8] Terrorism can be defined from either the perpetrator's or the victim's perspective. Be that as it may, in this study, terrorism refers to any attempt or act of force aimed at achieving political goals. Building on this, Islamist terrorism refers to the attempt or use of force to achieve political goals by mobilizing or referring to Islam as a source of justification. Yet, in any discourse of Islamist terrorism, one comes across three different typologies—the fundamentalist, extremist, and terrorist. The Islamist fundamentalist is a Muslim who is well-versed in the Islamic religious heritage and tenets. He knows whereupon in Islam to draw for references to justify his ideology and the rationale behind his affirmative belief. His belief is not a crime. He merely excels in drawing upon Islam's heritage. Neither is his preaching. The Islamist fundamentalist, if not guilty of committing violence, is not a criminal. If anything, a good Muslim must submit to the fundamentals of the *Koran* and to that extent, all good Muslims are fundamentalist. By the same logic, all good Christians, Hindus, Buddhists, and Sikhs are also fundamentalists. By itself, fundamentalism is not a problem.

The extremist, however, draws on the fundamentalist. He is dependent on the fundamentalist for the promise of sanctity of his actions to validate the facilitation of terror. The fundamentalist provides the extremist with a framework for planning operations. With the extremist's subscription to the ideological framework established by the fundamentalist, the extremist takes one giant step closer to the employment of violence that characterizes terrorism. The extremist may not be directly involved in the planning and execution of terrorist activities, but he is an important conduit that accounts for the conversion of an individual to terrorism. The extremist's enabling role to propagate and justify violence and the commitment to a radical ideology binds the individual or group together. This is what makes an extremist a threat of society. The extremist facilitates terrorism by providing information and logistical and financial support, links beliefs with action, and provides a rationale for violence that will be praised in the "House of God." The extremist, by definition, is largely intolerant and propagates the use of violence to "correct" what is considered as "wrong." While the extremist might not be "criminal," he nevertheless through his intolerant interpretation of religious texts is able to convert a fundamentalist, or even someone largely ignorant of the essence of what is in the text, to the cause of terrorism. This is primarily by providing the justifications for the action and, most important, the benefits of such acts, namely everlasting life in Heaven.

Thus, if religious terrorism is associated with the act of violence perpetrated in the name of God, it is equally important to understand the process by which an individual is transformed to become a terrorist. No individual is born a terrorist. He becomes one through a series of processes and influences. As an analogy, the rise of a terrorist can be equated to the food chain, indicating the symbiosis between fundamentalism, extremism, and terrorism. The fundamentalist is akin to a plant that provides the basic food in the ecosystem. The extremist is the rabbit in the food chain, which feeds on fundamentalism, the food, for his growth. The terrorist is the third tier of the food chain, the lion, known for its instinctive violence that feeds on the rabbit for survival. In reality, the typologies might not be that neat. Still one gets a sense of how someone steeped in religion can be easily manipulated to a distorted ideology culminating in acts of terrorism, as the perpetrator believes that what has been done is justifiable regardless of its brutalities. This is the crux of religious extremism and terrorism that is confronting Southeast Asia today.

STRUCTURE OF THE STUDY

Against this backdrop, this study aims to undertake an in-depth analysis of the most important terrorist organization to surface in Southeast Asia to date, namely the AJAI. Following the introduction of some of the key Islamic terms that are relevant to this study, Chapter 1 will shed light on the nexus between religion and terrorism. How religion has been used to construct a particular political milieu that justifies the use of terrorism in the region will be discussed. It is argued that when socioeconomic inequalities are politicized, issues related to injustice projected, and the ideology of *Jihad* mobilized and socialized, there is a great chance that terrorism is one of the many likely outcomes. Chapter 2 examines the region's experience with Islamist extremism. The study will focus on *Jihadi*-oriented terrorism in Indonesia, the Philippines, Thailand, and Myanmar. Chapter 3 analyzes the origins, structure, and strategy of the AJAI in achieving its goals as a regionwide terrorist organization. Chapter 4 evaluates the measures that have been adopted both by individual states and collectively to manage the terrorist scourge in the region, with the AJAI as the key target. Why the measures are described as "one step forward, two steps backward" and what the limits to counterterrorism are in the region, will be discussed. Finally, the future of AJAI and *Jihadi* terrorism in Southeast Asia will analyzed. The key aim is to examine the consequences of Talibanization for Southeast Asia. What does the failure to curb Islamist extremism mean for the region and beyond? What is the likely political-security landscape of Southeast Asia, and how will this impact upon the external world?

KEY ISLAMIC TERMS

Some of the key Islamic terms that will be referred to in this study are elaborated below:

Jihad

Jihad stems from the Arabic word *Jahada*, which means to strive for a better way of life. Specifically, it means "to strive" or "to exert to the utmost," and when placed within the context of *Islam*, it would encompass all forms of striving, including armed struggle, aimed at making the Word of God (Islam) prevail. Often, *jihad* has been conveniently, yet erroneously, defined as holy fighting in the Cause of *Allah* or any effort to make *Allah*'s words (*Islam*) superior. In actuality, the latter does not exist in Islam as it only refers to the Holy War of the Crusaders (Christians).

Similarly, *jihad* is not a war to force the faith on others, as perceived by many. It should never be interpreted as a way of compulsion of the belief on others, since the *Al-Koran* has explicitly said, "There is no compulsion in religion."[9] In actuality, the term *jihad* can be divided into two specific categories. The first is the *al-jihad al-akbar* or otherwise known as the greater *jihad,* while the other is *al-jihad al-asghar,* or lesser *jihad.* In the former, *jihad* is viewed as the struggle against evil and the maintenance of one's virtue, ethics, and morals. It also encompasses the inner struggle to overcome one's temptations and tendency to sin. The latter, on the other hand, refers to the fight against injustice and oppression as well as the defending Islam in general.

It is due to the ambiguity of the latter that the term *jihad* has often been utilized to mobilize Muslims to resort to armed struggles so as to achieve "divinely ordained goals." More often than not, religious entrepreneurs have, whether for personal or societal gains, unwisely decided to emulate the *jihad* as practiced during Prophet Muhammad's time. Such tendencies only serve to mislead since the society during that of the Prophet is certainly different from that of the modern day. Expectedly then, the term *jihad* at present is subjected to various radical and moderate interpretations, each guided by its particular circumstances or needs.

Even when engaged in an armed struggle, Islam does not condone terrorism, kidnapping, and hijacking, especially against civilians. Similarly, in an armed struggle, *Islam* prohibits Muslim soldiers from harming civilians, women, children, elderly, and religious men like priests and rabbis. Doing so would be a violation of Islamic laws, and the offender is liable to punishment under Islamic laws. As such, attacks on civilian populations as manifested in the September 11 attacks on the World Trade Center and Pentagon are totally unacceptable and condemned in Islam.

Khalifah

Khalifah, or the *Caliph,* is short for *Khalifatu Rasulil-lah,* which translates to the successor or representative of Prophet Muhammad. In Islamic traditions, this would refer to the first four rulers after the death of the Prophet. The four *Caliphs* were Abu Bakr As-Siddiq (632–34 A.D.), Omar Ibn Al-Khattab (634–44 A.D.), Othman Ibn Affan (644–56 A.D.), and Ali Ibn Abi Talib (656–61 A.D.). They were also referred to as the *Al-Khulafa'Ar-Rashidun* (The Guided *Caliphs*). As successor to the Prophet, the *Caliph* was the head of the Muslim community, and his primary responsibility was to preserve in the path of the Prophet, which included calling people to the worship of and submission to *Allah.* The first four *Caliphs* were known to be kind, merciful, just, and impartial in the course of their leadership.

The death of the fourth *Caliph,* Ali Ibn Abi Talib, saw the transfer of the *Caliphate* to the *Ummayad* Empire under the leadership of Mu'awiyya. Following the fall of the *Ummayad* Empire, the Caliphate was transferred to the Abbasid Empire. The later *Caliphs,* however, assumed the manners of kings and emperors, which then degraded the true spirit of equality of ruler and the role of *Caliphs.* The later *Caliphs* also manipulated the concept of *Caliphate* for their personal ends. This eventually led to the decline and eventual abolition of the *Caliphate* in the Muslim world. Sporadic attempts to revive the Islamic *Caliphate* have increasingly failed.

Shias and Sunnis

Shias form the largest non-*Sunni* branch of Islam. The *Shias,* in their various forms, represent some 10–15 percent of the Muslim world. *Shia* Islam holds that the *Caliphate* after Ali is illegitimate. The term *Shia* refers to the partisans of the fourth *Caliph* Ali, who was Muhammad's son-in-law through his daughter Fatima. *Sunnis,* on the other hand, form the main group in Islam, making up 85–90 percent of the religion's adherents. *Sunni* Islam claims to be the continuation of the Islam as it was defined through the revelations given to Prophet Muhammad. *Sunni* Islam has its name from its identification with the importance of the *Sunna* (the examples from the *hadiths*). The theological and ritual differences between *Sunni* and *Shia* Islam developed over centuries. For a long time, *Sunni* Islam was distinct from *Shia* Islam by its adherence to the *Caliph* as the leader of the Muslim world.

Despite various differences, the *Sunnis* and *Shias* share three core doctrines—namely, oneness of God, the belief in the revelations of Muhammad, and the belief in resurrection on the Day of Judgment. *Sunni* Islam has a different set of *hadiths* from *Shia* Islam. *Sunni* Islam puts more importance into the *haj* to Mecca, while *Shia* Islam places importance on other forms of pilgrimages. *Sunni* Islam reveres Ali but does not hold him up as the only true continuation of the tradition of Muhammad, and has no emphasis on him bringing on a divine light from the Prophet. In the *Sunni* world, there are four major schools of jurisprudence founded by *imams,* or scholars, from the ninth to eleventh centuries, namely, Imam Ahmad ibn Hanbal in Baghdad, and Imam Abu Hanifa, Imam Maliki, and Imam Idris al-Shafei in Egypt. These schools are respectively referred to as the *Hanbali, Hanafi, Maliki,* and *Shafei.* With regard to legal matters, these four schools give different weight in legal opinions to prescriptions in the *Koran,* the *hadith* or sayings of the Prophet Muhammad, the consensus of legal scholars, analogy (to similar situations at the time of the Prophet), and reason or opinion. Muslims are, however, not obliged to stick to any particular schools of thought since the belief in oneness of God and the Prophet forms the fundamentals of the religion. A Muslim can belong to any of the schools and is at liberty to consult any scholar from any of the schools of thought on religious matters.

Wahhabism

Dating back from the mid-1700s, *Wahhabism* is a purist movement seeking to cleanse the Muslim spirit and eliminate all innovations to Islam. *Wahhabists* reject innovation and consensus, favoring instead strict adherence to the word of the *Koran* and *Sunnah. Wahhabism* has no special practices or special rites than the Sunni body of Islam. It originated from Sheikh Muhammad ibn Abdul al-Wahhab, who was born in 1703 in Ayina, Saudi Arabia. He started the movement during a time when Islam was suffering a decline in Arabia. People were straying away from the path of Islam by worshipping idols and praying to tombs and shrines. After having studied under prominent Islamic scholars, Sheikh Muhammad became passionate about restoring the true faith of Islam and called for people to worship only *Allah* (*Tawheed*) and to return to the *Koran* and *Sunnah.* The people who followed Ibn Wahhab called themselves *muwahiddun,* the adherents of *Tawheed.* In many ways, the term *Wahhabism* was the creation of Wahhab's enemies and adversaries.

He traveled widely to spread his movement. He was banished from his hometown after cutting down trees that were being worshipped, bringing down the dome over the grave of Zaid ibn al-Khattab, and punishing a woman who had committed adultery the way it was prescribed in the *Koran.* He moved to Dariya where he stayed with Abdul al-Rahman bin Suwailim. It was during his stay here that prominent people came to know of Sheikh Muhammad and his movement, including Prince Muhammad bin Saud. The prince accepted the teachings of Sheikh Muhammad and promised to help and support him in his movement. Sheikh Muhammad started to gain a following, but with supporters also came enemies, who labeled the teachings of Sheikh Muhammad as *Wahhabism.* Prince Muhammad was asked by the Sheikh to lead the Muslims, and to this day the Saudi royal family follows

Wahhabism. This commitment was strengthened when descendents of Sheikh Muhammad helped the Saudi ruling family unify its kingdom in 1932.

Being a conservative and intolerant form of Islam, *Wahhabism* does not tolerate integration with other religions. *Wahhabism* gained popularity in the West and the Muslim world in the aftermath of the Iranian Revolution in 1979. In effect, *Wahhabism* was propagated by the Saudi royal houses to counter the *Shia* ideology that was emanating from Iran at that time. Religious schools, *madrasahs,* and mosques in Afghanistan, for example, were flooded with *Wahhabi*-oriented Islamic ideology. This greatly influenced the earlier batches of Afghanistan and Taliban veterans. The Islamist government in Sudan and the now-defunct Islamist Taliban in Afghanistan were both greatly influenced by the *Wahhabi* movement. The ideology of *Wahhabism* has also spread to Southeast Asia with the AJAI and its regional associates, such as MILF and *Abu Sayyaf,* as strong adherents.

Dar al-Islam, Dar al-Harb and Dar al-Sulh

In the conservative Islamist tradition, the world is divided into three components or houses. This consisted of the *dar al-Islam,* or the house of submission; *dar al-Harb,* or the house of war; and *dar al-Sulh,* or the house of treaty. The terms are used to describe those lands administered by Muslim and non-governments. *Dar al-Islam,* also the house of Islam, signifies a geographic location or territory controlled by Muslims and where Islamic *Sharia* law prevails. The *dar al-Islam* is also said to include areas where Islam is dominant.

Dar al-Harb, or the house of war, on the other hand, refers to the territory controlled by non-Muslims or nonbelievers. Many have argued that this would also encompass secular Muslim–majority countries. The *dar al-Harb* is viewed as an active and a potential threat to the *dar al-Islam* and is always viewed with hostility. *Dar al-Sulh,* or the house of treaty, are territories that are not under Muslim control but has friendly relations with Islamic territories. In Islamic history, an example of the *Dar al-Sulh* is the treaty that the Prophet Muhammad entered into with the Christian city state of Najran. Numerous Islamic militant movements argue that the *dar al-Islam* should be expanded at the expense of the *dar al-harb,* with the sole intention of creating a universal Islamic community. More importantly, such movements would contend that this is the true meaning of *jihad.*

Religious Extremism and Terrorism:
A Conceptual Framework

INTRODUCTION

The aftermath of September 11, 2001, saw not only a "War on Terror" but also a proliferation of literature on the nexus between religion and politics, especially with a focus on Islam and terrorism. Unfortunately, the literature on both terrorism and Islam has clouded rather than clarified the link between the two concepts. While both terrorism and Islam are widely accepted notions, the ambiguities and vagueness within them have not been helpful in elucidating the problem that is believed to be plaguing mankind today. Similarly, the concept of terrorism has also been imbued with great difficulties. It is useful to note that terrorist groups and individuals such as the Jewish *Haganah, Irgun Zeva'i Le'umi,* and *Stern* Gang made a simple transition from being terrorists hunted by the British to becoming legitimate and respected political leaders of Israel later on. The cliché of "today's terrorists being tomorrow's nationalists" highlight the difficulties in defining terrorism and individuals who resort to violence to achieve political goals. This study attempts to locate this nexus within the concept of Talibanization. The example of the Taliban and the concept of Talibanization demonstrates how one can, through a selective reading of Islam, seek to achieve political goals that are linked between religion and politics. In essence, Talibanization encompasses aspects from symbolic group politics and communal definitions through "authenticity"—that is, a specific reading of Islam and reconstructing Islamic tradition to actual practices such as the institution of an Islamic state.

Prior to understanding the practice of Talibanization, it is important to note that political violence rooted in fundamentalism and extremism has never been accepted as something natural or normal in Islam. It is more expedient to approach Talibanization as a "political" rather than a "religious" or "Islamic" movement.[1]

An analysis of this requires one to revisit the Cold War era to locate the literal seeds of the Taliban. Primary to the focus is how Islam has been a convenient source of legitimacy and validation, not only for Islamists, but also for the United States, as evident in the Afghanistan resistance movement against the Soviets. The United States rallied the idea of a "good *jihad*" to contend the Soviets during the Afghanistan invasion.[2] While *jihadi* overtones have encouraged the stereotyping of Islam as a backward, decadent, and violent religion, the "Afghanistan factor" together with the extremist interpretation of Islam is paramount in explaining the rise of the AJAI and its violent operations.

In the post–September 11 environment, Islam has been accused of providing the foundation stone of terrorism. This is unfortunate as Western scholarship has ignored historical origins of concepts such as "fundamentalism" that bears American Protestant roots.[3] There are also the various cases of non-Islamist terrorism, ranging from the Sri Lankan Tamil Tigers (which has indulged in the highest number of suicide bombings), the Sikh *Khalistanis,* the Irish Republican Army, the *Aum Shinrikyo* group (which perpetrated the 1995 Tokyo subway gas attack), Timothy McVeigh's bombing of Oklahoma City, and the spreading of anthrax by American rightist Christians. This is not to ignore the secular "terrorist" groups such as the German Red Army *Fraktion,* the Italian Brigade Rose, the neofascist *Ordine Nuvo,* the French Action *Directe,* and the Basque ETA.[4] It is thus essential to depart from a single-minded focus on the essence of a "religion" to one that is more "political" in nature in unraveling religious extremism and terrorism.

THE CHALLENGE OF TALIBANIZATION

In this study, Talibanization refers to the growing propensity to adopt extremist religious ideological interpretations and practices in Muslim societies, especially in Southeast Asia. Even though Southeast Asian governments have been able to make tactical claims of deaths and arrests of many extremists and terrorists, this is only a pyrrhic victory. This is due to the fact that extremist Islamist ideology has burrowed deep roots into the region. Since the 1990s and especially following the 9/11 Incident, the region has been experiencing a form of Talibanization with varying and uneven intensity, especially in the Muslim-dominated states of Indonesia, Malaysia, and Brunei. Muslim minorities in Singapore, Thailand, and the Philippines are similarly exposed to this radical Islamist ideology. Talibanization as a process refers to the concerted adoption at the mass level of extremist Islamist ideas, something most Southeast Asian governments have been almost helpless in countering. As long as the trail of Talibanization is unchecked, no matter how many terrorists or extremists are killed or arrested, Southeast Asia's counterterrorism strategies are bound to fail and the triumph of religious extremism and militancy assured.

The concept of Talibanization is directly related to the Taliban's governance of Afghanistan from 1994 to 2001. Conceptually, *Taliban,* the plural of *Talib,* means "students." The term *Taliban* shot to fame in September 1994 following the emergence of an extremist militia force in Kandahar, southern Afghanistan, which became the political and spiritual heartland of the *Taliban*. In the first *Mujahidin* struggle in Afghanistan from 1979 to 1989, the *Taliban*'s role was largely insignificant. However, when the Soviets and the triumphant West withdrew in 1989, Afghanistan was left to the victorious but highly fragmented *Mujahidins*. A bloody civil war broke out among the *Mujahidins* in April 1992 as they struggled for predominance and control of Afghanistan. In reaction to the lawlessness and chaos, an essentially ethnic *Pashtun* (who make up 40 percent of Afghanistan's population) militia force emerged under the leadership of Mullah Muhammad Omar in September 1994. They were referred to as *Talibans* as they were the "children of *Jihad*" who grew up in the refugee camps in Pakistan. They were students from the *Deobandi madaris* (plural for *madrassas*) who had been indoctrinated in the ideology of *Sunni Wahhabism* and *salafism*. Most of the *Deobandi madaris* were linked to political-religious parties such as the *Jamiat Ulema-i-Islam* (JUI) and other breakaway elements of JUI such as *Sipah-e-Sahaba* Pakistan, *Harkatul Mujahidin, Tehrikul Jihad,* and *Jaish-e-Mohammed*. These seminaries churned out *Talibans* by the thousands, and hence the intense radicalization of Afghan society following the Soviet and Western withdrawal from the war-ravaged country.

The *Talibans* won the second *Mujahidin* struggle, which was essentially an internecine civil war. Even though Mullah Omar struggled against the Soviet invasion of Afghanistan and, later, against the communist regime of Najibullah, he became extremely disillusioned with the factionalism and criminal activities of the *Mujahidin* leaders. Schooled in *Wahhabism,* his promise to bring peace won him support from many former *Mujahidin* commanders, religious clerics, and the people at large. Supported by Pakistan, some Gulf states such as Saudi Arabia, and even the West, which hoped to negotiate with whoever was in control of the country to gain access to the rich energy resources of Central Asia, the *Talibans* swept aside most of the opposition and took control of Kabul in September 1996. By 2000, most of Afghanistan was controlled by the *Taliban*.

Taliban was adopted as the name of the regime to distinguish it from the *Mujahidin* political parties that struggled for power since April 1992. Mullah Omar's grand design was not so much to grab power as much as to cleanse Afghan society. As an adherent of *Wahhabism,* he adopted a rigid interpretation of *Sharia,* or Islamic law. This fuelled Islamic extremism with intolerance towards non-Muslims and Muslims who did not adopt ultraorthodoxy. Islamic militancy and extremism became the *Taliban*'s key defining features, something that flourished in a war-weary, poor Afghan society that lacked formal education. To that extent, Talibanization became synonymous with extremism. As extremism is inversely proportional to socioeconomic conditions of a country, Afghanistan was ripe and ready for Talibanization, almost the same manner China was ripe for the communists in 1949. Projecting itself as the "true believers of Islam," the *Taliban* imposed restrictions on men and women alike, installing an almost Khmer Rouge–type regime with the aim of purifying society from evils of the West and decadent Islam. Mullah Omar was himself named *Amir-ul-Momin* (Commander of the Faithful), signalling clearly the significance of radical and extremist Islamists as the key driving force behind his brand of governance. As purifiers, Mullah Omar and the Taliban returned Afghanistan to the medieval ages, with the Department of Vice and Virtue policing every aspect of Afghan society. In short, the *Taliban* drew an ideological wall around Afghanistan, opposing any idea that was in conflict with its orthodox interpretation of Islam. The adoption and practice of extremist and radical ideas by the Taliban have come to be seen as the hallmark of Talibanization. Wittingly and unwittingly, this process is also in vogue in Southeast Asia, making the region's "war on terror" difficult to win in the years to come.

CONCEPTUALIZING TALIBANIZATION: THE NEXUS BETWEEN RELIGION AND POLITICAL VIOLENCE

This study of Talibanization departs from the historical accounts of Islamic fundamentalism as a novel phenomenon. It is pertinent to locate the politics of Talibanization in the 1970s or even earlier. Nazih Ayubi has traced the "politics" of Talibanization to the 1960s, essentially to the failure of secular regimes in the Middle East, the closing of secular channels for the opposition, and the Islamists' adoption of an "authentic ideology" of protest through the selective reading of Islamic texts.[5] While Ayubi has credited these trends of Talibanization as the cause of the Iranian Revolution in 1979, Ahmed Rashid has shown how the Taliban mastered these processes of challenging secular regimes through "Islam."[6] It is apparent from these studies that understanding the concept of Talibanization requires engagement, as it is not merely confined to Afghanistan or the Taliban; on the contrary, it has transnational implications and applications. This phenomenon has been responsible for the increasing number of Islamist-oriented domestic and foreign policies, leading observers to lament about the successes of the Islamist extremism.[7]

The various facets of Talibanization, including the pursuit of terrorism and excessive terror as shown by events such as the bombings in New York, Bali, Madrid, Jakarta, London, and Bombay, should not, however, foreclose scholarly engagement of the distinct politics of Islam. It is imperative for scholars to understand the "political" premises of the selected reading of the Islamic religious heritage, particularly concepts like *jihad,* where Islamists from their world of *Dar al-Islam* (camp of Islam) declare and pursue holy war on *Dar al-harb* (camp of War). Similarly, Edward Said[8] and Armando Salvatore[9] have noted the complexities and inertia of Western scholarship to engage any "Islamic" phenomena except in the negative. This study is interested in tracing the politics of Talibanization in its qualitative aspects, including its ideology and roots. One cannot ignore the observation of scholars such as Gilles Kepel, who has noted the evolution of political Islam in the past quarter of a century to a more violent, terrorist-oriented dimension of Talibanization.[10] However, rather than focusing on a "clash of civilizations" as advocated by Samuel Huntington,[11] Francis Fukuyama,[12] Daniel Pipes,[13] and Barry Rubin and Judith Rubin,[14] this study aims to analyze Talibanization as a "political" rather than a "religious" discourse. The phenomenon of violence is not a manifestation of Islam, the religion but reflects the "militant strand" of Talibanized Islam as constructed by Islamists.[15]

The aim is not to present an exhaustive scientific approach to political Islam but to study how Talibanization exemplifies the nexus between religion and terrorism. Despite the encouraging turn to more objective analyses in the discipline of "terrorism studies," the phenomenon of political Islam deserves much more attention as Western studies, in general, continue to be plagued by the stereotyping of Islam. In this section, the evolution to Talibanization is attempted by accounting for Islamist motivations and political ambitions that, more often than not, are manipulated from Islamic religious heritage. Islamists usually draw from Islamic concepts of *jihad* (holy war), *jahiliyyah* (state of ignorance/infidelity) and *hakimiyyah* (the sovereignty of God) as sources of validation to justify their acts. In this connection, the Islamist political project in the Southeast Asia can be seen as part of their quest to establish an Islamic order at the national and regional level, being an important manifestation of Talibanization that is creeping and scoring successes in the region.

UNRAVELING TALIBANIZATION

In this study, Talibanization encompasses Islamist political endeavors, including the resort to violence and terrorism, that is legitimized through selective reading and interpretation of Islam. What is pertinent is that the rich religious tradition of Islam has been appropriated and manipulated to further the cause of Talibanization. In Francis Fukuyama's assessment, Islamists, labeled as "Islamofascism," are referred to as politically ambitious terrorists who have manipulated Islam to justify indulgences in extreme terror. Islamists, to Fukuyama, are detached from the present realities as they cling to an ancient Islamic heritage. The Orientalist scholar, Bernard Lewis, in assessing Islam as a historical tradition, noted the nexus between religion and terrorism in political Islam as a violent manifestation bearing its roots in an Islamic heritage.[16] Similarly, another Islamic scholar, Emmanuel Sivan, analyzed the nexus between religion and terrorism by locating Talibanization in its violent manifestation within the Islamic religious heritage, in "age-old Islamic ideas."[17] Abdelwahab Meddeb, in a similar train of thought, noted how the nexus between Islam and terrorism lie in Islamists' drawing upon the religious traditions and heritage of Islam.[18] However, more insightful scholarship on Talibanization has analyzed it as a "political" phenomenon in which Islamist political actors have utilized Islam for achieving specific political aims, including the grabbing of state power.[19]

One such analysis is Nazih Ayubi's interesting text on Talibanization as a sociopolitical phenomenon.[20] According to Ayubi, the roots of the nexus between religion and terrorism lay in the Islamists' attempt to radically change the social settings within which they perceive themselves to be victims of deprivation. For example, he links the nexus to the disenfranchisement and unemployment in the societies in which Islamists are operating. As the secular order and elites are blamed for the deprivations and ensuing oppression, the Islamists seek the violent overthrow of the existing order as a panacea for their problems. In order to resort to violence, including terrorism, the Islamists turned to selected religious heritage to legitimize their aim of achieving their political goals. Ayubi, in viewing Talibanization as a vent for Islamists' frustration in the secular order, noted that "Islamists are not angry because the aeroplane has replaced the camel; they are angry because they could not get on to the aeroplane."[21]

In this study, the concept of Talibanization as a sociopolitical phenomenon is adopted to elucidate the development of Islamist extremism in Southeast Asia. This explains the political struggles that are taking place where there is a clear nexus between religion and terrorism. This is manifested in the violent attempts to replace the secular regimes in the region by groups such as the AJAI, the Moro Islamic Liberation Front, *Gerakan Mujahidin Islam Pattani,* and even the *Gerakan Aceh Merdeka.* The quest for greater autonomy in southern Thailand is also part of the Talibanization endeavor, just as it is for the concept of DIN. The AJAI enters into the political radar as it epitomizes the perpetuation of terrorism against secular regimes in the region. Equally important is the need to understand how the notion of Talibanization has taken on a transcontextual mode, being appropriated in Southeast Asia from Afghanistan. Of equal significance is the need to understand Talibanization not only in a national context through the concept of *Darul Islam,* but also its regional equivalent through the extranational concept of DIN. Even though most Islamist groups were "nationally organized," the AJAI has altered this through its concept of DIN, in turn, linked to the creation of an Islamist *Caliphate* or *Khalifah* for the whole world.

Before charting a provisional map of facets of Talibanization, it is interesting to note how scholars like Eqbal Ahmad, who is known for countering Western stereotypical images of Islam, have interpreted the religion-terrorism nexus as one that has dangerously culminated in the rise of Talibanization.[22] In assessing terrorist motivations, he noted how, through extremist and radical interpretations, Islamic tenets have been manipulated and distorted. This is the key to Talibanization. This is aimed at legitimizing excessive violence, actions that Eqbal posits as belonging to the realm of "crime" and "pathology." Devoid of rationality, to Eqbal, Islamists rely purely on religious motivations to pursue their political goals. These religious motivations are important considerations for understanding the dangerous nexus as Islamists, especially the more religiously extremist terrorists, remain motivated to committing atrocities that are beyond the sensibilities of other more secular terrorists. For Eqbal, Talibanization is a political phenomenon with dangerous transnational implications.

How should Talibanization be defined? According to Kouser Azam,[23] there are various ways of looking at it, including:

1. A religious interpretation of world history, with the Islamists being divided into a camp of *Dar al-Islam* (world of Islam) in violent contention with the rest of the world, *Dar al-Harb* (world of war);

2. A total rejection of the existing world order from the position of negating it and rejecting it as an order of *kafirs* (infidels) and atheism, with a strong belief in changing it;

3. A reversal of the historical evolution back to the era of the Islamic State, marking a return to the Caliphate period;

4. A rejection of common universal values;

5. Antagonism towards science, secularism, and enlightenment.

The factors that fuelled Talibanization were many. Among others, these include:

a. The dilemma of backwardness under which a vast majority of Muslim population live in extreme poverty, destitution, ignorance, and disease, leading to deep divisions between rich and poor within the Islamic world as well as at the international level;

b. The prevalence of military, totalitarian, and autocratic systems in the entire Arab world and a total absence of democracy and human rights, not only on the economic and political level, but also in the family sphere. Rigidly patriarchal traditions still constitute the basic value system that generates the way of thinking that encourages antagonism and rebellion, unemployment, inhibition, suppression, and frustration that radicalizes the younger generations. This creates circumstances in which there is no gleam of hope for change and reformation as an alternative to the status quo in the Arab and Islamic worlds;

c. The negative influence of petrodollars within the Islamic world.

Understanding the constituents of Talibanization and what fuelled the process are important, as this helps in unraveling the nexus between religion and terrorism. The study of Islamist extremism in Southeast Asia cannot theoretically and practically divorce itself from the general process and phenomenon of Talibanization, due to the ideological sharing and infusion that has been taking place between Southeast Asia and the discourse of radical Islam. This was particularly so when many Southeast Asian *mujahids* participated in the Afghan war to evict the Soviets, as well as due to the socialization of Talibanization through various mediums ever since.

THE TALIBANIZATION IN SOUTHEAST ASIA

To understand the threat, it is of prime importance to be cognizant of the ideology and roots of Talibanization. It is clear that Talibanization lays less in Islam and more in the reconstruction of Islam for political purposes. Particularly important is the concept of *jihad,* which has been extensively manipulated by Islamists to declare war on political enemies and justify any means to institute the supposed Islamic ends. Even though this study does not account for the concept's origins in the *Koran* or the *Hadiths* (Traditions of the Prophet), or provide a historical evolution of the concept, an understanding of Islamists' reconstruction is essential to the understanding of Talibanization. Similarly, the dichotomies that Islamists from Afghanistan to Southeast Asia frequently evoke—namely, *Dar al-Islam* and *Dar al-harb*—are not strictly "Islamic," but rather political constructs of Talibanization. These metaphorical categories, which are not even in the *Koran,* have been utilized to justify extreme political violence.

Majid Khadduri[24] takes a useful step in this direction by noting that the concept of *jihad* is not a singular concept, but bears diverse representations from its violent to nonviolent manifestations. Khadduri has historically traced how it is only in certain periods of Islamic history that individuals and groups have manipulated the concept of *jihad* to make it appear as a concept singularly marked by violence, concealing its nonviolent basis.[25] Talibanization places much emphasis on *jihad* being a violent war, in line with Islamists' aims of justifying the terror to which they frequently resort in pursuit of their political aims. Here, Islamists have largely pursued the Islamic concept as one that should be declared against *jahilli* societies to radically change them. Talibanization as such involves extreme reconstructions of concepts like *jihad* for "political" ends. As many Islamic thinkers have argued, there are important *Hadiths* clarifying Prophet Muhammad's ideas of *jihad* for Muslims, with the focus being essentially aspiritual and even "apolitical" in nature. This is in stark contrast to the definition of *jihad* in Talibanization as being a strictly violent concept and a violent struggle to change society and replace political orders they define as infidel and ignorant.

Islamists, through Talibanization, seek to implement strict religious codes according to the *Sharia* for their societies as a panacea for the ills that they believe must be cured for Muslims to claim their place in this world. In this regard, a number of orthodox religious schools have emerged in the Muslim world with thinkers such as Hassan al-Banna, Maulana Maududi and Sayyid Qutb, providing the intellectual stimulus for "Islamic revivalism and reformation," through their writings and discourses. Common among these Muslim thinkers was their belief that contemporary Islamic societies were undergoing sociocultural degeneration, mainly caused by Western education and culture.[26] In order to emancipate the Muslims, these thinkers believed that the adherents should "return to the fundamentals of Islam" as "Islam is a comprehensive, self-evolving system, that efforts must be made to integrate the *Koranic* injunctions and Prophet's traditions into individual and communal lives, and that Islam is applicable in all times and in all conditions."[27]

Hassan al-Banna was among the first to opt for the "Islamist route," believing that the *Al-Ikhwan-al-Muslimin* (Muslim Brotherhood), or *al-Ikhwan* for short, that he started in 1928 would act as a catalyst of reform in Egypt. Adopting the tenets of *Wahhabism,* he believed in the establishment of a complete Islamic state with *Sharia* as the key guiding principle.[28] While aiming to implement *Sharia* at home, he also envisaged the internationalization of the *al-Ikhwan* to the Islamic world to free it from Western colonialism. While the movement suffered a setback following his assassination in 1949, his ideas continued to influence the discourse of Islam internationally. Among others, al-Banna believed that:

> So long this government is not established, Muslims are, all of them, guilty before God Almighty of having failed to install it. This betrayal in the bewildering circumstances of the times was a betrayal not only of Muslims but of all humanity.[29]

The role of al-Banna is important as he was critical in providing an intellectual basis for Islamists' activism worldwide and providing the grounds for anti-Westernism.

The Arabs' humiliating defeat at the hands of Israel in 1967 further awakened Islamists' nationalism, prodding them towards militancy and violence.

Undoubtedly, al-Banna was a key thinker in providing Muslims with a "road map" to achieve their "messianic vision." Even so, two Islamic fundamentalist ideologues have largely been accused of providing the intellectual and religious bases for Islamist militancy, extremism, and violence as well as rationalizing the achievement of the "Islamic Revolution" through *jihad*, or "holy war." They are Abu al-Ala Maududi, the ideologue of the *Jamaat-e-Islami Pakistan*, and Sayyid Qutb, the ideologue of the Muslim Brotherhood. The latter was executed under Nasser's regime, while the former escaped execution once in Pakistan.

Maududi has emerged as one of the leading Islamist thinkers of the twentieth century. A proponent of Islamic fundamentalism, he believed that Islam can be transformed into a powerful ideology that can address the plethora of challenges Muslim societies are confronting the world over. Even though from Pakistan, he believed that his diagnosis and prognosis was relevant to all Muslim societies, especially wherever corrupt and degenerated social and political orders existed. He distanced himself from violence and argued that Islam's moral high ground would account for its success, just as the Prophet, through his exemplary behaviour and actions, succeeded in launching "the greatest 'bloodless' revolution in Islamic history which no other civilization can match." Maududi's book on *al-Jihad fil-Islam* (*Jihad* in Islam) greatly influenced and inspired the Muslim Brotherhood in Egypt, the *Fidaiyan* in Iran and the *Jamatis* in Pakistan.[30]

While the works of al-Banna and Maududi are extremely important, another Islamist thinker, Sayyid Qutb, is increasingly seen as the "father of modern *Jihadists*," including Osama bin Laden and his band of extremists. Unlike Maududi, Qutb openly celebrated the use of violence to achieve the goals of Islamic revolution. For him, *Jihad* and the resort to violence were legitimate means to eradicate political and moral decadence in Muslim societies as well as to terminate Western imperialism. Of Egyptian origins, disgruntled and disillusioned with Western civilization, he sought salvation by returning to the roots of Islam. In 1951, he joined the Muslim Brotherhood and advocated the adoption of *Sharia* and transforming of Egypt into an Islamic state. Arrested on a number of occasions, he was executed in August 1966. One of his most important works, *Fizlal-al-Koran* (in the shadow of *Koran*), a 30-volume commentary on *Koran,* was completed in prison, and where he forwarded fundamentalist and extremist solutions to overcome societal ills in Muslim states. Another influential work, the *Milestones,* which was partly inspired by Maududi, has also acted as an ideological fountain for Islamists seeking to resort to political violence based on religious influences. For Qutb, a fundamental part of the problem confronting Muslim societies was the existence of decadent and corrupt regimes in the Gulf States and North Africa. He advocated their overthrow. These governments and societies were equated to those of the *Jahilliya* era, prior to the Prophet's *Koranic* revelations. In this endeavor, Qutb referred to the writings of Ibn Tamiyya (1268–1328), who believed that *jihad* could be waged against anyone who was a *Jahilli*. As such, Qutb's writings declared war not only against the West, who were believed to be continuing the "Crusades" against Islam but also against Muslims who were undermining Islam from "within" through their actions and thinking. This is "Qutb Syndrome" at its best, with Osama bin Laden viewed as one of Qutb's best students. As was argued by Iqbal Hussain, the Al Qaeda's 9/11 attack on the United States was only a "by-blow" as the real strategy was:

> not to penetrate the heartland of America but the deserts of Saudi Arabia, Egypt and other Gulf States where the *Jahilli* scandal is being perpetrated to perpetuate the corrupt and repressive regimes of the *Jahilli* monarchs.[31]

Other than minor exceptions, most discussions of Talibanization have ignored how Maududi and Qutb reconstructed *jihad* for "political" ends to challenge secular orders that are perceived to be preserving and promoting Western hegemony. In the same vein, ideas contained in Talibanization challenges the *jahilliyas*. The adherents of Talibanization believe that in the present era, Islamic principles have been discarded and replaced by secularism. Through Talibanization, *jahilliyas* should be cured of this illness that stem from ignorance. Here, the concept of *hakimiyyah,* or rule of God, a manifestation of God's centrality, a notion allowing Islamists to declare any regime *kafir,* is also important.

Islamists like al-Banna, Maududi and Qutb have, just as in the Middle East, been evoked in Southeast Asia for the reconstruction of Islam to achieve political goals. Using *Al-Ikhwan*-type ideas, Islamists in Southeast Asia have created a regional political ideal to challenge existing secular orders. Primarily, within these Islamists' postulations, is the notion of Islam as not merely a "religion" but also a "political" instrument. Such a reading of Islam has allowed the Talibanization of al-Banna, Maududi, and Qutb in their attempts to replace secular orders with Islamic political orders. Such a definition of Islam has prompted these Islamists to condemn secular regimes, even Muslim ones as *kafir* and as indulging in *kufr.* Developing an Islam for political purposes, Islamists like al-Banna, Maududi, and Qutb reconstructed *jihad* to challenge secular orders and tolerated excesses like violence and terror by describing secular orders as *kafir* and even *jahilli.* Utilizing the rhetoric of the "rule of God" over the "rule of Man", these Islamists used Islamic categories to legitimize political violence against any regime.

A discussion on Talibanization will be incomplete without an account of "Qutbism." This is a popular slogan that has colored the processes of Talibanization that Islamists have indulged in from the *Ikhwan* (Muslim Brotherhood) and Muhammad Abdul al-Salam Faraj (the assassin of the Egyptian president, Anwar Sadat) and more recent Islamist terrorism. It is worth highlighting here the life and ideas of Qutb as a starting point of analysis. Qutb's *Ma'alim fi-l-Tariq* (*Milestones*), which marked his radical transformation from a secular reformist in the 1930s to a radical Islamist in the 1950s has evolved into a *jihad*-manual.[32] Qutb's imprisonment and incarceration with other members of the Brotherhood from 1954–1964 led to his contempt for secularism on the whole, and culminated in an Islamist consciousness that only the institution of an Islamic state and Islamic law could prevent such abuses. However, there were larger processes that culminated in Qutb's condemnation of *jahilliyah* as a condition/state that must be resisted by violence. In the *Milestones,* Qutb draws upon his experiences in America and under the secular regime (which Qutb declared as Western in spite of Gamal Abdel Nasser's anti-Western rhetoric) to declare any non-Islamic state as *jahilli*.[33] Simultaneously, Qutb politicizes the faith, Islam, through calling for the mandatory institution of *Sharia,* that is, a complete system extending into all aspects of life from religion to politics, in all Muslim societies.

Qutb's adoption of radical Islamist doctrine was partly influenced by his career. This was evident in his writings, such as the *al-Tafsir al-Fanni fil-Quran (Artistic Representation in the Quran),* and his extensive commentary on the Koran, *Fi zilal al-Qur'an (In the Shade of the Quran),* carried similar themes of disenchantment and disillusionment that were to form significant aspects of the revolutionary declarations of *Milestones*.[34] It was indeed in the latter "*jihad*-manual" that Qutb laid out the foundations of Talibanization through creating an Islamist ideology that was transmitted to various contexts to justify attacks on regimes declared as *jahilliya*.[35] Unlike Islamic intellectuals who saw the value in alternative political systems, Qutb held rigidly to "Islam" as the only system of morality, justice, and governance that should be abided to, and called for the immediate imposition of *Sharia* through any means possible. Ultimately, he was concerned with the radical institution of a complete Islamic system (covering aspects from law to culture) over the dominant, secular notion of the nation-state. It is in such ideological foundations of Qutbism that scholars of the Middle East like Fred Halliday have located the *Al Qaeda* and its diverse local affiliates.[36]

The ideology of Qutbism is particularly evident in Qutb's characterization of Muslim and non-Muslim societies as having reverted to a pre-Islamic state of ignorance characterized by the aforementioned *Koranic* concept of *Jahilliya.* Such a ideological conception allowed Qutb—and subsequently, has allowed later Islamist endeavors at Talibanization—to declare any society (even Muslim ones like Egypt) as *kafir*.[37] This declaration of someone as *kafir* was a radical call for all Muslims to resist any political system they were in and facilitate the processes of Talibanization. Qutb as such preceded even the Taliban in conceiving a "revolutionary vanguard" to fight *Jahilliya* through a double-pronged method of *dakwah* (preaching) and *jihad* (physically abolishing the *Jahili* system).[38]

Qutb had in his work laid out a transnational ideology that was to permeate the mindsets of Islamists, from Egypt such as Faraj to the Southeast Asian Islamists to be discussed below. The revolutionary movement he charted was one not of merely aiming at establishing an Islamic state in Egypt, but one that aimed globally. Qutb openly celebrated the need for violence in *Milestones* by arguing that this "movement" will be constantly attacked by defenders of *Jahilliya,* such as *ersatz*-Muslims, Jews, and Westerners. While earlier Islamists like Ibn Tamiyya, Maududi, and Wahhab had utilized the Koranic concept of *Jahilliya* to condemn contemporary Muslim societies and develop a radical Islamist movement, none of these Islamists had developed such a prolific application of the concept and attained such a popular appropriation.

The ideology of Qutbism was pursued by Muhammad Abdul al-Salam Faraj, who emerged after Qutb as Egypt's most important Islamist revolutionaries.[39] In spite of being unsuccessful like Qutb in overthrowing the secular regime in Egypt and establishing an Islamic state, the implications of Qutb and Faraj lie in the contemporary, transnational ideology of Talibanization. For example, Faraj played an integral role in the post-1966 *Salafist* movement. Faraj's radicalism was evident in his rejection of contemporary *Salafists* and even the Muslim Brotherhood for attempting to integrate with the secular political orders and adopt a nonviolent path of reconciliation.[40]

In Faraj's work such the *Al Farida al Ghaiba* (*The Neglected Obligation/Forgotten Duty/Missing Commandment*) which was released as a complementary *jihad*-manual to Qutb's *Milestones,* Faraj represents *jihad* as the sixth *rukn* (or pillar) of Islam.[41] According to Faraj, *jihad* is a *fard 'ayn* (a mandatory religious duty) that requires immediate imposition. Declaring any deviation from *jihad* as *kufr* itself (through even dismissing Muslims' *kafir*), Faraj advocated the immediate Islamist infiltration of society, government, and security forces, and the militant contention of the regime. Faraj's Qutbism was so radical that he had to split from a group called the *Jama'at al-Jihad* (Group of Holy Struggle) to form his own organization under the same label in 1981.[42] *Al-Jihad* began a guerilla war of absorbing Islamist cells striving towards a Talibanization of Egypt, and began carrying out terrorist attacks against the secular regime, ultimately culminating in the assassination of President Sadat at an army parade. The success of Faraj's *jihad* was itself evident in how this Islamist ideology had pervaded even the military; Sadat's assassin—personally sanctioned by Faraj— was an army officer (Lieutenant Khalid Islambouli) who was integral to the parade. Scholars who have ignored Faraj's significance to Qutbism and Talibanization on the whole have also simultaneously ignored how Ayman al-Zawahiri of the *Al Qaeda* was also one of the members of *Al-Jihad* arrested after Sadat's assassination.

Another prominent Islamist, Ustad Abdul Rasul Sayyaf, who was integral to the *jihad* against the Soviet occupation of Afghanistan, is worth highlighting. Sayyaf is a *Wahhabi Pashtun* warlord, leading a *Pashtun* militia financially supported by Saudi Arabia, and held leadership of the *Itihad-i-Islami Baraye Azadi Afghanistan* (United Islamic Front for the Liberation of Afghanistan).[43] This study is particularly interested in the Qutbism that determined Sayyaf's anti-Western ideological stance from his membership in the Muslim Brotherhood based in Afghanistan. This base of the *Ikhwan,* established by Gulbuddin Hekmatyar and Syed Burhanuddin Rabbani in 1969, became a conduit for the transnational networks of Qutbists.[44]

The transnational aspect of Islamism was evident in how Sayyaf's *Wahhabism* led to his affinity with Osama and their alliance in instituting a network of training camps to bunkers in Jalalabad.[45] Interestingly, it was Sayyaf who invited Osama to return from his Sudanese exile in 1996.[46] Sayyaf's Islamism characterizes as such, a synthesis between the doctrines of *Wahhabism* and Qutbism, and stands starkly apart from the majority of Afghan Sunni Muslims who abide by the Hanafi *madhab* and the Shias (such as the *Hazaras*). For a fuller understanding of Sayyaf's Islamist ideology, it is important to understand how like Qutb, Sayyaf suffered periods of incarceration by the Communist People's Democratic Party of Afghanistan in 1978.[47]

There is a need to study Islamists such as Sayyaf for the influential and transnational role they have played in the post-Afghan War context. The camps Sayyaf established with Osama were utilized to indoctrinate recruits from Chechnya, Bosnia-Herzegovina, Indonesia, Malaysia, Thailand and the Philippines with his synthesis of Qutbism and Wahhabism.[48] Southeast Asian Islamist endeavors at Talibanization can be located in an Islamist rubric of Qutbism, *Wahhabism* and their practical culmination in Sayyaf's camps and training for *mujahidins*.

This practical culmination is best evident in how Sayyaf has through permeating the *Loya Jirga* in Kabul since 2003 (through elections), endeavored towards instituting Talibanization in the post-Taliban Afghan state. Imposing gridlocks on the drafting of a constitution, Sayyaf has been able to extract a clause prohibiting legalities "offending Islam."[49] Similarly, the appointment of Sayyaf's ally, Fazal Hadi Shinwari, as chief justice of the Supreme Court has revived the Taliban's dreaded "Ministry for the Promotion of Virtue and Prevention of Vice."[50] Sayyaf's integrality to transnational endeavors at Talibanization lies in his characteristic synthesis of Qutbism and Wahhabism, and his practical embodiment of this Islamist ideology.

As far as Southeast Asian Islamist extremist and terrorism are concerned, most of the *Mujahids* who traveled to Pakistan and Afghanistan became associated with Rasul Sayyaf and his interpretation of Islam. The Afghanistan *Mujahidin* Military Academy, the training camp for Southeast Asian *jihadists* was located at Towrkham, where Sayyaf was based. Initially, this camp was referred to as *Jamaah Negara Islam* Indonesia Camp. Later, it was renamed the *Al Jamaah Al Islamiyah* Camp. All leading Southeast Asian *jihadists* were trained in this camp, including Hambali, Zulkarnean, and other militants from Indonesia, the Philippines, and Thailand.[51]

It is also pertinent to study the evolution of Talibanization in the thought of Abdullah Yusuf Azzam (born in 1941) who witnessed and perceived "Western atrocities" during his upbringing in the West Bank (in Jordan) and participation in a *jihad* against "Israeli occupation."[52] However, his expression of Talibanization was manifest in his adoption of an academic position in Saudi Arabia and exposure to Wahhabism.[53] Azzam developed a conviction that military contention was obligatory for the *Ummah*'s progress and disregarded alternative avenues.[54] For instance, he argued, "*jihad* and the rifle alone: no negotiations, no conferences and no dialogues" in dealing with the "enemies."[55] From his exposure to Qutbism in the Muslim Brotherhood's operation in the West Bank, Azzam's exposure to Wahhabism culminated in a drive to put Islamist doctrine and theories into practice. This was evident in his leave from his tenure at the King Abdul-Aziz University in Jeddah (Saudi Arabia) and travels to Pakistan and Afghanistan to participate in the Afghan *jihad*.

Following the Soviet invasion of Afghanistan, he arrived in Pakistan and became a lecturer at the Islamic University in Islamabad. He then moved to Peshawar to support *Mujahidin* organizations that were fighting in Afghanistan. He established the *Beit ul Ansar* (House of Supporters) to assist the *Jihadists* fighting in Afghanistan. His writings and travels helped to globalize the Afghan War and moved Muslims to support the *Jihad* through manpower and materiel. According to Yoram Schweitzer and Shaul Shay, Azzam became "a symbol and leader of the *jihad* organizations and radical Islamic circles worldwide, and his impact on the global *jihad* movement lasted beyond his lifetime."[56] Initially, Azzam was also Osama's spiritual mentor. Though Azzam was assassinated in November 1989, his impact on Islamist radicalism remains important. This includes:

a. The setting up of Islamic "international" organizations based on volunteers recruited from all over the Islamic world on behalf of the *jihad* in Afghanistan;

b. The establishment of international networks of Islamic terror cells supported by radical Islamic movements around the world;

c. The victory of the *mujahidins* in Afghanistan created an aura and ethos of bravery around the Muslim fighters, inspiring Muslims all over the world; and

d. The establishment of an extensive network of Islamic fighters imbued with a sense of mission and combat experience and who have served as the vanguard defending Islam and attacking its foes.[57]

The "war on terror" rhetoric that the United States has flirted with since the 9/11 Incident is partly an endeavor to conceal a reality of the event being closely integrated, with deep roots in Talibanization. In a discussion of Talibanization, it is pertinent to note the evolution of a certain form of Islamic thought that colors the imaginations of many Islamists. This is the rigid *Wahhabi* form of Islam, which has evolved from Saudi Arabia to an Islamic ideological imagination that edges and religiously influences Islamists from the Arab world to regions in South and Southeast Asia. A myriad of theological literature has accounted for the history of the *Wahhabi* order, marking its evolution through borrowing from earlier radical *Sunni* orders such as the *Hanbali,* which limited liberal readings of the Islamic religious heritage.[58] The *Wahhabi* order encompasses a rigid, selective reading of Islam that has allowed Islamist borrowings to justify the utility of extreme terror to challenge regimes defined as un-Islamic or *kafir.* This is motivated by the need to use political Islam as a political project.[56] For the purpose of this study, the roots of Talibanization lie in how Southeast Asian Islamists have appropriated *Wahhabism* in diverse forms, from Moluccan and Acehnese reliance on on-line *fatwas* from Saudi Arabia, to the curriculum of the Saudi-sponsored colleges in Southern Thailand.

The spread of Talibanization, legitimizing Islamic-sanctioned violence, is also in part due to the easy accessibility of *Wahhabist* ideologies and organizational models through the *Taliban, Jamaat-e-Islami,* and *Al-Ikhwan.* What is critical is that one understands the political parameters of Talibanization. In this regard, the roots of Talibanization lies not within Islam but rather in Cold War and social scientific dynamics of various societies that allow Islamists to "plough the fields so that seeds can grow and be harvested" to achieve specific goals of Islamic revolution. The DIN ideal, as championed by the AJAI in Southeast Asia, for example, is a political project of Islamists that want to replace the essentially secular, so-called un-Islamic or even anti-Islamic orders in the region with an Islamic caliphate—if necessary, through the use of political violence and terror. As such, in spite of the reference and deference to Islam in rhetoric that is often mobilized, in reality Islam figures merely as a tool for the furtherance of the goal of Talibanization so that a new political order can be created in the region.

CONCLUSION

This study is not arguing the *Talibans à la Mullah Omar* in Afghanistan are going to take over Southeast Asia. It is also not arguing that Southeast Asia will be transformed into the Afghanistan of the period from 1996 to 2001. What the Talibans operationalized in Afghanistan was a function of the conditions found in the society following the Soviet invasion and the *Mujahidin* struggle against the invaders that wrecked the society and provided conditions for the rise of what can be termed as "extreme of the extremism." Afghan Talibanization was also in part a *Pasthun* phenomenon. Such a situation is unlikely to take place in Southeast Asia.

Instead, due to various internal and external imperatives, Islamist radicalism is fast digging roots in the region. Radical piety has increasingly become a fact of life. With problems arising from poor governance and the perception that the West, often in collaboration with governments in the region, have launched a "war against Islam," many Muslims have been mobilized into action to defend "Islam." The task of mobilization has been greatly facilitated by the rise and penetration of Islamist radicalism into the region. Islamist radicalism is fast penetrating into the region through the adoption of radical ideas and concepts that originated from the Middle East and actualized in the Islamic revolution in Iran and the *Mujahidin* struggle in Afghanistan. Writings of scholars such as al-Banna, Maududi, Qutb, Faraj, Sayyaf, and Azzam have deeply penetrated into the conscience of most Muslims in Southeast Asia. Such radical ideology describes not only how the "West" has launched a war against Islam, but even more important, why it is imperative for every Muslim to take action against both the "*kafir* West" and "*Jahilliya* Muslims" who are undermining and threatening Islam. It is against this backdrop that Southeast Asia is witnessing the process of Talibanization. Unlike in Afghanistan, it is a more open concept, but the final outcome is the same; rising exclusivity, Islamist radicalism, and war against both Muslims and non-Muslims who are viewed as threatening Islam in Southeast Asia. Also, the key defense prescribed by these radicals against such a threat is for societies to adopt *sharia* and establish *Dauliah Islamiyyah* nationally and regionally. While for many Muslims, radicalism was learned from the textbooks of scholars such as al-Banna, Maududi, and Qutb, many Southeast Asian radicals, personally saw and heard what modern radicals such as Faraj, Sayyaf, and Azzam had to say. This had a lasting impact on their outlook, which has culminated in the trail of Talibanization in Southeast Asia.

Southeast Asia's Experience with Old and New Islamist Extremism and *Jihadism*

THE SOUTHEAST ASIAN POLITICAL LANDSCAPE

As a norm politically, Southeast Asia is defined as the geographical region that lies south to southeast of India, south to southwest of China, northwest of Australia, and astride the important sea lanes of communications between the Indian and Pacific oceans. Collectively, it is made up of 10 countries, namely Brunei, Cambodia, Indonesia, Laos, Malaysia, Myanmar, the Philippines, Singapore, Thailand, and Vietnam.[1] As the region is located at a major crossroads of the world, historically it has been highly accessible to external influences. It has witnessed settlement, occupation, colonization, control, and war over the region's people, territories, and resources. Indian traders, mainly Hindus from India, and Arabs, mostly Muslims from the Middle East, were among the first to traverse the Indian Ocean with the monsoon winds to trade. Later, from the north came Chinese traders and settlers. In the final major movement of history, the European colonizers captured the region through force of superior arms, controlled the vast region for more than three and a half centuries, and, in many ways, continue to dominate the economies of the region.

Due to the geographical importance that was accompanied by various riches, from the very beginning, Southeast Asia had played an important role in world history. Being essentially a maritime region, it drew international attention due to its location among the major trade routes of the world; hence, its importance in the trading system of the Indians, Chinese, Muslims, and later, Europeans. In addition to growing competition among key international actors, one major and lasting manifestation of the importance of the region and the impact of external players was the transplanting of major external religions and ideologies into the region. This culminated in the establishment of an Islamic arc in southern Southeast Asia, mainly in Indonesia, Malaysia, Brunei, southern Thailand, and southern Philippines. Chinese Confucian values were deeply entrenched in northern Vietnam. The rest of the region, primarily mainland Southeast Asia, consisting of Myanmar, Cambodia, Thailand (except the south), Laos, and southern Vietnam was influenced by *Theravada* Buddhism. The entry of Europeans brought in its wake Christian influences and values that dominate the Philippines (except in the south), with pockets of presence in other parts of the region.

Due to these penetrations, including the integration of the region into the modern economic system of the West, Southeast Asia has witnessed, almost on a continuous basis, the collision between the largely stronger, external political-economic-social-cultural forces with what can be regarded as largely local patterns and system of political, economic, and social organizations. This explains the largely fragmented nature and the continuous social-cultural fault lines that exist in the region. These weaknesses have allowed external and internal forces to operate in the region and often challenge the political authorities of various states in the region. Even though many countries in the region gained various degrees of independence from the colonial powers, due to their geographical position and richness, the region was easily sucked into the global rivalries that ensued following the end of the Second World War. The entry of the Cold War into the region, mirroring the clash of the two superpowers, was not unexpected, and gravely impacted upon the politics, security, and economies of Southeast Asia. Similarly, the end of the Cold War did not bring any "peace dividends" as the region continues to be embroiled in various conflicts, with it being viewed as a major front and theater of the global "war on terrorism." This stems in part from the fact that Southeast Asia houses one of the largest concentrations of Muslims in the world.

Southeast Asia is a very violent region. Since time immemorial, interstate wars have in one way or another characterized the region. While this was halted by Western colonization of the region from the fifteenth century onwards, latent conflicts, many of which were exacerbated by the manner in which the postcolonial order emerged in the region, have resurfaced, leading to Southeast Asia emerging as the arc of instability in the Asia-Pacific region. Two categories of conflicts dominate the region, namely, those that are essentially interstate in character, and those that can be subsumed as intrastate conflicts.

Most Southeast Asian states have land or maritime disputes with each other. Malaysia has territorial disputes with Singapore, Indonesia, Thailand, Brunei, and the Philippines. There have been skirmishes along the Myanmar-Thailand border. The latter's relations with Cambodia have also been tense due to various conflicts, including xenophobia. Besides territorial disputes, Malaysia and Singapore have not resolved many bilateral issues, including Malaysia's dispute with Singapore over deliveries of fresh water, land reclamation, bridge construction, maritime boundaries, and ownership of *Pedra Branca Island/Pulau Batu Putih,* the last of which has been referred to the International Court of Justice (ICJ). In addition, Malaysia has a one-kilometer segment at the mouth of the Golok River in dispute with Thailand. Malaysia is also involved in a complex dispute with China, the Philippines, Taiwan, Vietnam, and Brunei over the Spratly Islands and the waters surrounding the islets in the South China Sea region. The Philippines retains a dormant claim to Malaysia's state of Sabah in northern Borneo, based on the sultanate of Sulu's granting the Philippines government the "power of attorney" to pursue the sultanate's sovereignty claim. The Indonesia-Malaysia dispute over Sipadan and Ligitan islands was settled through adjudication when the ICJ awarded them to Malaysia in 2002.

Brunei and Malaysia have disputes over ownership of oil and gas resources in their offshore and deepwater seabed, similar to the ones that exist between Indonesia and Malaysia. Malaysia's land boundary with Brunei around Limbang remains in dispute. Brunei established an exclusive economic fishing zone encompassing Louisa Reef in southern Spratly Islands in 1984 but made no public territorial claim to the offshore reefs. The 2002 "Declaration on the Conduct of Parties in the South China Sea" has eased tensions in the Spratly Islands but fell short of a legally binding "code of conduct" desired by several of the disputants. Significant differences remain between Myanmar and Thailand over boundary alignment and the handling of ethnic rebels, refugees, and illegal cross-border activities.

There continues to exist persistent land boundary disputes between Cambodia and its two powerful neighbors, Thailand to the west and Vietnam to the east. Cambodians have claimed that Thailand and Vietnam have moved or destroyed land boundary markers—that is, their maritime boundary with Vietnam is hampered by dispute over offshore islands, and Thailand obstructs access to the *Preah Vihear* temple ruins awarded to Cambodia by the ICJ in 1962. While Laos's boundaries with Cambodia, Thailand, and Vietnam are peaceful, several areas, including the Mekong River's islets, remain in dispute with Thailand. Vietnam's demarcation of the land boundary with China remains in dispute. China continues to occupy the Paracel Islands that are also claimed by Vietnam and Taiwan. Both countries are also parties to a complex dispute with Malaysia, Indonesia, Philippines, Taiwan, and Brunei over the Spratly Islands.

In addition to the existence of various interstate conflicts, the persistence of intra-state conflicts has helped to create a perception that the region is a zone of conflict. There are a vast array of conflicts, ranging from center-periphery conflicts in Aceh and Papua in Indonesia, the conflict in southern Philippines and southern Thailand, and uprisings by various ethnic groups such as the Karens in Myanmar and the Was in Thailand. Historically, almost every noncommunist Southeast Asian state, including in Malaysia, Thailand, and the Philippines, was plagued by challenges from commu-nist movements. Due to problems of nation building and the refusal to accept the authority of the central government, states in the region had to confront separatist movements, be it in Indonesia, the Philippines, Thailand, or Myanmar.

THE "OLD" NATIONAL *JIHADI* MOVEMENTS IN SOUTHEAST ASIA

Introduced not by Arab armies but by *Sufi* mystics, starting in the middle of the fourteenth century, Southeast Asian Islam adapted not only to Hinduism and Buddhism but also to older animist practices. While Indonesia is the largest Muslim country, its brand of Islam—especially practiced by the Javanese, the majority of

Indonesians—is really a mixture of many dissimilar elements. Southeast Asia is the cultural and geographical crossroads of Asia, where Sinic, Hindu, Islamic, and Western civilizations have met and interacted for almost a millennium. The struggles played out in the region have resonated beyond the region. For instance, how Indonesia deals with the issues of democracy and political and religious diversity could well influence the course of events in Asia and the larger Islamic world.

Due to this heterogeneity, Southeast Asian Islam had adapted to modernity more easily than the orthodox Islam of the Middle East and North Africa. While secular nationalists such as Gamal Nasser and Ahmed Ben Bella in postcolonial Egypt and Algeria, respectively, failed to deliver on their promises of bread and freedom, Mahathir bin Mohamed in Malaysia and Suharto in Indonesia succeeded in bringing significant material benefits to their peoples. Yet at the same time, economic growth in Southeast Asia, as elsewhere, also generated grievances among groups that were marginalized. In both Muslim-majority Indonesia and Malaysia, as well as in Singapore, the southern Philippines, and southern Thailand where sizeable Muslim minorities exist, there emerged a number of Islamist movements whose *raison d'etre* (at least outwardly) sought to redress grievances through violence. Some of these radical movements seek to separate themselves from exploitative secular governments or to overthrow them. Others expressed in religious terms what in reality were worldly disputes with non-Muslim communities, such as rivalries over land rights and access to jobs and livelihood. Ultimately, all these movements have sought to create states governed by *Koranic* law—namely, Islamic states that would be strong enough to resist the invasion of Western influences being promoted by cultural globalization. This force is identified as the root cause of the backwardness of Muslims everywhere.

The emergence of what can be described as "ethnocratic regimes" is also partly blamed for conflicts in the region. This arises when one ethnic group gains control of the state machinery and uses it to maintain its ethnic identity at the expense of the other groups within the state. The controlling ethnic group achieves this position of power by recruiting only members of its ethnic group to positions of power within the state machinery, such as the civil service and armed forces. In the process, the national identity of the population is determined by the cultural attributes of the dominant ethnic group, including the adoption of the governing group's language. One result of this is that the institutions of the state, such as the constitution and laws, favor and reinforce the monopolization of power by the dominant ethnic group. There are varying degrees of this element in Southeast Asia. While in Malaysia, the regime is a ruling coalition representing the different ethnic groups, it can still be considered ethnocratic because the dominant party represents the Malays and the constitution grants the Malays a "special position" which, amongst other things, gives them special access to government employment. A similar case can be made in Myanmar, Thailand, Singapore, and the Philippines with the Burmans, Thais, Chinese, and Christian Filipinos, respectively, dominating politics and the economy, often at the expense of the national minorities.

As a rule, whichever group dominates national politics would always attempt to rationalize its political, economic, and social policies in terms of national interest as well as in pursuit of its nation-building effort. However, the apparent failure of various "nationalist projects" to deliver political, economic, and social goods has led to counteractions in a Muslim majority and minority region. These include the adoption of the "Islamic mode" of political, economic, and social development, and even the use of terrorism and violence, to remedy what are perceived as national, regional, and international injustices. This is clearly evident in the various national *jihadi* movements in the region, especially in Indonesia, the Philippines, and Thailand.

INDONESIA

According to the U.S. State Department, in 2006, with 216.04 million Muslims out of a population of 245.5 million, Indonesia is the world's largest Islamic country.[2] Islam has a long history in modern Indonesia, and most of the violence is related to the quest for setting up of an Islamic state. The struggle for an Islamic state in Indonesia, however, did not always take a violent form, as various social and political organizations with aspirations for an Islamic state often adopted parliamentary and electoral approaches. Traditionally, Indonesian Islam has been syncretic in form, incorporating traditional Islamic practices with earlier Hindu and Buddhist influences. Most *santri* (devout) Muslims are associated with the *Nahdatul Ulama* and the *Muhammadiyah,* both of which are moderate, inclusive organizations, encouraging the practice of Islam within the framework of a secular Indonesian state. As elsewhere, Indonesian Islam has become increasingly *santricized,* partly influenced by the spread of the austere Saudi Arabian *Wahhabi* doctrines. As the Indonesian public became more pious in their religious practices and aware of their Islamic identity, it also widens the corridor for things religious, including the move towards greater radicalism and violence in their political behavior. Historically, two *Jihadi-*oriented movements have stood out, namely, the *Darul Islam* and the Aceh struggle.

The *Darul Islam* Challenge

The predecessor of what was to emerge as the *Darul Islam* (DI) was the *Hizbullah,* the Army of *Allah,* which was initially created by the Japanese during the occupation of the country from 1942 to 1945. Following the Japanese surrender in August 1945, the *Hizbullah*, though not directly under the Indonesian Army, fought a guerrilla war against the Dutch to win national independence. The *Darul Islam* challenge was a direct function of the Linggajati Agreement that was signed between the Dutch and the Indonesian government on November 15, 1946.[3] By this agreement, The Hague recognized the Republic's *de facto* authority in Java, Sumatra, and Madura, and where the Indonesian Republican leaders agreed to a federal structure, the United States of Indonesia. The agreement was only ratified by the Netherlands in March 1947. Due to the Linggajati Agreement, both parties agreed to withdraw their troops to the established demarcation lines. A direct consequence of this was the need for the Republican *Siliwangi* Division in West Java to withdraw to Central Java. This was opposed by Deputy Defense Minister Kartosuwiryo,[4] a former leader of the *Partai Syarikat Islam Indonesia* (PSII), or Indonesian *Syarikat Islam* Party. The Linggajati Agreement, a deal between Socialist Prime Minister Sutan Sjahrir and the Dutch, was opposed by Kartosuwiryo as it was perceived to be disadvantageous for the republic.

Kartosuwiryo opposed Sjahrir and Jogjakarta's position on grounds that since the Republican Army was in control of territories in Java and elsewhere, they should not succumb to Dutch diplomatic and military pressure, as the Socialists and the Jogjakarta leadership under Sukarno-Hatta were prepared to do. This was a consequence of the debate between those who proposed *diplomasi* (diplomacy) and those who proposed *perjuangan* (struggle) as the best way to gain independence from the Dutch. The Republican Army was made up of mixed elements, including various *laskars* or militia groups. There were many Islamic-oriented *laskars* in West Java, a group to whom Kartosuwiryo appealed. Thus, when the Republican Army withdrew to Central Java, the Islamic-oriented *laskars* stayed on and continued fighting the Dutch. These *laskars* controlled vast territories in West Java, partly a consequence of the vacuum left by the vacating *Siliwangi* Division.

Following the signing of the Renville Agreement in January 1948, a cease-fire was declared between the Dutch and the Republican Army. Among others, this permitted the *Siliwangi* Division to return to West Java. This was opposed by Kartosuwiryo and the Islamic *laskars* in West Java, leading to the outbreak of conflict between the *Siliwangi* and *laskars*. Kartosuwiryo felt that since the *Siliwangi* had "shamelessly" abandoned the territory and that it has been in the *laskars'* control, the former had no right to return to West Java to control the territory. The contest for control between the two forces led to the outbreak of a military conflict that was to eventuate in the birth of *Darul Islam* (DI) and the *Negara Islam Indonesia* (NII) in July 1949.

Sections of the *Hizbullah* established the DI, or "House of Islam," and created its armed faction called *Tentara Islam Indonesia* (TII) or Indonesian Islamic Army. On August 7, 1949, the DI under the leadership of Kartosuwiryo, based essentially in West Java, refused to place his military units under the command of the regular army and proclaimed an Islamic state. Kartosuwiryo accused the moderate and largely secular nationalist leaders such as Sukarno and Mohammed Hatta of committing "crimes against Islam" as they had rejected "Islam as the sole foundation of the state."[5] As the DI was created to set up an Indonesian Islamic state (*Negara Islam Indonesia,* NII), it eventually established nine political and military commands, in Lampung, Sumatra, Kalimantan, Sulawesi, East Java, Central Java, Jakarta, West Priangan (Serang-Banten, Bogor, Garut, and Bandung) and East Priangan, the last two in West Java being the strongholds of the DI.[6]

What started as Kartosuwiryo's challenge in West Java eventually spread to different parts of the country, with a number of DI rebellions breaking out throughout the country. In central Java, Amir Fatah and his associates launched a DI rebellion against the Republican government. More ominous was the DI rebellion in South Sulawesi. During the revolutionary war, the military governor for South Sulawesi was Kahar Muzakkar. Following the Linggajati Agreement, all Republican troops could not withdraw as was stipulated in the agreement. As such, the fighting continued. Once the cease-fire was declared in 1949, like that of the Dutch government, the Republican government refused to recognize Kahar's forces as part of the Republican Army. Kahar felt betrayed by the Republican Army, particularly Sukarno, Hatta, Sudirman, and Nasution. He then raised arms and fought against the Republic and the Republican Army. Later, he joined forces with Kartosuwiryo, leading to the expansion of DI to South Sulawesi. Like Kartosuwiryo, Amir Fatah and Kahar Muzakkar fought against the Dutch during the "war of revolution," in South Kalimantan with Ibnu Hadjar leading the guerrillas. Just as in West and Central Java, and in South Sulawesi, following the Renville Agreement, clashes broke out between the Republican Army and forces of Ibnu Hadjar, leading to the latter joining forces with Kartosuwiryo's DI and the rebellion spreading to Kalimantan. The last major region to support the DI rebellion was Aceh, in September 1953.[7]

Even though the DI was militarily suppressed and its leader, Kartosuwiryo, captured by the *Siliwangi* Division on June 4, 1962, in Gunung Rakutak (later in September, he was sentenced to death), in all sense, the concept, roots, and aspirations of the DI, TII, and NII remained fresh in Indonesia's body politic. However, it was never allowed to surface and pose a challenge to the political order, especially under Suharto. DI's insurgency in Indonesia, mainly in Java, Sumatra, and Sulawesi, lasted until 1962, when Kartosuwiryo was executed. In South Sulawesi, Kahar led the insurgency that lasted much longer. Even though DI's military threat was contained and neutralized, as an organization it remained intact, especially various commands in Java, Sumatra, and Sulawesi. Under Suharto, the activities of the DI were closely monitored and its leaders pursued.

The Conflict in Aceh

Located on the westernmost tip of Indonesia, Aceh is renowned for its prominent role during the Indonesian struggle for independence against Dutch colonial rule. A province of more than four million people, located at the head of the Malaccan Strait, it lies astride one of the most strategic waterways in the world, linking the Pacific and Indian oceans. Having violently resisted Dutch colonial rule for decades, the Acehnese were finally forced in the early 1900s to submit to an uneasy peace with their colonial masters. The Dutch stationed their troops in Aceh until the Japanese invasion of 1942. In 1948, with the help of the Netherlands, the province was annexed by the newly created Indonesian state.

Since becoming part of the Republic of Indonesia, Aceh has revolted on two occasions against the state, namely in 1953 and 1976. In 1953, Aceh declared itself a part of DI's revolt. The rebellion was Islam-inspired and led by Teungku Chik di Tiro of Pidie. It was led by the Acehnese *ulamas* (religious leaders) demanding greater autonomy for Aceh regarding religion, *adat* (customary law), and education. Indonesian troops quelled the unrest. When the DI rebellion erupted in parts of Java and in Aceh, a movement that wanted Indonesia to become an Islamic state, it never advocated independence for Aceh, and this accounted in part for its weakness in Aceh. The DI movement disintegrated in Aceh when its leaders were co-opted into the

government and Aceh was given special provincial status. A shaky truce was negotiated with Jakarta in 1959, and Aceh was granted the status of "Special Region" with
autonomy in matters of religion, education, and social customs.

In reality, however, the Acehnese felt that they were cheated of the right to exercise
their autonomy, and the majority of the Acehnese felt that they did not benefit by
integrating into the Republic of Indonesia. Despite its great wealth, Aceh has
remained one of the poorest and underdeveloped provinces in Indonesia. What
Aceh contributes to the central government in terms of oil, natural gas, and other
resources, and what the Acehnese people receive in return, was perceived to be
profoundly unequal, representing a clear case of "internal colonialism." For instance,
in 1997–98, the central government collected more than 32 trillion Rupiah and gave
to Aceh only 290 billion Rupiah.[8]

The economic exploitation, among others, made some Acehnese bent upon
fighting for the independence of Aceh by joining the guerrilla movement, the Aceh
Sumatra National Liberation Front, Free Aceh Movement, *Gerakan Aceh Merdeka*
(GAM). In October 1976, the Acehnese revolted and declared independence, marking the beginning of an era of oppression by the Indonesian regime.[9] Instead of
working to ameliorate sociopolitical and economic conflict through dialogue, Jakarta
mobilized the military to institutionalize state violence and counterinsurgency
against suspected members of the independence movement, leading to military
brutalities, abuse of power, and massive casualties on both sides. Jakarta's oppression
of Acehnese separatism was understandable, as it wanted to preserve the territorial
integrity of the state and profit from the vast resources found in the province, as well
as use the territory for resettlement of Javanese from Java.

While Hasan di Tiro's GAM has been the key separatist group in Aceh, now
renamed *Nanggroë Aceh Darusalam,* or NAD, due to internal differences, a splinter
faction led by Dr. Hussani (a former cabinet minister in GAM) has emerged, calling
itself the MP-GAM (*Majelis Pemerintahan–Gerakan Aceh Merdeka*). The conflict
between GAM and the Indonesian government has continued despite a number
of efforts at peacemaking. On May 12, 2000, representatives of the Stockholm-
based GAM and the Indonesian government signed a formal accord in Geneva,
Switzerland. Referred to as a "truce" or "humanitarian pause" by then-Indonesian
President Abdurrahman Wahid, this agreement was the culmination of secret
negotiations that begun in February 1999. On June 13, 2000, a six-point agreement,
"The Permanent Procedure of the Joint Committee on Security Modalities," was
signed in Banda Aceh, the capital of the province. Despite the designation of certain
areas in Aceh as "peace zones," the deal broke down, and armed conflict continued
until a new peace initiative under President Susilo Bambang Yudhoyono was
signed in August 2005. Through the good offices of Finland, the Indonesian
government and GAM signed a "peace treaty," and this appears to be holding.
While the military conflict seems to have ended, the radicalization of Acehnese
society seems to be proceeding unabated with *sharia* law being applied locally.
How this Acehnese radicalization in a peace setting will impact upon Indonesian
society remains to be seen.

PHILIPPINES

Islam took root in the Philippines in 1380, even though some scholars date it as far as the early 1200s. The inhabitants of Sulu were among the earliest converts to Islam in the country. These converts retained much of their pre-Islamic beliefs because the conversions were mostly done by Arab Muslim traders and not religious scholars. By the early 1700s, the sultan of Sulu defeated the sultan of Maguindanao, signaling the rise of the Sulu sultanate in Mindanao and the spread of Islam. The Spaniards made several attempts to control Jolo, the capital of Sulu, but failed. The coming of Islam brought about dramatic transformations in the lives of the converts. A rigid and uncompromising monotheism was introduced, with Islamic laws, ethical standards, and new outlooks shaping the lives of the people. The Arabic script was adopted for writing local languages and the Arabic language itself was used for ritual and theological matters. Moreover, Malay became the commercial and court language, helping, in the process, to make the Philippine Muslims increasingly an integral part of an expanding Islamic Malay world.

The political and ideological cohesive character of the Philippine Muslim principalities was the principal reason impeding the Spanish subjugation of Mindanao and Sulu, unlike other parts of the Philippines. The confrontation between the Spaniards and the Muslims in the Philippines flamed into the so-called Moro Wars—a series of bitter wars of attrition that continued for more than three centuries. These bitter wars have made the Philippine Muslims what they are today and helped to define their attitudes to all non-Muslim foreigners as well as to non-Muslim Filipinos. The premise of Spanish historians that the so-called Moro Wars were waged primarily by the Spaniards to curb piratical incursions of Muslim sultans and their followers is not only too facile an explanation of the facts, but was actually a rationalization for the conquest, colonization, and Christianization of the Muslims.

Four main factors underscored Moro separatist sentiment.[10] First was the fear of a weakening religious, cultural, and political tradition through forced assimilation into a Catholic-dominated Philippine republic. In fact, governments in Manila aimed at both political domination and religious conversion in Mindanao. It reflected a general unwillingness to subscribe to Manila's secular civil, political, judicial, and penal constitutional system. Second was the resentment of Catholic transmigration from the north. This has not only dispossessed many Muslims of ancient and communal land rights, but also reduced the Moro population to a minority in their own homeland. Third was the frustration with Mindanao's lack of economic development. Currently, 15 of the Philippines' poorest provinces are located in the south, which additionally has the country's lowest literacy rate (75 percent) and life expectancy (57 years). Exploitative economic policies and uneven investment flows, which have mainly benefited industries in the northern Philippines, have exacerbated disparities between Catholics and Muslims, further fueling perceptions of local alienation and deprivation. Fourth is a tradition of warlordism, banditry, and blood feuds.

MORO NATIONAL LIBERATION FRONT (MNLF)

The Moro rebellion has dominated the Philippines' politics for the longest period, having its roots in Spanish and American colonialism of the country. When the Spanish halted the Islamization of the Philippines in 1565 and drove the Moros southward, the war between the essentially Islamic Moros and the largely Christian north, be it under Spain, the United States, or the Philippines, has continued almost unabated.[11] The Moros[12] fought the Spanish for nearly 350 years. Following the American colonization of the Philippines, the Moros contested Washington's control of the Muslim territories and again, the war continued. The same pattern continued under Philippines rule, only that the situation was worsened by the influx of Catholic settlers in the south, the occupation of Muslim lands by the northern settlers, the growth in landlessness of the Muslims and growth in economic deprivation. This was worsened by brutal military repression by the essentially Catholic-dominated Armed Forces of the Philippines.

Due to the accumulation of grievances, in May 1968, under the leadership of Datu Udtog Matalam (a Muslim), the former governor of Cotabota, the Mindanao Independence Movement (MIM) was established with the avowed aim of establishing an independent Islamic state constituting of Mindanao, Sulu, and Palawan islands.[13] The other Islamic militant organizations, Union of Islamic Forces and Organizations (UIFO), and the *Ansar El Islam,* were also established during this period, mainly with support from the Middle East. An important catalyst for the establishment of the MIM, UIFO, and other militant groups was the Filipino Muslims' reaction to what has come to be known as the *"Jabidah* Massacre," or the Corregidor Incident. In March 1968, the Philippines Armed Forces massacred 28 Muslim military trainees who refused to be sent to Sabah and Sarawak to agitate the civilians to demand annexation by the Philippines. Once this became public, Kuala Lumpur broke off diplomatic relations with Manila and began supporting the Moro struggle, among others, permitting the establishment of military training camps in the country.[14] Kuala Lumpur's support for the Moros was critical in the growth and development of the separatist movement in the Philippines.

In reaction to the formation of the MIM, Manila sponsored the establishment of various "Christian defenders groups," the most notorious being the *Illaga* Movement. This intensified Muslim-Christian violence in the south, thereby worsening the security situation. An important consequence of this emerging conflict was the emergence of a group of new and younger Muslim leaders, gravely altering the tempo and depth of the conflict. A key leader in this regard was Nur Misuari, a Tausug, who founded the Moro National Liberation Front (MNLF) in 1972. Following this, the MIM was dissolved, with the Organization of Islamic Conference (OIC), Islamic Conference of Foreign Ministers, and Libya supporting the MNLF. Initially, the MNLF defined itself according to three main beliefs—that the Moro people constituted a distinct *bangsa* (nation) that has a specific Islamic historical and cultural identity; that the *bangsa Moro* has a legitimate right to determine their own future; and the MNLF has both a duty and obligation to wage a *Jihad* against the Philippine state.[15] The *Bangsa Moro* Army, the military arm of the MNLF, conducted a bitter guerrilla war with the Philippines army, forcing President Marcos to declare martial law in 1972. Due to the intensity of the fighting, the Philippines government sued for peace, resulting in the 1976 Tripoli Agreement that was brokered by the OIC. Rather than independence, Nur Misuari accepted autonomy for 13 of Mindanao's 21 provinces. The agreement broke down, however, and warfare continued. A new deal was signed in 1996 that brought a modicum of peace to southern Philippines as far as the MNLF was concerned. Nur Misuari's deal with Manila, however, fragmented the Islamic insurgency as a breakaway faction intensified its goal of establishing an Islamic republic that would be based on "*Koranic* principles."[16]

MORO ISLAMIC LIBERATION FRONT (MILF)

A split in the MNLF saw the establishment of the Moro Islamic Liberation Front (MILF) and the MNLF Reformist Group. Particularly important was the former, which was established on December 26, 1977. Unlike the essentially leftist credentials of the MNLF, the MILF emphasized its Islamic identity with the goal of establishing an independent Islamic Moro state.[17] Its leader, the late Hashim Salamat, formerly Vice-Chairman of the MNLF, was strongly supported by many Muslim religious leaders and a powerful military wing, the *Bangsa Moro* Islamic Armed Forces (BMIAF) that is believed to greatly outnumber the MNLF. While the MNLF draws its support from the Tausug ethnic group and is based in Sulu, the MILF has the support of the two largest ethnic groups in Mindanao, the Maguindanaos and Maranaos. The BMIAF is highly proficient militarily, as many of its members have combat experience in Afghanistan fighting alongside anti-Soviet *Mujahidin* fighters. According to Hashim Salamat, the avowed political objective of the MILF was to create a separate Islamic state in areas where Muslims were a majority in the southern Philippines. These areas have been defined to include central Mindanao, parts of the Zamboanga peninsula, Davao, Basilan, Sulu, Tawi-Tawi, and Palawan. The purpose of this polity, to be known as the Mindanao Islamic Republic (MIR), was to establish a system of government that upheld and applied *sharia* (Islamic law) in all aspects of daily life. Such a goal was to be achieved through a combined strategy of *da'wa* (Islamic preaching) and *jihad* (holy war).[18]

In view of the growing insurgency in southern Philippines, with the support of the OIC and particularly Indonesia, Nur Misuari negotiated a peace deal with Manila. However, in addition to the challenge posed by the MILF, the establishment of an extremist Islamist movement, the *Abu Sayyaf* in 1991 by Amilhussin Jumaani and Abdurajak Abubakar Janjalani, complicated the state of Islamic separatism in the Philippines. The founders of the *Abu Sayyaf* were religious scholars (or *Ulamas*) who had been trained in the Middle East. Even though compared to the MNLF and MILF, the *Abu Sayyaf* is a much smaller outfit, it is extremely ruthless, with most of its members being veterans of the anti-Soviet war in Afghanistan. Being extremely anti-Christian and not prepared to negotiate, it has been involved in some of the most brutal attacks in the south. It has also been able to increase its membership, mainly drawing support from ex-MNLF members who have become disillusioned with Nur Misuari. Abdurajak was killed in a gun battle with security forces in December 1998. His younger brother Khadafi took over *Abu Sayyaf*'s leadership, and he was killed in September 2006. In early 2007, Yasser Igasan was installed as *Abu Sayyaf*'s new leader Despite the government's claim that the *Abu Sayyaf* has been annihilated, the extremist group has been able to survive and poses a serious security threat to the Philippines all the more as it has successfully linked up with various international terrorist groups.

THAILAND

The Muslim minority of approximately six million accounts for about 5 percent of the total population of Thailand. The vast majority of these Muslims are Malay in origin, the remainder being Pakistani immigrants, ethnic Thai Muslims, and a few Chinese Muslims. The majority of the Muslims are Sunnis, though the Shias are also sizeable in some of the areas. About 10 percent of the total Muslim population is Wahhabi. The Muslims are concentrated in the provinces of Songkhla, Satun, Pattani, Narathiwat, and Yala at the southern end of Thailand bordering the northern states of West Malaysia. Historically, the area occupied by these Muslims has generally been much poorer than the rest of Thailand.[19]

The Islamic sultanate of Pattani, historically referred to as Langkasuka, was considered by historians as one of the cradles of Islam in Southeast Asia. Thailand's history of Islam dates back to the Ayutthia Dynasty (1350–1767). Islam arrived from various directions: the Malay-Indonesian archipelago, Yemen (Hadhramawt), Persia, India, Burma, China, and Cambodia. The establishment of Islam in Malacca, during the reign of Sultan Iskandar, led to the spread of the early syncretic Islam in the Southeast Asian archipelago, reaching Pattani by 1387. The upper southern Thai province of Songkhla marks the language border between Malay- and Thai-speaking Muslims. There was minimal spreading of Malay Islamic religiosity beyond Songkhla. This was partly due to consolidation of the orthodoxy of Singhalese (*Theravada*) Buddhism, which had been introduced into the Indo-Chinese peninsula by the Mons of Burma. This was disseminated further by the Thais a century following the decline of Hindu Sanskrit culture and Mahayana Buddhism in the Menam and Mekong basins.

Historically, the region consisting of the provinces of Satun, Songkhla, Pattani, Yala, and Narathiwat has long served as a dumping ground for corrupt and incompetent civilian and military officials, a trend that has alienated the local population from the central government. Another major problem facing the region, particularly in urban areas, is the higher level of common banditry and acts of lawlessness in comparison to the other regions of Thailand, making it sometimes very difficult for authorities to differentiate between lawlessness committed by criminals and terrorist acts committed by Thai terrorist and Muslim separatist groups.[20]

The bulk of the region now occupied by the Muslims in southern Thailand was annexed by Thailand in 1902 as a buffer against British Malaya. Fearing that the region would drift into the hands of British Malaya, Thailand annexed Pattani and six other sultanates, placing the region under Bangkok's direct control. Since the 1902 annexation, there has always been local resistance against Bangkok's control over the region. While the sultan and their siblings fled to present day northern Malaysia, Abdul Kadir, the last sultan, stayed behind to fight the new Siamese rulers. His resistance was quickly put down, and he was charged with treason and sentenced to 10 years in prison. Following diplomatic pressure from the British colonial authorities (especially Governor Sir Frank Swettenham), he was released as the British feared Kadir's jailing would become a rallying point for the locals in northern Malaysia. This was because people on both sides of what is today's Thai-Malaysian border saw themselves as one community.[21] Kadir was granted royal amnesty on the condition that he no longer participate in any kind of political activities. However, in 1915 he was discovered engaging in active politics and was again imprisoned for another two years and eight months.

At the end of his prison term, Kadir sought political asylum in Kelantan and lived there until his death in 1933. Thereafter, Tengku Mahmud Mahyideen, his youngest son, continued his father's mission of trying to liberate Pattani from Thailand. While in Kelantan, Abdul Kadir maintained links with his own people in the southernmost provinces of Thailand and motivated them to take political action in the form of aggressive illegal movements, such as the Nam Sai Rebellion in 1922. Tengku Mahmud Mahyideen also cooperated with some religious leaders in the southernmost provinces of Thailand to liberate Pattani state from Thailand. He had also brought together all the descendants of the seven sultans and formed the *Gabungan Melayu Pattani Raya* (GAMPAR), or Association of Malays of Greater Pattani, on March 5, 1948. Following the Border Agreement on the Suppression of Communism in December 1948, the British colonial authorities in Malaya and the Thai government arrested most of GAMPAR's leaders, sounding the death knell of the association.

King Rama VI did his best to reduce political tension between Pattani and other neighboring regions through carefully crafted sociocultural integration and nation-building policies. However, the ethnicity-based nationalistic attitudes of the Malay ethnic groups in the northern states of Malaya towards those in the southernmost provinces of Thailand had been obviously so strong and sensitive that the former were prepared to extend their possible political support to the latter. These attitudes also served as a warning to the Thai government that suppression of the Malays and cultural identity would be met with opposition from the Malay Muslims in the region.

The Japanese invasion of Thailand and Malaya in 1941 and the beginning of the Second World War gave the separatist movements some hope. As the Thai government was allied with the Japanese, in return for support, the British promised the Muslims an independent Pattani state. The British governor, Sir Frank Sweetenham, later reneged the understanding, as the post–Second World War Thai government decided to ally itself with the United States. The Muslim separatist movement in Thailand has its modern-day roots in the late 1940s, and is characterized by internal divisions, factions, and constant reorganizations. Neighboring Malaysia provided another widely used propaganda theme. In 1957, all regions in West Malaysia, then called Malaya, became independent states. As a consequence, some Thai Muslims in the southern border provinces realized that they would not be able to enjoy similar privileges and freedoms granted to the Malays by the Malay government if they continued to live under Thai rule. Armed resistance did not begin until 1960, when Field Marshall Sarit Thannarat ignited the powder keg with his decision to bring all Islamic schools in the south, known as *pondoks,* under the control of the Thai Ministry of the Interior. Sarit's government saw the *pondoks* as a rallying point for separatists. One hundred and fifty of the 355 *pondoks* in the region protested the government's decision by shutting themselves down. One in Narathiwat challenged Sarit's decision by taking up arms and fled to the jungle to wage a military insurgency.

Following GAMPAR's demise, three separatist movements have dominated the struggle in the south, namely, the *Barisan Revolusi Nasional* (BRN), the *Barisan Nasional Pembebasan Pattani* (BNPP), and the Pattani United Liberation Organization (PULO). The BRN, or National Revolution Front, was founded in 1960 and was essentially a leftist organization that worked closely with the Communist Party of Malaya, which had sanctuaries in southern Thailand. Having pan-Malay ideals, it adopted armed struggle as a means to first unite the four Muslim-dominated provinces in the south and later seek a union with Malaya (later Malaysia). The BRN was, however, greatly weakened by internal divisions, and two splinter groups emerged from it. The first was the *Partai Revolusi Nasional* (PARNAS), or the National Revolutionary Party, in 1965. This proved to be ineffective.

A more effective splinter from the BRN was the BNPP, or Pattani National Liberation Movement, that was formed in 1971 in Kelantan under the leadership of Tengku Abdul Jalil. The BNPP is believed to have some support from Kelantan and various Middle East countries, including the Islamic Secretariat, Arab League, and the Palestine Liberation Organization. Later in 1986, the BNPP renamed itself the *Barisan Islam Pembebasan Pattani* (BIPP, or the Islamic Liberation Front of Pattani) to underline its stronger commitment to Islamist politics and conform to the struggle launched by separatist Muslims throughout the world. As its ideology was unclear at the time of its establishment, the BNPP also attracted a large number of followers from a broad spectrum of Pattani society. But the BNPP's main weakness was its apparent lack of direction and ideological coherence. Its goal of national liberation remained vague, and many of its members were concerned about the dominance of traditional elites and aristocrats. The organization ceased its activity in Thailand until early 2002. It is believed to have been involved in some attacks during the recent spate of violence.

The BNPP is headquartered in Kelantan and participates in Malaysian state–level politics. At present, it is led by Badri Harridan and Sumsuddin, who organized a temporary army called *Tentera Nasional Pembebasan Rakyat Pattani* (TNPP). It is believed that the members of the TNPP are several hundred in number, recruited from Pattani, Yala, and Narathiwat provinces and divided into subdivisions, consisting of 10–20 staff members. Their immediate goal is to restore or revive the former

Pattani state, which was prosperous in the past, and the topmost goal is to unite the Pattani state with the Federation of Malaysia. As it is, the BNPP has been in operation for a long time and has played a significant part in the struggle for separation, with special emphasis on the public relations by means of which adequate information about Pattani was well publicized—so much so that the people both inside Thailand and beyond have been kept well informed. Much of the focus was on the people in the Arabic world. Under the support by the BNPP, the young Malay-Muslims were sent to study at universities in the Middle East, such as Egypt and Saudi Arabia. After completing their studies, the young graduates returned to their home place, working under the direction and supervision of the BNPP.

The PULO was established in 1967 in India. It was, however, launched in Mecca, Saudi Arabia, in January 1968.[22] By far, it has been the most important separatist group in southern Thailand. Believing in seceding from Thailand and sanctioning the use of force, it established the Pattani United Liberation Army, PULA. As most of PULO leaders were foreign-educated, they had established a fairly extensive international network, especially with the Middle East countries. It has achieved some degree of international recognition, being an observer at the World Muslim League Conference.[23] Like most groups, it suffered from splits, and three main factions have emerged. The PULO Leadership Council is led by Arong Muleng, PULO Army Command Council is led by Hayihadi Mindosali, and the original PULO is under Tengku Bira. Dr. Arong's faction is often referred to as the New PULO.

In 1995, rifts emerged among the core leaders of the new PULO movement. As a result, Dr. Arong decided to split his group from the movement to set up a new organization called "PULO 88," or the *Abu Jihad* PULO. The other group, led by Haji Habeng Abdul Rohman, named its armed unit as "Caddan Army," choosing to pursue the goal of internal autonomy through less dramatic but more consistent actions than its parent organization. To this end, the focus has been on carrying out minor attacks that were intended to harass the police, local authorities, and other symbols of Thai sociopolitical suppression, particularly public schools.

Command headquarters of the two factions are located in Malaysia. In common with PULO, it is alleged that the group's ability to carry out assaults have been aided by passive Malaysian support, not least because its leaders are believed to have had the benefit of operating out of secure safe havens in the jungles of Kelantan. After some leaders of the old and new PULO movements were arrested in early 1998—including Haji Da-Oh Thanam, the group's military leader, and Rohman Bazo, the group's chairman—confusion immediately occurred within this organization. As a result, morale became very low and some of its members, who lost faith in the group, surrendered to the Thai government. In view of the worsening security situation in southern Thailand, in April 2005, the remerger of all the PULO factions was announced under the leadership of Abdul Rahman Betong.[24]

Additionally, in line with the increasing radicalization of Muslims in southern Thailand, mainly due to the participation in the Afghan struggle, a new group, the *Gerakan Mujahidin Islam Pattani* (GMIP) was established in 1985. It aimed to carry out a struggle to liberate the southern border provinces and establish an "Islamic

State." GMIP elements were commonly known as *Mujahidin Pattani* members. The front's goal is also to consolidate the various resistance organizations into a single entity. It has placed an emphasis on conducting personnel training and political work. Its main headquarters is located in Malaysia. Most of its core leaders were elements that split from the BNPP. However, the front's performance has not been particularly successful.

The United Front for the Independence of Pattani, or BERSATU, was formed with an idea of unifying all splinter terrorist groups together. On August 31, 1989, core leaders of all terrorist movement groups, namely the BIPP, the BRN Congress, the BNP, the new PULO, and GMIP, held a joint meeting called "the gathering of the fighters for Pattani." The meeting agreed to set up a "*Payong* (umbrella) Organization" to unify all the movements and to carry out the struggle in the same direction in order to avoid creating confusion in accepting financial donations from foreign countries. In 1991, the name of the organization was changed to "The United Front for the Independence of Pattani," or BERSATU, as it is still referred to currently. The group has carried out a series of coordinated attacks (code-named "Falling Leaves"), aimed at killing state workers, law enforcement personnel, local government officials, school teachers, and other perceived symbols of Thai repression. Between August 1997 and January 1998, no fewer than 33 separate attacks were carried out as part of this effort, resulting in nine deaths, several dozen injuries and considerable economic damage.[25]

These groups have employed the tactic of deploying small armed bands to carry out guerrilla activities in the jungles. They set up no permanent bases on Thai soil. Instead, they are on the move all the time and avoid engaging in armed clashes with Thai government authorities. If a brief clash should occur, the terrorists would see to it that they must withdraw from the scene of fighting immediately. Fighting must not be protracted. If an opportunity should arise, they would resort to ambush tactics or launch a surprise attack on the government authorities and positions. They choose to retaliate against government suppression drives by conducting sabotage activities against public facilities in town or on the plain.

Since 1997, there has been a resurgence of violence in the southern provinces. This is due to several factors, including unemployment caused by the "Asian Financial Crisis," which hit Thailand in August 1997, as well as the growing drug problem. Both these factors resulted in an expanded pool of discontented youth that are prime targets for recruitment by terrorists. Youth returning from overseas Islamic schools have also have been recruited. For several years since, terrorist activities in the southern provinces included the occasional bombing of soft targets, extortion, armed robbery, assassination for hire, and protection services for narcotics traffickers. Local criminals also have masqueraded as terrorists, sometimes making it difficult to distinguish activities among the different groups. In the last few years, terrorist groups have lost many fighters both in armed clashes and from the Thai government's public relations campaign, prompting terrorists to begin relying on the media as a primary tool.

The geographical contiguity of Malaysia provides an important explanation as to the impetus to armed irredentism among the Thai Malay-Muslims. The visible

economic development in neighboring Malaysia, where "kindred Malays are dominant politically and are also reaping economic benefits from the pro-*Bumiputra* (sons
of the soils or natives) New Economic Policy, provided an unwelcome comparison."[26]
Moreover, the free flow of information across the Thai-Malaysian border has enabled
the Thai Malay-Muslims to reinforce their cultural, ethnic, and religious identity in
the face of concerted efforts directed towards assimilation on the part of the Thai
government. Malay Muslims in the southern border provinces of Thailand and those
in the northern border states of Malaysia are very close to each other religiously,
racially, and culturally, sharing similar sociocultural backgrounds. The leaders of the
two are also closely related by blood. Although the Malaysian government has denied
any involvement in supporting armed separatist in southern Thailand, Thailand has
repeatedly accused Malaysia of sponsoring armed separatism and sanctioning the
operation of separatists from bases in Kelantan.

Since the 9/11 incident and Thailand's support for the U.S. "war on terror," the
situation in southern Thailand has worsened dramatically, especially since
January 2004.[27] More than 2,000 people have been killed from January 2004 to
February 2007.[28] The repression of the Thaksin Government was a key factor in this
escalation, especially following the Krue Se Mosque and Tak Bai incidents, where
Thai security forces killed nearly 200 Muslims. The Krue Sae Mosque incident
occurred on April 28, 2004, and the Tak Bai Incident on October 28, 2004. The
Muslim separatists have retaliated with almost daily violence, killing members of
the security apparatus, Thai bureaucrats, monks, and Muslims suspected of being
agents for the intelligence agencies. Not only have the attacks become more lethal
and coordinated, what is interesting is that the perpetrators have never claimed
responsibility for their acts. For instance, on February 18, 2007, the separatists staged
49 coordinated bombings in the south that killed nine people and wounded 44.[29]
This was despite the conciliatory policies of the military-installed government that
came to power in September 2006.

MYANMAR

Myanmar is home to more than two million Muslims, or 4 percent of the population. Due to repression by the Myanmarese military junta, there are more than 1.5
million Myanmar Muslims living in Bangladesh, Pakistan, and the Middle East.[30]
There are at least four ethnically distinct Muslim communities in Myanmar, all of
which are Sunnis.[31] The largest, and also the poorest, are the *Rohingyas*. They reside
along the Myanmar-Bangladesh border and share many common cultural traits with
Bangladesh's Bengali Muslims. Most of the Myanmar *Rohingyas* live in the
northwestern Rakhine state.[32] In addition, there is a small community of Chinese
Muslims, known as the Panthay, whose origins lie in an Islamic sultanate that
dominated southern Yunnan in the mid-nineteenth century. Even though during
the colonial government and during the democratic era, Muslims held senior
positions in Myanmar's public service, following Ne Win's military coup in 1962,
they have been heavily discriminated against and marginalized, fuelling resentment

and hostility.[33] Under various regulations since 1982, most of Myanmar's Muslims have been denied full citizenship, refused permission to build new mosques, and had some of their older places of worship destroyed. Mainly due to these pogroms, many Myanmar Muslims have opted for *jihad,* and this largely explains the struggle against the state.

The poverty of the *Rohingyas* as well as the overt discriminatory policies and violence perpetrated against them has led many to seek refuge in neighboring Bangladesh. Between 1978 and 2001, some 250,000 *Rohingyas* are believed to have fled to Bangladesh to escape from military-instituted violence against them.[34] As the Yangon government openly views Islam as a "national security threat," a near-apartheid situation exists in Myanmar, even though the state is located in a region with many Muslim-dominated states in South and Southeast Asia.[35] It is against this backdrop that Islamic-based self-determination armed groups have emerged to challenge Myanmar.

For some decades, there have been a number of small Muslim armed groups based in the Rakhine state and engaged in the struggle for human rights and federal democracy. For them, national *Jihad* had been the rallying cry. Some Muslims have also joined the Burmese Communist Party. There are also a number of Muslim armed opposition groups based along the Myanmar-Bangladesh border. In the past, there was also a Muslim armed group, the *Kawthoolei* Muslim Liberation Front, established on the Myanmar-Thai border in the mid-1980s that fought alongside the Karen National Liberation Army. However, in general, only a small proportion of Muslims in Myanmar have advocated armed struggle, and only a few have actively sought for international assistance. Even fewer favor links with extremist pan-Islamic organizations. Some *Rohingya* insurgent groups have been at pains to refute suggestions that they are in any way associated with radical movements of this kind. Over the past decade, however, it appears that the Bangladesh-based *Rohingya* Solidarity Organization (RSO) has developed connections with Muslim extremist organizations in Bangladesh, Pakistan, and possibly even the Middle East.[36]

The most prominent political Islamic group in Myanmar is the *Arakan Rohingya* National Organization (ARNO) and is essentially an armed self-determination movement. This group seeks to protect the rights of the minority *Rohingya* and hope to establish an autonomous state of Arakan in Myanmar.[37] Many of the ARNO recruits are from refugee camps, and this is a major backlash of Myanmar's repressive policies. To make the situation worse, there has been a growing radicalization of the ARNO, with many ARNO members believed to have established ties with radicals from the *Taliban* and *al Qaeda.*

Historically, the ARNO originated from the *Mujahid* Party, Arakan. The *Mujahid* Party was formed under the *Dobboro Chaung* Declaration in 1947. It was led by Jafar Hussain, popularly known as Jafar Kawal. The *Mujahid* Party (which was guided by a *Jihad* Council) then consisted of *Rohingya* elders who supported a *jihad* movement in Arakan. The aim of the *Mujahid* Party was to create a Muslim Autonomous State within the Federal Union of Burma. By the early sixties, due to the lack of the international community's support and recognition, the movement withered away.[38]

In April 1964, the *Rohingya* Independent Force (RIF) was formed at Maungdaw, Arakan, under the leadership of Master Sultan Ahmed and Jafar Habib (popularly known as B.A. Jafar). The aim of the RIF was to create a *Rohingya* autonomous state under the Union of Burma. In 1969 the name of RIF was changed to AIR (*Rohingya* Independent Army) and led by Jafar Habib.[39] On September 12, 1973, near Sack Dala on the Myanmar-Bangladesh border, AIR renamed itself the *Rohingya* Patriotic Front (RPF) and was led by Jafar Habib. After the independence of Bangladesh, there were many changes in RPF, and in June 1974 RPF was again reconstituted under the leadership of Jafar Habib. The aim of the RPF was to create a *Rohingya* autonomous state within the Union of Burma.[40]

Since 1978, factionalism and disunity have caused serious disintegration within the *Rohingya* movement and the mushrooming of factional groups. This led to infighting within the *Rohingya* movement.[41] In 1995, the then-existing two *Rohingya* organizations, the Arakan *Rohingya* Islamic Front (ARIF) and the *Rohingya* Solidarity Organization (RSO), formed an alliance under the umbrella of *Rohingya* National Alliance (RNA). The two groups agreed to combine their resources and efforts, and to work together in several fields—political, military, sociocultural, educational, and other national activities—in the interest of their people. A Joint Declaration of Alliance was signed and issued on July 10, 1995.[42]

This alliance did not last long, and in a matter of months, the RSO was divided into two factions, RSO (led by Dr. Mohammed Yunus) and RSO (led by Mohammed Zakaria). Bitter rivalry and intense infighting between the two factions of RSO resulted in indiscipline and total loss of command among the rank and file. Since then, the alliance has almost been nonfunctional.[43] The ARIF and RSO factions realized the importance of unity among them and opted for a broad-based single representative organization. The leaders of the ARIF, RSO (Yunus), and RSO (Zakaria), together with *Rohingya* elite, academics, and intellectuals, and after long deliberations and discussions on all issues and problems relating to the *Rohingya* movement for about two years, finally evolved a best-suited formula and framed a constitution and policy guidelines for the future course-of-action programs.[44]

All three organizations were officially declared as dissolved and merged into a single representative organization, the Arakan *Rohingya* National Organization (ARNO). A new Central Committee was formed with Mr. Nurul Islam as its president. To this end a joint declaration of the merger of the all-*Rohingya* organization, dated November 28, 1998, was signed, issued, and circulated. It should be stressed that the emergence of ARNO, through the merger of all *Rohingya* organizations, has given a fresh impetus to the *Rohingya* freedom struggle, and it has become a symbol of hope and confidence for the entire *Rohingya* people.[45]

THE "NEW" *JIHADISTS* IN SOUTHEAST ASIA

The Talibanization of Southeast Asia is riding on the birth of many new Islamist groups that came into being in the 1980s and 1990s. What distinguished the new movements were their intense militancy, extremism, and increasing propensity to resort to or condone violence to achieve their political goals. Similarly, more often than not, their national and regional objectives are synchronized with global *jihadi* objectives. In some ways, Islamist extremism and militancy were part of the rise in global religious extremism. While the Western media has focused on Islamist extremism as the most dangerous threat to Western civilization following the end of the Cold War, in actuality, religious extremism is not the sole monopoly of Islam. All religions have been experiencing revitalization, revivalism, and tendency towards greater extremism. The resurgence of religious extremism has enhanced interethnic and interreligious conflicts, especially in the post–Cold War era, a notion best highlighted by Samuel Huntington's thesis of "The Clash of Civilizations."

Many factors have contributed to the rise of Islamist militancy. Politically, there is a sense of disillusionment with national politics and political processes. In many Muslim societies, political repression, especially by secular regimes, has aggravated the situation. From the economic standpoint, there is disillusionment with economic programs of various states, especially the exploitation of the poor by the rich. The existence of unfair distribution of economic goods in spite of countries being well endowed has also provided ready recruits for the extremist cause. The existence of a sense of injustice that the country is being exploited by "global capitalism" and the "capitalists," often through collusion with local elites, has merely widened the "us versus them" gap. As far as sociocultural factors are concerned, the poor and repressed have blamed the spread of "global [mainly Western] values" through a mass media that is allegedly often controlled by various Jewish groups.

Added to these domestic considerations is the whole array of international factors. Many Muslims are disillusioned with the international system, mainly dominated by the West and particularly the United States, that is often portrayed to be practicing double standards. Though viewed as a democracy and champion of human rights, the United States' pro-Israel policies and sanction of Israeli repression of the Palestinians and Arabs, as well as its own largely anti-Islamic policies—evident in its almost nonaction when Muslims were being butchered in Bosnia—have riled many into launching a *Jihad* against the United States, Israel, and their supporters. Also, international (read, Western) support for repression of Muslims by various secular governments is also a source of anger and motivation. The lack of objection by the West to the repressive policies of Egypt, Algeria, Pakistan, and Suharto's Indonesia against their Islamic militants has led to the burgeoning of Islamic militancy and extremism in these countries.

The failure of "nationalist projects" to deliver political, economic, and social goods has led to counteractions—namely, the adoption of the "Islamic mode" of political, economic, and social development (including the use of terrorism and violence), to remedy what is perceived as national, regional, and global injustices. In this context, three important sources of Islamic extremism are worthy of note. One is the failure of secular governments to promote good governance and economic development in most Islamic countries. Many governments in the Muslim world have failed to address the challenges of development arising from rapid political, economic, social, and demographic changes over the last century, and particularly in the last 25 years.

Governmental failures have led to the emergence of poor masses in large- and medium-sized towns as well as in the rural areas, and this has made them particularly susceptible to extremist appeals. As governments failed to deliver the "goods" or simply ignored a large section of the populace, the extremist religious groups have gained dominance and tried to answer various material and psychological shortcomings through the resort of religious revivalism and extremism. This is because national and international injustices are usually blamed for the populace's backwardness, and violence (*Jihad*) is often recommended as the only alternative to overcome the national, as well as the *ummat*'s (Islamic community) problems worldwide.

Additionally, external forces have played a major role in the rise of many extremist Islamic groups in the Middle East, South Asia, and Southeast Asia. Particularly important here was the funding provided by the United States and the conservative regimes in the Middle East (especially Saudi Arabia) to prop up or create extremist groups, among others, to counter the Soviet invasion of Afghanistan and Israel's occupation of Palestine and its inhuman policies towards Palestinians and Arabs in general. The rise of extremist groups was also a function of the fact that the West, especially the United States, was supporting various conservative, feudal, and oppressive regimes in the Middle East, mainly for geopolitical and geoeconomic reasons, leading many to blame Washington and its allies for the rise of extremism in the region. A related factor is the rise of crisis within Islam. There has been a decline of the established tradition of *ijtihad,* interpretation of the *Koran* by Muslim clerics to apply *Koranic* laws to changing circumstances and dynamic developments that are confronting all societies, not just more Islamic ones. One consequence of this has been the rise of rigid and narrow interpretations of various religious precepts, especially as governments have failed to deliver political and economic goods as well as failed to build institutions, let alone democracy.

While many factors have contributed to the rise of new radical organizations and *Jihadists* in Southeast Asia, in the context of worldwide Islamic revival, the goals and character of "new Islam" has fundamentally altered the sociopolitical architecture of the region. The influx of funds and ideology from the Middle East and the trend toward Arabization of Islam, as well as efforts to "purify" the religion, to a large extent has accounted for this new phenomenon. Increasingly, unlike the past, concepts of an Islamic caliphate and Muslim Brotherhood as well as calls for a more "assertive defense" against attacks by "*kafirs*" (infidels, usually described as Christians and Jews) have been more openly adopted. While the role of the Iranian Revolution and the *Mujahidin* struggle in Afghanistan had a definite impact in radicalizing Islam, Saudi-funded schools and charities, spreading *Wahhabism* as well as "spark plugs" such as *Hizbut Tahrir* and *Jamaah Tarbiyah,* have played a key role in radicalizing Islam in the region.

While all, if not most, Islamist organizations have seen the intensification of radicalism, be it in Malaysia, southern Thailand, and southern Philippines, it is in Indonesia that the process of Talibanization is most acute and apparent. This is a function of both internal and external developments. Many radical groups are essentially home-grown, even though the influence of external developments is also important. There are also many groups that are closely affiliated with the Middle East. Whatever the origins and source of inspiration, the net effect has been the radicalization of Muslims in Indonesia and the region as a whole. A clear evidence of this is the efflorescence of radical and extremist groups in Indonesia. Some of these are operating as innocuous religious organizations even though they adhere to radical ideas and ideology.

The *Dewan Dakwah Islamiyah Indonesia* (DDII), or Indonesian Islamic Faith-Strengthening Body, was established in 1967 to continue the ideals of the *Masjumi* Party, which believes in promoting *Sharia* and the establishment of an Islamic state in Indonesia. Even though *Masjumi* was banned by President Sukarno and implicated in the American-sponsored regional rebellions in 1958 in Sumatra and Sulawesi, President Suharto gave his blessings to DDII for assisting him in toppling Sukarno and the PKI.[46] Under the leadership of Muhammad Natsir, a former prime minister and leader of *Masjumi,* the DDII send Indonesian students to the Middle East, especially Saudi Arabia. Scholarships were provided by Saudi Arabia. The DDII even opened an office in Riyadh, Saudi Arabia. Later, the Indonesian government took over the program, with more than 500 Indonesians benefiting from the program.

These graduates were later to play a leading role in Indonesia's radicalization, especially in spreading *Wahhabism,* becoming leaders of the *Tarbiyah* and *Dakwah Salafi.*[47] Natsir and the DDII were also instrumental in the establishment of *Lembaga Ilmu Islam dan Arab* (LIPIA), or the Institute for Islamic and Arab Studies, in Jakarta, which was, in effect, a branch of the Muhammad Ibnu Saud Islamic University in Riyadh. The LIPIA was principally instrumental in producing thousands of graduates that latter became key *salafist* actors in the *Tarbiyah.* The DDII was also instrumental in establishing the roots of radicalism in Indonesian campuses through its *Mujahid* Training Programme at the *Salman* Mosque at the Institute of Technology, Bandung. This movement eventually culminated in the establishment of the Campus *Dakwah* Institute. This movement provided the embryo for activists who later joined the *Tarbiyah, Hizbut Tahrir* Indonesia and the various *salafist* movements.

In 1987, the DDII sponsored the establishment of *Komite Indonesia Untuk Solidaritas Dengan Dunia Islam* (KISDI), or the Indonesian Committee for Solidarity with the Islamic World. According to Martin van Bruinessen, even though KISDI "claims as its founding date 1987 but its first public appearance was in 1990, around the same time that ICMI was established."[48] Since its establishment, KISDI, even under the Suharto regime, had been, despite various constraints, attempting to spearhead Islamization of Indonesia, especially at a time when Suharto had made his peace with political Islam. As was argued by a leading observer on Indonesian Islam:

> Its founders belonged to the most "hard-line" wing of DDII, were firm believers in a Western Jewish and Christian conspiracy to weaken or destroy Islam, and were generally hostile to non-Muslims. It would have been unthinkable for a group like this to operate publicly during the 1980s, but during Suharto's last years they came to dominate the streets. Their first actions were demonstrations of solidarity with Palestine—a very

acceptable cause in Indonesia, which has never recognized Israel—and later they took up the causes of oppressed Muslims in Bosnia, Kashmir, Chechnya, and Algeria.[49]

While spreading political Islam through various cultural programs, at the same time, structurally KISDI was involved in politics. Its leader, Adian Husaini, argued that the agenda of "political *dakwah*" was to spread the message of Prophet Muhammad. This saw KISDI leaders such as Husien Umar and K.H. Kholi Ridwan involved in initiating the passage of laws with regard to religion and national education.[50]

However, it was just prior to, and particularly following, the fall of Suharto that saw the proliferation of many radical Islamic organizations in Indonesia. One of the first to surface was the *Forum Komunikasi Ahlus Sunnah Wal Jamaah* (Communication Forum of the Followers of the *Sunna* and the Community of the Prophet). This was established in February 1998. The paramilitary organization, *Laskar Jihad,* was established by the Forum in January 2000 under the leadership of Jafar Umar Thalib, a charismatic preacher who fought with the *Mujahidins* in Afghanistan. This is a leading neo-*salafi* organization. Another group, *Kesatuan Aksi Mahasiswa Muslim Indonesia* (KAMMI), or the Muslim Students' Action Union, which had clandestinely operated in the campuses since the 1980s, surfaced in early 1998. Greatly influenced by the Muslim Brotherhood's *Tarbiyah* ideology, it became a leading radicalizing force in most Indonesian campuses. It later became the key recruiting ground for the *Partai Keadilan,* which renamed itself as *Partai Keadilan Sejatera.* Another Islamic radical body, *Himpunan Mahasiswa Muslim Antar Kampus* (HAMMAS), Inter-University Muslim Student Association, also emerged and has been involved in a number of violent actions in support of various Islamic causes.[51] The *Front Pembela Islam* (Islamic Defence Front), led by Habib Rizq Shihab, emerged on the Indonesian scene following the fall of the Suharto regime. It also has a paramilitary wing, the *Laskar Pembela Islam,* a group noted for its raids on brothels, bars, and gambling joints.

The *Majlis Mujahidin Indonesia,* MMI (Council of Indonesian *Jihad* Fighters) under the leadership Abu Bakar Baasyir (as its *Amir al-mujahidin,* Supreme Leader) tried to induct under its umbrella most of the former DI members. The MMI has tried to promote *Sharia* and the Jakarta Charter. This group's importance lies in the fact that its leader, Abu Bakar Baasyir, is currently alleged to be the spiritual leader of the most dangerous terrorist group threatening Southeast Asia, AJAI. What is important is that all these groups are essentially home grown. There is also the *Jamaah Ikhwan al-Muslimin* Indonesia, a group that is closely affiliated with *Al-Ikhwan-al-Muslimin* in Egypt. This is led by Habib Husein al-Habsyi. There is also the *Hizb al-Tharir Indonesia* (Indonesian Party of Liberation), originally established in Jordan but with deep roots in Indonesia. There are also a number of other "militias" that gained notoriety in Indonesia in the post-Suharto period. These include *Laskar Mujahidin Indonesia* (Indonesian Holy Warriors Force), *Barisan Pemuda Ka'ba* (Ka'ba Youth Squad), *Pam Swakarsa* (Self-Service Security Force), *Pendekar Banten* (Banten Warriors), *Gerakan Pemuda Islam* (Muslim Youth

Movement), and *Front Hizbullah Bulan Bintang* (God's Army Front of Crescent Moon Party).

There has been a similar upsurge of Islamist radicalism in other parts of Southeast Asia. Many existing separatist groups have adopted "Islamism" as the basis of its ideology. This is particularly evident in Thailand.[52] The BRN and PULO have become more Islamized and increasingly resort to calls for *jihad* in its mode of operations. PULO, long known for its factionalism, reemerged in May 2005 to form the "new united PULO." The BRN is believed to have formed a radical wing in late 2005, the *Runda Kumpulan Kecil,* and to have been established in close collaboration with Indonesian radicals based in Bandung. This group is believed to be behind some of the worst violence in southern Thailand since 2005. At the same time, the *Jemaah Salafi* group led by Abdul Fatah, the comrade-in-arm of Hambali, Hashim Salamat, and other *Jihadists* at Camp Sadda in Afghanistan during the *Mujahidin* struggle against the Soviets, is equally active, promoting hard-line *Wahhabi-salafist* ideas in southern Thailand.

Even though there are many groups that subscribe to Islamic radicalism, what unites them is their adoption of *salafism* as a religious ideology. Politically, they also adopt the ideology of *khilafatism,* supporting the establishment of an Islamic caliphate for all Muslims. It is against this backdrop that the rise of the AJAI should be understood, being one of the most important fallouts of the trend towards Talibanization in Southeast Asia.

CONCLUSION

A survey of the past shows that there has been widespread experience with Islamist radicalism in the region. Despite this challenge, the Southeast Asian region succeeded in maintaining a balance in favor of moderate Islam and kept the ensuing radicalism at bay. However, as Southeast Asia entered into the twenty-first century, the balance appears to be shifting in favor of the radicals. This was essentially a function of many factors, both internal and external, with a definite swing towards Islamist radicalization the clear trend. This development is foreboding and ominous. Until the discovery of the AJAI in the post-9/11 setting, the construction and definition of the Islamist terrorism problem in Southeast Asia was understood from a number of perspectives. First, every movement was largely viewed from a national perspective. The aims of DI and GAM were Indonesia-centric. Similarly, the goals of the MNLF, MILF, and *Abu Sayyaf* were Philippines-centric in the same way PULO's were Thailand-centric. Second, while there were external linkages and influences, especially from the Middle East, such as the assistance provided by Libya to the MNLF and GAM, and by other Middle Eastern countries to MILF and *Abu Sayyaf,* the aid, material and moral, were aimed more at assisting these groups to achieve their national goals, be it greater autonomy in Islamic affairs or in the establishment of a breakaway Islamic state. Third, there was hardly any cooperation or synergy between the Islamic groups in each country with other like-minded organizations in the region. Hence, there is little evidence in terms of PULO's cooperation with GAM, or for that matter, MNLF, MILF, or *Abu Sayyaf*'s cooperation with either GAM or PULO. If anything, some of these groups cooperated with other groups in the country, be it PULO with the Communist Party of Thailand or the MNLF with Maoist New People's Army. Fourth, in almost every instance, the Islamic-oriented groups in Southeast Asia had launched a *jihad,* a holy war nationally to counter repressive national secular governments, as was the case in Indonesia (DI and GAM), Thailand (PULO), and the Philippines (MNLF, MILF, and *Abu Sayyaf*). A paradigmatic shift, however, took place with the discovery of the AJAI, and this was mainly due to the rise of the phenomenon of *Global Jihad* following the nurturing of Islamic militancy, extremism, and terrorism by the United States and its allies to defeat the Soviet Union in Afghanistan from 1979 to 1989. Significantly, there were also other important forces and developments that strengthened the hands of the Islamist radicals in the region. With the rise of the AJAI as the single most important signal that the radicals have emerged as part of the Southeast Asian security architecture, and that the process of Talibanization is undoubtedly in vogue in Southeast Asia.

The Rise of *Al-Jama'ah Al-Islamiyyah* as Southeast Asia's Leading Transnational Terrorist Organization

INTRODUCTION

Even though the AJAI has been accused of being the premier and most dangerous terrorist organization in Southeast Asia in recent times, much controversy remains about its origins, establishment, structure, leadership, activities, and linkages. This has been exacerbated by the fact that many—including its alleged current spiritual leader, Abu Bakar Ba'asyir, have denied its existence. Others have been argued that AJAI is nothing more than a figment created by the United States and its regional allies (especially in Australia, Singapore, Malaysia, and the Philippines), or the various intelligence agencies that are bent on undermining and suppressing Islam in general and Indonesia in particular. At the same time, it is often argued that there are two different AJAI organizations. The first and the older one, established probably in the early 1970s, is believed to be largely religious in character, though characterized by its hard-line expositions. This is believed to be led presently by Abu Bakar Ba'asyir, the radical and firebrand preacher who is openly committed to the creation of an Islamic state in Indonesia along the lines of his historical inspiration Kartosuwiryo, the late leader of the *Darul Islam.* However, it is the second AJAI, believed to be operating clandestinely and undercover, even under the auspices of the original AJAI, that is the terrorist organization beyond detection. The fact that the United Nations and a number of countries such as the United States, United Kingdom, and Australia, and even the European Union, have identified and listed the AJAI as a terrorist organization justifies analyzing the origins of this largely elusive organization, believed to be behind most of the major terrorist activities in the Southeast Asian region since the late 1990s.

TERMINOLOGY

Since Singapore's Internal Security Department (ISD) arrested 15 persons believed to be "members of a radical, regional Islamic group called *Jemaah Islamiyah* (JI)" in December 2001,[1] the AJAI has become an important and even key element of the discourse on terrorism in Southeast Asia. Yet, a closer examination reveals that what is alleged to be a regional terrorist organization, namely the *Jemaah Islamiyah,* is spelled differently by various people and countries.[2] In some ways, the term *Jemaah Islamiyah* is problematic, especially when used in the Southeast Asian context, or for that matter in any context where there is a sizeable Muslim presence. In literal translation, *Jemaah Islamiyyah* means "Islamic Community" or "Islamic Congregation." To accuse a country's "Islamic Community" or its "Islamic Congregation" of being a "terrorist organization," or perpetrating terrorism, is synonymous with labelling the entire community of a country as being terrorists or terrorists' supporters, something that is both politically repulsive and suicidal. It was mainly due to this that the former Indonesian Religious Affairs Minister Said Agil Husein Al Munawar argued on August 30, 2003, "the terminology of *Jemaah Islamiyah* should not be used. It is better just to describe such persons as terrorists" rather than implicating the entire Islamic Community.[3]

In addition to denigrating the entire Islamic Community, the term has also been spelled in various ways. The Singapore government "popularized" the regional terrorist organization as "*Jemaah Islamiyah.*" Yet, other spellings refer to the same organization with both words, "*Jemaah*" and "*Islamiyah,*" spelled in different ways. The first word "*Jemaah*" has also been spelled as *Jema'ah* or *Jama'ah.* Similarly, "*Islamiyah*" has been spelled as *Islamiyyah* or *Islamiah.* Interestingly, individuals and documents closely associated with the terrorist organization have consistently adopted a particular terminology. Sheik Abdullah Sungkar, the alleged brains and founder of the organization, described his organization as "*Jama'ah Islamiyah,*" which is the proper Arabic transliteration.[4] According to a key document of the organization that was captured by Indonesian security forces, the actual name of the group is "*Al-Jama'ah Al-Islamiyyah,*" meaning "The (or An) Organization of Muslims."[5] While the differences in spelling may be important only semantically, it is vital that these differences be noted. While describing the organization as either "*Jemaah Islamiyah*" or "*Ja'maah Islamiyah*" might be offensive to many Muslims, somehow "*Al-Jama'ah Al-Islamiyyah*" might be more acceptable as it does not "taint" every member of the Islamic community. In this study, the term *Al-Jama'ah Al-Islamiyyah,* or AJAI for short, will be used, and this refers to the same organization that has been popularly described as *Jemaah Islamiyah* since 2001.

AJAI'S ORIGINS

Very little is known of the AJAI. Like the *Al Qaeda,* it is essentially a secretive and clandestine organization.[6] The terrorist organization is also the only one that is regional in character. The origins of the AJAI can be attributed to one of the following explanations:

a. An offshoot of the *Darul Islam,* created to continue its struggle through a new organization following its suppression by the Sukarno regime.

b. An offshoot of the *Darul Islam* that emerged as a consequence of power struggle in the Islamic militant organization, especially under the Suharto regime.

c. A "black operation" by the Indonesian military under the Suharto regime that went out of control.

d. A front of the *Al Qaeda* in the region, formed by various returning *jihadists* following the completion of their operations in Afghanistan.

As an offshoot of the DI, the AJAI is believed to have been created, as has been alluded to by Abdullah Sungkar in 1997, to continue the struggle to create an Islamic state in Indonesia. Even though Kartosuwiryo and other leaders, including Kahar Muzakkar, of the DI, were arrested and executed by the Sukarno regime, many Islamists felt that they had as much right to be politically active as they played a critical role in containing and neutralizing the communist threat. However, the newly installed Suharto regime pursued anti-Islamist policies and was bent on nipping any aspiration that would eventuate in an Islamic state. For that reason, AJAI was established to resist Suharto and his apparently anti-Islam policies. Even though the AJAI was believed to be established for missionary work, it had eventually took on a bigger political role of resisting the New Order and its supporters, especially the West. It is within this context that the AJAI's origins could be understood.[7] Thus, even though the AJAI was originally created for *Tabligh* (educational) and *Dakwah* (missionary) activities, it became increasingly political when its key leaders fled to Malaysia and linked up with other like-minded individuals, groups and organizations, a linkage facilitated mainly by their common and mutual support for the *mujahidin* struggle in Afghanistan in the 1980s.

Somewhat related to the above, the AJAI's origins can also be understood from the manner the DI leadership in Central Java evolved. Following the arrest and execution of Kartosurwiryo, the nine commands of the DI were believed to have become autonomous with almost no central authority directing the movement. In this context, the Central Java command was headed by Ateng Djalaeni and later, Ajengan Masduki. The latter, a Sundanese, was unacceptable to many, including Sungkar and Ba'asyir, who originated from the city of Surakarta (Solo) in central Java and Jombang in east Java, respectively. Sungkar also accused Masduki of *Sufi* tendencies.[8] Both Sungkar and Ba'asyir had differences with Masduki and did not accept his leadership. Following their *hijrah* (strategic migration) to Malaysia, rather than face expulsion, they are believed to have established a new organization, the AJAI.[9] As was argued by the International Crisis Group, "in the studies of *Jemaah Islamiyah,* Ajengan Masduki is best known as the man whose differences with Abdullah Sungkar led the latter to break from *Darul Islam* and found JI in 1993."[10] In this context, the AJAI can be seen as the successor to the DI that was based in Central Java and emerged out of an internal power struggle in the organization.

A somewhat different view argues that the AJAI was nothing more than a "black operation" by the Suharto government that went wrong. According to the

International Crisis Group (ICG), as part of its attempt to manage the challenge posed by political Islam, especially during the 1977 general election and mainly through the Islamic party organized under the PPP, the national intelligence agency BAKIN, through Ali Moertopo, decided to reactivate the former DI members, many of whom had been inducted into the military. According to the ICG, "the argument provided by BAKIN was that, with the fall of South Vietnam in 1975, Indonesia was in danger of Communist infiltration across the Indonesian-Malaysian border in Borneo, and that only the reactivation of the *Darul Islam* could protect Indonesia."[11] Following this (through mid-1977), the Indonesian government arrested many who were accused of being members of the *Komando Jihad*, "committed to following the ideals of Kartosuwiryo and establishing the Islamic state of Indonesia (NII)."[12] Among those arrested in 1978 were Abdullah Sungkar and Abu Bakar Ba'asyir. Following their *hijrah* to Malaysia, they continued their anti-Suharto and anti–New Order activities from abroad. However, once President Suharto's regime collapse in May 1998, the democratization and liberties provided the members of the AJAI, including Sungkar and Ba'asyir, to return home. With the Indonesian military greatly weakened by the new political paradigm, the AJAI has been able to operate independently of any control and has emerged as a radical and militant Islamic movement bent on transforming Indonesia into an Islamic state, including through the use of terrorism.

A final version argues that the origins of the AJAI can be found in the common experience of many Indonesians and their like-minded compatriots who were involved in the *Jihad* against the Soviet Union in Afghanistan. Many of them were also involved in the DI, past and present, and as such, it was almost natural for them to respond to the call for *Jihad* in Afghanistan. As the United States was involved in the Cold War against the "evil empire" of the Soviet Union, Washington supported Osama bin Laden and his *jihadi* activities against the Soviet occupation of Afghanistan.[13] In this endeavor, the United States condoned the mobilization of *jihadists* all over the world, including Southeast Asia. The AJAI is believed to be created in this context. Unsurprisingly, many "first generation" AJAI operatives in Southeast Asia had spent time either fighting the Soviets or training in military camps in Afghanistan and Pakistan. To that extent, what eventually emerged as the AJAI was largely a function of the global *Mujahidin* against the Soviets in Afghanistan. This is where the *Mujahids* from Southeast Asia first met, and this later formed the basis of the regionwide network. In this regard, the United States was largely instrumental in bringing the regional *Mujahids* together, and an important consequence of this experience was the birth of a Southeast Asian "*Mujahidin*-oriented" organization that came to be known as the AJAI.

As all these operatives were involved in the *jihad* against the USSR, and once this war was terminated, many of them returned and continued their struggle in their home countries, partly due to the various injustices that they disliked as well as the belief that the West, particularly the United States, was dominating Muslim lands. As Osama bin Laden, the leader of the global *jihad* movement in Afghanistan, turned against his former patron the United States, especially the Central Intelligence Agency, a similar turnaround could be detected from the *jihadists* that returned to their home countries. This largely explains the anti-West character of the AJAI, even though it is believed to have originated in the context of the *jihadi* operations against the Soviets and, more importantly, with U.S. support. In many ways, the Afghanistan experience was particularly critical in the transformation of various national *jihadi* movements into something larger than what they had been before. This metamorphosis was largely a function of the U.S. policy of nurturing global Islamic fundamentalism and terrorism as part of its Cold War struggle against the Soviet Union, with the immediate goal of "rolling back" the Soviet occupation of Afghanistan.

DOES THE AJAI REALLY EXIST?

Most of the leading AJAI leaders have denied the existence of the *"Jemaah Islamiyah."* The only exception was Nasir Abbas, who, following his renunciation of links with AJAI, wrote a book titled *Exposing the Jamaah Islamiyah.*[14] According to Abu Bakar Ba'asyir, since time immemorial, dating back to the Crusades, the enemies of Islam have tried to destroy it through two means. First, through the use of force and weapons, be it the Crusades of the past or what George W. Bush has tried to do in Afghanistan and Iraq and now is threatening to do in Iran. Second, through the nonuse of force, mainly by infiltrating into Islam, creating divisions, and then destroying it from within.[15] In this connection, Abu Bakar Ba'asyir has argued that "the notion of *Jemaah Islamiyah* as a terrorist organization" is a fiction created by the United States, Israel, and countries like the United Kingdom, Australia and Singapore that have always expressed enmity towards Islam."[16] Hence, the *Jemaah Islamiyah,* or AJAI, does not exist, as "it is a creation through conspiracy to discredit Islam in general and the Muslims whose religious consciousness has been awakened to challenge the interests of the West and their supporters."[17]

In the same vein, Akh. Muzakki has argued that there is a credible school of thought in Indonesia that does not accept the existence of the AJAI. This view argues that AJAI is essentially a function of a "political campaign of other countries" and that it is "a fictitious organization." He argues that AJAI "is not well recognised by Indonesians" and most had "no prior knowledge of its existence."[18] Alfitra Salamm, a researcher from the Indonesian Institute of Social Sciences, argued that "JI is not real, but only a fictitious organization set up by Malaysian and Singaporean governments to silence the criticism of Islamic radical groups in their respective countries."[19]

The view that the AJAI is a "creation" by its enemies has been strengthened by emerging evidence that some of the "terrorists" were actually "agents" of Indonesian and Malaysian intelligence agencies.[20] In this connection, two key AJAI figures have stood out, namely Nasir Abbas and Hambali, both of whom were alleged to have been planted by Indonesian military intelligence to penetrate the Islamist radicals. Omar Al-Faruq, who was reportedly shot dead in Iraq in 2006, was another key suspect in this "terrorist-intelligence" nexus.[21] While Hambali is believed to have been planted to penetrate the Islamist radicals that "migrated" to Malaysia in the mid-1980s, Nasir, according to a senior retired police officer, was "turned around" following his disillusionment with *Mantiqi* 1 and 2 leadership that carried out bombings from 2000 onwards.[22] According to a senior military intelligence officer in Jakarta:

whatever Hambali was alleged to be doing or have done in terms of violence in the late 1990s until his arrest in August 2003, his existence as an extremist began with the Indonesian military intelligence "planting" him in Malaysia to penetrate the radicals there. Hambali had long been an informer of the *Siliwangi* Regional Command in West Java. He was a good source of information on the radicals. He was later lost to the radicals' cause, either because of his disenchantment following his experience in the *Mujahidin* war in Afghanistan and conversion to radicalism, or simply that was what was required of him, especially in the light of the political change in Indonesia and the rising anti-TNI movement following Suharto's fall.[23]

A number of scholarly writings have also alluded to the "terrorist-intelligence" nexus. According to Damien Kingsbury and Clinton Fernandes:

The case of Hambali is illustrative of the complex nature of "terrorist" and military/intelligence links....according to *Laksamana.net,* an "intelligence source" revealed that in the 1970s Hambali had been a Special Operations (opsus) plant into JI. He was given the code-name G-8 and tasked with building the financial structure of JI. The aim of the operation was to discredit political Islam and to legitimise repressive action by the New Order government. A similar link was establish between the TNI and Fauzi Hasbi, an Acehnese whose father was a leader of the *Darul Islam* movement in Aceh, who had a history of links with TNI intelligence dating to 1977. Hasbi was later identified as the link between TNI intelligence and three men (one of whom, Edi Sugianto, was also associated with Kopassus) charged with a bombing on Christmas Eve 2000 in Medan. On 22 February 2002, Hasbi was abducted from a hotel in Ambon and murdered. His son [Lamkaruna Putra] claimed he was taken and killed by the police. Journalist Martinukus has noted that his killing could have been to prevent him from being investigated as a link between the TNI and *Jema'ah Islamiyah.* As senior *Jema'ah Islamiyah* researcher Sidney Jones noted: "If you scratch any radical Islamic group in Indonesia, you will find some security forces involvement."[24]

An almost similar report, confirming the "terrorist-intelligence" nexus was made by *SBS Dateline* on October 12, 2005. A security analyst, John Mempi, argued that the terrorist violence blamed on the Islamist radicals is actually the work of a "state within a state ruling this country."[25] Similarly, former President Abdurrahman Wahid argued that the bombings in Indonesia "may be the work of the police or armed forces. The orders to do this or that came from within our armed forces, not from the fundamentalist people."[26] Revealing more details about Fauzi Hasbi, *SBS Dateline* reported:

Lamkaruna Putra's father (Fauzi Hasbi) was an Achenese separatist leader descended from a long line of Achenese fighters. He went on to become a key figure in *Jemaah Islamiyah*. Fauzi Hasbi who used the alias Abu Jihad was in contact with Osama bin Laden's deputy. He lived for many years in the house next door to Abu Bakar [Ba'asyir] in Malaysia and was very close to JI operations chief Hambali. Umar Abduh is an Islamist convicted of terrorism and jailed for 10 years under the Suharto regime. He belonged to a group that attacked police stations and hijacked a Garuda flight to Bangkok. He remembers Fauzi Hasbi as a hardliner who traded arms and was willing to commit acts of violence.[27]

According to Umar Abduh:

Fauzi Hasbi was so relaxed among the militants and they with him, that he even took his son to a critical meeting in Kuala Lumpur in January 2001 as JI was preparing for its violent campaign. The attendance list was a who's who of accused terrorists.[28]

Lamkaruna Putra noted:

There was someone from MILF in Mindanao, his name was Ustad Abu Rela, commander of the *Abu Sayyaf*. Ustad Abdul Fatah from Pattani was there. People from Sulawesi and West Java came to the meeting. The organization was managed by Hambali.[29]

According to *SBS Dateline:*

Hambali and company would have known their colleague Fauzi Hasbi had been captured in 1978 by this Indonesian military special force unit but they wouldn't have known that he became a secret agent for Indonesian military intelligence. The commanding officer that caught him was Syafrie Syamsuddin, now a general and one of Indonesia's key military intelligence figures. [Presently, the Secretary General in the Department of Defense, Indonesia]. These documents obtained by *Dateline* prove beyond doubt that Fauzi Hasbi had a long association with the military. This 1990 document, signed by the chief of military intelligence in North Sumatra, authorised Fauzi Hasbi to undertake a special job. And this 1995 internal memo from military intelligence HQ in Jakarta was a request to use brother Fauzi Hasbi to spy on Acehnese separatists not only in Indonesia but in Malaysia and Sweden. And then this document, from only three years ago, assigned him the job of special agent for BIN, the national intelligence agency.[30]

According to John Mempi:

The first *Jemaah Islamiyah* congress in Bogor was facilitated by Abu Jihad, after Abu Bakar Ba'syir returned from Malaysia. We can see that Abu Jihad played an important role, he was later found to be an intelligence agent. So an intelligence agent has been facilitating the radical Islamic movement.[31]

This led *SBS Dateline* to argue that:

The extraordinary story of Fauzi Hasbi raises many important questions about JI and the Indonesian authorities. Why didn't they smash the terror group in its infancy? Do they still have agents in the organization? And what information, if any, have they had in advance about the recent deadly spate of terror attacks?...The man who held all the secrets, Abu Jihad was disembowelled in a mysterious murder in early 2003, just after he was exposed as a military agent. His son, Lamkaruna Putra died in a plane crash last month [September 2005].[32]

Evidently, there are many "conspiracy theories" about terrorism being constructed by regimes in the West and the developing world to divert public attention from domestic woes and the role of Christian, Jewish, and Islamic ideologues in wanting to spread their faith as well as the role of the defense industries in wanting to expand their exports worldwide. Other, more realist-oriented analysts have argued that the "9/11" Incident and the "war on terror" following it is nothing more than a "clash of two fundamentalisms," namely between Islam and the largely Christian and capitalist West. For instance, according to Vikram Sood, the former chief of Research and Analysis Wing (Indian Intelligence Agency), "in today's context, when we talk of international terrorism, we invariably refer to Islamic/*Jihadi* terrorism. Unfortunately, the response to this, described as the global war on terror is neither global nor is it against terror." According to him, what George W. Bush has declared as the litmus test of winning the war against terror in Iraq has actually succeeded in creating "more terrorists than it has destroyed." Due to this, "the battle has become globalized capitalism versus global Islam." In the so-called "war on terror," one party, the West, was "affluent, powerful, politically empowered, mainly Christian but running out of resources; the other is poor, politically un-empowered and Muslim and resource rich". Arguing from the realist perspective, Vikram argues that what has euphemistically been dubbed as a "war on terror" is actually nothing more that the attempt by the West to gain unhindered access to finance, markets, and resources required to retain its primacy and Global Islam's strive for an Islamic Caliphate that wants to practice puritan Islam and return to the former glory."[33]

Yet, when one traces the actions of Abdullah Sungkar, Abu Bakar Ba'asyir, Hambali, Abu Jibril, and many others, it is obvious that there was a pro-DI Islamist community that "migrated" to Malaysia due to the repression of Suharto's New Order. In Malaysia, partly due to opposition to Suharto, the need to overthrow the New Order and towards the creation of a *Daulah Islamiyah* as well as influences from abroad, mainly Afghanistan, the largely Indonesian-based community was severely radicalized. This saw the community, following being imbued with Islamist radicalism of *Qutbiyyah* and Sheik Abdullah Azzam, organizing itself regionally and for violent actions on grounds of *Jihad*. This organization, established in January 1993, was named AJAI, had regionwide linkages as well as with the *Al Qaeda,* and was primarily responsible for the violence in the region, especially Indonesia. Due to AJAI's violence, the international community listed it as a "terrorist organization." Thus, it is difficult to deny the existence of AJAI.

THE UNITED STATES, THE AFGHANISTAN "*BLOWBACK*" AND THE BIRTH OF GLOBAL *JIHAD*

What essentially transformed the nationalist-oriented *jihadists* into groups that were prepared to collaborate with like-minded movements and organizations outside their home countries and led them eventually to support AJAI's activities in Southeast Asia was their ideological, political, and military experiences in Afghanistan from 1979 to 1989. The success of Khomeini's Revolution in Iran in 1979 was also important in demonstrating the possibility of securing an Islamic state. However, it was the war in Afghanistan that proved to be catalytic in sowing the seeds for Global *Jihad* and the emergence of the AJAI as a regionwide terrorist organization with close links with hitherto national-oriented *jihadists* as one of its major consequences. To that extent, the Afghanistan War can be regarded as the cradle from which many terrorists and militants have emerged to threaten the world. The perpetrators of policies aimed at encouraging the growth of Islamic militancy, extremism, and even terrorism should be regarded as the midwives of these terrorist groups that have come to haunt most civilized states in the world. The primary responsibility for this lays with the United States and its allies, namely, Pakistan, Saudi Arabia, the Gulf States, and all those who directly and indirectly fuelled Islamic fanaticism as an instrument to reverse the Soviet invasion and occupation of Afghanistan.[34]

When the Soviet army marched into Kabul in December 1979, the Carter administration, and later the Reagan administration, launched a massive support and training campaign to support the Afghan *Mujahidin*.[35] According to Robert Gates, the former CIA director, covert operations to assist the *Mujahidin* began in June 1979.[36] In 1998, this was confirmed by Carter's national security adviser, Zbigniew Brzezinski.[37] Between 1979 to 1989, identifying Pakistan as the "frontline state" in the struggle against global communism, some US$6 billion was funnelled into the country to support and train the Afghan *Mujahidin* with the Pakistani Inter-Services Intelligence (ISI) as the principal conduit. The CIA and ISI worked closely with the seven key Afghan resistance movements, including the radical group led by Gulbuddin Hikmatyars, who later became Afghanistan's prime minister and is presently one of Washington's greatest sworn enemies. Other hard-liners, including the Saudi-born Osama bin Laden, were also recruited for the rollback of the Soviet Union from Afghanistan.[38] Osama ran the *Maktab al-Khidmat lil Mujahidin al-Arab* (Afghan Services Bureau) in Peshawar, Pakistan, recruiting would-be *Mujahidins* from all over the world.

At the heart of the CIA plan was to destabilize the USSR through the spread of Islamic fanaticism against its Muslim-dominated Central Asian Republics.[39] In this endeavor, the United States funded the establishment of a massive *madrasah* (Islamic religious schools) network aimed at propagating *jihadi* Islam as well as using them as a base for recruiting *Mujahidin* fighters for the war against the "Godless Russians" in Afghanistan. Zia ul Haq's government promoted the proliferation of these *madrasahs* in order to gain support from the religious political parties as well as to recruit troops for the war in Afghanistan. The number of *madrasahs* increased from nearly 1,000 in 1979 to 10,000 by the end of the Afghan War. Here, the CIA played a key role by financing the training and indoctrination of the *Mujahidin*, where guerrilla training was integrated with the teaching of hard-line Islam.[40] Training camps were built in Pakistan and Afghanistan, from where the *Mujahidin* attacked the leftist government in Kabul, and later the Soviet occupation force. In addition to training and recruiting

Afghan nationals to fight the Soviets, the CIA also encouraged the ISI to recruit Muslim extremists from around the world to join in the Global *Jihad* regardless of its long-term consequences.[41] According to Ahmed Rashid:

> Between 1982 and 1992, some 35,000 Muslim radicals from 43 Islamic countries in the Middle East, North and East Africa, Central Asia and the Far East would pass through baptism under fire with the Afghan *Mujahidin*. Tens of thousands more foreign Muslim radicals came to study in the hundreds of new *Madrasahs* that Zia's military government began to fund in Pakistan and along the Afghan border. Eventually, more than 100,000 Muslim radicals were to have direct contact with Pakistan and Afghanistan and be influenced by the *Jihad*.

In camps near Peshawar and in Afghanistan, these radicals met each other for the first time and studied, trained, and fought together. It was the first opportunity for most of them to learn about Islamic movements in other countries, and they forged tactical and ideological links that would serve them well in the future. The camps became virtual universities for future Islamic radicalism. None of the intelligence agencies involved wanted to consider the consequences of bringing together thousands of Islamic radicals from all over the world.[42]

In 1985, President Reagan ordered the escalation of the conflict in Afghanistan by channelling sophisticated weaponry, including antiaircraft *Stinger* missiles, to bleed the Soviet occupation force. According to Steve Coll, "President Reagan signed National Security Decision Directive 166 which authorised stepped-up covert military aid to the *Mujahidins* and it made clear that the secret Afghan war had a new goal: to defeat Soviet troops in Afghanistan through covert action and encourage a Soviet withdrawal."[43] The CIA-*Mujahidin* partnership proved to be effective, and in 1989, the last Soviet soldier left Afghanistan. While the U.S. interest diminished with the Soviet withdrawal and the CIA markedly reduced its presence in Pakistan, the ISI continued training and channelling funds to the *Mujahidins*. In 1992, Kabul fell to the *Mujahidins*.

Following the Soviet withdrawal from Afghanistan, thousands of triumphant non-Afghan *jihadis* returned to their home countries. For the battle-hardened *jihadis,* their heightened political consciousness combined with their strong ideological convictions made them realize that there was also a need for a national and possibly regional *jihad,* as various secular governments at home were just as much client regimes of the United States as was Najibullah a client of the Soviet Union. Worse still, there was a large army of well-trained religious zealots who believed in the export of their brand of Islam. In many ways, the phenomenon of globalization of Islamist radicalism went hand in hand with the struggle to undertake national and regional *jihad*. What also drew these *jihadis* together was the formidable network they had built up during their sojourn in Afghanistan leading them to be labelled as the *Afghanis*. When the national and regional *Afghanis* joined forces, there was the synergy of a powerful and dangerous network of terrorism that has since come to haunt the world. As many of the *Afghanis* would also like to propagate their interpretation of Islam to the rest of the Muslim *Ummah,* the targeting of various secular regimes in the Muslim world was something natural. This partly explained the *raison d'être* of Osama and his supporters in targeting the United States. In Osama's mind, the United States was trying to save the heart (Saudi Arabia) of the Muslim world from falling into the hands of radical Islam.

While the Afghan endgame was being played out, in 1988, with U.S. knowledge, Osama created the *Al Qaeda*, a conglomerate of quasi-independent Islamic terrorist cells spread across at least 26 countries, and now believed to have extended to some 60 countries.[44] Washington, however, turned a blind eye, confident that it would not directly impinge on the United States and its interests. Once the Afghan War was over, there was a surplus of *jihadis* in Pakistan and Afghanistan. These surplus *jihadis* were unleashed for *jihadi* missions elsewhere, and therein lay one of the most important factors accounting for the spread of Islamist extremism and terrorism the world over through the 1990s to the present period. Later, many joined *Al Qaeda* and turned against the United States, Saudi Arabia, and others. Even though the Afghan War ended in 1989, the country was torn apart by internecine conflict. The Najibullah regime collapsed in 1992, and Kabul was taken over by the *Mujahidins,* who now fought a bloody civil war with each other for the spoils of *jihad* in Afghanistan. In September 1996, Mullah Omar's created Taliban (drawing mainly students from the *madrasahs*) came to power in Kabul. Despite the Soviet defeat in 1989, *jihadi*-oriented training, sponsored by the various Islamist groups and often with the backing of the ISI, continued with many "surplus *jihadis*" now unleashed for the liberation of Kashmir and elsewhere, including Bosnia and Chechnya. In some ways, Afghanistan as a "breeding ground" for terrorists in the post-Soviet period represented the second phase with Kabul, especially the Taliban providing sanctuaries and training to various groups, including those from Southeast Asia. This continued in Afghanistan until a new political paradigm emerged in the world following the 9/11 attacks that eventually led to the *Taliban*'s overthrow by a U.S.-led invasion in December 2001.

To that extent, even though the short-term geopolitical interest of the United States was achieved in Afghanistan, which probably also assisted in the dismantling of the USSR and its communist empire, in the long run, Washington's Afghan policy was primarily responsible for unleashing the many hydra-headed monsters of *jihadi* terrorism the world over.[45] In many ways, both Carter and Reagan were responsible for the creation of a Frankenstein monster of global terrorism that is threatening the world, including the United States.[46] The origins of the 9/11 attacks on the United States can indeed be found in the shortsighted policy of the preceding American administrations. In the words of Jagmohan Meher, "the indecisive American policy towards Pakistan and Afghanistan seemed to have boomeranged in the form of its former allies becoming the sources of largest terrorist networks worldwide, which led to the attack on American on September 11, 2001."[47] The menace of global terrorism *a la Al Qaeda* is hence partly self-made. Whatever one calls them—the *Afghanis,* "the Afghan Boys," the "Afghan Veterans," or "the *Mujahidins*"—these groups were germinated and nurtured by short-term American geopolitical interests. The long-term ramification of this has been the proliferation of various national and regional terrorist organizations, including the AJAI in Southeast Asia. In many ways, it reminds one of an old Javanese saying: *"siapa menabur angin akan menuai badai,"* literally translated to mean, "he who sows winds will eventually harvest hurricanes." Ironically, Washington's secret program of supporting the Afghan *Mujahidin* was called "Operation Cyclone."

THE GROWTH OF AJAI

What eventually emerged as the AJAI was a function of anti-Suharto *jihadists* and Southeast Asian *Afghanis* coalescing into a regional group with largely national and regional, and at times international, objectives. What has bound them together, at least in the initial instance, was their *jihadi*-oriented experience in Afghanistan, where as *Mujahidins,* they were encouraged by their success in rolling back the mighty Soviets. In short, originally, the AJAI was nothing more than an Afghan alumni. It was only later that other variations developed to make it into a regionwide terrorist organization. In the initial instance, as a regionwide organization, the AJAI was the brainchild of Indonesian radical Islamists in exile in Malaysia, of which the key members included Sheikh Abdullah Sungkar, Abu Bakar Ba'syir, Riduan Isamuddin (Hambali alias Nurjaman), Mohammed Iqbal Rahman (Abu Jibril, alias) Fikruddin Muqti), Ali Ghufron alias Muklas, Fathur Rahman Al-Ghozi and Agus Dwikarna.

Even though little is known about the origins of the AJAI, which like the *Al Qaeda,* denies involvement in any act of terrorism,[48] there is no doubt that the organization exists. Whichever explanation one subscribes to, it is clear that the roots of present-day AJAI can be traced to the DI, especially its branch in Central Java. This has been stated by none other than AJAI's founder, Abdullah Sungkar, in an interview in early 1997. While analysing various Islamic movements in Indonesia, he described the adoption by his organization, of which he was the *Amir* (leader), of a noncooperative approach towards the Indonesian government, as follows:

> *Jama'ah Islamiyah* which has the purpose of establishing *Dawlah Islamiyah* by applying the strategies of *Eeman* (preaching), *Hijrah* (strategic evasion) and *jihad* (struggle). The embryo of this *Jama'ah,* which is more well known as *Darul Islam* (DI/TII) has already declared its proclamation as the Islamic Nation of Indonesia (NII) on the 7th August 1949 in Malangbong, West Java. Furthermore, at that time *jihad* was taking place in order to defend its existence in opposition to the Dutch *Kafir* Government and the Secular Regime of the Indonesian Republic (which is best known as the "triangular war") until 1962.

> In fact, the element of hope is still extant within the *Jama'ah.* And further more this *Jama'ah* tried to demand and bring about a return to the consciousness of its obligation to establish *Dawlah Islamiyah* by following the way of *jihad.* Nowadays they are quite active in bringing about methods and approaches of *Da'wah* aimed at the various social strata of the Islamic Community, and in doing so, they at least carry on the struggle of *Jama'ah Islamiyah.*[49]

It is apparent that the AJAI grew out of the DI. This is a position adopted by many AJAI analysts, including the Singapore government. In the *White Paper* published in 2003, the origins of the AJAI were described as follows:

> Historically, AJAI traces its roots to the *Darul Islam* (DI, or House of Islam), an organization which emerged in the 1940s and which fought together with the Indonesian revolutionary army against the Dutch colonial rule. After Indonesia gained independence in 1949, the DI continued its armed and violent struggle for the establishment of an Islamic State in Indonesia.

> The Indonesian government tried to suppress the group after independence but never completely succeeded. In 1985, several radical DI elements fled to Malaysia to avoid arrest by the Suharto government. They settled there, and later regrouped and renamed themselves Jemaah Islamiyah.[50]

Though somewhat simplistic, as the *White Paper* missed many other important developments that eventually led to the DI elements to set up the AJAI, one cannot ignore and disconnect the AJAI's establishment from the extremists found in the DI. This was because even though the DI's rebellions were crushed by the Indonesian military and its leaders arrested and executed, its ideology remained alive. The AJAI's struggle for an Islamic state (*Daulah Islamiyah*) can be understood as a continuation of the DI goal, even though a goal expansion did take place from an Islamic Indonesia to Islamic Southeast Asia (*Nusantara*).

Largely due to the repressive, particularly anti-Islamist policies of Suharto's New Order, the centralized structure of the DI was destroyed. This, however, led to the emergence of essentially autonomous branches of the DI, led by various local leaders. Particularly important in this regard was the DI branch in Central Java, then led by Sheik Abdullah Sungkar and Abu Bakar Ba'asyir.[51] From the mid-1950s onwards, both Sungkar and Ba'asyir were closely affiliated with the *Masjumi,* being leaders of its student group, the *Gerakan Pemuda Islam Indonesia*. Both men were actively involved in various proselytization activities, Sungkar for Masjumi and Ba'asyir for the *Al-Irsyad* Organization. In 1967, both moved to Solo and, with the backing of Hasan Basri, founded the Radio *Dakwah Islamiyah Surakarta* (Islamic Proselytization Radio of Surakarta), a pirate radio station, broadcasting calls for *jihad* in Central Java. This was shut down in 1975. In 1971, the pair founded the puritanical *al-Mukmin Koranic* Studies boarding school, which in 1973 moved to Ngruki village, east of Surakarta (Solo). The roots of the AJAI are allegedly found in this school, known popularly as *Pondok Ngruki*.

Sometime in February 1977, Sungkar and Ba'asyir founded a group called the *Jemaah Mujahidin Anshorullah* (JMA). It was essentially a DI organization, founded and supported by DI members in Central Java. This group is believed to have metamorphosed into the AJAI. In November 1978, Indonesian security apparatus jailed Sungkar and Ba'asyir for nine years for participating in the activities of a clandestine Islamic militia, the *Komando Jihad.* Most analysts are, however, in agreement that the *Komando Jihad* was in actuality a creation of the Indonesian intelligence to entrap the

Islamist extremists opposed to the Suharto regime. According to the Indonesian government, *Kommando Jihad* was led by Haji Ismail Pranoto and Haji Danu Mohammad Hasan, both of whom were closely associated with the DI struggle. Pranoto was put on trial in September 1978, and Danu in 1983. Charged with subversion, both maintained that they were collaborating with the Indonesian military to halt the communist threat, even though the government charged them with attempting to regroup and establish an Islamic state.

Alongside Pranoto and Danu, both Sungkar and Ba'asyir were alleged to be part of a plot to establish an Islamic state in Indonesia. According to the Indonesian government, Pranoto inducted both of them for his cause, and in February 1977, Sungkar was allegedly installed as the military governor of the Indonesian Islamic State for Central Java as well as head of JMA. On appeal, in late 1982, their sentence was reduced to three years and 10 months, with both of them being released from prison. While they returned to *Pondok Ngruki,* the country witnessed an escalation of Islamist-oriented militancy and violence. This was in part a reaction to Suharto's announcement of the *"asas tunggal'* or "sole basis" policy that mandated every organization to adopt *Pancasila* as the sole ideological basis. The Islamists were outraged, and in September 1984, more than 100 Muslims were massacred by the Indonesian security forces at Tanjong Priok, on the outskirts of Jakarta, for rioting. This led to retaliations, with many bombings taking place from 1984 to the middle of 1985.

Against the worsening security situation, the Indonesian Supreme Court acceded to the prosecution's appeal against the reduced sentence of Sungkar and Ba'asyir. The court issued summons for the rearrest of both men. Before they could be rearrested, like many of DI leaders from Central Java, Sungkar and Ba'asyir fled to Malaysia. According to the ICG Report, Sungkar and Ba'asyir have described their departure from Indonesia not as a "flight from injustice, but on a religiously-inspired *hijrah* (emigration) to escape from the enemies of Islam, similar to the Prophet's *hijrah* from Mecca to Medina."[52] According to Abu Bakar Ba'asyir, "his intentions were purely religious and he wanted to join the *Jaamah Sunnah* and*Islam* (Islamic community) in Malaysia, based in Kuala Pilah where Ustad Hashim Ghani had invited him and provided the necessary hospitality."[53] In an interview with the author, Ba'asyir argued:

> The *hijrah* was necessary due to Suharto's policies. The *"asas tunggal"* policy of *Pancasila* as the sole basis of any organization, especially political ones, was an act of sacrilege. For me, there is only the *Koran Sunnah,* not *Pancasila* as my *asas tunggal. Pancasila* did not place God as the centre of all things. As I could not accept this and more important, I could not challenge it, I had no choice but to *hijrah* to Malaysia, where I lived as a farmer, selling traditional medicines and preaching Islam.[54]

Malaysia proved to be a safe haven, and many Islamic political dissidents congregated there. In addition to Sungkar and Ba'asyir, the other key players included Hambali, alias Riduan Isamuddin, alias Nurjaman, originating from Cianjur, West Java; Abu Jibril alias Fikruddin Muqti alias Mohamed Iqbal Rahman, from Lombok;

Ali Ghufron alias Muklas, Fathur Rahman al-Gozi, originating from Madiun, East Java; and Agus Dwikarna. The coming together of these anti-Suharto Islamic radicals and the like in Malaysia is often viewed as the germinating ground for what was eventually to emerge as the militant and extremist AJAI. Even though the AJAI and its leadership were believed to have originated from this source, Ba'asyir has argued that the AJAI is "only a Koran reading group."[55] Regardless of Ba'asyir's denials, what cannot be ignored is that the AJAI has emerged as a major terrorist organization, had more than a decade to grow and extend its tentacles regionwide, and tends to be led essentially by Indonesian militants.

Sometime between 1985 and 1987, being out of Indonesia and outside the DI, TII, and NII frameworks, Sungkar and Ba'asyir broke away from the DI and established the AJAI. By 1993 or so, a decision was made to establish a regionwide AJAI network, with Hambali and Abu Jibril tasked by Sungkar to set up the militant cells in Southeast Asia. Between 1996 and 1997, the AJAI's regional network was in place. Many of its members had fought the Soviets in Afghanistan and received military training. Following Suharto's fall, both Ba'asyir and Sungkar returned to Indonesia, their home and main base of their struggle, to continue their activities. When Sungkar died in 1999, the leadership of AJAI fell into the hands of Abu Bakar Ba'asyir, with Hambali controlling the field operations in the region. Due to the widening political space provided by *Reformasi,* the activities of Abu Bakar Ba'asyir widened, as evident in the establishment of *Majlis Mujahidin Indonesia* (MMI), or the Indonesian *Mujahidin* Council, established on August 7, 2000. It aimed to champion the adoption of strict Islamic *sharia* law in Indonesia.[56] It is widely believed that the MMI and AJAI interact closely, just as the AJAI is believed to be working closely with the *Al Qaeda.* For many, especially Western analysts, the AJAI is believed to be the front of the *Al Qaeda* in Southeast Asia.

Ba'asyir was the AJAI's *Amir* and the "ideological general"—in other words, the spiritual leader. He is believed to have inspired most of the *Jihadists* that were involved in the struggle against Indonesia for the establishment of an Islamic state.[57] However, before long, the field commander and operations chief of the AJAI in Southeast Asia was Hambali. As Hambali was appointed by Sungkar, a person to whom Hambali looked up and from whom he took his orders, following Sungkar's death, there appears to be a division between Ba'asyir and Hambali, with the former being unable to control the latter. This partly explains Ba'asyir's confidence in operating the way he does in Indonesia, as, until recently, it was difficult to charge him with anything other than the fact that he was tried and charged in 1984, and he escaped justice by absconding from the country. Following Hambali's arrest and the arrest of many first-generation AJAI operatives, it is difficult to pinpoint with certainty as to who is leading the terrorist organization. The author was informed by a number of senior counterterrorism officials in Indonesia that following the arrest of Abu Bakar Ba'asyir and Hambali, Abu Rusdan became the *Amir.* After Abu Rusdan was arrested, the leadership of AJAI is believed to have fallen into the hands of Abu Dujana, who was the Secretary to both Ba'asyir and Rusdan. Currently and until his capture, Indonesian counterterrorism specialists assume that Abu Dujana was the *Pelaksana Amir,* or the acting *Amir.* The capture of Abu Dujana in June 2007 was important as it clarified somewhat the leadership structure of AJAI. What became clear was that after Abu Rusdan's arrest, Nuaim alias Abu Irsyad alias Zarkasih became the interim *Amir.* Abu Dujana admitted leading the military wing of AJAI while reporting to Zarkasih, who, until his arrest in June 2007, was overall in charge of AJAI.

STRUCTURE AND ORGANIZATION OF THE AJAI

Due to the secretive nature of the AJAI, until recently, there was very little data on the structure and organization of the AJAI. Most of the information on its structure has been published by governments that have captured AJAI operatives. One important source in this regard has been the information provided by the Singapore government following the arrest of a number of AJAI operatives in the country in 2001 and 2002. A more detailed and probably accurate picture of the AJAI's organizational structure emerged following the capture of the *Pedoman Umum Perjuangan Jemaah Islamiyah* (PUPJI) in late 2002 in Indonesia.[58] One startling fact is the very close resemblance between the structure of the *Al Qaeda* and AJAI, indicating the influence of the former on the latter, primarily due to the Afghanistan experience of the AJAI founders (see Figures 3.1 and 3.2).[59]

Organizationally, at the top of the AJAI hierarchy is the *Markas* (Headquarters) and below it is the Regional *Shurah* (Consultative) Council. Below this, the AJAI is believed to be divided into a number of regional and territorial divisions or *mantiqis,* with the main ones being in Indonesia, Malaysia, southern Philippines, and Australia.[60] The *mantiqis* are further divided into *wakalahs* or branches. AJAI branches are believed, for instance, to be found in Singapore, Johor, Kelantan, Selangor, and

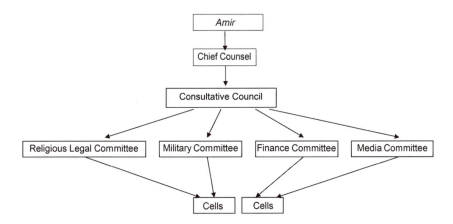

Figure 3.1   Organizational Structure of the Al-Qaeda

Source: See "The Nuts and Bolts of Terror," *Newsweek,* October 15, 2001, 36.

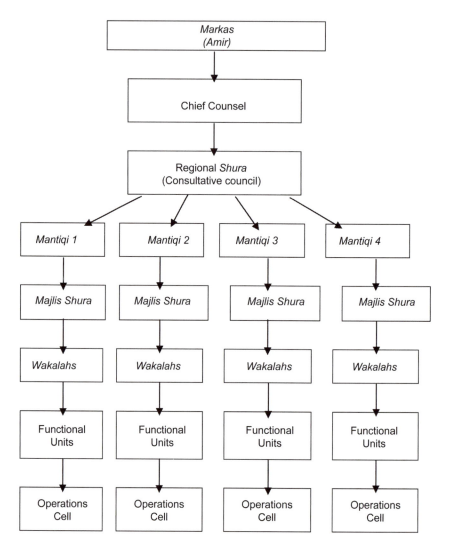

Figure 3.2   The AJAI Organizational Structure in Southeast Asia

Source: "White Paper: The Jemaah Islamiyah Arrests and the Threat of Terrorism"
(Singapore: Ministry of Home Affairs, 2003), 10.

Negri Sembilan. In terms of geographical expanse, the AJAI is believed to be operating in most of Southeast Asia, with the focus on Indonesia, Malaysia, Singapore, southern Philippines and southern Thailand.[61] Below these are the *Kaitbahs, Kirdas, and Fiahs.*

Organizationally, the AJAI is led by an *Amir,* or leader. Abdullah Sungkar was the first *Amir,* and this is believed to have been passed to Abu Bakar Ba'asyir following the demise of the former in 1999. When Abu Bakar Ba'asyir became more active in the MMI, Abu Rusdan, alias Thoriquddin, took over as caretaker *Amir* until he was arrested. Since then, Abu Dujana was believed to have taken over as the caretaker *Amir* of AJAI, even though in actuality it was headed by Zarkasih, a relatively unknown AJAI operative. According to the PUPJI, in carrying out his duties, the *Amir* is assisted by the *Majlis Qiyadah* (MQ; Leadership Council), *Majlis Syuro* (MS; Consultative Council), *Majlis Fatwa* (MF; Fatwa Council), and *Majlis Hisbah* (MH; *Hisbah* Council). The MQ is composed of the *Majlis Qiyadah Markaziyah* (Central Leadership Council), *Majlis Mantiqiyah* (*Mantiqi* Leadership Council), and *Majlis Qiyadah Wakalah* (*Wakalah* Leadership Council). The *Amir* is nominated and appointed by the MS. The central and all-powerful figure in the AJAI is the *Amir,* who appoints all key office holders, decides on key operations, collects donations, metes out sanctions, and establishes relations with other groups and organizations. The members of the *Majlis Qiyadah Markaziyah, Majlis Syuro, Majlis Fatwa,* and *Majlis Hisbah* are appointed by the *Amir.* The organizational structure of the AJAI as found in the PUPJI is much more detailed than the one provided by the Singapore government. (see Figures 3.3–3.7).

Partly due to the familiarity of the key AJAI leaders with the Indonesian territorial structure of the TNI as well as the need to conduct a struggle beyond Indonesia, a regionwide territorial network spanning most of Southeast Asia was established. In addition to a clear hierarchical structure, the AJAI has four key territorial divisions, or *Mantiqis,* covering most of Southeast Asia as well as probably covering Australia, Papua New Guinea, and newly independent East Timor. (see Table 3.1). The first covers Malaysia, Singapore, Thailand and Myanmar. The second covers Sumatra and Java in Indonesia. The third covers Indonesia's islands of Sulawesi as well as various islands in eastern Indonesia, including Maluku, Kalimantan, Sarawak, Sabah, Brunei, and southern Philippines. The fourth cell covers Australia, the Indonesian province of Papua and possibly Papua New Guinea, East Timor, and the Maldives. Indonesian intelligence officials have described the AJAI regional network as follows: *Mantiqi 1/Ula,* covering Sumatra, Singapore, Malaysia, and southern Thailand; *Mantiqi 2/Sani,* covering Java, Bali, and eastern Indonesia; *Mantiqi 3/Thalid,* covering Philippines, Kalimantan, and Sulawesi; and *Mantiqi 4/Ukhro,* covering Australia and Papua.[62]

Following the arrest of various key AJAI operatives and capture of various documents, more information has surfaced about the manner in which the terrorist organization has been operating in the region, especially Indonesia. One of the most starting revelations was the depth and breadth of the organization, whose zone of operation extended from Afghanistan and Pakistan to the whole of Southeast Asia and as far as Australia and possibly the Maldives. In line with the PUPJI, the Indonesian police was able to piece together the AJAI structure that existed up to 2002, prior to it being dismantled following the arrest of key leaders such as Hambali, Abu Rusdan, Mukhlas, and Mohammad Nasir. While the key elements were as revealed by the various intelligence agencies, in reality the AJAI organization was much more structured hierarchically, from the *Amir* at the very top to the *Fiah* at

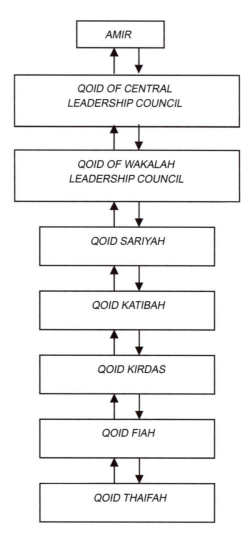

Figure 3.3   AJAI's Basic Procedures on Communications, Information, and Education

Source: Pedoman Umum Perjuangan Al-Jama'ah Al-Islamiyyah (General Guidelines
on the Struggle of Jemaah Islamiyah) (Kuala Lumpur: Issued by Majlis Qiyadah
Markaziyah, Al Ja'amah Al Islamiyyah, May 1996).

the lowest rung. While AJAI is a very loose and unstructured organization today,
until about late 2002 and early 2003 it was well structured, with Abu Bakar Ba'asyir
as the *Amir* heading the *Markaz,* assisted by the chief executive of the *Amir,* Abu
Rusdan, and the chief of the Military Wing, Zulkarnain; a regional *Shura* headed
by Hambali; and a Working Party under Mustofa and Achmad Roichan. Below this

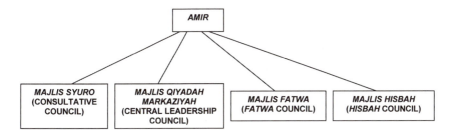

Figure 3.4   *Majelis* (Councils) Assisting the *Amir*

Source: Pedoman Umum Perjuangan Al-Jama'ah Al-Islamiyyah (General Guidelines
on the Struggle of Jemaah Islamiyah), (Kuala Lumpur: Issued by
Majlis Qiyadah Markaziyah, Al Ja'amah Al Islamiyyah, May 1996).

were the four *Mantiqis,* then the various *Wakalahs,* and then, interestingly, two
additional structures that were not well publicized before this, namely the *Khatibah*
and *Qirdas,* and below them were the various *Fiahs* or cells.

Equally important, partly in response to its largely Indonesian origins based on a
territorial structure, and in addition to the four *Mantiqis,* captured Indonesian AJAI
operatives revealed the existence of what was referred to as the "AJAI's regions of operation" (see Figure 3.8). In this regard, from the initial training grounds in Afghanistan
and Pakistan to the ultimate realization of the Indonesian Islamic State, three regions
were established in Southeast Asia. The first, under *Mantiqi* 1, referred to as the
"economic region" encompassed Singapore, Malaysia, southern Thailand, Sumatra,
Java, Riau, and the Malukus. Under the leadership of Mukhlas, this region was tasked
with collection of financial resources of the organization, both internal and particularly, external. The second, under *Mantiqi* 2, referred to as the "regions of conflict,"
overlapped with various territories under *Mantiqi* 1 and 2 as well as covered Poso,

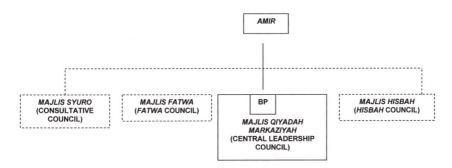

Figure 3.5   *Majelis* (Councils) Assisting the *Amir* in Times of Emergency

Source: Pedoman Umum Perjuangan Al-Jama'ah Al-Islamiyyah (General Guidelines
on the Struggle of Jemaah Islamiyah), (Kuala Lumpur: Issued by
Majlis Qiyadah Markaziyah, Al Ja'amah Al Islamiyyah, May 1996).

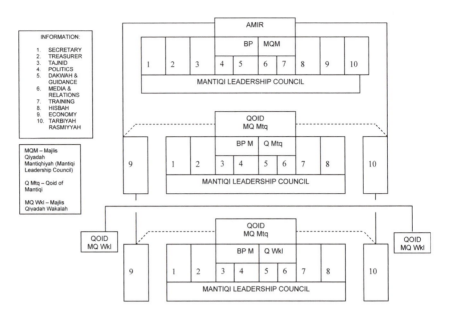

Figure 3.6   Working Mechanism of *Majelis Qiyadah* (Qiyadah Councils)

Source: Pedoman Umum Perjuangan Al-Jama'ah Al-Islamiyyah (General Guidelines
on the Struggle of Jemaah Islamiyah), (Kuala Lumpur: Issued by
Majlis Qiyadah Markaziyah, Al Ja'amah Al Islamiyyah, May 1996).

Ternate, and Ambon. Under the leadership of Abu Irsyad, AJAI fighters were involved
in various bloody conflicts, and many received their baptism of *jihad* in this zone.
Some AJAI members even referred to this as the "*Jihad* Zone." The third, under
Mantiqi 3, referred to as the "training region" encompassed Mindanao and the surrounding regions. Under the leadership of Mohammad Nasir Abbas, a Malaysian,
the various AJAI training camps such as Camp *Abubakar,* Camp *Hudaibiyah,* and
Camp MILF were located mainly in MILF-controlled regions in the Philippines.

Each *Mantiqi* is in turn subdivided into a number of *Wakalahs.* For instance,
Mantiqi 1 is believed to have *wakalahs* in Indonesia, Malaysia, Singapore, Thailand,
Myanmar, and even Cambodia (see Figure 3.9). Within its ambit and area of
responsibility, each *wakalah* has a number of functional groups dealing with
economic matters, *dakwah* activities, communications and operations. For instance,
the Singapore *wakalah* was headed by Ibrahim Maidin (now in detention), and
later he was succeeded by Mas Selamat, who was arrested in February 2003 by the
Indonesian police while on a bus in Tanjung Pinang in Bintan. He is presently in
detention in Singapore.

The aim of the AJAI, just as the DI, is to develop and establish an Islamic nation
through *dakwah* (peaceful means) as well as the use of force and revolution. Both
Sungkar and Ba'asyir are believed to view Kartosuwiryo as their role model.

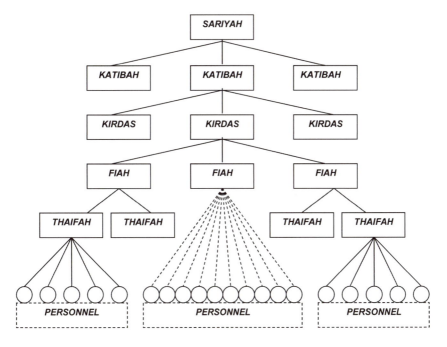

Figure 3.7 AJAI'S Personnel Building and Training

Source: Pedoman Umum Perjuangan Al-Jama'ah Al-Islamiyyah (General Guidelines
on the Struggle of Jemaah Islamiyah), (Kuala Lumpur: Issued by
Majlis Qiyadah Markaziyah, Al Ja'amah Al Islamiyyah, May 1996).

However, unlike the DI, the goals of the AJAI are far wider. While the DI wanted to
create an Islamic state only in Indonesia, the AJAI's goal is to create a *Daulah Islamiyah Nusantara,* or a Southeast Asian Archipelagic Islamic State encompassing the
whole of southern Southeast Asian, including Singapore and Brunei.[63]

AJAI'S STRATEGY AND OPERATIONAL GUIDELINES

Despite the existence of a wide-ranging debate about the efficacy and organizational strength of the AJAI, it is clear that, at least in the beginning, it was not a loosely
organized group of violent Islamists operating without any direction or strategy.
The AJAI started as a highly organized and structured organization, with clear rules
of operation and engagement, leadership hierarchy, and goals as well as operational
procedures. In early 1997, Abdullah Sungkar stated that his organization had clear
"guidelines" to realize an "Islamic Community" and this was by "the materialization
of three strengths." These were "a) *Quwwatul Aqidah* (Faith's Strength); b) *Quwwatul
Ukhuwwah* (Brotherhood's Strength); and c) *Quwwatul Musallaha* (Military
Strength)."[64] Sungkar's claim cannot be dismissed lightly, as he was speaking with

Table 3.1   The AJAI Regional Structure

Mantiqi 1:	Malaysia, Singapore, Southern Thailand, and possibly Myanmar
Mantiqi 2:	Indonesia (Java, Sumatra, Eastern Indonesia)
Mantiqi 3:	Indonesia (Sulawesi, Kalimantan), East Malaysia (Sabah, Sarawak), Brunei, and Southern Philippines (Mindanao)
Mantiqi 4:	Australia, Indonesia (Papua) and Papua New Guinea, and East Timor

the foreknowledge of the existence of an elaborate plan and strategy to achieve his organization's stated goal, namely "to establish a *Daulah Islamiyah* (Islamic State) as a basis towards the restoration of *Khilaafaah Alaa Minhajin Nubuwwah*." This was stated in the hitherto secret manual called the *Pedoman Umum Perjuangan Jama'ah Islamiyah* (PUPJI), or General Guide to the Struggle of the *Jamaah Islamiyah,* that was captured by Indonesian security forces in Solo, Central Java, in December 2002. The PUPJI that was issued by the Central Leadership Council of the *Ja'maah Islamiyyah* in May 1996 was authored with the blessings of Abdullah Sungkar, Ba'asyir, and Mukhlas, by Ahmad Roichan, alias Saad, who is presently in custody in Jakarta.

The strategies and game plan adopted by the AJAI in its struggle were elucidated in the PUPJI (see Appendix 1) under four main headings, namely, *Ushulul-Manhaj Al-Harakiy Li Iqomatid-Dien* (the 10 principles on which all of its activities are based), *Al-Manhaj Al-Harakiy Li Iqomatid-Dien* (the various programs

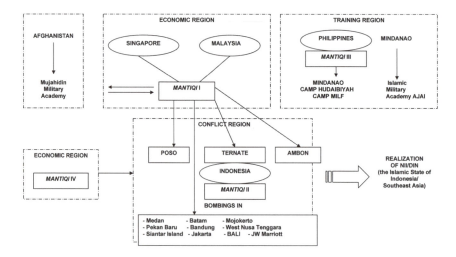

Figure 3.8   Logic of AJAI's *Mantiqi* Regional Structure

Source: Author's interviews with Indonesian Officials involved in counterterrorism

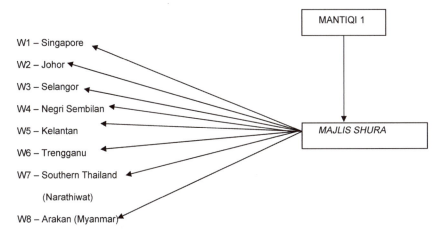

Figure 3.9   AJAI *Mantiqi* 1 and Its Subunits (*wakalahs*)

based on the 10 principles), *Al-Manhaj Al-Amaliy* (Operational Guidelines), and *An-Nidhomul-Asasiyb* (rules and regulations governing the *Jama'ah Islamiyah*).

The *Ushulul-Manhaj Al-Harakiy Li Iqomatid-Dien,* or 10 principles adopted in its struggle to uphold Islam and the eventual establishment of a *Daulah Islamiyah* that would eventuate in the *Khilafah Islamiyah,* includes the following:

1. Our aim is to seek *Allah's* pleasures in the ways prescribed by him and his messenger;

2. Our *Aqidah* (belief) is based on the *Aqidah* of the Sunnis subscribed by the *Salafus Solih* (Pious predecessors);

3. Our understanding of Islam is comprehensive based on the understanding of the *Salafus Solih;*

4. Our objective is to make man submit to Allah only by restoring the *Khilafah* (Caliphate) on earth;

5. Our path is *Iman* (faith), *Hijrah* (migration), and *Jihad Fie Sabilillah* (*Jihad* in the cause of Allah);

6. Our resources are: knowledge and *taqwa* (piety), confidence and *tawakkal* (resign to the will of Allah), thankful and perseverance, leading *zuhud* (renunciation of worldly life and pleasures) and giving priority to the hereafter, and *Jihad Fie Sabilillah* and martyrdom;

7. Our love is for Allah, the messenger and the faithful;

8. Our enemies are Satan and evil men;

9. Our *Jama'ah* is bound by unanimity of objective, *Aqidah* and understanding of Islam; and

10. Our practice of Islam is pure and total starting from the *Jama'ah* followed by the *Daulah* and *Khilafah.*

As for the *Al-Manhaj Al-Harakiy Li Iqomatid-Dien,* or programs of AJAI, two stages are identified. The first stage, the preparations needed to establish the *Daulah Islamiyah,* involves the building of three main "strengths." The first is that of the *Jama'ah.* This encompasses the following:

a. Formation of *Qiyadah Ar-Rosyidah*

b. Formation of *Qo'idah Solabah*

c. Implementation of *Tanzim Sirri* (clandestine groups and organizations)

d. Development of *iman* and *as-samu'w wath thaatu*

e. Enjoinment of good and forbidden of evil

f. *Hisbah*

Second is the building of the strength and power of AJAI through:

a. Education (knowledge)

b. *Dakwah* (missionary work)

c. *Hijrah* (migration)

d. *Jihad* (armed struggle)

e. Tajnid (military training)

f. *Qoidah Aminah* (building of safe areas/bases and sanctuaries)

g. *Diklat* (education and training)

h. *Jasus* (spying and intelligence gathering)

i. Cooperation and networking with like-minded groups

Third involves the exercise of the various strengths that have been garnered. This could be operationalized through *Dakwah* (*indzar*) or armed *Jihad.*

The second aspect of the program involves the establishment of the *Daulah Islamiyah.* There are also three components. First is *Daulah.* This involves "a. *Tandhim (Hukumiy)* or establishment of laws and regulations; b. *Tajnid* (military training); c. *Jihad;* d. *Tahkin* (arbitration or judiciary); e. *Tamwil* (finance); f. Establishment of a Muslim Community; and f. *Tarbiyah* (education). Second is *Tatsbitud-Daulah,* or strengthening of the state. Third is *Tansiq bainad-Duwal,* or collaboration with other countries. Once the two aspects of the program are in place, the AJAI believes that the next phase would involve the establishment of the *Khilafah,* or Caliphate or worldwide Islamic governance.

The third aspect of the strategy involves *Al-Manhaj Al-Harakiy Li Iqomatid-Dien.* This refers to the guidelines to uphold Islam and covers both the operational and administrative aspects. Though sounding ubiquitous, this covers the military aspects, and the details are akin to that of a military manual. As far as "strategy of operations" is concerned, it covers the following: a. Definition of strategy; b. Procedures of Operations Strategy (general and detailed); and c. Conduct of Operations. Demonstrating

AJAI's military competency, the detailed procedures on how to engage its enemies are stated in the following sequence:

a. To observe and analyze the *Jama'ah,* its enemies, and surrounding;

b. To make a frank assessment of the effectiveness of the *Jama'ah*'s strengths;

c. To look for targets for attacks against the enemies;

d. To make plan for programs and operations;

e. To discuss with the leadership and the person to execute the plan;

f. To conduct final testing;

g. To decide on the operations strategy; and

h. To execute the plan.

The PUPJI also identified four types of operations—intelligence, development of strength, deployment of strength, and combat. In dealing with its "enemies," the PUPJI clearly stressed the importance of *Jihad fi sabilillah* and three "developments" of an individual are emphasized. First, intellectual development "to enlighten members on the justification to carry out *Jihad* as well as on its laws and ethics. Second, spiritual development "to instill self-discipline, patience and trust in God." Third, skills development "to maintain *i'dad* (state of preparedness) and to pave the way for others to achieve the level of preparedness" as well as "to involve members in *Jihad*". In this regard, particular emphasis is paid to "*Jihad Musallah*" or "armed *Jihad*." This requires its members "to fight the enemies of Allah such as non-Muslims authorities, the hypocrites, apostates, *zindiq* (atheists), *mustabdil* and their allies in the cause of Allah and His Messenger." Seven functions of armed *Jihad* were highlighted in this connection:

1. To destroy the influence of *toghut* (one who exceeds his legitimate limit; a transgressor) who has often prevented the setting up of an Islamic state according to the Prophet;

2. To eradicate cruelty and uphold the truth so that destruction on earth could be prevented;

3. To safeguard the existence and dignity of Muslims and to assist those who are weak;

4. To humiliate and raise alarm among Allah's enemies and prevent them from creating mischief;

5. To separate the infidels/hypocrites from among the ranks of Muslims and to pave the way towards martyrdom;

6. To test one's faith;

7. To maintain power on this earth to set up *Allah*'s law (*sharia* and justice) and live under *Allah*'s *minhaj.*

As far as the administration and development of its personnel are concerned, it covers personnel, territorial, and economic development as well as establishing a network with other groups that share the ideals of the AJAI. In order to enhance personnel development, four aspects are emphasized: information/recruitment, education, *tajnid,* and *hisbah.* Exhibiting the influence of the Indonesian military, which underpins its strategy on "territoriality," this aspect is determined by the geographical, demographic, and social conditions obtained at any one time.

The fourth aspect of the PUPJI refers to a set of rules and regulations that governs the AJAI. It is more akin to a "Constitution of the AJAI" and contains 15 chapters and 43 articles. This sets out clearly the command structure of the AJAI, the role and functions of the various bodies (*Amir, Majlis Qiyadah* [Leadership Council], *Majlis Syuro* [Consultative Council], *Majlis Fatwa* [Fatwa Council], and *Majlis Hisbah* [*Hisbah* Council]).

AJAI'S IDEOLOGY

The key thinkers and actors of AJAI, such as Abdullah Sungkar, Abu Bakar Ba'a-syir, Hambali, Abu Jibril, Mukhlas, Dulmatin, Umar Patek, Zulkarnean and Abu Dujana, were strictly *Wahhabist* and *salafist.* They believed in the creation of an Islamic state and in the implementation of *Sharia.* What is equally significant is that the key leaders of AJAI appeared to have undergone a metamorphosis as far as their ideology was concerned. When they all started their struggle, they were essentially followers of the DI and wanted to realize the dream of Kartosuwiryo, of creating Indonesia as an Islamic state. Hence, initially, when the Indonesian *Mujahidin* group operated in Pakistan and Afghanistan, they were known, according to Nasir Abbas, the former leader of *Mantiqi 3,* as *Jamaah NII* or Followers of the Indonesian Islamic State or at times as *Jamaah DI* or Followers of the *Darul Islam.*[65] Initially, this dream was pursued through *dakwah* or through peaceful means. However, over time, AJAI leaders became radicalized on two counts. First, their goal expanded from merely transforming Indonesia to converting Southeast Asia into an Islamic region. Hence, the shift from NII to *Daulah Islamiyah Nusantara,* DIN. Second, in addition to *dakwah,* the adoption of *jihad* was sanctioned to achieve the end.

The *Wahhabi-Salafi* orientation of the AJAI was clearly evident in Abu Bakar Ba'asyir's exposition of what he thought were the key principles of Islam. He argued that there were five key pillars that were critical in understanding Islam in the contemporary era. First, "Islam (*Din*) was based on the laws for living and these were the teachings of God transmitted to his Messenger, the Prophet." For him, this is not strictly confined to religion but affects all aspects of human existence, be it political, economic, and social-cultural. According to him, "the corridor of Islam should be widened as broadly as possible." Second, "since Islam is a religion from God, Man had no right to interfere, intervene or amend it. If anything, Man's actions should be judged, at least for Muslims, by the yardstick of Islamic religion." According to him, "the fundamentals of the Islam were based on the teaching of God, as transmitted by the Prophet and practices that were introduced by the companions of the Prophet." Third, "Islam should be proselytized through *dakwah,* peacefully, winning over adherents through discussions and advice, and not through force or inducements." Fourth, "Islam condones the use of force to defend itself. If Islam is attacked by arguments, then it is only right that Muslims responded likewise. However, if Islam is attacked through weapons, then the religion condones and legitimizes the use of force." Fifth, the propagation, promotion, and protection of the religion are the duty of the government, not just individuals. The state, through its power and authority, can do far more than an individual. If a country has a Muslim majority, it is only right that *Sharia* be adopted and implemented."[66]

A consistent theme in the radical discourse is the righteousness of force to further the goals of Islam. This includes sacrificing oneself either to defend Islam from attacks or to promote its good image. According to Abu Bakar Ba'asyir:

> Defending Islam is both a duty and obligation. While death is certain, yet there are different kinds of death. Some are of low or high quality and others somewhere in the middle. For Islam, the highest value of death comes to a person when he/she dies a martyr or *mati sahid*. Undertaking suicide is forbidden by Islam as this is done by people who have lost all hope in living. However, a martyrdom death is highly valued and prized. When one dies for Islam, one gets closer to God as his chosen one. This is what all *Jihadists* strive for and is permissible in Islam. Since the days of the Prophet, the idea of dying for Islam was to weaken the enemy, both directly and indirectly. As long as these goals are achieved, then death in not in vain. It is highly valued and hence, should be both encouraged and praised. It emanates from higher ideals and intentions with the sole purpose of getting closer to God and to defend Islam in the face of attacks by its enemies.[67]

Abu Bakar Ba'asyir, as one of the key preachers of AJAI, argued that Muslims were suffering from the disease of "*Wahn.*" In short, they were sick. This was the malaise of "loving the world but fearing death." Muslims were becoming materialists, thinking of accumulating wealth, but not giving thought to after-death. Because of this illness, the vast majority of Muslims were becoming weak; their spirits weakened, and hence they were easily manipulated by others, especially the *kafirs,* or infidels. He blamed the governments in Muslim countries for this situation, as leaders in such countries had also gone astray, mainly to please to global Western powers that wanted to weaken and exploit Islamic countries. Hence, the need to support *dakwah* and *Jihad* whenever necessary to achieve the goals of *syaria* and *Daulah Islamiyah.*[68]

The adoption of *Salafi* thought, or "*Salaficazation,*" of Sungkar, Ba'asyir, and other AJAI leaders was due to a number of factors. This goal expansion from NII to DIN and the adoption of *Jihad* to achieve the goals were largely due to the AJAI's leaders' exposure and interactions with Middle East ideologues that preached and practiced violence, especially with regard to the struggle in the Middle East and Afghanistan. The success of the Iranian Revolution was also important, demonstrating that Islamists could rise to power and implement the causes of *Sharia* for Muslims. In some ways, by the time the AJAI leaders undertook their *hijrah* to Malaysia, they had already become radicalized due to the opposition to Suharto's New Order and what these leaders perceived as violent persecution of Islamists by Suharto and his security apparatus. While Sungkar and Ba'asyir started their careers as preachers and believed in the bottom-up *dakwah* process, as evident in the opening of the *Al-Mukmin Pesantren* in Solo, their persecution by the New Order compelled them to adopt a more radical and violent approach to attain their goals. According to Kumar Ramakrishna:

> The period of incarceration from 1978 and subsequent targeting by the New Order Regime may have been the "tipping point" in terms of providing them with the final insight that *dakwah* in the absence of *jihad* would be an exercise in futility. In other words, they became not merely Islamists but radical Islamists who believed in *jihad* as the means to actualize an Islamized Indonesia.[69]

By most accounts, by 1985, the AJAI leadership were converted towards the Qutbiyyah-type thinking, believing that to defend and preserve the Islamic order, there was a need to wage a war against the "infidels" and their supporters, even if they happened to be Muslims. While *Sharia* was adopted as the blueprint for the Islamic order, at the same time, Western values and their "conspiracies" were blamed for weaknesses of the Muslim all over the world. By the time the *Mujahidins* won in Afghanistan, resorting to *Jihad* had become an article of faith for the AJAI leaders. In addition to the ideas of al-Banna, Maududi, and Qutb, the AJAI leaders were influenced by the teachings of Abdullah Azam, who played a critical role in mobilizing foreign *Mujahidins* to undertake a *Jihad* against the Soviets. Following the *Mujahidins'* success, Azzam expanded his mission to liberate other Muslim territories. According to him:

> *Jihad* is now...incumbent on all Muslims and will remain so until the Muslims recapture every spot that was Islamic but late fell into the hands of the *kuffar* (infidels)...The duty of *jihad* is one of the most important imposed on us by God.... He has made it incumbent on us, just like prayer, fasting and alms (*zakat*).[70]

In this connection, the radicalization of the AJAI's ideology was not only in terms of adopting violence to achieve its goals. Even more important was the resort to extreme violence in terms of targeting. Along Qutbiyyah lines, the AJAI *jihadis* believed that in addition to non-Muslim enemies, *jihad* could also be launched against apostate Muslim governments that were viewed as "agents" of the West. In addition to the shift in terms of means and targeting, there was also a clear goal expansion, with the AJAI endorsing the establishment of a *Khilafah* (global caliphate) that would unite all Muslims under a "single, righteous exemplar ruler."[71] In sum, the key ideological strands that dominate the AJAI's ideology include the establishment of Islamic state nationally, regionally, and eventually a global *Khilafah;* adoption of *Sharia* governance; adoption of *dakwah* to spread the message; and, where necessary, adopt violence to defend Islam from threats posed by Muslims and non-Muslims.

FUNDING THE AJAI'S OPERATIONS

For any terrorist organization, its success in achieving various goals, and ultimately its very existence, depends largely on its access to funds. In this connection, the manner in which the AJAI was organized partly reflected this consideration, with *Mantiqi* 1 and 4 being essentially the "economic" basis of the organization.[72] More specifically, there are a number of sources of AJAI's funding. First, there are donations from its members. Every member is expected to donate 5 percent of his income to the organization. The Head of a *Fiah* would collect the donations from its members and forward it to the head of *Wakalah,* who will in turn send the collections to the *Mantiqi* head. Keeping aside a certain amount for operational and other expenses, the total collections will then be forwarded to the *Markaziyah,* the AJAI's headquarters.

Second, there are the donations collected from the community, be it from various Islamic institutions or from recitations classes at mosques. Many non-Islamic institutions also make donations, even though they are not aware of how the donations are utilized. Third, there are the *Fisabillah* donations, specifically undertaken to promote Islamic-related struggles or *Jihads.* These donations are usually used for logistical support, training of personnel, transportation, and even purchase of weapons. Fourth, there are various obligatory donations, be they during the *Ramadhan* (fasting month), for propagation of Islam, and even a 2 percent wealth tax. Next, there are also funds from *Fa'i,* that is, "legitimate war booty" for *Jihad* accumulated from robberies, especially from *Kafirs.* Finally, there are donations from external sources and, in the case of AJAI, from the *Al Qaeda* and charities from the Middle East that support the propagation of radical Islam ideology in Southeast Asia. For instance, Abdullah Sunata, the leader of KOMPAK, admitted receiving US$25,000 from *Al Qaeda*'s Abu Muhamad. After using US$2,500, the rest of it was sent to the Head of *Mantiqi 3* in Mindanao to finance training of *Jihadists,* even though Nordin Top, a key leader of AJAI's "pro-bombing faction" wanted part of the largesse.[73]

AJAI AND STRATEGIC MARRIAGES—KINSHIP TIES THAT BIND

That a "network" exists is undeniable. The new Islamist terrorist network in Southeast Asia tends to be loose, unstructured, informal, and often based on personal and familial ties. Sidney Jones identified nine main sources of AJAI's network.[74] One of the most important in this regard is family and kinship ties, something unique in the annals of terrorism.[75] There are many marriages involving family members of key AJAI leaders and their operatives, helping to keep the AJAI organization a "close-knit one from every aspect."[76] What makes AJAI unique as a regional terrorist organization has been the compact manner in which it has held together since its official formation in January 1993 and the unity of cause expressed by its members since the mid-1980s. In addition to training, common experience in *Jihad* in various theaters, ideology, and loyalty to its leaders, family bonds through strategic marriages have accounted for the compact nature of AJAI. According to a *Straits Times* report, Indonesian "intelligence agents have uncovered a complex web of more than 100 marriages involving family members of key *Jemaah Islamiah* (JI) leaders, members and their operatives across the region."[77] The intricate web of strategic marriage alliances make the AJAI akin to a mammoth extended family bound by radical

Table 3.2 AJAI's Kinship Ties

Name	Family Links
Nordin Mohd Top	Married to Rahmah Rusdi, sister of Rais Rusdi, a key AJAI operative.
Fathur Rahman Al Ghozi	Married to Sheila Mubin, cousin of Amrozi, and is brother of Muhajir, involved in Mojokerto's bombing.
Faiz Bafana	Brother of Hashim Bafana, AJAI member. Their sister is married to Shukri Omar Talib, a key AJAI member.
Mohd Nasir Abbas	Three of his sisters married to key AJAI operatives, including Mukhlas. His brother Hashim was involved in the Pekan Baru and Batam bombings.
Taufik Abdul Halim	His sister is married to Zulkifli Hir, a AJAI member.
Jaafar Anwarul	Three of his brothers are also AJAI members.
Amrozi	Brother of Ali Imron and Mukhlas.
Muchlis	Married to Sungkar's daughter.
Noralwizah Lee Abdullah	Hambali's wife and believed to head the AJAI's Women Wing. Her sister Norfadilah Lee Abdullah (Daemugading) is married to Dadang Suratman, a key AJAI leader.
Dulmatin	His wife's sister is married to Hery Kuncoro, an important AJAI operative.
Abu Dzar	Father-in-law of Omar al-Faruq.
Abu Fatih	Brother of Abdul Rochim, a teacher at *Pondok Ngruki*.
Abu Rusdan	Son of Mohd. Faleh, a *Laskar Hizbullah* and DI fighter.
Datuk Rajah Ameh	Father-in-law of Johnny Hendrawan, a Bali bomber.
Jaafar Bin Mistooki	His wife is sister-in-law of Rasul, a teacher at Lukmanul Hakiem.
Wahyudin	Son-in-law of Abdullah Sungkar.
Taufik	Sister married to Zulkifli Hir, still on the run.

Islamic ideology. The marriage diplomacy of comrade-in-arms has cemented the AJAI, and this partly explains its staying power.

Marriage alliances have been struck across the board, involving brothers, sisters and in-laws. There are cases of a number of brothers being involved in the AJAI cause. In this regard, there are the Bali bomber brothers, Ali Ghufron, Ali Imron, and

Amrozi. Two other brothers were also implicated in the first Bali bombing, namely, Herlambang and Hernianto. Fathur Rahman Al-Ghozi and Ahmad Rofiq Ridho are also brothers with Ahmad, later marrying his brother's widow. Fathurrahman's cousin, Gempur Angkoro was also an active AJAI member who was killed by police. Two other brothers active in AJAI were Hambali and his Rusman Gunawan (Gun Gun); the latter was arrested in Karachi, Pakistan. From Singapore, two brothers were arrested for being AJAI members, Faiz and Fatihi bin Abu Bakar Bafana. Another sibling linked to terrorism is from the family of Achmad Kandai. Achmad's brother, Nasir, worked closely with Sungkar and Abu Bakar Ba'asyir. Achmad's sons, Farihin, Abdul Jabar, Mohammed Islam, and Solahudin have all been implicated in AJAI-linked bombings.

As far as in-laws are concerned, there are a number of notable cases. Ali Ghufron married Farida, younger sister of Nasir bin Abbas, former leader of *Mantiqi* 3. Syamsul Bahri, an AJAI member, is also Nasir's brother-in-law. Taufiq Abdul Halim is the brother-in-law of Zulkifli Hir, a Malaysian *jihadi*. Datuk Rajah Ameh, involved in the Christmas Eve bombing in 2000, is the father-in-law of AJAI member Joni Hendrawan. Muhammad Rais, part of the Marriott bombing team, is the brother-in-law of Nordin Top. Two sisters, Noraliza Abdullah and Noral Falida, married Hambali and Abu Yusuf, respectively.

There are also cases of fathers and sons involved in the terrorist endeavor. Abdul Rohim, Abu Bakar Ba'asyir's son, was the cell leader in Karachi. Abu Dzar, whose father was a close associate of Hambali, and two of his uncles were AJAI members. In addition, arranged marriages have also been used to cement the AJAI. Abdullah Sungkar married two of his stepdaughters to two senior *jihadists,* Ferial Muchlis bin Abdul Halim, head of Selangor AJAI cell, and Syawal Yassin, a South Sulawesi AJAI leader. In the same vein, Haris Fadillah, leader of *Laskar Mujahidin,* married his daughter to Omar Al-Faruk

Hence, AJAI is bonded together through a network of brothers, sisters, brothers-in-law, and sisters-in-law. One can only agree with Noor Huda Ismail when he argued, "Understanding kinship ties in the *jihadi* network in Indonesia and beyond is critical. Without such ties, many alienated young Muslim men would not have become or remained *jihadis.* Kinship is particularly important in a clandestine organization like AJAI where maintaining relations of trust and confidence is crucial for survival."[78] In short, what makes AJAI unique as a terrorist organization is not merely its violence and regionwide expanse, but also its role as a "terrorist tribe cemented by kinship."

THE AJAI CELL AND CUT-OFF SYSTEM—A KEY TO ITS RESILIENCE AND SURVIVAL

In many ways, the AJAI, like most terrorist groups, is organized and structured like most communist groups. They tend to operate clandestinely and are organized in cells, the basic unit of the AJAI.[79] As such, due to high motivation, commitment, and oath of secrecy, it is difficult to detect the groups, their motivation, plans, and ultimate objectives. At the same time, they tend to operate in small numbers, and this makes detection as well as understanding their *modus operandi* extremely difficult. This is one of the keys ensuring the survival of AJAI. For instance, even though AJAI was formally established on January 1, 1993, it was only in late 2001 that it was detected in Singapore, and it took a much longer time to crack it down in other Southeast Asian countries. Even tiny Singapore, known for its control, did not detect AJAI's existence until some nine years later, thereby giving the terrorist organization a head start in its "war" against governments in Southeast Asia. What is particularly significant as far as the structure of the AJAI is concerned is not merely the clandestine nature, organization, and operations based on the cell as the basic unit, but more important is the practice of what is known as the "cut-off" system. Using the analogy of the electrical system, there will be an automatic shutdown of electricity if a short circuit takes place anywhere in the system, thereby ensuring that the whole system is not harmed or undermined.

In the AJAI's cell setup, while there is no apparent clear-cut hierarchy, in reality it exists. There is a system of triangulation, whereby information is always shared between a small group of people, often organized along the lines of a triangle. There is also a clear code of conduct of not seeking information about other operations and operating on the need-to-know principle. Otherwise, if one is too inquisitive about the organization and its operations, there are always the suspicions that he/she might be an intelligence plant. The cutoff system operates as follows (see Figure 3.10): In the first triangle, called Alpha, cell members 1, 2, and 3 are known to each other. In triangle Bravo, cell members 3, 4, and 5 are known to each other. In triangle Charlie, cell members 5, 6, and 7 are known to each other. However, only cell member 3 knows about the existence and operation of triangles Alpha and Bravo simultaneously while cell member 1 and 2 are totally oblivious of triangle Bravo just as cell members 4 and 5 are cut off from triangle Alpha. Similarly, cell member 5 knows about triangles Bravo and Charlie, but cell members 6 and 7 are cut off from triangle Bravo just as cell members 3 and 4 are cut off from triangle Charlie. If any one member of the cell is caught by the security apparatus, the danger to the organization tends to be minimal except when a key member is caught. The key members in the above hypothetical setup would be 3, 5, and 7.

THE AJAI NETWORK: NATIONAL, REGIONAL, AND INTERNATIONAL

The AJAI draws its network from varied sources. In addition to kinship ties, there are a number of other important sources. The first basis of AJAI's network involves the *Darul Islam.* As the AJAI literally grew out of the DI, the latter remains one of the most important reservoirs of recruits for the group. Second, are the linkages forged during the Afghanistan experience, something that united many of *Mantiqi* 1 leaders and operatives. An important factor accounting for the "internationalization" of the AJAI was the coming together of *Jihadists* from Southeast Asia who met in Pakistan and Afghanistan; this essentially brought together the future regional network of AJAI, namely the KMM, MILF, GMIP and Abu Sayyaf. Third, there is

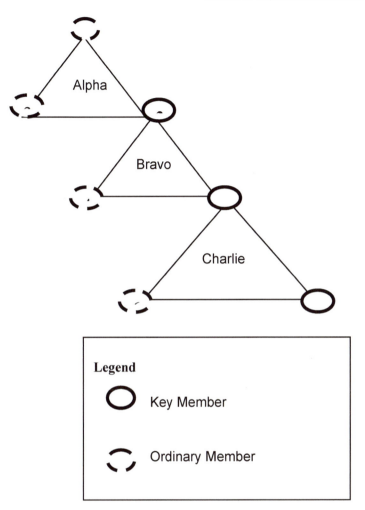

Figure 3.10   The AJAI Cell and Cut-Off System

the "old school network," essentially involving *Pondok Pesantren Islam Al-Mukmin* in Ngruki, Solo, Central Java, *Pondok Pesantren Al-Islam* in Tengguluh, Lamongan, East Java, and the *Pondok Pesantren Lukmanul Hakiem* in Ulu Tiram, Johor, Malaysia. The fourth source refers to the network that grew out of the "terrorist military academies," essentially the training camps located in MILF territories in southern Philippines. Fifth was the common experience engendered through the experience of *Jihad* in Poso and Ambon. The last two sources of bonding arose either from business relations or due to experience in prison and detentions.

What has made the AJAI terrorist organization is also its ability to link up with like-minded organizations in Southeast Asia and beyond. Even though the AJAI was essentially born in Indonesia and largely Indonesian-led, over time it has developed extensive collaboration with various radical groups in Southeast Asia. There are essentially two aspects of AJAI's regionalism. First is its regionwide network, as evident in its structure and organization. What makes the terrorist organization a force to be reckoned with is its regionwide expanse covering the whole of Southeast Asia, best evident in the operationalization of the four *Mantiqis*. At the same time, what makes the AJAI a full-fledged organization, and the first Southeast Asian regional terrorist organization, is not merely its regionwide expanse but also its close collaboration with like-minded Islamists, extremists, and terrorists in the region. Also, partly due to the first-generation AJAI's leadership experience in Afghanistan, there is every reason to believe that close ties with the *Al Qaeda* have been established. These unique features have made the AJAI the epicenter of terrorism in Southeast Asia. Hence, it is important to unravel the national, regional, and international network of the AJAI in order to understand its goals and *modus operandi*.

AJAI'S GUIDELINES ON NETWORKING

According to the AJAI's constitution or PUPJI, only the *Amir* has the authority to "establish relations with other parties that may benefit the *Jama'ah*." This is further elaborated under Chapter XIV (Communications), Article 41, which states:

1. Relations with other Islamic organizations that share the AJAI principles and objectives, shall be based on the spirit of brotherhood and cooperation;
2. All *Qoid* shall establish relations with other organizations and institutions with the approval of the *Amir;*
3. Every member shall establish relations with those outside the AJAI circles with the approval of the respective *Qoid;* and
4. Every member of the *Jama'ah* shall deliver talks to people outside the AJAI circles with the knowledge of the respective *Qoid* and should report it to his *Qoid*.

In further clarifying cooperation with other groups (*Tansiq bainal Jama'ah*), it is explicitly stated that there is a need "to cooperate with other groups so that the objectives of the *Jama'ah* can be achieved." Clear guidelines and criteria are established for such cooperation to take place. Collaboration, according to the PUPJI, can take place only with groups that satisfy the following two conditions:

1. Groups whose *aqidah* (faith), objective, and *wasilah* (way) are similar to ours;
2. Groups whose *aqidah* and objectives are similar to ours but different *wasilah,* yet still acceptable under Islamic teachings.

The purpose of cooperation is threefold:

1. To create *tafahum* (understanding), *ta'awaun* (cooperation), and *takaful* (solidarity) among all Islamic groups with a view to share a common responsibility and objective

of establishing a *Daulah Islamiyah* (Islamic State) and *Khilafah* (Islamic system of governance);

2. To step up *I'dadul Quwwah* (physical/mental preparation);
3. To create a united Muslim community that will be able to counter its enemies.

Against these philosophical underpinnings, the AJAI network in the region and beyond will be analyzed.

THE AJAI REGIONAL NETWORK

One aspect that differentiates the AJAI from previous and other terrorist organizations in Southeast Asia is its ability to synergize with like-minded groups in the region. While this is undertaken in line with its stated "philosophy and guidelines," as obtained in the PUPJI, what is vitally important is that such cooperation and collaboration is real, essentially with like-minded *Jihadi*-oriented organizations in the region. This principally explains the danger of AJAI's terrorism in the region and beyond. The AJAI is closely affiliated with *Kumpulan Mujahidin Malaysia* (KMM), sharing its founders and top leaders, namely Abu Bakar Ba'asyir and Riduan Isamuddin (Hambali). In addition to the MMI headed by Ba'asyir, the AJAI is also linked to *Laskar Jihad,* one of Indonesia's top militant groups until its militia wing was disbanded. *Laskar Jihad* is headed by Jafar Umar Thalib. Jafar, a veteran of the Afghan war, is believed to be behind much of the violence in Ambon and the Malukus. Similarly, the AJAI has close ties with *Laskar Jundulla.* The AJAI is also believed to be cooperating closely with the *Abu Sayyaf* group, one of the most violent radical groups in the Philippines. Additionally, the AJAI is also linked to the Moro Islamic Liberation Front, an Islamic radical group in the Philippines that surpasses the *Abu Sayyaf* in numbers and scale of threat. Due to AJAI's close connections with various radical groups in Southeast Asia, the former FBI chief, Robert Mueller, singled out the AJAI as *Al Qaeda*'s foremost Southeast Asian collaborator. There are also reports that Islamic militants from Myanmar, particularly the Arakan *Rohingya* National Organization, may also have linked up with the *Al Qaeda* and has become part of the "regional network" of terrorists. Similarly, the AJAI is believed to be working closely with a relatively new terrorist group in Pattani, southern Thailand, namely *Gerakan Mujahidin Islam Pattani.* There are also reports that the AJAI has established ties with some groups in Cambodia (see Table 3.3).

AJAI'S SYNERGY WITH ISLAMIST EXTREMISTS IN SOUTHEAST ASIA

It is crucial to note that the majority of identifiable terrorist groups operating in the region are in fact based in religious fundamentalism and Islamic militancy. The AJAI in Indonesia, Malaysia, Singapore, the Philippines, Cambodia, Thailand, and possibly Myanmar, the *Abu Sayyaf* and MILF in the Philippines, and the

Table 3.3   AJAI's Regional Partners and Linkages

Malaysia	*Kumpulan Mujahidin Malaysia,* Al-Muanah
Indonesia	*Majlis Mujahidin Indonesia, Laskar Jihad, Laskar Jundulla,* GAM, FPI, DI, Jammah NII, *Laskar Mujahidin,* Mujahidin KOMPAK, ABB, AMIN, and RP11
Philippines	*Abu Sayyaf* Group, MILF, MBG, BI/RMS)
Thailand	*Gerakan Mujahidin Pattani Islam*
Myanmar	Arakan Rohingya National Organisation

Gerakan Mujahidin Islam Pattani in Thailand, to name a few, have been identified as active terrorist groups operating in the region. As far as the identity of the various terrorist groups are concerned, long before the United States experienced the September 11, 2001, attacks, the ASEAN region had to reckon with various terrorist groups, with the security forces in Indonesia and the Philippines engaged in a violent struggle to stem these groups. Terrorism in the region is, however, not a sole monopoly of the Islamic groups, with a number of non-Islamic groups also active and posing a danger to various states in the region. The New People's Army and the Alex Boncayao Brigade, both essentially Maoist groups, have been operating in the Philippines for quite some time.[80]

However, since September 11, 2001, Islamic terrorism has been increasingly focused upon, and many such groups are believed to be operating in Southeast Asia. A number of factors have made the region particularly important in the global war against terrorism. First, as the United States has traditionally been the major target of most terrorist groups, and since it is heavily involved and has widespread interests in the region, it is natural to assume that Southeast Asia has grown in importance as far as terrorism and counterterrorism is concerned. Second, historically, due to various political, economic, and social-cultural problems as well as long-standing insurgencies, the region has been home to various terrorist groups, especially in Indonesia and the Philippines. Third, as Islamist terrorism has risen in importance, the region's importance has concomitantly increased, as it houses one-fifth of the world's Islamic population. The "Islamic Sea" of Southeast Asia has provided a convenient cover whereby "Islamist terrorists" (the "fish") can easily mingle ("swim") and take cover without raising suspicions, all the more as the region has close political, economic, and social-cultural ties with various countries of the Middle East. The then Singapore's Deputy Prime Minister Lee Hsien Loong argued that "Southeast Asia offers plausible possibilities [as new beachheads and safe havens for the *Al Qaeda*]. The majority of Muslims in the region were moderate and peaceful but a small minority had imported the "viruses of terrorism."[81] For instance, the United States believes that Malaysia was "the perfect place for Arabs to lie low" all the more, as Muslims could enter and leave the country without visas.[82] It was mainly due to this factor that the FBI concluded that Malaysia was a "primary operational launch pad for the September 11 attacks".[83] Together, the region's importance has increased with regard to the presence of Islamist terrorism as well as the need to counter it. The importance of Southeast Asia in global terrorism and counterterrorism is evident in a country-study of Indonesia, the Philippines, Malaysia, Thailand, and Singapore as far as the presence of terrorist groups is concerned.

INDONESIA

As the most populous Islamic country in the world, the danger posed by Islamist terrorism has been endemic, with various radical elements wanting to convert the country into an Islamic theological state. This was best evident by the danger posed by *Darul Islam,* which fought a bloody war with the security forces through the 1950s until it was suppressed in the early 1960s. Since then, there have been various groups that have championed the Islamic cause in Indonesia, with the separatist war in Aceh the most important telltale of this threat. Many of these groups are also believed to have links with the *Al Qaeda.* The United States believes that the *Al Qaeda* set up a cell in Indonesia in the beginning of 2002.

Since the September 11, 2001, incident, a number of Islamic terrorist groups have been identified in Indonesia:

The Free Aceh Movement (Gerakan Aceh Merdeka)

This group has been in operation for many years with explicit aims of establishing an Acehnese independent state. Though exuding Islamic characteristics, it has been driven more by Acehnese nationalism. Described by many analysts as belonging to the "A-list" of world-class terrorists, the group has received international support, facilitated in part by its area of operation being in northern Sumatra, lying across the Straits of Malacca. Arms are also believed to have been smuggled from Thailand, Malaysia and even India. However, through a peace treaty, this group has been somewhat neutralized.

Laskar Jihad

Even though the existence of this group was known long before, the conflict between the Christian and Muslims in Maluku since 1999 that claimed thousands of lives, brought this group to prominence. The *Laskar Jihad* sent thousands of men from Java and Sulawesi to Maluku to defend the Muslim community. Its leader, Jafar Umar Thalib, is believed to have joined the Afghanistan *Mujahidin* in the war against the occupying Soviet forces. He also boasted of meeting Osama bin Laden but publicly despised the Saudi terrorist on grounds that Osama "knew nothing about true religion." The *Al Qaeda* is also believed to be in contact with *Laskar Jihad* even though Jafar Umar Thalib dismissed the *Al Qaeda* as "a different sect which is not in line with true Islam." The *Jihad* warriors were believed to have undertaken military-style training at a camp at Munjul Village near Bogor, on a seven-hectare plot belonging to the *Al Irsad* Foundation even though the group's headquarters is at Yogyakarta. While Jafar Umar does not share totally the AJAI's ideology as propagated by Abu Bakar Ba'asyir and the MMI, in terms of defending Islam from the "near and far enemies," *Laskar Jihad* has collaborated with AJAI, as happened in Ambon and Poso.[84]

Islamic Defenders Front (FPI)

This group has been most active in terms of establishing a "purified" Islamic state and established its reputation by attacking bars, night clubs, and brothels in major towns such as Jakarta. Its leader, Habib Rizieq Syihab, boasted having several thousand members and even demanded an end to diplomatic relations with the United States. He argued that "as long as there is no evidence linking Osama to the 11 September attacks in the United States and he has sworn he is innocent, then he is not guilty. So when he called for a *Jihad* for the truth, we accepted his call."[85]

Darul Islam (New Group)

Even though little is known about this group, its spokesperson, Al Chaidar, has claimed that it has close collaboration with the *Al Qaeda* group. For instance, Al Chaidar maintained that "every year since 1989, there has been cooperation in military training, and we have sent between 100 and 200 people each year to Afghanistan to be trained to be good soldiers of Islam."[86]

Jamaah Negara Islam Indonesia

The Kartosuwiryo-led DI, which aimed to create a *Negara Islam Indonesia* (NII), or Indonesia Islamic State, though badly crippled by Sukarno and Suharto's pogroms, have remained active throughout the 1960s right up to the 1990s. As a result, when many Islamic radicals from Indonesia fled to Malaysia in the mid-1980s, most of them were associated with the *Jamaah NII* or NII community. According to Nasir Abbas, who interacted closely with *Jamaah NII* members in Pakistan and Afghanistan, the group was also referred to as '*Jamaah DI*' of the DI community.[87] Even though the *Jamaah NII* group later split, with AJAI emerging as the key component from it, members of the NII have continued to support AJAI in various activities, especially terrorism and other logistical support.[88] However, the Sungkar-Ba'asyir split with *Jamaah NII* was somewhat healed when both groups began collaborating in the Ambon and Poso conflicts.

Laskar Jundullah

Laskar Jundullah, meaning "Army of Allah," has been active in the Ambon and Poso conflicts as well as various other violent incidents in Sulawesi. LJ is closely associated with a group that supports AJAI, namely, *Komite Persiapan Penegakan Syariat Islam* (KPPSI), or the Preparatory Committee for Upholding Islamic Law, directly led by Agus Dwikarna. While many groups have referred themselves as LJ, the primary one is associated with Agus Dwikarna, a key AJAI leader best known for his role in acting as a guide to *Al Qaeda*'s leaders when they visited Indonesia. LJ, which is based in Makassar, Sulawesi, is made up of various components, including former members of the DI that operated in the region, the breakaway *Himpunan Mahasiswa Indonesia* (HMI) group, known as HMO-MPO, and local fighters in Poso.[89] In addition to Agus Dwikarna, Tamsil Linrung is the other key leader of LJ, both of whom were arrested in the Philippines for smuggling arms in March 2002.

Laskar Mujahidin

This refers to the militia-linked Ngruki and other pesantrens that are associated with Abu Bakar Ba'asyir. They were extremely active in the Ambon and Poso conflicts. The first commander of *Laskar Mujahidin* was Haris Fadillah, alias Abu Dzar, the father-in-law of Omar al-Faruq. Following Haris's death, Arynato Aris took command of LM. This group works closely with AJAI and is often referred to as the "armed forces of the Ngruki Network."[90]

Majlis Mujahidin Indonesia (MMI)

Since its founding in August 2000, the MMI, under the leadership of Abu Bakar Ba'asyir, has been alleged to have betrayed and diverged from Sungkar's aim, which required its key leaders to remain "underground."[91] Yet, there is no doubt that both AJAI and MMI collaborates closely, as most of AJAI's leaders support the MMI and vice versa. Many of MMI's key leaders, such as Irfan Awwas, have been among the most vocal supporters of Abu Bakar Ba'asyir and his struggle for the adoption of *sharia* in Indonesia.

Mujahidin KOMPAK

The *Komite Aksi Penanggulangan Akibat Krisis* (KOMPAK), or Action Committee for Crisis Response, was established in 1998 under the aegis of DDII. KOMPAK had been established in Solo and was led by Arismunandar, an important AJAI member. An alumnus of *Pondok Ngruki,* Arismundar originated from Boyolali, adjacent to Solo.[92] Though established to assist bona fide causes of Islam, KOMPAK members were also active in violence, especially in Ambon. Agus Dwikarn, while heading LJ, also simultaneously headed the KOMPAK's branch in Sulawesi. When the conflict in Ambon worsened, leading AJAI members such as Zulkarnean and Dulmatin trained members of the fighters of *Mujahidin* KOMPAK. Thus, even though KOMPAK was not part of AJAI, it helped AJAI to achieve its goals.[93]

Abu Bakar Battalion

This is a splinter group from DI. Established in 1999, it called itself the Abu Bakar Battalion (ABB) and worked closely with *Laskar Mujahidin,* especially its leader, Haris Fadillah. Though involved in various *Fa'i* activities, it was also involved in the Ambon and Poso violence.

Angkatan Mujahidin Islam Nusantara

Having established itself as the most radical and violent group in the ABB, it broke away and established the *Angkatan Mujahidin Islam Nusantara,* or AMIN.

Republik Persatuan Islam Indonesia

The *Republik Persatuan Islam Indonesia* (RPII), or the Unitary Islamic Republic of Indonesia, was a splinter DI group, drawing its supporters from followers of Kahar Muzakkar. In some ways, the RPII members had close ties with AMIN and ABB, and supported the aims and goals of what was seen as the key umbrella organization, AJAI.

Medical Emergency Relief Charity (MERC)

According to Indonesian police, MERC is closely associated with a Saudi charity, the International Islamic Relief Organization, and has been alleged to channel funds to AJAI. Even though MERC was established to assist Muslims caught in the sectarian conflict in the Malukus, it has been closely identified with AJAI leaders such as Abu Jibril, Agus Dwikarna, and Aris Munandar. In Indonesia, MERC has 12 branches and is concentrated in areas affected by sectarian violence, with some observers arguing that it is a front for the AJAI.

PHILIPPINES

Moro Islamic Liberation Front (MILF)

This group has had a long history and has been trying to cooperate with the authorities in Manila in an effort to negotiate various political concessions. It remains a formidable force with thousands of armed fighters. Its founding leaders, particularly Hashim Salamat, was close to AJAI leaders, having shared not only a common radical ideology, but also having being actively involved in the *Mujahidin* struggle in Afghanistan. MILF's close ties and support for AJAI is evident from the various training camps that are located in MILF-controlled territories in southern Philippines. According to Carlos Agustin, the president of National Defense College, Philippines, AJAI's training grounds include Camp *Hudaybah,* Camp *Kararao* 1 and 2, Camp *Abubakar,* and Camp *Jabal Huda.*[94]

Abu Sayyaf

Probably the most violent terrorist group in the region after GAM, it has been in the international limelight due to its high-profile kidnapping operations in the Philippines and Malaysia. It is also believed to be behind the bomb attack on the Philippines' ambassador in Jakarta. The group is believed to have been founded by one of Osama's top associates, Jamal Khalifa, and was initially led by Abdurajak Janjalani, a Filipino Muslim who found alongside the *Mujahidin* in Afghanistan against the Soviets. Abdurajak was killed in a gun battle by the police in December 1998. Like the AJAI, it also promotes Islamic radicalism, as is evident in Janjalani's statement, "Islam must govern not only in Sulu but in the whole world. This is the objective of the Islamic movement...Even the entire Philippines, as mandated by Allah."[95] His brother Khadaffy replaced him as leader, and following his death in 2006, a new leader, Yasser Igasan, is now leading the group.

MNLF/Misuari Breakaway Group

Even though initially the MNLF did not promote Islamic radicalism, and its leader, Nur Misuari, did collaborate with the Philippines government, in 2001, a faction of the MNLF became radicalized. When Nur Misuari led a rebellion in Jolo, ending in his incarceration, his supporters established a group that has come to be known as the Misuari Breakaway Group (MBG). The MBG is active in southern Philippines and has become increasingly radicalized, working with radicals from the MILF, Abu Sayyaf, and AJAI.

The *Balik Islam* and Raja Solaiman Movements

These refer to Christian Filipinos who became Muslim converts and, in the process, became extremely radicalized. While the *Balik Islam Movement,* essentially based in Luzon, tends to be more religious than political, it has become vulnerable to penetration by other groups, as many of its members have become associated with various radical groups. However, it is the *Raja Solaiman Movement* (RSM) that is presently the center of extremism among the converts. Founded by Hilarion Santos, alias Ahmad, in 2001, the group is believed to have close ties with many radical groups, including the MILF, Abu Sayyaf, and AJAI. A prominent AJAI member, Fathur Rahman Al-Ghozi, had close ties with the RSM.[96]

MALAYSIA

Al-Ma'Unah (Brotherhood of Inner Power)

Though espousing to be a mix of Islam and martial arts, it supports the use of violence to overthrow the government and establish an Islamic regime. It leaped to prominence when 29 of its members walked into two army camps (Banding and Grik) in Perak, northern Malaysia, and drove off with an arsenal of 119 high-caliber modern weapons on July 2, 2000. It is believed to have supporters and followers in Singapore and Brunei. In the ensuing encounter, two security personnel were brutally killed and the movement subdued only on July 6, with its members being given long prison sentences.[97]

Kumpulan Mujahidin Malaysia (KMM; Malaysian *Mujahidin* Group)

This group is regarded as one of Malaysia's most active Islamic terrorist groups and one that has close cooperation with its counterparts in Indonesia, Singapore, and the Philippines. The KMM is also often referred to as *Kumpulan Militant Malaysia,* or Malaysian Militant Group. Essentially it was formed by a group of *Mujahidins* who fought in Afghanistan. Following their return from Pakistan, under the leadership of Zainon bin Ismail, the group was established in 1996. Even though many of its members have been detained, its network is still believed to be formidable, with many members still at large. The KMM also worked closely with Nurjaman Riduan Isamuddin, better known as Hambali, who is believed to have close ties with the *Al Qaeda* and who was tasked to expand the *Al Qaeda* network in the ASEAN region. The KMM is believed to be working closely with two other Islamic terrorist organizations, namely, AJAI and the *Jihad* Gang, even though there is little information on the latter two groups. For instance, a key suspect, Yazid Safaat, who was arrested by the Malaysian authorities, is believed to a member of AJAI and a close associate of Hambali. Yazid is also believed to have worked closely with a number of the terrorists that were involved in the September 11, 2001, attack. The KMM is also closely associated with various Thai *jihadists* operating in southern Thailand.

The Malaysian AJAI

Working on the instructions of Sungkar and Abu Bakar Ba'asyir, Hambali and Abu Jibril are believed to have established the Malaysian AJAI in 1994. Among the key members were the many Indonesian migrants as well as university lecturers and students from the Technology University of Malaysia, based in the state of Johor in the south of the country.

THAILAND

Even though not of the same strength as Islamist terrorists in Indonesia, Malaysia, and the Philippines, Thailand has five groups that are worthy of mention. These include the Pattani United Liberation Organization, New Pattani United Liberation Organization, *Gerakan Mujahidin Islam Pattani,* the *Barisan Revolusi Nasional,* and *Jemaah Salafi.* Of the five, the GMIP and *Jemaah Salafi* have close ties with AJAI. For instance, the founder of *Jemaah Salafi,* Muhammad Haji Jaeming, alias Abdul Fatah, trained in the Sadda Camp together with the Indonesian *jihadists.* He was also one of the few invited to attend *Rabitatul Mujahidin* meetings in Malaysia in 1999–2000. On the whole, the activities of the Thai Islamists have largely been confined to southern Thailand and tend to be local and national rather than international in character, even though there is a significant cross-border activity on the Malaysian side as far as support and sanctuary are concerned.

SINGAPORE

Al-Jama'ah Al-Islamiyyah

The existence of this group came to known when the Singapore authorities detained 13 members of the group that were planning to undertake a series of bombing in the republic. The group is believed to have links with the *Al Qaeda,* even though the Singapore government has accused Abu Bakar Ba'asyir as being the mastermind behind the plot.

OTHER ASEAN COUNTRIES

Even though other ASEAN countries such as Brunei, Cambodia, and Myanmar have Islamic communities, the existence of Islamist terrorist organizations or groups, though not absent, is unknown. Many Muslims, especially from Myanmar, are studying in Pakistani *Madrasahs,* the breeding grounds of Islamist extremists and the extent of the threat from this sector is yet to surface. Similarly, AJAI operatives have operated in Cambodia, where there is a sizeable Muslim community, especially in Kampot province. Islamists from Thailand and Malaysia are believed to have operated from Cambodia in the past. Hambali also took refuge in Cambodia from October 2002 to early 2003.[98] Many Myanmar extremists area also believed to be operating in Bangladesh, especially under the auspices of HUJI.

While most of the terrorist groups are nationally based and motivated by causes specific to particular countries, increasingly there have been groups that have been operating on a transnational basis. It is believed that the *Jemaah* Islamic Movement and KMM, as well as *Al-Ma'Unah* have followers, supporters and operatives in Indonesia, Malaysia, Singapore, Philippines, Thailand, and possibly Brunei. For the present, however, despite the presence of various Islamist terrorist groups in the ASEAN region, significant Islamic terrorist activity is mainly concentrated in two countries, Indonesia and the Philippines.

Since the September 11, 2001, incident, attention has been increasingly focused on the links of Islamist terrorist groups in Southeast Asia with the *Al Qaeda* and in this regard, a number of groups are believed to be part of this global terrorist network. The *Abu Sayyaf* has been linked directly to the *Al Qaeda* network and been accused of sending millions of dollars, gained through their kidnapping operations, in support of the *Al-Qaeda.* Similarly, of the many terror groups operating, most have been linked in some way or other to the popularly termed "network of terror,"[99] with the United States increasingly focusing its attention, in addition to the *Abu Sayyaf* group, to the more illusive AJAI, which has come to be perceived as the *Al Qaeda*'s "point" in Southeast Asia.

The AJAI, or Islamic Group, is believed to have cells in Indonesia, Malaysia, Singapore, and the Philippines. The group was believed to be directed by an Indonesian cleric, Hambali. Hambali was believed to be *Al Qaeda,* and Osama's point man in Southeast Asia. The overriding aim of the group was to overthrow secular governments in the region and create an Islamic state linking Malaysia, Indonesia, Brunei, southern Thailand, southern Philippines, and Singapore. While prior to September 11, security agencies in the region believed that these groups only had a domestic agenda, the discovery of a regionwide network has been disconcerting, highlighting the breadth and depth of the intentions of AJAI. As was pointed out by an American security official, "what is alarming are the regional links. It is not just one country that they have infiltrated. It is at least four."[100]

It is therefore impossible to ignore the role that religious extremism plays in defining and linking together these terrorist groups. The root of the problem is not based in religious dissatisfaction. Rather, it is through regional and domestic issues such as the lack of political representation or the perceived oppression of a particular group, or it is directed at the dismissal of specific concerns of these groups by the state government. According to Singapore's then deputy prime minister, "Without stability, there can be no economic development. And without economic development, there would be political chaos and abject poverty, the ideal conditions for extremism."[101] Terrorism in Southeast Asia is still bound conceptually by the traditional definitions—where a group dissatisfied either by political, social, or religious strife seeks, through means of terror and guerrilla operations, to advance its interests; or quite simply, to make a point. However, a major shift that has come to light since the 9/11 Incident. While it was assumed that these terrorist groups operated independently and nationally, now one sees a vast network that each operates within. Though they may promote independent and varying causes, many are bound by the very "network of terror" that has been brought to light since September 11, 2001. This realization is critical to the issue of combating terrorism in the region.

Following the arrest of the second batch of AJAI operatives in Singapore in 2002, it was revealed that by 1999, a regional network of Islamic militant groups bent on using terrorism, among others, to pursue their political objectives, had already been set up. The AJAI is said to have initiated an alliance called *Rabitatul Mujahidin,* involving among others, the MILF, the *Abu Sayyaf,* and *Gerakan Mujahidin Islamic Pattani.* It is highly possible that the *Majlis Permusyawaratan Gerakan Aceh Merdeka* (MP-GAM) led by Dr. Hussani, which has been fighting for an Islamic state in northern Sumatra and where the *Al Qaeda* leadership paid a visit to facilitate cooperation, might also be involved in this alliance.[102]

AJAI'S COOPERATION WITH OTHER TERRORIST GROUPS

One feature that makes the AJAI extremely dangerous and a source of national, regional, and global concern is its linkage with the *Al Qaeda,* especially organizationally, and how many of the AJAI leaders are believed to be close to Osama bin Laden and his terrorist network. In addition to being Muslims, what binds the AJAI with

Al Qaeda is the single-minded belief in *jihad*. Initially, it was this ideological affinity that brought individuals from the Southeast Asian region into contact with Osama and his network, especially when they were involved in the "global *jihad*" against the Soviets in Afghanistan, mainly with the backing of the United States. Once the war in Afghanistan tapered off and the *Mujahidin* fighters returned home, they continued their struggle, with Osama and his *Al Qaeda* organization coordinating, funding, and giving direction to the various "local *jihads*" around the world, including in Southeast Asia.

In this connection, the key AJAI leaders such as Abu Bakar Ba'asyir and Hambali, for instance, were staunch supporters of Osama and his global causes, especially against the United States. For instance, Abu Bakar Ba'asyir has described Osama as a "true Islamic warrior" and publicly stated, "I support Osama bin Laden's struggle because his is the true struggle to uphold Islam, not terror—the terrorists are America and Israel."[103] In the case of Hambali, he also spent time fighting the Soviets in Afghanistan. Even more important, the *Al Qaeda* succeeded in establishing close ties with various radical Islamic groups in the region, including the *Abu Sayyaf* group and the MILF in the Philippines, *Laskar Jihad* and *Laskar Jundullah* in Indonesia, as well as various other Islamic groups such as GAM in Aceh, the *Gerakan Mujahidin Pattani* and possibly, the *Rohingyas* in Myanmar. In addition to sharing common causes on *jihad* in Afghanistan, another source of *Al Qaeda*'s infiltration into the Southeast Asian region was through the *Madrasahs* in Pakistan that were largely controlled by the *Taliban*. However, the single most important conduit of *Al Qaeda*'s penetration into Southeast Asia was through the AJAI, leading many to conclude that the AJAI was *Al Qaeda*'s point in Southeast Asia. The AJAI can also be compared to as the *Al Qaeda* of Southeast Asia, as it coordinated many terrorist activities through its regional network, *Rabitatul Mujahidin,* that grouped all the key Islamic radical movements in the region and that was established in 1999 under the leadership of the AJAI.

The potency of the AJAI's linkage with the *Al Qaeda* is best evident from the various cooperative endeavors and operations that are believed to have been undertaken and planned in the region or against targets outside Southeast Asia as follows:

- Indonesia's *Darul Islam* leader, Al Chaidar, admitted supporting *jihad* activities in Afghanistan and receiving financial assistance from Osama.[104]
- KMM's hosting of Zacarias Moussaoui, a Frenchman who is believed to be part of the group that planned and involved in the September 11, 2001, attack in New York and Washington.
- *Laskar Jundullah,* through Agus Dwikarna, is supposed to have organised a terrorist training camp in Poso, Sulawesi in Indonesia in cooperation with the *Al Qaeda.*
- Emergence of Hambali as one of the top six leaders of the *Al Qaeda.*
- Claims by Omar Al-Faruq, the *Al Qaeda* operative in Southeast Asia (who was under American detention in Bagram Air Base, later escaped, and was killed in Iraq in September 2006) that he was given orders by two senior *Al Qaeda* leaders, Abu Zubaydah

and Ibn al-Shaykh al-Libi, to undertake large-scale attacks of American targets in Southeast Asia and that Abu Bakar Ba'asyir was his key collaborator in the region.

What is unique about the regionalization of the AJAI threat in Southeast Asia has been its ability to link up with various radical groups, many of them well established and in a position to threaten the security of various states. In this connection, the AJAI has played a catalytic role in synergizing regional terrorism, especially in close collaboration with the *Al Qaeda.* According to Singapore Minister of Home Affairs Mr. Wong Kan Seng, the ability of the *Al Qaeda* to "franchise and indigenise its violent expertise and agenda" was something unique in the annals of terrorism in the region.[105] The extent of *Al Qaeda*'s penetration into the Southeast Asia region was evident from the manner, among others; the AJAI operatives reported and sought "clearance" from Osama and his key lieutenants for various operations in the region. For instance, a videotape, showing various American targets in Singapore was recovered from the house of Abu Hafs, alias Mohd. Atef, a key military leader of Osama, who was apparently killed by American bombing of Afghanistan in December 2001. The videotape was shown to him by members of the Singapore AJAI who went over to Afghanistan for military training.[106]

AJAI'S OTHER "TRIBUTARIES": SAUDI ARABIA AND PAKISTAN

If the *Al Qaeda* is analogous to AJAI's principal "river," then the main "tributaries" can be found in Saudi Arabia and Pakistan. Historically, Saudi Arabia and to some extent Egypt were regarded as the principal centers for Islamic studies and spiritual inspiration for Southeast Asians. *Al Azhar* University in Egypt, the centre of modernist and reformist Islam, and Mecca and Medina, the traditional historical centers of Islamic civilization, had always attracted thousands of Islamic scholars and students from the region. In the main, the purpose tended to be theological rather than political, and this explained the general tolerance exhibited by governments in Southeast Asia towards these exchanges. Sunni Islam dominates Southeast Asia and, hence, the ideological proximity between the Saudis and Southeast Asia. There are four main "schools" of Sunni Islam, namely, *Hanifiyyah, Malikiyyah, Shafiyyah, and Hanbaliyyah.* Even though Saudi *Wahhabism* is more akin to *Hanbaliyyah,* which tends to be rather conservative and fundamentalist, for a long time there was a high degree of peaceful coexistence among the Sunnis in the region. The character and intensity of these exchanges and interactions underwent a marked transformation in the late 1970s right through to the present period and this was largely due to the political character of the influences that were taking place, in particular through Pakistan and Afghanistan.

As analyzed earlier, due to the Afghan War from 1979 to 1989, the Pakistani government, with the support of the United States, fostered Islamic militancy and extremism in order to bleed the Soviets in Afghanistan. Pakistani *madrasahs* were structured to breed extremism and sponsor *jihadis* for Afghanistan and, later Kashmir. Pakistan was home to five main types of *madrasahs,* namely, the *Deobandi* and *Bareili* variety of Sunni Islam, the *Ahl-e Hadith* or the Saudi-sponsored *Salafi Islam (Wahhabi)* variety, the *Shia-type,* and finally, those aligned with *Jamaat-e-Islami.* A number of factors contributed to the radicalization of Islam in the 1970s and 1980s, including the Iranian Revolution, the Soviet invasion and occupation of Afghanistan and the Iran-Iraq War. As far as the *madrasahs'* role in breeding extremism and terrorism were concerned, two main types were particularly active in Pakistan. There were first those that produced *jihadi* literature, mobilized public opinion, recruited, and trained *jihadi* forces such as the *Jamaat-e-Islami's Rabita Madrassahs.* Next, there was also a multitude of independent *madrasahs* such as those administered by *Jamiat-e-Ulema Islam,* though opposed to Zia ul Haq but were prepared to support the *jihad* in Afghanistan.

Radical Muslims from all over the world were encouraged to join the *madrasahs* and eventually become *Mujahidins* to liberate Afghanistan. Many from Southeast Asia also participated in this *jihad,* even though the exact number is unclear. However, they must run in the thousands, and this represent one of the most important linkages between Pakistan and Southeast Asian terrorism, especially the AJAI and its regional allies. Southeast Asians have been found to be involved in various religious and paramilitary activities administered by Pakistani organizations such as the *Jamiat-Ulema-i-Islam,* which created the *Hizb-ul-Mujahidin* for the liberation of Kashmir; the *Wahhabi*-oriented *Ahl-e Hadith; Hizb-i-Islami; Harkat-ul-Mujahidin; Makraz ad-Da'wa Wal Irshad* and its military wing, *Lashkar-e-Taiba; Harakat-ul-jihad-al-Islami; Jaish-e-Mohammad;* and *Lashkar-e-Jhangvi,* the last five being members of Osama's International Islamic Front that was created in 1998.

While specific details are difficult to come by, there is ample evidence to prove that a small number of Muslims from Myanmar, Thailand, Malaysia, Indonesia, Singapore, and the Philippines have participated in various activities related to Islamist militancy and terrorism via Pakistan. According to one report, probably since 2002, "of the 190 students from Southeast Asia in the *madrasahs* in Sindh, 86 were from Malaysia, 82 from Thailand and 22 from Indonesia; 151 in the *madrasahs* of Pakistani Punjab, of whom 61 were from Malaysia, 49 from Thailand and 41 from Indonesia; and the 59 *madrasahs* in the volatile Northwest Frontier Province, of whom 21 were from Indonesia, 20 from Malaysia and 18 from Thailand. Thus, there were 167 Malaysians, 149 Thais and 84 Indonesians in the various *madrasahs* of Pakistan."[107] It was also reported that "since March 2002, about 200 *jihadis* from Malaysia, Indonesia, the Philippines and Thailand had joined the *jihadi* groups of *Harakat-ul-Mujahidin,* the *Lashkar-e-Taiba* and the *Harakat-ul-jihad-al-Islami* and had gone into Afghanistan to fight against the allied troops led by the USA after the US started its military action on October 7 2001 but they reentered Pakistan after sustaining casualties when Kabul fell to the Northern Alliance and US and the Taliban decided to melt away for the time being. The HUJI subsequently helped these dregs from Southeast Asia to escape to Bangladesh, from where they were to sneak their way back to their respective countries."[108]

This was brought to light most clearly in 2003. In September, 20 Southeast Asians from Indonesia, Malaysia, Indonesia, Myanmar, and Singapore, believed to be AJAI members, were arrested by Pakistani security officials.[109] They were found in a number of religious schools and hostels in Karachi, including Abu Bakar Islamic University, Ashraful Madaris, *Jama Darasitul Islamiya Madrasa, Darul Islam Madrasah,* and some private hostels in eastern Karachi, in Gulshan-e-Iqbal district. Among those detained was Gungun Rusman Runawan, Hambali's brother, who acted as a supervisor of the Southeast Asian students. Hambali's brother has also been described as the likely bridge between *Al Qaeda* operatives in Pakistan and the Afghan and AJAI networks in Southeast Asia. Some of them had military training in *Al Qaeda* camps in Afghanistan. According to security officials from the region, the detainees included "children of those who were involved in AJAI activities in Malaysia and Indonesia" and that "these students were not being trained as foot soldiers but as a second or third echelon of leaders."[110] It is now evident that while the AJAI had four territorial divisions, or *Mantiqis,* there were also two other divisions, one based in Karachi, Pakistan, and another in Kandhar, Afghanistan. This clearly demonstrates the linkages between AJAI and centers of Islamic radicalism and terrorism worldwide, especially Pakistan and Afghanistan.

What this arrest signified was the continued role of Pakistan, especially its *madrasahs,* in producing *jihadis* for regional and international terrorism. Out of the 500 students in Abu Bakar University, nearly 200 are foreigners, including from Malaysia, Thailand, and Indonesia. Following the arrest of Hambali's brother, a Thai student studying in one of *madrasahs* was reported to have argued, "Islam is against terrorism but Islam is for *jihad* against the oppressor of Muslims. If American and Jews want to conspire against Muslims, then we should wage war against them."[111] Equally important was the role of *Jama Darasitul Islamiya Madarasa.* This is a religious seminary administered by *Jamaat-ud Da'awa,* the political wing of the banned Pakistani Kashmiri militant group, *Lashkar-e-Taiba.* While the LET, known for its violence in Kashmir, is not known to have been active in Southeast Asia in the past, it is clear that some Southeast Asians have been influenced by its *madrasahs* and most likely, its political ideology and *modus operandi.*

CONCLUSION

On hindsight, AJAI's origins were largely a function of Indonesia's repression of Islamists, past and present, particularly the *Darul Islam* and its followers. In this regard, efforts and attention should be focused on two key individuals, Abdullah Sungkar and Abu Bakar Ba'asyir. The trail left behind by them makes it clear that they were instrumental in the establishment, organization, and sustenance of what came to be known as the AJAI. Their inspiration, motivation, and single-minded determination to establish an Islamic state in Indonesia can be traced to their commitment to the cause and ideals of DI. However, what spurred their single-mindedness to the goal was the repression they and their followers suffered at the hands of Suharto and his repressive state machinery from the 1970s through to the 1990s. What essentially crystallized as opposition to Suharto and his regime eventually coalesced into a movement with goals beyond Indonesia, encompassing the

Southeast Asian region. This was largely a function of the various Islamist experiences in the Afghan *jihad,* as well as the repression (or perceived repression) that each of the Islamist groups or individuals suffered in their respective home country, be it in the Philippines, Thailand, Malaysia, and/or even Singapore.

Comprehension of the origins and structure of AJAI is not a mere academic exercise. What makes the AJAI particularly important and unique in the history of terrorism in general, and religious terrorism in particular, in Southeast Asia is its regional character. Never has such regional terrorism confronted the Southeast Asian region. This makes the understanding of its character and network important if it is to be effectively managed, contained and neutralized. While the indigenous goal is either a national or supranational Islamic state, the AJAI also works closely with *Al Qaeda* and other terrorist organizations to support global *jihadi* activities as evident in the "Singapore Plan," in which Western political, military, and commercial targets were identified for attack.

Counterterrorism in Southeast Asia: One Step Forward, Two Steps Backward?

INTRODUCTION

Even with the arrest of key leaders of the AJAI and the perpetrators of the October 2002 Bali bombings, the persistence of the terrorist acts continues to pose serious threats to the security of the Southeast Asian region. Despite the detentions of several key AJAI leaders such as Hambali, Omar al-Faruq, Mukhlas, Imam Samudra, Agus Dwikarna, Abu Jibril, Abu Bakar Ba'asyir, Abu Rusdan, and the killing of the "Demolition Man" (Dr. Azahari Husin) in October 2005, the 2003 car bomb blast that tore apart the J. W. Marriott Hotel in Jakarta, the Kuningan bombing in 2005, and the second Bali bombing in 2005, sent a compelling message that the AJAI is not toothless. The 2002 post-Bali bombings have demonstrated the AJAI can strike anywhere, anytime, and that it is still a major threat to be reckoned with. This is mainly due to the fact that it seems to have an unending supply of adherents and recruits who have been captivated by AJAI's goals and objectives.

THE AJAI MILITARY OPERATIONS IN SOUTHEAST ASIA

What has made the AJAI such a force to be reckoned with is not merely the fact that it is religiously motivated and organized and has a regionwide network. Probably even more important has been its willingness and ability to destabilize the region by undertaking violent terrorist activities. So far, analysts have attributed the following attacks (planned, aborted, and implemented) in the region to the AJAI:

- Bomb explosion in a Philippines Airline passenger plane in 1994
- *Oplan Bojnka* (plan to assassinate the pope and President Clinton in Manila as well as explode 11 American airliners in the Pacific region in 1995
- Bombing of *Istiqal* Mosque in Jakarta in April 1999

- Attempted assassination of then Vice-President Megawati Sukarnoputri of Indonesia
- Bombing of Protestant church in Jakarta in May 2000
- Bombing of Santa Ana Church in Medan in July 2000
- Bombing of Christian Church of the Republic of Indonesia and its pastor in Medan in August 2000
- Grenade attack on the residence of the Philippines' ambassador to Indonesia in Jakarta in August 2000
- Bombing of Jakarta Stock Exchange in September 2000
- Bombing of 17 churches that killed 22 and wounded nearly 100 in Jakarta, West Java, North Sumatra, Riau, Bandung, East Java, and *Nusatenggara* on Christmas Eve, December 2000. This included:[1]

  1. Jakarta
     a. Jakarta Cathedral
     b. Kanisius Church
     c. Santo Yosef Church
     d. Oikumene Protestant Christian Church
     e. Koinonia Church
     f. Anglican Church
  2. Bekasi
     a. Protestant Church
  3. Bandung
     a. Bomb goes off prematurely, killing three bombers
  4. Sukabumi
     a. Sidang Kristus Church
     b. Huria Kristen Batak Protestan Church
  5. Ciamis
     a. Premature explosion of bomb in front of Hotel Kencana
  6. Pekanbaru
     a. HKBP Church
     b. Jalan Sidomulyo Church
     c. Third Church
  7. Batam
     a. Protestant Church
     b. Bethel Indonesia Church
     c. Pentecostal Church of Indonesia
     d. Santo Beato Church
  8. Medan
     a. Protestant Church of Indonesia
     b. GKPS Stadion Teladan

  c. Kemenangan Iman Indonesia Church

  d. GKII Sisimangaraja

  e. HKBP Church

  f. Santo Paulus Church

  g. Cathedral Church

  h. Kristus Raja Church

  i. Home of Pastor James Hood

  j. Home of Pastor Oloan Padaribu

  k. Home of Pastor El Imanson

  l. Catholic Vicarage

 9. Pematang Siantar

  a. Home of Pastor Elisman Sibayak

  b. Gereja HKBP Damai

  c. Kalam Kudus Church (Pastor's home)

  d. Building in Jalan Merdeka

 10. Mojokerto

  a. Santo Yoseph Church

  b. Kristen Allah Biak Church

  c. Kristen Ebinezer Church

  d. Bethany Church

 11. Mataram

  a. Protestant Church of Western Indonesia (Immanuel)

  b. Pentecostal Church Pusat Surabaya

- Bombing of five targets in Manila on December 30, 2000
- Involvement in the Maluku fighting that killed more than 5,000 people
- Hosting by Malaysian AJAI cell of *Al Qaeda* operatives that were involved in the bombing of the USS *Cole* and the September 11, 2001, attack on New York and Pentagon
- Bombing of HKBP Church and Santa Ana churches in Jakarta in July 2001
- Atrium bombing in August 2001
- Bombing of Atrium Mall in Jakarta in August and September 2001
- Hand grenade thrown at Australian International School in Jakarta in November 2001
- Bombing of Petra Church in Jakarta in November 2001
- Bombing of Protestant Church in Pekanbaru in December 2001
- Arrest of nearly 100 AJAI operatives in Malaysia and Singapore in 2001 and 2002 that were planning to attack Western and national targets in the two countries
- Hand grenade explosion near American embassy in Jakarta in September 2002
- The October 2002 Bali bombing that killed nearly 200 people

- Police headquarters in Jakarta is bombed in February 2003
- Bombing of Terminal 2 at the Sukarno-Hatta International Airport in Jakarta in April 2003
- Bombing in the vicinity of the United Nations office in Jakarta in April 2003
- The August 2003 bombing of J.W. Marriott Hotel in Jakarta that killed 11 people
- Kuningan bombing outside Australian embassy in Jakarta in 2004.

In this connection, the Bali bombing can be regarded as the single most critical event that has highlighted the threat of terrorism in Southeast Asia, and in particular the danger posed by the AJAI and its various national, regional, and international collaborators. This terrorist act was probably the most serious since the September 11, 2001, attack on New York and Washington. The Bali attack on October 12, 2002, took the lives of 202 holiday makers, mostly from Australia.[2] A number of arrests have been made, including of Imam Samudra and Amrozi. Both of them are believed to be part of the AJAI network and close associates of Hambali and Mukhlas, the regional leaders of the AJAI. In fact, Amrozi and another two of his brothers wanted in the Bali bombing, namely Ali Imron and Ali Fauzi, are younger brothers of Mukhlas, who had, prior to his arrest in December 2002, reportedly took over responsibility for AJAI operations in Southeast Asia from Hambali.[3] Following new jurisdiction to trial and convict terrorists, Amrozi has been found guilty and sentenced to death for involvement in the Bali bombings by the Denpasar District Court in Bali.

THE AJAI IN SINGAPORE

Even though Singapore is essentially a Chinese-majority state, historically, the republic has been confronted with threats and challenges from various Islamic groups. Some of these challenges include:

- Maria Hertogh riots in 1950
- The agitation by the Malay National Party and PMIP for *Melayu Raya (Great Malay)* in 1950
- The threat posed by *Angkatan Revolusi Tentara Islam* (Revolutionary Islamic Army) in 1961
- The bloody communal riots in 1964 and 1969
- The threat posed by the Singapore People's Liberation Organization in 1981
- Attempts by the *Hizbollah* to recruit Muslim Singaporeans in 1990 and later in 1998, through Ustad Bandei, an Indonesian extremist, to bomb American interests in the republic

The activities of Islamic militants in Singapore are a function of three main variables. First, it is due to the sizeable presence of Muslims in Singapore, constituting about 16 percent of the republic's population. That many Singapore Muslims believed that they have been systematically marginalized and discriminated by the

Chinese-dominated government have provided various internal and external elements with a ready-made disgruntled group to be exploited for various religiously oriented causes. Second, being located in the heart of the Malay world and where Singapore's immediate neighbors are dominated by Islamic majorities, especially in Malaysia and Indonesia, means that the republic cannot escape from any development that involves the Malay-Muslim population. Third, as Singapore is geostrategically located and closely intertwined with the region and world, any development that involves the regional and global Islamic population would have an immediate and direct impact on the republic, particularly its Muslim population. Finally, Singapore is viewed as a close strategic partner of various Western powers, especially the United States. The republic is perceived to be supporting various controversial American policies that are deemed anti-Islamic in character, such as Washington's invasion of Afghanistan and Iraq. Also, the republic's close defense and military ties with Israel, a Jewish state that is ideologically believed to be anti-Islamic as seen in its persecution of the Palestinians, has combined to make Singapore an attractive, even natural target of Islamist terrorism from the region and beyond.

In this connection, even though the AJAI was not home-grown in Singapore, and despite the republic being alleged to be a "tightly-organized state," the activities of the AJAI cell in Singapore remained undetected for nearly a decade. Singaporeans are believed to have been involved in AJAI activities, mainly in Malaysia as early as 1990. A Singapore AJAI cell, as part of a regionwide organization, was believed to have been formally established in 1993 following the return of its leader, Ibrahim Maidin, from military training in Afghanistan.[4] The Singapore AJAI cell, known as the Singapore AJAI *Wakalah* (SAJAIW) reported to AJAI leaders in Malaysia (*Mantiqi* 1), especially Abu Jibril, Hambali, and Mukhlas. Even though it long maintained a low profile, the SAJAIW began enhancing their activities in 1997, working closely with the *wakalah* in Johor, the southernmost state in Malaysia that borders Singapore (see Figure 4.1).

Organizationally, the SAJAIW was organized into a number of functional groups. Among others, there was the Operations Group, involved in intelligence and military activities; the Security Group (*Tajnid*), tasked with ensuring that the SAJAIW was secured from infiltration and detection; the Economic/Finance Group, overseeing financial affairs; the Communications Group, which managed electronic and non-electronic linkages, including security; the *Dakwah*/missionary Group, which imbibed its members with hard-line teachings; and the Educational (*Tarbiyah Rasmiyah*) Group, which focused on general educational matters.[5]

As a terrorist group, the members of the SAJAIW started military training as early as 1990. The bulk of the military training of the Singapore cell took place in Malaysia, even though some members were also trained in Afghanistan and in camps ran by the MILF in southern Philippines. In the main, there were four main phases of military training involving the SAJAIW. From 1990 to 1994, the emphasis was essentially on physical fitness training, and where the trainees had no real inkling that they were being prepared for sinister military operations in Singapore. The actual basic military training started in 1995. From 1997 onwards, the members were given

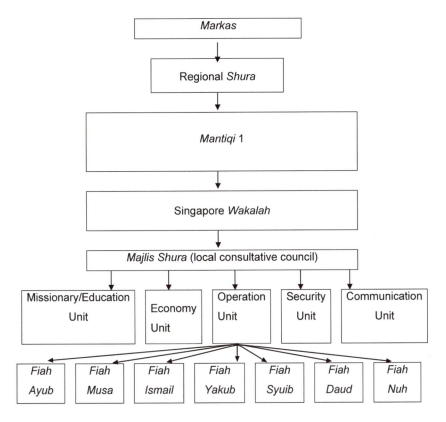

Figure 4.1   The Singapore AJAI Structure

advanced military training, involving ambushes, infiltration, etc. From 2000 onwards, members were taught the tactics of urban warfare, preparing them essentially for military operations in Singapore.

ARRESTS AND DISCOVERY OF AJAI'S OPERATIONAL CELLS (*FIAHS*) IN SINGAPORE

On January 6, 2002, the Singapore Internal Security Department served 13 of the 15 persons arrested in December 2001 for terrorism-related activities with Orders of Detention for two years under Section 8 (1) (a) of the Internal Security Act.[6] They were: Haji Ibrahim b Haji Maidin, 51, condominium manager; Mohamad Anuar bin Margono, 31, driver; Mohamed Khalim bin Jaffar, 39, printer; Ja'afar bin Mistooki, 40, dispatch driver; Faiz bin Abu Bakar Bafana, 39, businessman; Fathi Abu Bakar Bafana, 36, businessman; Mohamed Ellias, son of Mohamed Khan, 29, manager; Mohamed Nazir bin Mohmmed Uthman, 27, ship traffic assistant; Adnan bin Musa, 36, technician; Halim bin Hussain, 41, supervisor; Hashim bin Abas, 40, service engineer; Andrew Gerard, alias Ali Ridhaa bin Abdullah, 34, technician; and Othman bin Mohamed, 42, supervisor. The other two persons arrested were released on Restriction Orders.

Of the 13, eight had gone to Afghanistan for training in *Al Qaeda* training camps. As part of their preparations for training in Afghanistan, all of them underwent military and religious training in Negri Sembilan, Malaysia. All of them were believed to have entered Afghanistan illegally. For this, covert arrangements for their entry into Afghanistan from Pakistan were made by their leader in Malaysia, Hambali, and a Malaysian permanent resident of Indonesian nationality. Training in the *Al Qaeda* camps included use of AK-47s and mortars and study of military tactics. One of the Singaporeans had gone to Afghanistan for training on three separate occasions between 1991 and 2000. Among the documents recovered from IT forensic investigation of Khalim Jaffar's encrypted diskette was a letter nominating Mohd Ellias and Mohd Nazir for special training in one of three areas—ambush/assassination, sniper activity, and "field engineering," that is, bomb construction.

On August 16, 2002, the Singapore government announced the arrest of another 21 persons, mostly AJAI members. Those arrested, all Singaporeans, were: Abdullah Wahab bin Ahmad, 42, delivery man; Syed Ibrahim, 30, dispatch clerk; Simon bin Sabtu, 38, canteen operator assistant/proprietor; Mohamed Noor bin Sulaimi, 32, project coordinator; Munain bin Turru, 41, driver; Naharudin bin Sabtu, 33, part-time trainer; Sanin bin Riffin, 40, driver; Nordin bin Parman, 39, taxi driver; Mohd Jauhari bin Abdullah, 37, assistant engineer; Salim bin Marwan, 31, butcher; Mahfuh bin Haji Halimi, 40, manager; Azman bin Jalani, 39, unemployed ; Abdul Majid, s/o Niaz Mohamed, 40, driver; Said bin Ismail, 45, fitter; Faiz Abdullah Ashiblie, 37, unemployed; Zulkifli bin Mohamed Jaffar, 42, used car salesman; Habibullah, s/o Hameed, 45, part-time foot reflexologist and religious teacher; Husin bin Abdullah Aziz, 52, businessman; Fauzi bin Abu Bakar Bafana, 37, technical officer; Mohammad Hisham bin Hairi, 34, transport worker; and Sajahan bin Abdul Rahman, 54, businessman.

Almost all the 31 men detained are believed to be members of the AJAI.[7] The Singapore AJAI is part of a larger AJAI network with cells in Malaysia, Indonesia, and others parts of Southeast Asia. The Singapore network reports to a Malaysia-based leadership structure called a regional *"shura,"* or consultative council. Following the arrest and detention of Mohammad Iqbal Abdul Rahman, alias Abu Jibril, by Malaysian authorities in June 2001, the regional *shura* was headed by Hambali. Since Hambali's arrest in 2003, little is known of the leadership structure.

The AJAI organization in Singapore is headed by a leader (with the title *Qoaid wakalah*) and is organized into various functional cells or *fiahs*.[8] These included cells for fund-raising, religious work, security, and operations. Ibrahim Maidin was the leader of the AJAI in Singapore, and Faiz bin Abu Bakar Bafana was a leading figure in the AJAI's regional *shura*. The rest of those detained were mostly members of the security unit or of the various operations cells. The operations *fiahs* are the cells assigned for terrorist support or terrorism-related activities. AJAI's terrorism-linked activities began long before the September 11, 2001, terrorist attacks in the United

States. Ibrahim Maidin, in fact, had gone to Afghanistan for military training in 1993. The surveillance activities of the first AJAI cell in support of terrorist targeting began as early as 1997.

The oldest operations cell was called *Fiah Ayub*. This cell, led by Khalim bin Jaffar, is believed to have started exploring terrorist targeting in Singapore as early as 1997. They conducted target surveillance of locations that were frequented by Americans in Singapore. This cell is believed to have made two well-developed plans. The first was to target a regular shuttle bus service conveying what was expected to be U.S. personnel between Sembawang Wharf and the Yishun MRT Station. Khalim made a detailed reconnaissance of the Yishun MRT Station. He prepared a videotape of the reconnaissance, with commentary in English by one of those detained, Hashim bin Abas. The videotape and some handwritten debriefing notes in Arabic were later found in the rubble of an *Al Qaeda* leader's house in Afghanistan.

The plan was apparently developed and ready for activation. Khalim briefed *Al Qaeda* leaders on this plan when he went to Afghanistan for training between August 1999 and April 2000. The *Al Qaeda* leaders showed interest in the plan, but for reasons not known, they did not subsequently pursue it. The second developed plan appeared to be a bomb attack against U.S. naval vessels along the northeast waters of Singapore between Changi and Pulau Tekong. Found among Khalim's possessions was a MINDEF map with markings indicating observation posts both in Singapore and Johor and a "kill zone" in the channel between Changi and Pulau Tekong.

Also found among Khalim's possessions was a list of over 200 U.S. companies in Singapore. Three of them were highlighted as potential targets, apparently because the office-bearers were regarded as fairly prominent members of the American community in Singapore. Other items included two tampered Singapore passports, 15 forged Malaysian and Philippines immigration stamps, night vision binoculars, and literature on bomb-making and survival techniques.

The second operations cell was called *Fiah Musa*. Members of the cell include Fathi Abu Bakar Bafana, Mohd Ellias, Mohd Nazir, and Adnan bin Musa. In April 2001 they used Andrew Gerard, another AJAI member who was a technician in Singapore Technologies Aerospace (STA), to photograph Paya Lebar Airbase and the American aircraft there as a potential target for terrorist attacks. Gerard was also directed to collect information on STA and Paya Lebar Airbase facilities, and on the movement of personnel. He took more than 50 digital photos of the airbase and aircraft as instructed, and handed them over to the cell members. These photographs were recovered from the possessions of one of those detained, Khalim bin Jaffar.

In September–October 2001, the cell was approached by a mixed group of foreign elements to assist in a plan for terrorist bombing against specific targets in Singapore. These foreigners were known to the local cell members only by code name. The linkup with the cell members with these foreigners was made by the ex-Singaporean detained, Faiz bin Abu Bakar Bafana. (Faiz is the brother of Fathi Abu Bakar Bafana and a member of the AJAI regional *shura*.)

Two of the foreigners (one of Arab extraction calling himself "Sammy" and believed to be linked to the *Al Qaeda* organization; the other of Indonesian extraction, calling himself "Mike" and described as a trainer and bomb-maker with the Moro Islamic Liberation Front) came to Singapore in October 2001. Assisted by the cell members, they conducted surveillance of several establishments, including the U.S. Embassy, the Australian High Commission, the British High Commission, the Israeli Embassy, commercial buildings where there are American companies, and also the MINDEF Complex at Bukit Gombak. They video-recorded what they surveyed for use in their planning. A copy of the video recording was found in the office of Fathi Abu Bakar Bafana. Both "Mike" and "Sammy," identified as Fathur Rahman Al-Ghozi and Jabarah Mohamed Mansur, respectively, were later detained in the Philippines and Oman, respectively.[9] Following his escape, the former was killed by Philippines' police.

"Sammy" and "Mike" who were the directing figures, also informed the cell that they needed 21 tons of ammonium nitrate for construction of several truck bombs. As they already had four tons in Malaysia with Faiz bin Abu Bakar Bafana, they instructed the cell members to procure the remaining 17 tons of ammonium nitrate. They also directed them to try and locate suitable warehouses for a secure site to construct truck bombs. Mohd Ellias subsequently attempted to purchase 17 tons of ammonium nitrate through a contact from a local vendor. Mohd Ellias was arrested by ISD before he could complete the transaction.

The third operations cell was called *"Fiah Ismail."* It was formed after the September 11, 2001, terrorist attacks in the United States. Members of the cell included Halim bin Hussain. They conducted some preliminary surveillance and observations of a few targets, including U.S. companies. Following the arrest of the second batch of detainees in August 2002, the Singapore authorities discovered that there were additional *fiahs* in the Singapore AJAI setup. Four operational *fiahs*, namely *fiah Yakub, fiah Syuib, fiah Daud,* and *fiah Nuh,* were uncovered, even though their specific targets and tasks are unknown.

AJAI'S STRATEGY IN SINGAPORE

Around 1999–2000, the AJAI stepped up its militant orientation. This was reflected in an increased number of reconnaissance and surveys of potential targets. It was also seen in greater efforts to recruit more AJAI members into the operations cells and prepare them for military training abroad. This change in orientation was initiated by regional AJAI leader Hambali, who reportedly wanted the AJAI to convert all its cells (that is, *dakwah* or missionary work, etc.) into operations cells. The AJAI planned to send as many men as possible for training abroad in Afghanistan or Mindanao. Other programs, which were not focused on these immediate objectives, were dropped.

Hambali's strategy was to prepare the AJAI in Malaysia and Singapore operationally to mount a series of terrorist incidents at the time of his choosing. Targets in Singapore would include the water pipelines and the Ministry of Defense. The aim was to create a situation in Malaysia and Singapore that would be conducive to overthrow the Malaysian government so that an Islamic state could arise in Malaysia.

The attacks on key Singapore installations would be portrayed as acts of aggression by the Malaysian government, thereby generating animosity and distrust between Malaysia and Singapore. Hambali aimed to stir up ethnic strife by playing up a "Chinese Singapore" threatening Malays/Muslims in Malaysia; he hoped that this would create a situation which would make Muslims respond to calls for *Jihad* and turn Malaysia and Singapore into another "Ambon," where religious clashes have broken out between Christians and Muslims since January 1999, resulting in many deaths and injuries. In this plan, Hambali was assisted by a small group of Malaysian AJAI members based in Johor. This group met with Singapore AJAI leaders, including Ibrahim Maidin (Ibrahim was detained in January 2002) on at least five occasions between December 2000 and July 2001. The leadership core working with Hambali resided in the Malaysian AJAI.

In 1999, the AJAI initiated an alliance with other *Jihad/*militant groups in the region, called the *Rabitatul Mujahidin.* The alliance facilitated cooperation and the sharing of resources among the groups, in terms of training, procurement of arms, financial assistance, and terrorist operations. The objective was to unify the Islamic militant groups in the region, with the ultimate goal of realizing the *Daulah Islamiyah*—i.e., an Islamic state comprising Malaysia, Indonesia, and Mindanao, following which Singapore and Brunei would eventually be absorbed.

The Singapore AJAI is important to the regional AJAI organization as a source of funds. In the early 1990s, many Singapore AJAI members had to contribute about 2 percent of their monthly salaries; in the latter half of the 1990s, the amount was raised to 5 percent of their monthly salaries. There were others who gave a fixed sum monthly. Apparently, 25 percent of the funds raised would be given to the Malaysian AJAI, and another 25 percent to the Indonesian AJAI. This sum of money would be personally handed over to the Malaysian AJAI, and the amounts meant for the Indonesian AJAI would then be forwarded by a Malaysian representative. The funds for Singapore AJAI were used for various purposes to fund the expenses of the *fiahs* (cells) and to assist local AJAI family members who were in need. AJAI funds were also used to send local AJAI members for military training abroad, and to purchase equipment that included walkie-talkies and binoculars.

THE AJAI'S THREAT TO SINGAPORE

Almost all of the AJAI operatives arrested in Singapore had undergone some kind of military training in Afghanistan, in Malaysia, or in MILF camps in the Philippines. Some of them had trained in Afghanistan at *Al Qaeda* facilities, such as Mahfuh bin Haji Halimi (Mahfuh) from September 1990 to January 1991. Another AJAI member, Habibullah, s/o Hameed (Habibullah), attended a short training stint in 1995 with the MILF. He attended further training in 1996 and 1997. A staunch supporter of the MILF, he also organized visits to the MILF's Camp Abu Bakar for several AJAI and non-AJAI persons. The AJAI had also been conducting a training camp in Malaysia since 1990. Up to 1994, the training was focused mainly on maintaining physical fitness, such as jogging and trekking. From

1995, however, the training camps held in Gunung Pulai, and Kulai began to also teach "military" skills (without firearms training). For instance, AJAI members were taught to make Molotov cocktails, learn knife-throwing skills, topography, jungle survival skills, and trekking. In 1997, additional modules like guerrilla warfare, infiltration, and ambush were included. Around 2000, reconnaissance and observation courses were conducted in Kota Tinggi; these classes were dubbed "urban warfare." The AJAI even conducted "Recall and Operation exercises" to ensure that members were operationally ready. Fourteen (including the three who went to Afghanistan) of the 21 arrestees participated in such training camps in Malaysia.

In addition to military training, the severity of the AJAI threat to Singapore was best evident from the reconnaissance of military and nonmilitary targets in Singapore. The AJAI leaders assigned at least eight of these operations cell members to conduct "casing" (which involves surveillance and reconnaissance) of a range of potential targets in Singapore. These targets include water pipelines, Changi Airport and Biggin Hill Radar Station, Jurong Island, MINDEF, and American targets in Singapore.

THE AJAI IN INDONESIA: A CASE STUDY

Following the 9/11 terrorist attack in the United States; authorities in Southeast Asia began to take notice of the terror network operating in the region. When Singapore's Senior Minister Lee Kuan Yew commented that regional terrorist leaders are roaming freely in Indonesia, he was not incorrect. In fact, prior to the October 2002 Bali bombings, there were denials over the existence of the AJAI terror network in Indonesia, if not accusations that the AJAI is a mere construct and a tool of the U.S. Central Intelligence Agency (CIA) and their "Zionist conspirators" to gain control of Indonesia. With the arrests and court trials of key AJAI leaders and perpetrators of terrorist activities, the Bali bomb attack is an important watershed to the recognition and, more importantly, the understanding of the AJAI, and in particular its terrorist network in Indonesia.

Despite the origins of the AJAI in the *Darul Islam* (DI), an organization that had long emerged in Indonesia in the 1940s, a mere cursory glance of the chronology of the AJAI's evolution in Indonesia would reveal the relative currency of its terror operations. With the fall of Suharto's New Order regime in 1998 and the subsequent return of Abdullah Sungkar, Abu Bakar Ba'asyir, and other members of the AJAI to Indonesia, the terrorist organization began to hit headlines with the series of bomb attacks in the country. It is ironic that the fall of the authoritarian New Order regime and the increased optimism for democracy in Indonesia have, in fact, led to the greater militancy of Islamic groups and especially the AJAI. However, it is of no mere coincidence that democratization has led to the emergence of the AJAI among other terrorist organizations in Indonesia. The current Singapore Prime Minister Lee Hsien Loong has argued that "the armed forces are the strongest institution [in Indonesia], which can safeguard the unity of the country. But the armed forces are wary of being accused of human rights violations, if they act against the militants as they had done in the past."[10] Indeed, democratization in Indonesia has meant that the Islamic constituency has become all-powerful politically and thus rivalling traditional political agents such as the armed forces, thereby weakening the government's ability to deal with hard-line Muslims and their organizations in the country, lest it be accused of undertaking Suharto-type anti-Islamic programs that in the past were endorsed by the Western world, especially the United States.

The democratization process in post-Suharto Indonesia has also provided opportunities in the political space for Abu Bakar Ba'asyir and other Muslim activists. Ba'asyir, who has taken over the role of the *Amir* or leader of the AJAI following the death of Sungkar, founded the *Majlis Mujahidin Indonesia* (MMI) together with Irfan Awwas Suryahardy and Mursalin Dahlan. According to an ICG report, Ba'asyir apparently believes that it is not an opportune time for further armed struggle, as U.S. and Indonesian authorities are clamping down on Islamic activists.[11] Instead, Ba'asyir argued in MMI-AJAI-held meetings that the increased political openness in the post-Suharto environment offered opportunities for the establishment of the Islamic state (*Daulah Islamiyah*) through the conventional political system. Ba'asyir's advice did not go down well with the younger and more belligerent group, including Hambali. The ICG is not wrong to suggest that the AJAI has started to fracture. The younger militant faction in the AJAI believes that the MMI is contrary to the teachings of Sungkar and the latter's intention for the AJAI to remain underground until the time is ripe. This younger militant group is adamant about furthering their causes through terrorist activities.

While the focus of court trials has been placed on Ba'asyir as the *Emir* of the AJAI, he is more likely the spiritual leader. This is not to say that Ba'asyir is not tainted by the crimes of the AJAI. However, notwithstanding the possibility that he gave his blessings to the terrorist operations, Ba'asyir is unlikely to be the mastermind behind the deadly Bali bomb attacks, among other operations. According to a Malaysian security official, if Ba'asyir was AJAI's "godfather" following Sungkar's death, then Hambali was the *"consigliere."* That is to say, while the AJAI members recognize Ba'asyir as the *Emir* of the AJAI, it would be more accurate to suggest that Ba'asyir is the *de jure* leader of the AJAI, and Hambali is the operations chief.

THE *"NGRUKI* ALUMNI"

Notwithstanding the apparent split in the leadership of the AJAI, one key element that continues to tie Ba'asyir, Hambali, and other members of militant organizations in Indonesia is the *"Ngruki* alumni" network. In 1971, Ba'asyir and Sungkar founded the Islamic school *Pesantren al-Mu'min,* which moved to the village of Ngruki in 1973 and became known as *Pondok Ngruki.* This religious boarding school near Solo, Central Java, adopted an ideological outlook of Middle Eastern Islamic radicalism and viewed the *Darul Islam* rebellions as important inspirations. More disturbingly, the teachings of Sungkar had an anti-Christianity tinge, which was attributed to his association with the Indonesian Islamic Propagation Council (*Dewan Dakwah Islamiyah Indonesia,* or DDII).[12] Both Sungkar and Ba'asyir were arrested and discredited in 1978 for alleged involvement in *Komando Jihad,* the shadowy Indonesian intelligence–created Islamic militia responsible for arson and bombings of churches, cinemas, and nightclubs. The pair was accused of preaching and circulating a book called *Jihad and Hijrah,* about urging *Jihad* against Islam's enemies. They were charged for not flying the Indonesian flag at the *pesantren* and for being anti-*Pancasila.*

After their release in 1982, Sungkar and Ba'asyir fled to Malaysia in 1985. A core group of the "Ngruki network" followed the two founders of the *pesantren* to Malaysia. Sungkar continued his teachings and founded *Pondok Pesantren Luqmanul Hakiem* in Johor, Malaysia. This Ngruki network thus expanded and became the foundations and breeding ground for the AJAI. Association with the Ngruki network does not equate to membership of the AJAI terror network. Yet, what this Ngruki network meant to the bonding of the AJAI members, in terms of its loyalty to the teachings of Sungkar and Ba'asyir, its commitment to the cause of *Jihad,* its shared experience radicalized by repression during Suharto's Indonesia, and its sheer membership, cannot be understated.

THE OPERATIONS CHIEF—HAMBALI

While the media's attention has been placed on the court trials of Abu Bakar Ba'asyir and the perpetrators of the Bali bombings, the capture of Hambali on August 11, 2003, in Ayutthaya, Thailand, was regarded as a significant triumph in the region's battle against terrorism. Thai police sources have said that Hambali had travelled from Chiang Khong border district in Chiang Rai to hide among the Muslim community in Ayutthaya. Hambali confessed during interrogation that he was plotting to bomb the backpacker area of Khao San Road and the embassies of the United States, Israel, and Japan. He was also planning to attack planes at Bangkok International Airport with missiles. Also, Hambali's capture has prevented a possible deadly terrorist attack during the forthcoming APEC meeting, which brings together prime ministers, presidents, and chief executives from 21 Asia-Pacific economies. More importantly, as one of the few top leaders aware of the complete operations picture, Hambali's arrest is a major blow to the AJAI organization.

Just as the AJAI is a clandestine organization, little is known about Hambali, the terrorist mastermind. What is clear is that Hambali operated with different pseudonyms, including Riduan Isamuddin. Born Encep Nurjaman in Kampung Pabuaran, subdistrict Karang Tengah, Cianjur, West Java, in 1964, Hambali attended a *madrasah* and graduated from the *Al-Ianah* Islamic High School in 1984. In 1985, at the age of 20, Hambali left Indonesia for Malaysia. It was not a surprising path, given that many Indonesian migrants had left for neighboring Malaysia to find work. However, Hambali's search for greener pastures took a major detour, and he left subsequently for Afghanistan to fight with the *Mujahidin.*

The Soviet-Afghan war (1979–1989) provided the formative experience for radicals from Southeast Asian countries who fought alongside the *Al Qaeda* members. Zachary Abuza noted that Pakistan's Inter-Service Intelligence (ISI) began to recruit radical Muslims from around the world to fight with the *Mujahidin* since 1982.[13] The U.S. CIA had monitored about 1,500 Indonesian students travelling to the Middle East. However, about 30–40 percent had never arrived at their stated destination. It is strongly believed that many of these students joined the *Taliban* in Afghanistan. Along with other Muslim radicals of his generation, his three-year stay as a *Mujahidin* in Afghanistan essentially transformed Hambali in terms of his world outlook and strengthened his firm commitment to the cause of *Jihad*. On Hambali's unyielding faith in the way of *Jihad* on his return to Malaysia in the late 1980s, Abu Bakar Ba'asyir commented that "Hambali, just like me, encouraged people to carry out *Jihad,* which at that time was not known in Malaysia."[14] Following a forgettable time as a *satay* and *jamu* hawker after his return from Afghanistan, Hambali the preacher began to captivate his audiences with his Afghan experiences in Malaysia. Anecdotes of his time spent fighting the Soviet and his encounters with Osama bin Laden were inspirations to other radical Muslims in his congregations.

By 1993 or so, as Sungkar's protégé, Hambali was tasked to set up the militant cells in the Southeast Asia region. Modelling the AJAI along Osama's *Al Qaeda,* Hambali divided the AJAI's structure into independent operation cells. This is to ensure the survival of the organization even if some cells were busted. Also, with the decision made to establish a regionwide AJAI network, Hambali took on a bigger role to establish links with the KMM, MILF, the *Abu Sayyaf,* and other Islamic militant organizations. In 1994, Hambali set up a business company called Konsojaya Sdn. Bhd., seemingly to trade palm oil with Afghanistan. The firm was in fact a cover for acquiring funds and logistical support, including, among others, buying bomb materials for terrorism.

Not only was he a key leader in the AJAI organization, Hambali was also the *Al Qaeda*'s link man for Southeast Asia. He had served in the *Al Qaeda*'s media and military committee in his second stint in Afghanistan. Hambali took part in the foiled attempt to bomb American airliners over the Asia-Pacific. He has also hosted a meeting of *Al Qaeda* members, including two of the September 11 hijackers, in Kuala Lumpur in January 2000. Hambali arranged the meeting for the attack on the U.S. destroyer, USS *Cole* in Yemen in October 2000. He also provided assistance to Zacarias Moussaoui, the 20th would-be hijacker of September 11, when the latter visited Malaysia in September and October 2000.

Hambali is believed to be the mastermind behind the operations in Southeast Asia—among others, the "Singapore Plan" in 1999, the Christmas Eve bombings in Indonesia in 2000, the attack on the residence of the Philippine ambassador in Jakarta in 2000, the Bali bomb blasts in October 2002, and the J.W. Marriott Hotel car bomb explosion in Jakarta in August 2003. Also, the capture of Hambali on August 11, 2003, meant the foiling of a possible terrorist attack on a forthcoming APEC summit involving prime ministers, presidents, and chief executives from 21 Asia-Pacific economies. While the arrest of Hambali the operations chief is a tremendous blow to the terrorist network, the question is whether the separation of the AJAI into many independent operation cells by Hambali has successfully ensured the survival of the terrorist organization. Chances are that this amoeba-like terrorist organization would produce another Hambali before long.

SUICIDE BOMBINGS—UNIT *KHOS* IN THE BALI AND JAKARTA ATTACKS

For his disciples willing to die for the cause of *Jihad,* Hambali's magnetism lies in his comprehension of the sufferings of Muslims in Palestine, Bosnia, and Chechnya. In an interview with *Time* magazine, Sobri, a former disciple of Hambali, revealed the sense of reverence members had for the preacher, "Whatever happens I can never forget him. For me, he opened a window into the world of Muslim sufferings."[15] It is this appeal that drew Muslim radicals into Hambali's *Jihad* project both at home and abroad. More disturbingly, Hambali taught these Islamic terrorists that violence was a sacramental act. For Hambali and his *Jihadists,* death in the name of *Jihad* meant martyrdom and eternal salvation.

Bali Bomb Blasts, October 12, 2002

It is in Bali in October 2002 that these suicide bombers first struck. Following the foiled Singapore Plan and the subsequent arrests of the AJAI members in Singapore and in Malaysia, Hambali made the critical decision, in a meeting held in southern Thailand, to move away from attacking well-guarded "hard" targets such as embassies and focus instead on "soft" ones such as bars and nightclubs frequented by foreigners. Mukhlas emerged as the terrorist network's *Mantiqi* 1 commander at another meeting in Bangkok. He was also the eldest of the three Nurhasyim brothers behind the Bali bombings (the other two being Amrozi, who was sentenced to death by the Denpasar District Court for his role in the blasts, and Ali Imron). Final plans were drawn up by Mukhlas in Central Java in August 2002, and he identified Kota Beach in Bali as the prime target.

According to a statement by the detained AJAI treasurer, Wan Min Wan Mat, during the trial of Imam Samudra, Hambali had directed that about US$35,500 was sent to Mukhlas. It was also decided that Imam Samudra was named field commander for the Bali attack. By September 2002, Imam Samudra had targeted Paddy's Irish Bar and the larger Sari Club for the deadly attack. Mukhlas appointed Idris, the Bali cell's deputy commander, to help with the logistics. Amrozi subsequently bought a L300 Mitsubishi van and transported the bomb materials and the vehicle to Bali. Indonesian electronics expert Dulmatin and former Malaysian university lecturer Dr. Azahari were entrusted with the job of making the bomb. Ali Imron has disclosed that the bomb makers used 900 kg of potassium chlorate, 150 kg of sulphur, and 75 kg of aluminium to create the van bomb, which tore apart the Sari Club. The two other bombs used in Bali were smaller. He also told the Denpasar District Court that the detonating cord used in the Kuta attacks had been "made in the USA" and obtained in the Philippines, and that the TNT came from Ambon in Indonesia's Maluku Islands.

Imam Samudra had shortlisted and settled on three suicide bombers from among six names, all aged between 19 and 22. Iqbal was to drive in the vehicle bomb, while Feri was to wear the bomb in a vest, and Rohmadi was to drive into Sari Club on a motorcycle, wearing the bomb vest. However, Rohmadi was later found to be too incompetent in his driving ability and was subsequently dropped as a Bali suicide bomber. Following a trial run on October 11, the suicide bombers struck on the next day, October 12, 2002. Idris and Ali Imron detonated a cell phone bomb at the U.S. Consulate in Denpasar. (The phone is designed to emit a current from the battery to the detonator in a cell phone bombing. When it receives a call or an SMS, the bomb triggers off.) Moments later, Feri blew himself up at Paddy's, and Iqbal was also torn apart as his bomb went off at Sari Club.

A crucial oversight had led to the investigations and the capture of the perpetrators of the Bali bombings. While Amrozi had erased the chassis number and other features of the van used in the Sari bombing, he failed to realize that the vehicle had been used as public transport and overlooked a government stamp. The oversight provided a crucial lead for forensic experts, which eventually led investigators to the "Smiling Bomber," Amrozi. A month after the Bali bombings, Amrozi and Imam Samudra were captured by the Indonesian authorities in November 2002. In December, Mukhlas was nabbed and his brother, Ali Imron, was arrested a month later in January 2003. Idris was also taken into police custody in June 2003. Subsequently, Amrozi was found guilty and sentenced to death by the Denpasar District Court for involvement in the terrorist attack. Whether justice would be carried out remains unclear. What is certain is that 202 people had died as a result of the Bali bomb blasts, many of them holiday makers from Australia. For others who survived the deadly terrorist attack, the wounds suffered and the indelible physical and psychological scars have changed their lives forever.

J.W. Marriott Hotel, Jakarta Bomb Blast, August 5, 2003

Despite the arrests of the alleged leader of the AJAI, Abu Bakar Ba'asyir, and the perpetrators of the Bali bomb blasts, the J.W. Marriott Hotel car-bomb explosion in Jakarta on August 5, 2003, demonstrated that the terrorist network is all but crippled. Indonesian authorities have affirmed that the AJAI was likely to be responsible for the Marriott bomb, which was similar to those set off in Bali and one that injured the Philippines ambassador in 2001. The bomb used in the Jakarta hotel attack consisted of mobile phone detonators and a 150-kg cocktail of potassium chlorate and TNT packed in three containers, along with four jerry cans filled with a mixture of petrol and kerosene to create a fiery blast. The hotel bombing killed 11 people and injured 150.

Forensic results from Indonesia's investigations have certified that the DNA of a severed head found in the blast scene of the Marriott Hotel explosion belonged to suicide bomber Asmar. On August 5, Asmar had driven a Toyota Kijang van into the Marriott Hotel driveway. As security guards of the hotel approached the vehicle, Asmar triggered the bomb explosion that ripped through the hotel. However,

Indonesian investigators believed that the suicide bomber had blundered in the operations by activating the bomb too early and too far away from the hotel lobby front. Security sources have disclosed that a kamikaze act at the hotel lobby front could have killed at least 200 people, given the lunchtime crowd in the adjoining coffee house. Instead, the bomb explosion was thrust downloads, creating a two-meter-wide and one-meter-deep crater. Nevertheless, of the 11 killed in the bomb explosion were mostly Indonesian hotel security guards and taxi drivers, awaiting passengers at the hotel front.

Disturbingly, Asmar is believed to be one of the 10 or 15 suicide bombers recruited by Mustofa, a senior AJAI leader (Mustofa was arrested in Semarang in July 2003). Asmar belonged to *Unit Khos,* a special squad within the AJAI network made up of suicide bombers believed to be gearing up for more attacks. Sidney Jones, the project director of the ICG in Jakarta has likened *Unit Khos* to the Indonesian military's Kopassus Special Forces unit.[16] This *Unit Khos* special operations outfit specializes in bombings and assassinations. The suicide-bomber network is believed to be headed by Zulkarnaen (alias Arif Sunarso), who is reportedly the most senior AJAI leader after Hambali. Zulkarnaen commands AJAI's military wing *Aksari,* which reports directly to the leader of the AJAI, be it Abu Bakar Ba'asyir or Hambali (see Figure 4.2).

The 2004 Kuningan Bombing (Australian High Commission)

On September 9, 2004, a car bomb exploded outside the Australian High Commission at Kuningan District. Eleven people, including the suicide bomber, were killed, with more than 180 injured. The attack was blamed on the AJAI, with Azahari Husin and Noordin Mohammed Top blamed as the brains behind the attack. In November 2005, the Indonesian police arrested four men in Bogor, West Java, for the attack. They were accused of being members of the Banten Ring that was involved in the Kuningan attack. They were Sogir, Iwan Darmwan, Hasan, and Apuy. The Kuningan bombing demonstrated AJAI's great capacity for networking: even though it was essentially an AJAI operation, the operatives were non-AJAI, with a partnership struck with former DI members who were committed to *Jihad*against the West. In this case, Australia chosen was a target for its role in supporting the U.S. invasion of Iraq. In March 2005, Irun Hidayat, a religious teacher, was sentenced to three years in jail for helping to motivate others to carry out acts of terrorism. Irun was accused of having influenced Heri Kurniwan to undertake the suicide bombing.[17]

The Second Bali Bombing, October 2005

On October 1, 2005, a series of bombs exploded in Bali, the second time it was targeted by the AJAI. The attacks were on two tourist locations, Jimbaran and Kuta. Twenty-three people, including three suicide bombers were killed, with more than 100 injured. Like the earlier attacks in Bali and the two attacks in Jakarta, the AJAI was alleged to be behind it.

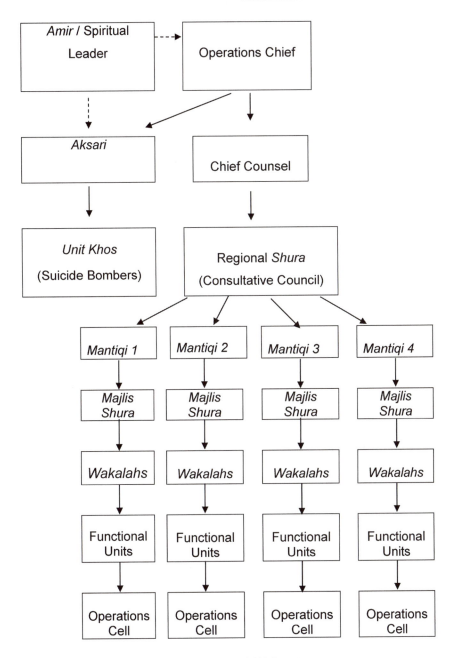

Figure 4.2   The *Aksari* Military Wing and the AJAI Structure

THE AJAI'S THREAT TO INDONESIA

The enactment of a new antiterrorism law in Indonesia, which allows police to arrest a person and detain him for seven days on suspicion of terrorism based on intelligence reports, signals an important change in the perception of Indonesia in the combat against terrorism. The resolve of Indonesia to stamp out the AJAI network is clearly demonstrated with the death sentences passed on Bali bombers Amrozi and Imam Samudra, and the life sentence on Ali Imron for his involvement in executing the October 2002 bombings in Bali. Yet, despite convictions in the Bali cases, Indonesia's fight against terrorism appears still to be an arduous task. While Indonesia's security agencies are pushing for the introduction of tougher, if not draconian antiterrorism laws and measures, politicians are out to score political points by opposing such moves or by denying that the AJAI even existed in Indonesia. On September 17, 2003, former President Abdurrahman Wahid has asserted that "none of the news that terrorists are here is convincing to me."[18] Such denials underscore that the politics of terrorism, especially the politicians' fear of a political backlash from the predominantly Muslim electorate as a consequence of heavy-handed measures against terrorism, affects how decisively and effectively Indonesia will be in combating the AJAI network.

Unlike the decisiveness demonstrated in the convictions of the Bali bombers Amrozi, Imam Samudra, and Ali Imron, the four-year jail sentence of Ba'asyir is a far cry from the 15 years that prosecutors had pressed for. Ba'asyir was found guilty for subversion with the aim of overthrowing the government by the Jakarta court. However, he escaped terrorism charges due to a lack of evidence to prove that he was the leader of AJAI. Ba'asyir's light jail term is sending mixed signals that Jakarta is "taking one step forward and two steps back" in its fight against terrorism. Doubts linger about Jakarta's credibility and commitment to fighting the AJAI terror. The political ramification of an indecisive stance against terrorism is stark: it offers hope for the terrorists to carry out acts of terrorism in the name of Islam.

MANAGING THE *AJAI* THREAT IN SOUTHEAST ASIA

Unlike the management of other terrorist organizations or even past terrorist organizations in the region, the AJAI threat can be managed through the adoption of comprehensive and wide-ranging measures. As it is a "nationally based" organization, specific local and national measures would be needed to contain, neutralise and eventually weed out the menace. As the AJAI is also a regional terrorist organization, regionwide measures would also be needed, either on a bilateral or ASEAN-wide multilateral basis. Finally, as the AJAI is connected with the *Al Qaeda* network and has an international agenda, either regionally or internationally to support the "global *Jihad* struggle," especially against the United States, international measures would also be needed to manage the threat. What measures have been taken thus far and how effective they have been will be analyzed here.

International

Prior to the September 11 attack, the ASEAN countries viewed the United States as a champion of democracy and human rights in the region, best evident in the manner Al Gore, the American vice president, championed for the release of the detained Anwar Ibrahim, the former deputy of Dr. Mahathir Mohammad. September 11 changed all this, with the Republicans under George W. Bush, already converts of *realpolitik,* reoriented American foreign and defense policies against international terrorism. In a way, there appears to be a new "cold war," only this time the enemy is not "international communism" but "international terrorism," often confined to Islam and not other religions.

Internationally, almost all countries in Southeast Asia supported the various counterterrorism measures that were being undertaken, especially by the United States and its allies. Most countries condemned the 9/11 attack as an attack on the civilized world. This was best evident in the stance adopted by the Singapore government. The republic strongly supported retaliations against the perpetrators, as she believed that there was no safety in silence. Singapore's leaders defended their support for the United States as follows:

> We have to stand up for our principles. It's not an attack just on the US. Its 7,000-odd casualties and more than 2,000 were from 80 different countries. So it's an attack on all civilised, open countries in the world. Singapore is also vulnerable. We are a financial centre, we are an economic hub, and we are an open city. It happened in the US. We can take precautions but we can never say it will not happen in Singapore. And indeed, such things have happened in Singapore.[19]

In the same vein, Singapore's Deputy Prime Minister Lee Hsien Loong argued that "we have to participate in the international effort against terrorism because it is our responsibility as an international citizen. This is something all countries have to do together."[20] Singapore made its clearest stance yet on the issue when its foreign minister, Professor S. Jayakumar, argued in a speech during the Ministerial Meeting on Counter-Terrorism at the United Nations Security Council that:

> Countering the threat of terrorism is clearly and rightly now a central global priority. The perpetrators of these horrendous crimes must not go unpunished. They must be brought to justice to deter others from contemplating similar horrific crimes. Singapore stands with the international community in this campaign against terrorism. This is not a fight against any religion. It is not a fight against the people of Afghanistan. It is a fight against the forces of violence, intolerance and fanaticism. It is a fight for civilisation and a fight that we must win. We must grid ourselves for a long effort. The threats will come in many different forms. Some will be more virulent than others, some waxes while others wane. And, like disease, even as one source of terrorism is eradicated, others will spring up or mutate. Only a determined, united, comprehensive and sustained global strategy will enable the international community to contain these malignant forces.[21]

ASEAN countries have been strongly encouraged to become parties and ratify the 12 international conventions and protocols relating to terrorism. Singapore and its ASEAN members also endorsed the various measures, especially financial in character, that were adopted by the UN Security Council in countering terrorism. One of the most important telling signs of growing international cooperation in stamping terrorism was the signing of the wide-ranging antiterrorist pact on August 3, 2002, in Brunei between the United States and ASEAN countries. The pact committed the parties to mutual assistance in the crackdown on the movement of terrorists, detection of fake passports, and movement of terrorist funds. It also called for improved intelligence sharing and stronger counterterrorism measures as part of the wide-ranging goal to prevent, disrupt, and combat international terrorism.[22] Since then, countries in the region, either bilaterally or regionally through ASEAN, have also initialled a number of agreements with a number of countries to demonstrate their commitment to eradicate terrorism from the region. This includes agreements with the United States, the European Union, China, India, and Australia.

Regional

What transpired in New York and Washington on September 11, 2001, was a testament to the global reach of terrorism and its spill over ramifications far and wide, especially in Southeast Asia. The region could not escape the consequences of whatever "order" that dominated the world, as it was plugged into the world strategically, politically, and economically. With Washington blaming Osama bin Laden and the *Al Qaeda* network for the terrorist attack, and declaring war on all those who supported and harbored such terrorists, particularly the *Taliban* regime in Afghanistan, the U.S. antiterrorist war eventually reached Southeast Asia, mainly due to links that were alleged to have existed between various terrorist groups in Southeast Asia and those targeted by the United States. For example, GAM, MILF, *Abu Sayyaf,* and the AJAI were believed to have close ties with Osama and the *Al Qaeda.*[23]

In this connection, particular attention was paid to Islamic terrorists that were alleged to be operating in Malaysia, Indonesia,and the Philippines, and eventually with a network discovered in Singapore in December 2001. Though motivated by differing considerations, ASEAN was jolted into action and this saw a number of policies being adopted by the regional body (see Appendix 2 on ASEAN's Agreements on Counter-Terrorism). The first important step was broached when all heads of governments, at the Seventh ASEAN Summit in Brunei, adopted the *ASEAN Declaration on Joint Action to Counter-Terrorism* (ADJACT) on November 5, 2001. Among others, the heads of ASEAN governments:

- condemned the September 11 terrorist attacks and extended deepest sympathy and condolences to the people and government of the United States. and the victims of the attacks;
- committed themselves to counter, prevent, and suppress all forms of terrorist acts;

- approved the initiatives of the Third ASEAN Ministers Meeting on Transnational Crime held in October 2001 to focus on terrorism and deal effectively with the issue at all levels and endorse the convening of an Ad Hoc Experts Meeting and Special sessions of the Senior Officials Meeting on Transnational Crime (SOMTC) and Annual Ministerial Meeting on Transnational Crime (AMMTC) that will focus on terrorism.

The pressing question is: how can ASEAN, in the light of its commitments to counterterrorism, implement what has been agreed upon? The ADJACT did provide a framework as far as the possible course of action was concerned. Among others, this was to include: reviewing and strengthening national mechanisms to combat terrorism; signing and ratification and accession to all relevant antiterrorist conventions; deepening cooperation among frontline law enforcement agencies in combating terrorism and sharing "best practices"; integrating relevant international conventions on terrorism with those of ASEAN's; enhancing information and intelligence exchange on terrorists and terrorist organizations, their movement, and funding; strengthening cooperation and coordination between AMMTC and other relevant bodies in ASEAN in countering, preventing, and suppressing all forms of terrorist acts; and enhancing regional counterterrorism capacities.[24]

In terms of counterterrorism operations, the ASEAN region also boasts of having established various mechanisms to manage the menace. Two key regionwide mechanisms in this regard are the Southeast Asian Regional Centre for Counter-Terrorism (SEARCCT), based in Kuala Lumpur, Malaysia; and the Jakarta Centre for Law Enforcement Cooperation (JCLEC), situated in Semarang, Central Java. In November 2002, through international efforts and assistance from the United States, the SEARCCT was established. Essentially, it aims to train and build the capacity of government agencies involved in counterterrorism. According to Ambassador Mohammad Hussin bin Nayan, Director of SEARCCT, many training seminars have been conducted with regard to interdicting terrorists, disaster scene management, prevention and crisis management of chemical terrorism, financial underpinnings of terrorism in Southeast Asia, and document management.[25] The JCLEC was established at the Bali Regional Ministerial Meeting on Counter-Terrorism and formally opened in 2004. Essentially a joint Indonesian-Australian venture, the Australian federal police and the Indonesian police have trained thousands of police and intelligence personnel in counterterrorism.

A number of other initiatives have also been undertaken in the "region's war on terror," and this includes among others:

- Undertake closer intelligence cooperation among ASEAN's partners, best evident in the "informal" meeting of the military intelligence chiefs in Kuala Lumpur in late January 2002.

- Provide intelligence and information to neighbors, among others, that led to the arrest of the alleged Indonesian bomb maker in the Philippines Fathur Rahman Al-Ghozi and *Al Qaeda* operative Mohamad Mansour Jabarah.

- A troika made up of the Philippines, Indonesia and Malaysia was formed to discuss joint policy. This antiterror pact was gradually expanded to include Thailand,

Cambodia, and Brunei. Singapore, however, indicated its preference for a bilateral approach, arguing that "we feel that the provisions in there [the expanded troika] are already covered by existing understandings by Singapore and the respective ASEAN countries."[26]

- Border cooperation between Indonesia and Malaysia has increased.
- An ASEAN Senior Officials Meeting on Transnational Crime (SOMTC), followed by a Special ASEAN Ministerial Meeting on Terrorism was held in May 2002 in Kuala Lumpur, Malaysia.

National

It is, however, at the national level that most counterterrorist measures have been undertaken by various countries, and it is here that Singapore's policy towards international terrorism and especially the threat posed by various Islamic militant groups is more obvious. Motivated by differing—and at times even conflicting—domestic concerns, countries in the ASEAN region have adopted a whole array of measures to combat the menace. Even though there is a lack of uniformity in the national countermeasures, it is clear that countries that have the will and are least constrained domestically, such as Singapore, Thailand, and the Philippines, have adopted wide-ranging measures to deal with the threat; compared to some others, such as Indonesia, that for different reasons had to be more circumscribed and restrained in managing the threat. The policies adopted by the Singapore government are an excellent manifestation of the determination some governments are prepared to go in managing terrorism in Southeast Asia.

In December 2001, the government announced the arrest of a clandestine group of 13 Singaporeans that had links with regional and international terrorists, and who were planning to bomb Western, especially American, commercial and military targets in Singapore. An additional two who were arrested were released with Restriction Orders (ROs), forbidding them from leaving Singapore without official consent. That the terrorists' threat to Singapore was real was further reinforced when the Singapore prime minister revealed on April 5, 2002, that five other members of the AJAI planned, a month following the arrest of 13 suspected terrorists, to hijack a plane and crash it into Changi International Airport in Singapore.[27] In August 2002, an additional 18 members were arrested. All those arrested were believed to be members of AJAI. An additional three members who were also arrested were subsequently released after being issued with ROs. Of the 31, 11 had received military training in *Al Qaeda* camps in Afghanistan. An additional three had trained with the MILF in the Philippines. Those arrested were described as "foot/ground soldiers" with the masterminds operating from abroad.[28] Many more AJAI operatives and cells are believed to be in the country, and apprehending them has been given a top priority.[29] The Singapore Ministry of Home Affairs also stated on September 21, 2002, that it believed that "about a dozen [AJAI] members are dispersed and in hiding in the region."[30] In this connection, the policy goals as far as managing Islamic militant groups, especially the AJAI, are as follows:

a. Investigate, unearth, and disrupt the AJAI network in the country.

b. Prevent violence and harm to life and property in the country.

c. Undertake preventive detention of all AJAI operatives in the country that are deemed dangerous.

d. Engage various government agencies to socialize the nature of threat to ensure that it does not undermine ethnic and social cohesion in the country and where the threat is not Islam, but terrorism.

e. Support various diplomatic and political efforts to designate the AJAI as an international terrorist organization.

It is against this backdrop that the antiterrorism policies of Singapore can be appreciated, which among others, includes:

- Using the Internal Security Act to arrest more than 40 (by October 2002) suspected terrorists belonging to AJAI.[31]

- Outline a new homeland security framework to enhance cooperation between the Defense and Home Affairs ministries, under the purview of the Security Policy Review Committee. A "special joint exercise" between the two ministries was organized in late January 2002, involving among others, the evacuation of casualties in a chemical plant that had been sabotaged and decontaminating firefighters who had come into contact with chemicals as well as disposal of bombs. All these activities are coordinated by the National Security Task Force that is under the charge of Deputy Prime Minister and Coordinating Minister for Security and Defense Dr. Tony Tan.

- Establish a National Security Secretariat to strengthen coordination between all security agencies.[32]

- Strengthened the Counter-Terrorism Division in the Ministry of Home Affairs, set up in 1988, as well as established the Joint Counter Terrorism Centre in January 2002 to coordinate intelligence efforts to combat terrorism.

- Passed the UN Act forbidding Singaporeans and foreigners in the republic from assisting terrorists financially or otherwise, thereby criminalizing such acts.

- Signed the International Convention for the Suppression of the Financing of Terrorism.

- Expand budget for intelligence and counterterrorism activities.

- Strengthen the Suspicious Transactions Reporting Office in order to stop money-laundering activities that might involve international terrorism.

- Support various diplomatic and political efforts to designate the AJAI as an international terrorist organization.

- Emphasis on interethnic harmony and peace through various mechanisms, including the establishment of Inter-Racial Harmony Circles throughout the country.

Indonesia is another country that has armed itself to counter the AJAI threat through a whole array of mechanisms. A number of laws have been passed to this effect. First, following the first Bali bombing, the government rushed through an antiterrorism law, Government Regulation In Lieu of Law (No. 1/2002). This was followed by Presidential Instruction Number 4/2002 that authorized the Coordinating Minister for Politics and Security to coordinate steps to fight terrorism. Following this, Presidential Instruction Number 5/2002 authorized the National Intelligence Agency to coordinate intelligence activities.

While these legal measures to counterterrorism were important, even more impressive were the actual measures to combat terrorism. Under the U.S. Department of State antiterrorism assistance program, the American Federal Bureau of Investigation trained the Police Counter-Terrorism Force, known as *Detachment 88* or *Gegana*.[33] This is Indonesia's war-fighting force that directly deals with the terrorists. First established in 1974, it has been reorganized in 1984, 1985, 1996, and 2001. In 1996, the *Gegana* Police Brigade was reorganized into four separate detachments. Following the first Bali bombing in 2002, Detachment 88 has been in the forefront in combating Islamist terrorists in Indonesia. However, more critical to Indonesia's counterterrorism efforts was the setting up of the Task Force on Counter-Terrorism (TFCT)—or in Indonesian, *Satuan Tugas Anti-Teror,* or *Tim Bom* for short—which was established in October 2002 following the first Bali bombing. This group has been described as the "silent warriors" that have been the key in containing and neutralizing the terrorists in Indonesia.[34] This has succeeded in mobilizing the best police officers in the country and reports directly to the Indonesian police chief. While in the public domain, most counterterrorism efforts are usually credited to Detachment 88, in actuality the most critical organization is the TFCT.

The prime mover behind the TFCT was Major-General (then Colonel) Gories Meri, presently the Deputy Head of the Criminal Investigation Board, CIB, under which Detachment 88 is one of the six divisions (see Figure 4.3). However, while Detachment 88 is part of the CIB, the TFCT operates autonomously; hence, in large measure, its success so far. Established under then–Police Chief Da'i Bachtiar, even though it is essentially an ad hoc organization, according to a senior TFCT officer, its success is due to the minimal bureaucracy, instant decision making, and tremendous flexibility that has accounted for most of Indonesia's counterterrorism successes, including the arrest of the two Bali bombers, those involved in the Jakarta bombings of Hotel Marriott and Kuningan. The TFCT was primarily responsible for the elimination of the "Demolition Man," Dr. Azahari Husin in October 2005, as well as the arrest of many others.[35]

In the same vein, Malaysia has used its ISA to detain suspected extremists and terrorists. In addition, arguing that the traditional Islamic schools were providing fertile grounds for fundamentalists, extremists, and terrorists, the Malaysian government has instituted strict measures to control these schools. Not only must the private Islamic schools be registered with the Ministry of Education, but even more important, every school's curriculum is to be scrutinized to ensure that it is in line with the national curriculum.[36] In the same vein, anti–money laundering laws, a task force to deal with terrorism, and support for international counterterrorism measures have been adopted by Malaysia as well as other ASEAN countries such as Thailand. In this regard, one country that has been active in adopting measures to neutralize the terrorism threat has been the Philippines.

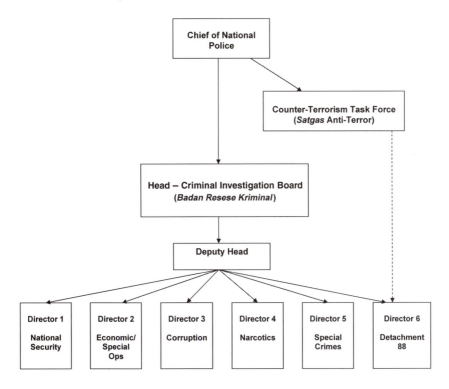

Figure 4.3   Indonesia's Counterterrorism Organizational Structure

Source: Counter-Terrorism Task Force, Indonesia Police Headquarters

In view of the AJAI threat, the Philippines have initiated a number of policies to counter the danger. Since the 9/11 incident, the Philippines government has been one of the strongest supporters of the U.S. "war on terror" and even agreed to deploy troops in Afghanistan and Iraq. On September 24, 2001, President Arroyo established the Inter-Agency Task Force Against International Terrorism to identify and neutralize suspected terrorists. On September 29, 2001, the Philippines Congress passed the Anti–Money Laundering Act. On October 12, 2001, President Arroyo announced a 14-pillar approach to combat terrorism, including the establishment of a Cabinet Oversight Committee on International Security as the leading antiterrorist body, called on the armed forces and police to address terrorist violence, sought regional consensus with Malaysia and Indonesia in the war on terror, and held accountable all public and private organizations that may be abetting terrorism.[37] Through General Order Number 2 on May 9, 2002, the armed forces were ordered to suppress lawlessness and violence in Muslim-dominated Mindanao. More important, through joint military exercises with the United States, the Philippines launched its own war on terror to neutralize the threat posed by the *Abu Sayyaf,* MILF-linked terrorists, and AJAI in southern Philippines. Admiral Dennis Blair, the then commander-in-chief of the U.S. Pacific Command, described the joint exercises as "the largest military operations against terrorism (outside Afghanistan)."[38] The Philippines also participated in the Southeast Asia Cooperation Against Terrorism exercise that was held in March 2002 in Thailand.

In the main, as each Southeast Asian country is confronted with its own home-grown terrorist problem, counterterrorism measures at the national level are particularly critical as governments and their policies will have to be accountable to the electoral process. Despite this constraint, countries faced with the terrorist threat, especially Indonesia, Malaysia, Singapore, and the Philippines, have undertaken various measures, including arresting suspects alleged to be involved in national, regional, and international terrorism. In the case of Singapore and Malaysia, this has been greatly facilitated by the resort to laws enacted by the British colonial authorities that provided for detention without trial. At the same time, all governments have committed themselves to antiterrorism policies even though the manner in which their commitments have been implemented has varied from country to country. Despite the public espousal to wipe out terrorism and to undertake cooperative measures, thus far only the Philippines have invited the United States to undertake "joint exercises," a euphemism for military support, in its war against the *Abu Sayyaf* terrorists in southern Philippines.[39]

Even though the challenge posed by religious-oriented terrorism is not new, the nature and character of the AJAI threat has forced the various governments in the region to become more proactive nationally, regionally, and internationally in order to overcome the menace. Not only does the AJAI poses a threat to the various regimes in the region, at the same time it has the potential to wreak havoc on the delicate ethnic and racial balance in various Southeast Asian countries such as Singapore, Malaysia, Indonesia, and the Philippines, as well as giving these countries a negative image to investors, tourists, and the West. As such, the stakes are indeed high, and managing the AJAI has indeed become a high-priority security issue, best evident in various laws and regulations as well as investments in propping up the security and intelligence services.

LIMITS AND OBSTACLES TO MANAGING *JIHADI* EXTREMISM AND TERRORISM IN SOUTHEAST ASIA

Even though governments in the region are in concert that the AJAI is a serious political, economic, and security menace, the fact that the terrorist organization has been able to germinate almost undetected for so long and reach various critical sectors of society would tend to indicate that there are serious problems that exist in the management of the threat. Uppermost in this regard, over and above the availability of resources, is the fact that the AJAI, as an "Islamic" organization, has been able to "melt away" and take cover in various legitimate religious activities, thereby making its detection and its threat-oriented activities that much more difficult to detect. At the same time, in Islamic-dominant societies such as Malaysia and Indonesia, there is the political cost of antagonizing the "Islamic vote bank," and governments are generally wary of appearing anti-Islamic and perceived to be persecuting radical Islamic groups at the behest of what appears to be the "anti-Islamic West."

Due to its strategic location, its political and economic importance to the world, and the presence of a large Islamic populace, Southeast Asia figures greatly in the international fight against terrorism. However, the first priority should be for governments in the region, possibly with U.S. assistance, to address the various domestic sources of tensions. According to Mohamed Jawhar Hassan, "the Muslim majority countries of ASEAN, noted for their essentially moderate and pacifist ways, can play a key role in mobilising the Islamic world in this endeavor."[40] He identified a number of steps that states in the region can take in the fight against terrorism. Southeast Asian states can contribute in the campaign against terrorism. This can be done by, among other things, cleaning up their own backyard and making the environment non-conducive to international terrorists and their overtures to local militants. There is also the need to intensify efforts to address both the symptoms and root causes of terrorism. The root causes included socioeconomic development in southern Philippines, economic recovery in Indonesia, greater determination in restoring law and order as well as apprehending militants in Maluku and Sulawesi to end the sectarian violence, as well as finding a peaceful solution to the problem in Aceh and Papua. Social cohesion and satisfaction as well as a just and able political administration are increasingly seen as natural barriers to both the recruitment and sustenance of terrorist elements. The object should be to make the ground infertile to terrorist appeals. Once the region is relatively free from strife, terrorism would not be able to root itself, almost in the same manner communism was rooted out in the region in the past.

As long as the United States is perceived to be selectively promoting certain countries and policies rather than fairly assisting the suppression of terrorism in the region, its antiterrorist policies are unlikely to succeed in the region. It is thus important for the United States. to be ready and willing to invest time, effort, and resources into Southeast Asia to assist in the maintenance of peace and stability. The approach should be to allow the United States to take a backseat and let ASEAN take care of itself in her own way—while still consistently providing assistance and expertise when required in combating the terrorist menace in the region. It is also crucial that regional forums such as the ASEAN Human Rights Working Group and the Asia-Pacific Dialogues be treated not as a vehicle for them to champion American interests and policies, but rather for them to show interest in the region itself and its problems. These include issues of good governance, human rights, and economic instability. In this regard, there is a serious need to overhaul America's hegemonic image in the region. The United States should make efforts to be seen as a supporter of peace and stability rather than one that is merely interested in advancing its own selfish, national interests in Southeast Asia.

Closely related to Washington's adoption of policies that are in principle sound, Walter Laqueur also observed that "the current resurgence of religious terrorism is largely identified with trends in the Muslim and the Arab World, much to the chagrin of the defenders of Islam and Islamists in the West and East."[41] This has the potential to complicate and undermine Washington's antiterrorism posture in general, and Southeast Asia in particular. This concern was clearly articulated by Mr. Goh Chok Tong, Singapore's prime minister, when he argued that the fight against terrorism is "not a fight against Islam. It is a fight against terrorists who misuse religion to rally support for their cause and to justify their violence."[42]

Southeast Asia is a region where Muslims who are nonmilitant in their interpretation of Islam form the majority of the populace. Yet, due to the increasing tendency towards "clashes of civilizations," the maintenance of racial-religious harmony is a great concern, not only to the region but also to the world at large. How the governments in the region manage the delicate ethnic balance in their respective societies, especially in states such as Indonesia, Malaysia, Brunei, Singapore, Thailand, and the Philippines—where there are sizeable Muslims—and how Washington relates fairly and prudently with these governments, will go a long way in determining the success of antiterrorism policies in the region. Any government that appears or behaves as nothing more than a proxy of Washington in its antiterrorism policy in the region is likely to gain the wrath of its citizens and be isolated regionally.

Closely related to a sense of fair play by governments in the region and the United States is the manner in which the politics in the Middle East has evolved. The U.S. policy in the Middle East, and particularly Washington's response to the Israeli-Palestinian crisis during the tenure of the hawkish Ariel Sharon, will have a major determining role in promoting or limiting the success of American antiterrorism policies in the region. If the United States adopts a one-sided policy of backing Israel at all costs, as is widely perceived in Southeast Asia, it will only succeed in heightening the general sense of injustice towards Muslims in general and the Palestinians in particular. If the United States fails to distinguish between Islamic fundamentalism and terrorism, with the former largely fuelled by the sense of injustice and helplessness in the face of state-sponsored violence by Israel, the net result is likely to be a paradigm shift in favor of greater religious fervor and fundamentalism, with extremist rather than moderate leaders gaining the cudgels of power in the region.

What cannot be denied is that U.S. policy in the Middle East has created an anti-U.S. sentiment in the Arab-Muslim world and provided the *leit motif* to oppose the U.S. and its policies. To some, the September 11, 2001, attacks were largely driven by this consideration. The Israel-Palestine saga during the prime ministership of Ariel Sharon, and in moments where the United States has fully backed the hardline policies of Israel, has succeeded only in creating more dissension in the region. In the face of seemingly pro-Israeli policies of the United States and Israel's excessive violence against Palestinians, many Islamic groups in ASEAN have volunteered to physically aid in the fight against Israel, just as they did during the Afghanistan bombings. As long as the Israel-Palestinian problem remains unresolved, it will only succeed in fanning the flame of anti-U.S. sentiments in the region, driven by what is perceived as U.S. double standards in its Middle Eastern policy. The empathy that is increasingly shared between the Muslim majority nations means that one cannot ignore their concerns, and anti-U.S. sentiments and elements will rise as long as Washington continues its hypocritical policies of supporting Israel's violence while objecting similar measures by other Islamic groups.

Washington's policies toward Indonesia, the most populous Islamic country in the world, have also weakened its global antiterrorism war. In its euphoria to undertake "democratic enlargement" at all costs, the Clinton administration supported the overthrow of Suharto and the subsequent democratization of Indonesia. This saw, among others, Indonesia's decision to abandon East Timor, the former Portuguese colony that it annexed in 1975. However, the mayhem that followed the United Nations' mismanaged referendum in August 1999 led the United States to cut all ties with the Indonesian military, the most important political force in the country and the most important pillar that is capable of countering Islamic extremism and terrorism in the country. As long as the U.S. Congress maintains its ban on military sales and training assistance, and continues to insist on "reforming the Indonesian military,"[43] there will be great limits to the ability of the latter to effectively manage and deal with the terrorist threat in the country.

Ironically, for Washington, democratization in Indonesia has meant that the Islamic constituency has become all-powerful politically, thereby weakening the government's ability to deal with hard-line Muslims and their organizations in the country, lest it be accused of undertaking Suharto-type anti-Islamic programs that in the past were endorsed by the Western world, especially the United States.[44] This was best evident in the decision of the Indonesian government to pardon Abu Bakar Ba'asyir on charges of subversion, and its intervention in seeking the release of Tasmsil Linrung and Abdul Jamal Balfas from detention in the Philippines.[45] That Washington's antiterrorism policies are facing problems in Indonesia was clearly evident in the allegations of Lieutenant-General Zen Maulani, the former head of National Intelligence, when he argued that the "sole Superpower" was using "anti-terrorism" to gain control of Indonesia:

> [S]ince Indonesia had many islands, a population of 220 million and some Muslim extremists, the U.S. analysts concluded that *Al Qaeda* network must exist here....The U.S. was trying to create the image that there is an *Al Qaeda* network in this country to force the Indonesian Government to act more firmly, more proactively in taking part in the fight against what the Americans label "terrorism." [However] the Washington's main aim was to weaken the forces of Islam in Indonesia and to control its abundant natural resources, to maintain its sole superpower position, its war and economic industries should survive, and they need oil. The world's largest oil producers are in the Islamic world and that is why there is a need for U.S. hegemony over the Islamic world. [In this endeavor] the U.S. was bent on dividing Indonesia into smaller states so that none would have the power to stand up to it. They are applying a preventive strategy to prevent Islamic countries, including Indonesia, from becoming advanced countries.[46]

Additionally, the nature of ASEAN, interstate differences as well as the strategic nature of the Islamic community in each country will also place brakes on the effectiveness of American antiterrorist posture and policies in the region. While ASEAN has come of age, it remains, relatively speaking, a weak organization. Regional politics has traditionally centered on noninterference and consensus between states as the basis for any discussion and policy in the regional organization.

It is this understanding that has successfully managed interstate tensions. It is precisely this approach that has also prevented the region from binding together in a collective effort against terrorism. ASEAN countries have been loathe to see interference in their domestic affairs by another neighbor, and this has greatly militated inter-ASEAN cooperation in counterterrorism. Ironically, some countries in the region, such as the Philippines, have found it easier to request military assistance from the United States rather than from a fellow ASEAN counterpart. The point being, most states in Southeast Asia find it easier to cooperate at the international level; however, most of them are faced with domestic tensions and conflicts at home because different groups have different opinions on this issue, leading to interstate relations being cohesive while intrastate ties tend to be more divisive.

Added to this, even though ASEAN has committed itself to combating the scourge of terrorism, its ability to do so has been greatly hampered by growing differences among its member-states over various issues. While disagreements over defining what terrorism covers is rather universal following the September 11, 2001, incident, what has come to the forefront has been the different approaches adopted by member states to tackle the menace and the preparedness of Singapore, a strategic U.S. ally and essentially a Chinese majority state with a sizeable Muslim minority, to openly criticize Indonesia for not doing enough to tackle terrorism in the country. Both of these developments have affected ASEAN's effectiveness to tackle terrorism in the region, thereby weakening the United States' ability to manage the problem in the region. What these problems highlight is the lack of a united front in Southeast Asia in the creation of a terrorist-free region. Additionally, due to the increasing political clout of political Islam in Indonesia, Jakarta finds it increasingly difficult to crack on the various hard-line Islamic groups, and is not prepared to tolerate actions being taken against suspected Indonesian terrorists in the region. This was evident in the Indonesian government intervention that led to the release of a number of terrorist suspects when they were arrested in the Philippines in 2002.

Finally, what has appeared to the most serious obstacle in stamping the terrorist threat in the region has been the presence of a large Islamic community that is not always supportive of government policies as far as antiterrorism is concerned. In countries such as Indonesia, Malaysia, Thailand, and the Philippines, there has always been a certain degree of unease and suspicion that antiterrorism is just another cloak to undertake anti-Islamic policies, and this has militated government's action against the bona fide terrorist groups. How to undertake counterterrorism policies against Islamic-oriented terrorist groups without appearing to be anti-Islamic is one of the most difficult challenges facing governments in the region, particularly in Indonesia, Malaysia, and Brunei, where the Islamic political constituency is also the largest and somewhat sizeable in Thailand, Singapore, and the Philippines. Together, these developments have placed limits on U.S. ability to undertake counterterrorist actions and ensure that strategically important Southeast Asia is free from the threat posed by terrorism, especially to American interests.

CONCLUSION

The emergence of a regionwide terrorist network that has been operating in a clandestine fashion for more than a decade and one that has global linkages is a new type of challenge confronting the Southeast Asia region. Unlike the Cold War challenge posed by communism, what makes the AJAI challenge all the more dangerous and difficult to manage lies in its ability to camouflage its activities behind the cloak of Islamic practices *albeit* radical in nature. In fact, many of its adherents have been seduced into the AJAI brand of terrorism through this route. As such, other than detecting and managing the AJAI, governments in the region are in a dilemma as they must be seen to be suppressing the threat posed by terrorism, and not Islam.

The Bali bombings and the Marriott Hotel explosion revealed that the AJAI terror network is very much alive and possibly more potent than before. The "Group of 272" formed from the number of Indonesians who fought in Afghanistan means that the terror network has the ability to reinvent itself very quickly. Moreover, the group of suicide bombers committed enough to the cause of *Jihad* has significantly increased the potency of terrorist attacks in Indonesia and the region as a whole. On the whole, the latent pool of militants in Indonesia means that another Hambali, and another cast of *kamikaze* bombers, would appear in the headlines before long.

Terrorism in Southeast Asia is very much a problem that needs to be addressed on various levels. There is a need for the Southeast Asian region to demonstrate to the international community that it is able to handle the threat of terrorism in a concerted manner. The creation of a regionwide consensus to coordinate efforts would go a long way towards centralizing the effort against terrorism as well as sound out to the world that ASEAN is united in eradicating terrorism in the region. Due to various developments, mainly domestic in nature, in spite of platitudes to eradicate terrorism, Southeast Asian governments have been unable to agree on a common approach in tackling the problem. At the same time, it is crucial for ASEAN and the United States to recognize that the root causes of terrorism often lie in the domestic sphere. Issues of political misrepresentation, socioeconomic concerns, and religious diversity should be dealt with fairly and expediently so that there is little or no ground for terrorist elements to latch on to. It is equally important that the more moderate Muslim community in the region assert itself onto the international Islamic consciousness and call for a more moderate stand. It is undoubtedly beneficial for the religion that the common misconception that Islamic extremism is the cause of terrorism be curtailed. The United States should also take an active interest to help to create a security network as well as provide aid and expertise to resolve the domestic problems plaguing the region. Washington should also reexamine its Middle Eastern policy, especially in the light of the unfolding Israeli-Palestinian conflict. Already being criticized for bias in its Middle East policy, the United States should reconsider its options in the Southeast Asian region, as the region remains central in the fight against international terrorism.

At the same time, it is also clear that as the AJAI terror network cuts across national borders, there is an urgent need to disrupt the regional network, even in the movement of AJAI operatives, finance, and weapons. While nationally, all governments in the region are said to be doing considerably, what appears lacking is the regional political will. All the original ASEAN founding members, namely, Indonesia, Malaysia, Singapore, Thailand, and the Philippines are seriously threatened by the AJAI and have a long history of security cooperation. Yet, when it comes to managing the AJAI threat, despite increased intelligence exchange and sharing, there does not appear to be a strong signal that ASEAN as a regional organization is prepared to stem the AJAI menace. There is no ASEAN Anti-Terrorism Task Force or the like. As Admiral Dennis Blair, the former commander in chief of the U.S. Pacific Command, has stated, the challenge of terrorism "is beyond the resources and authority of any single country and its armed forces." As such, until and unless the ASEAN governments, particularly the founding members, get their act together, the AJAI threat will take a long time to manage. Is ASEAN waiting for another Bali attack or another J.W. Marriott Hotel bombing to occur before it will act militarily as a regional grouping? Is it not time for ASEAN to become a security organization in the management of terrorism? In the last 20 years or so, ASEAN has done well in managing conventional threats from outside. However, when it comes to nonconventional threats, be it attacks from financial speculators, haze, or the AJAI, it is always found wanting. If this lesson is not learned, then it can expect more attacks in the future.

Conclusion

Southeast Asia's Failure in Its War on Terror against Islamist Extremism and the Road Ahead

INTRODUCTION

Historically, the challenge of terrorism in Southeast Asia, be it religious in character or otherwise, has always been a mere national concern. It has taken the national authorities a long time to overcome these threats; hence, the protracted nature of the security threat as evident in the GAM challenge in Indonesia, the MILF and *Abu Sayyaf* challenges in the Philippines, and the threat posed by PULO in Thailand. The AJAI challenge is something new as it is not only a national threat to a number of countries in Southeast Asia (particularly Indonesia, Malaysia, Singapore, and the Philippines), but rather due to the character of the organization and linkages, its concerns have become regional and global in character. The security implications of the AJAI threat stems mainly from the character of its composition, organization, linkages, ideology, and mode of violent actions.

IMPACT OF THE AJAI THREAT IN SOUTHEAST ASIA

As Southeast Asian states organized themselves to manage the terrorism threat posed by the AJAI, a plethora of ramifications have emerged from the various policies adopted by governments in the region. As managing the AJAI also involves issues dear to the heart of most Muslims in the region, namely the role and place of Islam, there was a need to be sensitive lest the anti-AJAI policies are perceived to be nothing more than anti-Islamic policies, be it in Muslim majority states such as Indonesia and Malaysia or in Muslim minority states such as Singapore, Thailand, and the Philippines. At the same time, governments in the region also had to pay attention to the various external players, be it the United States, the leader state that has launched a war on terror since the 9/11 Incident or for that matter, Muslim states in the Middle East that have adopted antiterrorist policies and yet are highly defensive of things Islamic. There are three key categories of implications that are noteworthy—on the AJAI itself, at the domestic level in each country, and at the international level.

Following the 9/11 Incident, even though attention was focused on neutralizing the *Al Qaeda* threat, some governments in the region began to adopt a proactive policy in tracking terrorists in the region. Even though the AJAI was known to exist prior to 9/11, and the Malaysian government had already arrested some of its operatives such as Abu Jibril, the first real breakthrough occurred following the arrest of 13 AJAI operatives by the Singapore government in December 2001. Following this was a domino effect, with arrests being made in Malaysia, Indonesia, the Philippines, Thailand, Singapore, and Cambodia in the next few years. More than 300 AJAI operatives are under detention and many have been killed (see Appendix 3).

Even though the Australian government has maintained that there are between 3,000 and 5,000 AJAI members in Indonesia alone, as an organization it has suffered greatly as a result of crackdown by governments in the region and beyond.[1] Though AJAI is a clandestine organization, the most dangerous terrorist group in Southeast Asia, and possessing trained men, weapons, and explosive materials,[2] the various crackdowns and arrest of its operatives and key leaders have gravely disrupted its activities. According to one source in August 2004, though somewhat contentious, the AJAI is believed to have been "stripped of its ability to strike big anytime soon."[3] Singapore Home Affairs Minister Wong Kan Seng said in January 2004 that "the inner core [of AJAI, at least in Singapore] has been broken and disrupted" even though he also realistically added, "it would be naïve of us to believe that we are out of the woods."[4]

However, AJAI being a dedicated organization, the various crackdowns have had two major impacts on the premier terrorist organization in Southeast Asia. First, AJAI is believed to have fundamentally regrouped itself. As many of its key leaders have been detained in Singapore, Indonesia, Malaysia, and the Philippines, best testified by the arrest of Hambali, Abu Jibril, and Abu Bakar Ba'asyir as well as the killing of Fathur Rahman Al-Ghozi and Dr Azahari. Due to the lack of a strong leader, especially following Hambali's arrest, the remnants of AJAI members are believed to have regrouped. Even so, due to the clandestine nature of the AJAI, its primary infrastructure remains intact. Two subgroups are believed to have emerged in Indonesia:

> The first is headed by little known Islamic militants whose main task is to ensure the survival of the group by remaining largely inactive and underground. The second subgroup is made up of what intelligence officials call "kamikaze" or suicide group, attackers' intent on pressing ahead with fresh assaults.[5]

At the same time, the AJAI is believed to have evolved itself in two main phases. From 1990, and more specifically January 1993, when it is believed to have been formally established, to sometime in 1999, it was largely on a preparatory mode to strengthen itself organizationally and to prepare itself for future *jihadi* actions.[6] During this phase, it focused its attention on recruitment, infrastructure, and organizational buildup. Due to its cause and existence of strong leaders such as Abdullah Sungkar, Abu Bakar Ba'asyir, and Hambali, there was a high degree of unity in AJAI, especially as *Mantiqi 1,* based in Malaysia, was in control of all AJAI operations. However, once AJAI entered into the second phase, namely the operational one with the launch of various bombing attacks best evident in the multiple Christmas bombings and the many other bombings that have followed ever since, the group is believed to have suffered serious internal splits. On August 4, 2004, Brigadier General Pranomo, Indonesia's police antiterrorist chief, remarked:

> The *Jemaah Islamiyah* has split into two groups. There are the hardliners and those who want to compromise. The ones who want to compromise are not interested in terrorist attacks anymore while the hardliners are planning more attacks.[7]

The various AJAI attacks, especially on civilian targets, are believed to have split the organization. There are some who want AJAI to abandon attacks on soft targets, as it is considered immoral and cruel. This group argues that pursuing this approach will not result in the establishment of an Islamic state by 2025, as the Islamic heartland in Indonesia in particular would have reacted negatively towards AJAI. Instead, this group would like to focus its activities on religious indoctrination and building a base in the country by winning the hearts and minds of the populace. Partially confirming this split, in July 2003 the police chief in Semarang, Didi Widayadi, informed the public that the police had captured an AJAI document in Central Java, where the Islamic boarding schools (*pondok pesantren*), Islamic scholars, and teachers (*Ulama, Kiai and Ustad*) were targeted for penetration by the terrorist organization.[8] Opposing this group are the hard-liners, who believe that bombings and assassinations should continue, especially of Western targets and the various governments in the region, as these are the main obstacles to the attainment of an Islamic state in Indonesia and Malaysia, as well as the *Dauliah Islamiyyah* in Southeast Asia. Many believe that Hambali, the late Dr. Azahari Husin, Mohammad Nordin Top, Zulkarnaen, Umar Patek, and Dulmatin, among others, belong to the hard-liner group and are behind most of the bombings, including the two Bali bombings, the one at Hotel Marriott, and the one in front of the Australian Embassy in Jakarta.

The burgeoning split in AJAI has been confirmed by AJAI operatives themselves. Nasir bin Abbas, a self-confessed AJAI leader, stated that there were three main factions in the group, essentially bifurcating the movement into the "hard-" and "soft-" liners.[9] According to Nasir, "the third group is extremely radical. I suspect that this radical group is behind the terror and bombings in many places."[10] He confessed that alleged AJAI spiritual leader Abu Bakar Ba'asyir and he "belonged to the more moderate faction of the group and were at odds with key Bali suspects such as Imam Samudra and Amrozi."[11] He maintained that Ba'asyir had always called for peaceful means to establish Islamic law. There might be some credence in this, as Ba'asyir, the firebrand cleric, is known more for his radical preaching than for terrorism.

This was clearly evident following his criticism of those who participated in the Bali and Hotel Marriott bombings. In February 2005, he argued that religious extremists were wrong to stage attacks in Indonesia as "the world largest Muslim country was not at war with anyone. If Muslims wanted to wage *Jihad* or holy war against the United States, they should go to countries like Afghanistan".[12] He categorically stated that, "I don't agree with the Marriott bombers. Maybe their intention was to defend Islam but their method was wrong. If they want to fight America they should go to Afghanistan. *Jihad* by taking up arms should only be carried in conflict areas."[13] In the same vein, while Abu Bakar Ba'asyir argued that he understood "Imam Samudra's anger and unhappiness with the West", he however "disagreed and did not condone the harming of innocent victims in Indonesia when the first Bali bombing took place in October 2002".[14]

Echoing similar sentiments, in a report in February 2004, the International Crisis Group stated that there were sharp divisions between the radicals and conservatives within AJAI, best evident from their approach to the conflict in Poso and Ambon.[15] In the main, there were sharp divisions between the leaders of *Mantiqi* 1 and 2. When the AJAI was first set up in 1993, there were only two *Mantiqis,* 1 and 2. The third *Mantiqi* was established only in 1997. This was due to logistical and command problems in coordinating activities in Indonesia, East and West Malaysia, and southern Philippines. Following the fall of Suharto in May 1998, most of the key leaders in *Mantiqi* 1 such as Abdullah Sungkar, Hambali, and Mukhlas believed that Indonesia was "ripe" for *Jihad*.[16] However, *Mantiqi* 2 leaders such as Achmad Roihan, who opted for caution due to shortage of resources and manpower, also believed that "there were no clear operational targets."[17] Unlike Soviet-controlled Afghanistan, *Mantiqi* 2 leaders believed that there were no clear enemies to fight in Indonesia and preferred to implement "a long term strategy to build up cadres and a target date of 2025 for establishing an Islamic state in Indonesia".[18] Abu Bakar Ba'asyir's acceptance of the MMI leadership was also opposed by *Mantiqi* 2 leaders who believed that it was unwise for a leader of a clandestine organization like AJAI to exist side by side with an open one. Also, there were worries that there would be too many demands on Abu Bakar Ba'asyir and that he might neglect the running of AJAI.[19]

DOMESTIC IMPLICATIONS OF AJAI'S TERRORISM

First and foremost, many countries in the region have been subject to violent attacks. Thus far, both Indonesia and the Philippines have borne the brunt of these attacks. In the case of Singapore, the planned attacks were neutralized by effective policing and law enforcement measures, while the other Southeast Asian states have not suffered any attacks. However, some of the violence in southern Thailand has been attributed to AJAI, even though the primary blame is usually credited to the various separatist groups located in the region.

Second, in view of the AJAI's threat, most Southeast Asian states have been compelled to adopt various measures to contain the threat of terrorism. This has seen a plethora of legal and other law enforcement and counterterrorist measures being put in placed since the 9/11 Incident, and in particular following the Bali bombing in October 2002, that marked the first most serious terrorist attack in the region, even though there had been other attacks prior to it. The region has witnessed the tightening of laws to deal with the threat of terrorism, with many human rights groups arguing that democracy and liberty have often tended to be sacrificed at the altar of law enforcement. Both Singapore and Malaysia have been targeted by critics for liberally utilizing the Internal Security Act that provides for detention without trial of suspects.

Third, most governments in the region increasingly have began paying attention to various Islamic-related educational institutions and other organizations that are believed to have acted as "feeders" in providing potential recruits to the AJAI. In particular, the more radical Islamic educational institutions such as the *Pesantren, Al-Islam,* and *Pesantren Al-Mukmin* in Indonesia have come under government scrutiny. In Malaysia, the *Luqmanul Hakiem* (Islamic School) in Johor has been closed down. In Thailand, the government has tried to modernize the curriculum of the *pondok* schools. Similarly, radical religious institutions, be it mosques, charitable organizations, or Islamic-oriented foundations, have been placed under scrutiny of the state security apparatus. Fourth, related to the control of various educational institutions and the mosques, the moderate elements in society, which at any one time constitutes the majority of the populace, has been persuaded to speak up and take up leadership in order to deny a vocal but radical minority the role of national leadership, especially in Islamic affairs.

In view of the sensitive nature of the threat posed by terrorism and, more important, its management, governments have tried to adopt "national-oriented" policies in order to ensure that fissures do not take place in the national fabric, especially between Muslims and non-Muslims or between radical and moderate Muslims. Hence, the importance of nation-building policies lies in their attempts to deny the radical Islamists any opportunity to undermine national unity in any of the targeted states in the region.

EXTERNAL IMPLICATIONS OF AJAI'S TERRORISM IN SOUTHEAST ASIA

First, Southeast Asian countries have increasingly realized that individually they are unable to manage the AJAI threat, as the danger posed by it is regional in nature. This has seen increasing cooperation between some member states even though the collaboration, due to various national sensitivities, is still largely limited. There is limited cooperation due to different national priorities, different interpretations of terrorism, and the unwillingness of some governments to appear as "lackeys" of the United States in being overzealous in taking action against AJAI and its members. Furthermore, due to domestic pressures and the different legal procedures, it is not always possible for countries to judiciously act against alleged terrorists, as is the case in Singapore and Malaysia that have access to the ISA. There are also conflicts and issues between governments in the region that limit cooperation as far as terrorism is concerned. The unwillingness of the Singapore government to sign an extradition treaty with Indonesia, and the tense relations between Bangkok and Kuala Lumpur with regard to the separatist problem in southern Thailand, have placed limits on cooperation as far as terrorism is concerned, despite the public pronouncements that are made in the name of ASEAN.

Despite growing collaboration between Australia and Southeast Asian countries, particularly Indonesia, in managing the threat posed by the AJAI, Australian-Indonesian relations have "roller-coasted" due to Jakarta's unhappiness with the manner in which the Australian government is perceived to have insensitively approached the problem. Against the background of poor relations following Canberra's intervention in the East Timor issue, the emergence of differences between the two governments have been one of the major casualties as a result of the AJAI threat. Four Australian policies are particularly noteworthy in this connection.

First, in December 2002, Australian Prime Minister John Howard announced, following the Bali bombing, that preemptive action in another country was a legitimate response to terrorism. This gravely alarmed countries in Southeast Asia. Indonesia's ambassador to Australia, Imron Cotan, following discussions with Australian leaders claimed, "Australia had assured Indonesia and other regional countries it would not deploy troops under the government policy of preemption against a terrorist attack."[20] Two years later, on December 20, 2004, Howard repeated his earlier stance, arguing, "If I believed there was going to be an attack, a terrorist attack on Australia, and there was no alternative but action being taken by Australia, I would unhesitatingly take it to prevent that attack occurring."[21]

Second, the Australian government, without consulting or informing the Indonesian government, made several travel warnings to its citizens to avoid Indonesia during the holiday season due to the threat of a terrorist attack. Australian Foreign Minister Alexander Downer claimed that his government had "credible information" that Western establishments, including the Hilton Hotel in Jakarta, would be attacked, something that did not eventuate. The Indonesian Ggovernment was upset as Canberra did not share the information on which the travel warning was based with Jakarta. Indonesian Foreign Minister Hassan Wirahuda wanted Canberra to share the information with Jakarta rather than make a public announcement:

> If it is true that Australia has credible information, we hope Australia will give us the information. In fact, there has been close cooperation between the two countries' police in dealing with terrorism.[22]

Other Indonesian leaders were more critical of the Australian stance. The chairman of the Indonesian People's Assembly, Nur Hidayat Wahid, slammed Canberra's position as one aimed at harming Indonesian tourism:

The [Australian] statement can create the impression that Indonesia is not safe, that there are terrorists in the country and that people must stay away and this is very bad for us. As a friendly neighbor, Australia should have communicated with the Indonesian government and law enforcers.[23]

Third, similar to Howard's preemptive strike declaration, another tendency towards unilateralism that harmed Australian-Indonesian relations was Canberra's announcement of a new maritime security zone that sanctioned the monitoring of ships up to 1,000 nautical miles (1,800 kilometers) from Australian shores. Calling it a Maritime Identification Zone, ships heading to Australia were required to provide details of journey and cargo, and the Australian navy was sanctioned to intercept any incoming ship that failed to comply with the order. The Indonesian government response to the Australian maritime initiative was totally negative, rejecting it as a violation of international law and an infringement of the country's territory and sovereignty.

The Indonesian foreign minister rejected the Australian proposal, as it was believed to violate the 1982 United Nations Convention on the Law of the Sea, to which both Indonesia and Australia are parties. Questioning the range of the surveillance zone, up to 1,850 kilometers, he argued, "that goes as far as the Halmahera, Sulawesi and Java Seas, which cover two-thirds of Indonesian waters."[24] He registered Indonesia's rejection as "it breaches our maritime jurisdiction. We view this concept as having the potential for violating international maritime laws."[25] Defense Minister Juwono Sudarsono similarly rejected the proposal, arguing that "we will deploy our naval strength to deter the possibility of Australian ships entering Indonesian waters."[26] Strumming a similar hard line, then Indonesian Armed Forces Chief General Sutarto responded by stating, "the claims amounts to Australia entering our sovereign waters and I am sure they do not want us to do the same."[27] In the same vein, the chairman of the Parliamentary Commission in charge of Foreign Affairs and Defense, Mr. Theo Sambuaga, argued that the Australian proposal was to be rejected, as "Australia cannot do as it like unilaterally. It is provocative and violates our sovereignty."[28]

Not only was the Indonesian government opposed to the proposal, but some Australian observers were equally scathing in the criticism of the initiative. For instance, an Australian security specialist, Dr. Michael McKinley argued that the proposal reflected Australian insensitivity to Asia and will only bolster the view of Australia as a regional American deputy sheriff:

It links in with the PSI—it's sort of chapter two of that. It will be seen as another instance of Australia being the deputy sheriff. We seem unable to integrate with the region in a sensitive way. This is another part of the testosterone-driven strategic policy of the Australian government. If you looked from afar you would say Australia is trying to be a regional policeman.[29]

Fourth, in line with the Australian government's general hype with regard to Islamist terrorism in general, especially with a focus on Indonesia, it has dramatically increased its defense budget, including its announcement of a decision to purchase long-range missiles. Of particular interest was John Howard's announcement to establish a special "task force" to combat terrorism in the "region." In September 2004, the Australian prime minister announced an A$100 million plan to establish "flying squads" that would be manned by the Australian federal police with capabilities to combat terrorism in the region. As part of a five-year-plan program, it hopes to create six new police teams—two specializing in high-technology surveillance, two on counterterrorism intelligence, and two on terrorism investigations. According to the plan, four of the units would be based in Australia, one in Indonesia, and one in the Philippines. In Canberra's thinking, if a terrorist threat is identified, "the teams could fly in on short notice with approval of these countries."[30] The Indonesian government did not comment publicly on the proposal.

The Australian government has also been applying pressure on the Indonesian government to do more as far as counterterrorism was concerned. In this regard, it has pressured Jakarta to adopt tougher policies against suspected AJAI operatives and in particular Abu Bakar Ba'asyir, the alleged *Amir* of AJAI. Abu Bakar was detained in October 2002 following the Bali bombing. He was jailed for three years. The Indonesian court cleared him of treason, but convicted him of minor immigration and document forgery charges. Once he had served his term, Canberra and its allies, especially the United States, applied pressure on Jakarta to prevent Abu Bakar's release. In fact Alexander Downer argued that "if he (Abu Bakar) is to be released, then that obviously would give *Jemaah Islamiyah* a bit of revitalization."[31] Since mid-2006, Abu Bakar Ba'asyir has been a free man, even though there is external pressure and attempts by the Indonesian police to charge him for being an accessory to the Hotel Marriott bombing but to no avail so far.[32]

An important external impact of the threat of terrorism in general and in Southeast Asia in particular was the general restriction placed on the movement of people and cargo into the West, in particular the United States. The targeting of Muslim countries, especially the strict visa requirements for entry into the United States, was a case in point. Following the 9/11 incident, the United States also moved to ensure port infrastructure and commercial shipping were rendered less vulnerable to maritime terrorism. From December 2002 onwards, the United States began working with the International Maritime Organization to develop an International Maritime Security Code to address various perceived vulnerabilities. This entered into force on July 1, 2003, covering cargo ships with more than 500 gross tons on international voyages, port facilities serving ships on international voyages, passenger ships, and mobile offshore drilling units.[33]

Following the various attacks that were attributed to the AJAI in Indonesia and the Philippines, the international community, largely in unanimity, also moved to take action against the AJAI, an organization alleged to be "the strategic point" of the *Al Qaeda* in Southeast Asia. Following the Bali bombing in October 2002, both the United Nations and United States, together with many other countries such as Australia, Brunei, Malaysia, the Philippines, Singapore, South Korea, Thailand, and Timor Leste, among others, designated the AJAI as a terrorist organization.

On October 23, 2002, U.S. Secretary of State Colin Powell announced that his government was designating the AJAI as a "Foreign Terrorist Organization" (FTO) under Executive Order 13224. At the same time, the UN was also to do likewise. In his statement, Powell declared that "today's actions mark the first time the United States has simultaneously designated a terrorist group as an FTO, designated it under Executive Order 13224, and requested the relevant UN sanctions committee to include it on the list of those against which sanctions should be applied."[34] Under American legislations, once a group is designated as FTO, it bounds the United States to block the organization's assets in U.S. financial institutions, criminalizes the knowing provision of material support or resources to the organization, and allows members of the organization to be excluded from the United States.[35] On October 26, 2002, the UN listed the AJAI as a terrorist organization.

Almost a year later, on September 5, 2003, U.S. Treasury Secretary John Snow, during a trip to Southeast Asia, announced that his government was designating 10 AJAI members as "Specially Designated Global Terrorists" (SDGT). According to Snow,

> This designation is yet another important step in the ongoing effort by the international community to shut down Jemaah Islamiyah terrorist operations in Southeast Asia. Today's action identifies ten individuals at the heart of the Jemaah Islamiyah network. These terrorists have worked to achieve al-Qaeda's terrorist goals in Southeast Asia. They have plotted to assassinate international leaders, they have planned and supported attacks such as the Bali bombing – a horrific act that tool the lives of 200 people and wounded 300.

In addition to Hambali (Nurjaman Riduan Isamuddin) and Abu Jibril (Mohd. Iqbal Abdurrahman, who was designated a SDGT on January 21, 2003), the following were added to the list on September 5, 2003: Yassin Sywal, Mukhlis Yunos, Imam Samudra, Huda bin Abdul Haq (Mukhlas), Parlindunga Siregar, Julkipli Salim Y. Salamuddin, Aris Munandar, Fathur Rahman Al-Ghozi, Agus Dwikarna, and Abdul Hakim Murad.

As part of the regional endeavor to manage the threat posed to AJAI, terrorism in general, and specifically with reference to maritime terrorism, the Five Powers Defense Arrangement (FPDA)—a military grouping established in 1971 that brought together Australia, New Zealand, Great Britain, Singapore, and Malaysia—for the first time in September 2004, staged a counterterrorism exercise at sea. It was argued that this would be the future direction of its strategy in view of the emergence of maritime terrorism as a potential threat in the region. According to Colonel Chew Men Leong, the Republic of Singapore Navy fleet commander:

> In the post–September 11 environment, it is insufficient for the FPDA to focus just on training against conventional threats. This will help position the FPDA to be able to deal and fight the growing terrorism threat in the region.[36]

WHITHER AJAI AS A TERRORIST ORGANIZATION

Due to the Islamic majority of Southeast Asia, political authorities in the region, especially in countries such as Indonesia, Malaysia, and Brunei, and even where there is a sizeable Muslim presence as in Thailand and the Philippines, are often in a dilemma in addressing challenges posed by Islamic organizations for fear of being accused of being anti-Islamic, as this could result in a backlash from the Islamic political constituency. It is due to this that authorities in the region, especially following the emergence of the AJAI threat, were quick to announce that the problem did not arise from Islam *per se* as much as it was from terrorism. While there were concerted efforts to distinguish the two, in reality this was more easily said than done. There have also been attempts to promote the rise and dominance of moderate Islam while ensuring that Islamic radicalism was stalled and stemmed in the Southeast Asian region. Even though the region by and large is dominated by *Sunni* Islam of the moderate variant, there are strong but influential pockets of radical Muslims in the region that have been the main source of inspiration, support, and recruits for the AJAI and its intents.

Yet, at the same time, it cannot be denied that political Islam is an important factor all the more in societies where there is a perception that the majority community discriminates the Muslim minority or, in Islamic-majority societies, where following the Asian Financial Crisis, there is a belief that secular politics and state management had failed to solve the problem of the majority of the people. This was clearly highlighted by Mr. Kobsak Chutikul, a member of Parliament in Thailand from the Chart Thai Party. According to him:

> There is no cause to be alarmist [about Islamic dominance in Southeast Asia]. The traditional, syncretic Islam of Southeast Asia, suffused with Indigenous Malay and other traditions, co-existing for centuries with many races and beliefs, is not the most fertile soil for Islamic fundamentalism. But then again, Islam itself has never been the problem. The vulnerabilities of the region stem not from the presence of a large Islamic population, but from the unique mix of relatively open, modernizing societies with a high degree of visible Western influence and presence coping with the after-effects of economic crisis and continued uncertainties in the midst of hard-core squalor and poverty in many areas—some of which correspond to ethnic and religious divides, creating disenchanted groups who in a globalized setting are now able to reach out for support from outside for their own domestic agendas and who, in turn, are susceptible to influence and manipulation for the wider external agendas of others.[37]

What makes the management of the AJAI threat all the more difficult and challenging is the fact that it operates like an amoeba. In fact, a senior Indonesian intelligence officer likened the AJAI to a hydra-headed monster. Thus, even if one country in Southeast Asia succeeds in containing and neutralizing the "national" AJAI threat, this is not a sufficient condition in the management of the AJAI danger. For the AJAI threat to be managed definitely, all the countries in the region, at least where the four AJAI *Mantiqis* are operational—Indonesia, Malaysia, Singapore, Thailand,

Myanmar, the Philippines, and Australia—must cooperate and undertake joint actions to manage the scourge. Otherwise, the threat posed by the AJAI as a regional terrorist organization will remained unmanageable, as it will be able to find safe havens and sanctuaries in one country or another. Particularly important here will be the policies of Indonesia, Malaysia, and the Philippines, the three countries that have become the primary "hosts" of the AJAI and its leaders and fighters. What this also implies is that as long as there are no regional mechanisms to manage the AJAI, the threat of terrorism from it will remain for a long time to come.

Until the September 11, 2001, attack, Southeast Asia did not figure prominently on the international "terrorism map" despite it being a victim of terrorism for such a long period. Only the *Abu Sayyaf* had figured prominently in the "who's who" list of terrorist organizations that was compiled by the U.S. government. Since then, the United States has added six new groups to the list of terrorist organizations. Two of these are non-Muslim organizations, the New People's Army and the Alex Boncayao Brigade, both of which are from the Philippines. All the rest are Islamic organizations, including the MILF from the Philippines, GAM from Indonesia, *Al-Ma'unah* from Malaysia, and the regionwide-based AJAI. This shows that Southeast Asia has emerged as an important front for the West, especially the U.S. war on terror, and this is best evident in the deployment of more than 1,000 American troops in southern Philippines (Exercise *Balikatan*) to contain the threat posed by the *Abu Sayyaf* and MILF. This also implies that there are international resources that can be tapped to manage the AJAI, as it is regarded as part of a global threat, especially to the West. It is thus imperative that countries in the region dovetail their national and regional policies in such a way that a three-pronged approach is adopted—national, regional, and international—to overcome the danger posed by the AJAI to peace and security in the region.

WHY IS SOUTHEAST ASIA LOSING THE WAR ON TERROR AGAINST ISLAMIST EXTREMISTS?

If Southeast Asia is likened to a beautiful placid blue-water lake, then what has been happening since the 1980s has been its steady pollution by poisonous weeds that endangers its ecosystem. Not only has the lake been losing its blue-water beauty and placidity through new turbulences, but even more ominous has been the introduction of dangerous weeds that is threatening the very existence of the lake community. The poisonous weeds are a consequence of Islamist extremism and terrorism. The rise in turbulence and loss of placidity are evident from the ascendancy of religious-based conflicts and violence, with Islamist terrorism and extremism being primarily responsible for this phenomenon. What is most worrisome about this process is the apparent inability of states in the region, especially in countries such as Indonesia, Malaysia, the Philippines, and even Thailand, to stall the march of Islamist extremism. It has become *de rigueur* to argue that there is no danger of Indonesia becoming an Islamic state because most Indonesians practice "a moderate strain of Islam and are tolerant of different religions" and that "the nation's founding fathers never wanted Indonesia to be an Islamic state." At the same time, what is undeniable is the rise of radicalism that is putting down roots and even becoming institutionalized, with both Muslims and non-Muslims as its victims.[38] If anything, most of the victims of terrorism perpetrated by Islamist extremists are Muslims. The process of Talibanization has been taking roots in the region, in turn, fuelling the threat by Islamist extremism.

The Talibanization of Southeast Asia can be understood from a number of perspectives. While the radicalization is not similar in terms of the same breadth and depth as it was in Afghanistan, what cannot be denied is the concerted adoption of radicalized Islam in the region. In many ways, while historically Southeast Asian Islam was described as "moderate" and "syncretic," what has gained momentum is the concerted efforts to "purify" the religion in the region. This means "returning to the fundamentals," eliminating "impurities" and the adoption of Islamic orthodoxy. In many ways, Southeast Asian Islam, particularly in Indonesia, is becoming an antithesis to its past image of openness and tolerance. There are also growing ties between political parties with fundamentalist Islamic groups, best evident in the rise of the *Partai Keadilan Sejatera* (PKS, or the Prosperous Justice Party) and *Partai Bulan Bintang* (PBB, or the Crescent Star Party) in Indonesia. These are also the two key parties that have been advocating the adoption of *Sharia* in Indonesia.

There is also the growing opposition of "decadent Western values and ideas," evident from the campaigns against alcoholic drinks, prostitution, and pornography. Religious minorities are also being marginalized and persecuted. With the inclusion into government of elements from the extremist parties, there is a rising sense of legitimacy of these elements, and society as a whole seems to be slipping towards radicalism. Most important of all, there is an attempt to nurture and promote the Islamic identity with Indonesia, Malaysia, and Brunei being projected as "Islamic states." It is within these interstices that Islamist radicalism is able to thrive and grow, and that makes the war on terror that much difficult to win. While the battle of killing a few terrorists might be won, the same cannot be said of the war, as there are many factors that militate this, as creeping radicalism is gaining center stage in many Southeast Asian countries. The Southeast Asian "lake" is being polluted with extremist ideology, and unless effective counterpollution and draining strategies are put into place, what has been dubbed as the "second front" in the war on terror stands the danger of emerging as the new front line of the threat.

The process of Islamist radicalization is evident on a number of counts. First, there have been widespread attacks on persons and properties of non-Muslims. While in Ambon and Poso, the attacks on Christians have continued, a similar trend is evident in southern Philippines and southern Thailand, where Christians and Buddhists have been targeted respectively. In Indonesia, dozens of churches and Christian houses of worship have been burned all over the country. For instance, according to the Indonesian Communion of Churches, in 2005, 23 churches were burnt in West Java alone.[39] Even more startling has been the concerted targeting of fellow Muslims who have been accused of being infidels and apostates. In Indonesia, throughout 2005, two groups of Indonesian Muslims were targeted. First, mobs organized by the FPI attacked mosques and buildings of *Ahmadiyah,* a minority Islamic sect that does not recognize Muhammad as the last prophet. Second, a new group, *Jaringan Islam Liberal* (JIL or Liberal Islam Network), which promotes tolerance and pluralism, was attacked and its offices closed in Jakarta.

In September 2005, the Malang District Court jailed Yusman Roy, a Muslim preacher, for introducing Indonesian translations of Muslim prayers (originally in Arabic).[40] With the spread of democratization, local administrations are also becoming more *Sharia*-oriented through the imposition of Islamic laws. Many local administrations have instituted bans on the sale of alcoholic drinks, as was instituted in Tangerang, Banten. In all these developments of creeping intolerance, the *Majlis Ugama Indonesia,* (MUI or Indonesian *Ulema* Council), Indonesia's highest Islamic authority, endorsed through its religious edicts or *fatwas* the persecution of the *Ahmadiyah* and JIL, signaling that Islamic radicalization was being increasingly institutionalized. The MUI declared *Ahmadiyah* a heretical sect. As was argued by Dr. Nur Syam from the *Sunan Ampel* State Institute of Islamic Studies, "radical movements have penetrated state structures through political parties, government bureaucracy and other institutions, including MUI."[41] While some would argue that what is taking place is actually *sharia*-mindedness, this has nevertheless widened the corridors for radicals to operate, with Talibanization as the ultimate consequence.

Radicalism is also gaining ground due to its ability to penetrate and imbue many *Pesantrens'* (religious schools) curriculum with radical ideologies. In 2004, the Indonesian police reported that an important AJAI document was seized that discussed the targeting of 140 *Pesantrens* in Central and Eastern Java as part of the bid to spread Islamist radicalism and militancy.[42] According to Didi Widayadi, the police chief in Central Java, "documents seized during the recent arrests of JI members had the names of 141 *pesantrens* and 388 Muslim clerics written down as targets to be imbued with their ideology."[43] As *pesantrens* penetrate into the poorest and most remote parts of Indonesia, the ability of Islamist radicals to penetrate these institutions could mark the turning of the tide in favor of radicalism in years to come. These efforts merely demonstrate the activism and strategies the AJAI and other radical groups have implemented in order to ensure that a *Dauliah Islamiyyah* emerges in Indonesia.

The state's unwillingness to offend local Muslims, fearing that it will be branded as anti-*Islam,* has also strengthened the hands of the radicals. As was argued by Azyumardi Azra, "radicalism is already there but sometimes it increases because of the failure of the government to enforce law and order."[44] A survey of JIL in 2005 showed that 18 percent of Muslims supported hard-line Islamic groups, with 6.5 percent being actively involved in it. According to Hamid Basyaid, JIL's executive, it "may be the number might seem insignificant but out of a population of over 200 million, it can be quite significant. It is enough to build their own country."[45]

As such, the rise of Islamic radicalism is clearly discernible, a process that is referred to in Indonesia as *"Santrinization."* While most Muslim scholars are loathe to concede that radicalism and Talibanization is on the ascendancy, what cannot be denied is the rising adherence to Islamic orthodoxy in the region. Despite initial assertions that Southeast Asian Islam tended to be "impure" due to its infusion with local beliefs and practices, many scholars had already observed the trend towards greater Islamic orthodoxy in the region.[46] From the 1980s onwards, the adoption of greater piety was particularly evident. At the same time, governments in the region also became more conciliatory towards Muslims, best evident in the establishment of various institutions such as Islamic banks and educational institutions (*madrassahs,* state polytechnics, and universities) to "co-opt" the growing assertive Islamic populace.

It was in view of these developments that in November 2006, Abu Bakar Ba'asyir was confidently arguing that the *Jihadists* and proponents of *Sharia* were winning in Indonesia. This, he argued, was due to a number of factors. First, this was inevitable as Indonesia was a Muslim majority state and it was only a matter of time before the consciousness would arise and awaken the masses. Second, the international community, especially the West under the leadership of the United States and Israel, had demonstrated how they intend to hurt, and how much they were hurting, Muslims all over the world—the latest being in Lebanon, with Israel's invasion being condoned by the global community. Third, Indonesia's democratization and, more important, the introduction of regional and local autonomy have allowed for a "bottom-up" approach with *Sharia*-oriented policies spreading throughout the archipelago as Western-induced polices of the republic have been at best counterproductive, and at worst have harmed and condemned Muslims to poverty and backwardness, while being suppressed and brutalized by the state apparatus.[47]

It was, however, the transnational factor that was particularly significant in radicalizing Muslims in the region. In a way, as far as Islam was concerned, the Southeast Asian region was historically always the periphery to the center based in the Middle East. As such, adopting ideas and practices from abroad, especially the Middle East, was not novel or difficult. Due to the various developments in the Middle East, there was a rise of "scriptural orthodoxy," and this was "exported" to Southeast Asia. In addition to the availability of information technology, the main conduit for this inflow was the many students and religious teachers who studied in the Middle East, as well as the many Middle Eastern teachers who visited the region to spread the new ideology of *sharia*-oriented Islam.

Many of the returnees also established Islamic presses to spread the Message. For instance, the *Al-Ishlahy* Press published the writings of Hassan al-Banna, Mustafa Masyhur, and Sa'id Hawwa. *Media Dakwah* published Sayyid Qutb's *Ma'alim fit Thariq* in Indonesian as *Petunjuk Jalan* (*Milestones,* or *Sign Post on the Road*). Over and above the role of Saudi *Wahhabism* and the 1979 Iranian revolution, radical ideas of Middle Eastern scholars such as Qutb, Maududi, and al-Nabhani, as well as movements such as *Al-Ikhwan-al-Muslimin* and *Hizb al-Tahrir,* have also inspired Muslims in the region. To these array of developments, the 9/11 Incident and the subsequent American invasion and occupation of Afghanistan and Iraq had the effect of dramatically radicalizing Muslims in the region. This proved the orthodox-oriented scholars right that the West, dominated by the "Jewish-Christian" power structure, had indeed launched a "war against Islam." All these developments created the image of the "Other" as the enemy of Islam, and one that had to be countered politically, ideologically, and even militarily.

The quantum leap towards Islamic radicalism and military is most vivid in Indonesia, the largest Muslim state, which has in the past been described as "moderate" and whose Islam is among the "least Arabized." While Indonesia has been experiencing "low-level" radicalization, in the main, radical Muslims and their teachings were held in check by Suharto's military-dominated New Order. While President Suharto adopted conciliatory policies towards Islam from the 1990s onwards, this was mainly to strengthen the moderate elements to undermine and marginalize the radical fringes, most of whom were operating from abroad or underground. The highly fragmented nature of the Islamic elite also proved helpful, and largely weakened and delayed the onslaught of the radicals. While Suharto's government was largely successful in checking the radicals at home, at the same time he was fighting a losing battle due to the growing influence of transnational forces, especially from the Middle East, that were "creeping" into Indonesia through the spread of scriptural orthodoxy. If anything, Suharto's authoritarianism forced many Muslims to seek refuge in religion, thereby widening the base of the radicals. Not only was the ruling GOLKAR party also affected by this "green virus," but so was the guardian of the New Order, the Indonesian military.

While leading Indonesian scholars such as Professor Azyumardi Azra remained in denial, arguing that "there is very limited room for radical discourses and movements in Southeast Asia in general. It is therefore simply wrong to assert that Muslim radicalism in the Middle East will find a fertile ground in Southeast Asia,"[48] unfortunately, the reality is just the reverse. Pockets of radicalism are already deeply entrenched in the region, especially in Indonesia. Even Professor Azyumardi has observed that "there can be little doubt that the September 11, 2001 tragedy did rapidly radicalize certain individuals and groups among Muslims in Southeast Asia, particularly in Indonesia."[49] As far as Indonesia is concerned, the 1997 Asian Financial Crisis and the rapid impoverishment of the country also strengthened the hands of the radicals. Following Suharto's fall, the emergence of weak governments led to the breakdown of law and order, and this provided hitherto unavailable channels for the radicals to operate and assert themselves. The democratization of Indonesia, and in particular the abolition of the "anti-subversion law," permitted, as far as Islamic radicalism was concerned, the "100 flowers to bloom." The weakening of law enforcement agencies (especially the military and police), were important factors that accounted for the rise of Islamic radicalism in Indonesia, now operating under various legitimate structures and institutions of the third-largest democracy in the world.

While reform and renewal in Islam has an age-old past, what is particularly important is the brand of Islam that has been increasingly promoted. As "guardians" of Islam, Saudi Arabia is also the capital of *Wahhabism,* a highly orthodox and puritanical Islam. As the Muslims have historically been weakened in the last few centuries, many have sought to regain strength by reinvigorating Islam from within, a process referred to as *tadjid* and *islah,* meaning renewal and reform, respectively. This can be undertaken both peacefully and by force. One of the most important renewal movements in Islam is the *Salafi* movement, closely identified with *Wahhabi* Islam. Professor Azyumardi distinguishes two types of *salafi* movements. "Classical *Salafiyyah*" is seen as peaceful, while "Neo-*Salafiyyah*" is viewed as being radical in nature.[50] Increasingly, in Indonesia, the neo-*salafists* have gained ground, and this largely explains the trend towards Talibanization in the country.

In a nutshell, following the heels of the United States, even though Southeast Asia launched its war on terror at the end of 2001, this war is not being won due to a number of reasons. First has been the ability of the radicals to exploit the anti-U.S. environment and public anger over the Iraq War, Lebanon, and other issues. As many have argued, the American actions worldwide, especially against Muslims, have been one of the main sources of recruitment for the cause of Islamist radicalism. Second, following from the above, is the growing perception that the U.S. "war on terror" is nothing more than a camouflage for a "war on Islam." This has resulted in many joining the ranks of radical groups to defend Islam. As was argued by Azyumardi Azra, "I think the problem now with this kind of U.S. foreign policy is that it alienates moderate and secular-minded Muslims. It is difficult for them when the radical take to the streets and it is difficult for the moderates to take sides with the U.S. on values like democracy."[51] Third is the increasing inability of governments in the region, especially in Muslim majority states to be proactive in the war on terror for fear of being labeled as anti-Islamic or pro-American lackeys. Fourth is the apparent failure of governance in most of Southeast Asia. While many radicals are motivated to launch *Jihad* for personal salvation, at the same time there are sufficient other causes to adopt terrorism, and these include the perpetual cycle of poverty, corruption, injustice, poor education, and religious and ethnic conflicts, flammables that have assisted in aggravating the situation in the region. Finally, due to the sophisticated manner in which the extremists are operating, it has become increasingly difficult to detect the growth of radicalism as they operate on a cell system and expand through a system of member-get-member. All these factors are signposts indicating that the region is fighting a losing war of terror against the Islamist extremists in the region.

MOVING AHEAD BUT THREADING CAUTIOUSLY IN OVERCOMING THE AJAI MENACE

From the manner in which all Southeast Asian countries have supported the United Nations' move to label the AJAI as an international terrorist organization, it is clear that all are united in recognizing the AJAI as a serious threat and want it to be stemmed out. Yet at the same time, it must be realized that not all countries in the region can adopt robust antiterrorist measures as have been adopted by the United States, United Kingdom, Australia, Singapore, or even the Philippines. This is primarily due to the influence, power, and sensitivities of political Islam and the manner in which the majority of its adherents in the largely Islamic-dominant countries, especially in Indonesia and Malaysia, view the problem. This is due partly to past experience of the United States' anti-Islamic stance and its present policy of condoning "state terrorism" of Israel against the Palestinians, as well as the Islamic populace's experience with their own government's persecutions, particularly in Indonesia. Most Muslims tended to be both cautious and wary of measures that are tantamount to be anti-Islamic in character.

This has serious short-to-medium implications for the Southeast Asian region in particular. As such, whatever is undertaken nationally, regionally, and internationally in the name of antiterrorism, governments must ensure that the Southeast Asian region does not become destabilized and, more importantly, make it difficult for moderate, secular-oriented Islamic leaders to rise and rule in Islamic-majority countries such as Indonesia, Malaysia, and even Brunei. This is because it is obvious that one of the long-term goals of the AJAI is to discredit and de-legitimize the ruling elites in the region and replace them through "internal or near *Jihad.*" If caution is not heeded, then the national, regional, and international community would, wittingly or unwittingly, be playing into the hands of the AJAI and assisting it to achieve its long-term strategic goal in the region.

In this connection, Western governments—particularly the United States, Britain, and Australia—have not helped, as they have adopted what can be interpreted as anti-Islam rather than antiterrorist measures. One example of this is the U.S. State Department's November 2001 decision to place more stringent visa application procedures on Muslim men from 25 Islamic countries, including Malaysia and Indonesia. This gave the impression that the United States was waging war against Islam, not against terrorism. Similarly, the heavy-handed manner in which the Australian security apparatus went around the country searching for AJAI operatives after the Bali bombing did not go down well in the region, leading Prime Minister Mahathir Mohammad to comment that if Southeast Asia was not safe for travel for Westerners, then similarly, countries such as Australia are not safe for Muslims.[52]

At the same time, both Indonesia and Malaysia, due to its increasingly democratic setup and culture—something the West played a role in promoting—cannot be expected to be heavy-handed against its citizens who subscribe to Islamic radicalism (not terrorism), as the ruling elite might suffer a backlash from its electorate. Hence, the need for caution in managing the AJAI threat cannot be understated. It is in this regard that while the war against terror has been launched, it cannot be fought with the same vigor and lack of sensitivity as it is being fought in certain parts of the world. If this is done, then it might unleash all kinds of complications, especially if outsiders are seen to be interfering in the internal affairs of a particular state and ignoring the due process that are in place, especially in countries that are increasingly democratic.

For this one need not go far to observe its consequence, as even neighbors are capable of causing irritations to one another. For instance, when Singapore Senior Minister Lee Kuan Yew described Indonesia as a "nest for terrorists" in January 2002, it immediately brought a negative reaction from Indonesian leaders and its people, accusing Lee Kuan Yew of being an "American puppet and mouthpiece" and the insensitive leader from a neighboring country in which he is known. Dewi

Fortuna, a foreign policy adviser to former President B. J. Habibie commented on Lee's comments in the following terms: "SM Lee's words do reverberate. What he says damages the image of Indonesia even further, especially when we are trying to refurbish our image."[53] One of the latest leaders to weaken the "united front" against terrorism in the region was Australia's Prime Minister John Howard, when he commented on December 1, 2002, that his country was prepared to undertake a "pre-emptive strike" against terrorists in neighboring Asian countries.[54] This immediately brought about negative reactions from the region, almost in the same manner when the Australian prime minister had earlier remarked in late 1999 that he was prepared to act as the "Deputy Sheriff" to the United States in the region.[55]

While the war against terrorism is being fought on a worldwide basis, in Southeast Asia, the AJAI has been identified as the key terrorist group that has to be neutralized. In the management of the AJAI threat, various sensitivities will have to be taken into cognizance, with each country neutralizing AJAI's ideology and operatives within the limits of its political, economic, social-cultural, and security parameters.

AJAI'S FUTURE?

With the detention of the AJAI's top leaders, including the *Amir* Abu Bakar Ba'asyir (who was later released), his successor Abu Rusdan, the operations chief Hambali, and the perpetrators of the two Bali bombings, the Marriott Hotel bombing, and the Kuningan bombing, the operations of the terror network have been severely crippled. This is more so as the AJAI's plan to extend its tentacles to other parts of the region has been successfully foiled with the arrests of Arifin Ali, Maisuri Haji Abdulloh, Muyahi Haji Boloh, and Waemahadi Wae-dao in southern Thailand, and an Egyptian, Esam Mohamid Khid Ali, and two Thais, Haji Ichiming Abdul Azi and Muhammadyalludin Mading, in Phnom Penh, Cambodia. Another 15 linked to Abu Rusdan, including a Malaysian national, Syamsul Bahri, alias Farhan, and a Universitas Semarang professor, Bambang Tutuko, alias Abu Umar, were captured in separate arrests in Jakarta, Central Java, and Lampung that began in the middle of August 2003. Their arrests have prevented the terrorist plot to blow up the Indonesian police headquarters. With the effective counterterrorism in the Southeast Asian region, it is thus worthwhile to ponder over the potential of the AJAI threat in executing terrorist attacks. Essentially, is AJAI "dead"?

The answer is a definite "no." Despite years of persecution, the survival ability of the *Darul Islam* (DI) organization, from which the AJAI originates, indicates the possibility that the AJAI will follow the same path. Notwithstanding the political repression by Suharto's New Order regime, the concept, roots, aspirations, etc., of the DI, *Tentara Islam Indonesia* (TII) and *Negara Islam Indonesia* (NII) remained in Indonesia's body politic, only that it was never allowed to surface and pose a challenge to the political order. Likewise, the AJAI and its unyielding commitment to the cause of *Jihad* and the establishment of a *Daulah Islamiyah Nusantara* has left its mark in the region.

This study has demonstrated that the decentralized organizational structure of the AJAI has led to its ability to reproduce itself very quickly despite the capture of members of various operation cells. The AJAI operates like an amoeba, or a hydra-headed monster. It will not be long before another Hambali or another cast of suicide bombers make the headlines. Also, the pool of previously dormant militants, or "sleepers," provides a ready supply of reserves for terrorist operations. Among other supporters of the AJAI, the potent force of the "Group of 272" in Indonesia consists of experienced war veterans who have fought in the Soviet-Afghan war. Furthermore, indoctrinated with fundamentalism, militant youths from the "Ngruki alumni" and other radical Islamic schools' alumni networks are ready to die for the cause of *Jihad.*

So long as the root causes of terrorism remain, the persistence of the AJAI organization or other terror network is ensured. The failure of "nationalist projects" to deliver political, economic, and social goods has led to counteractions, namely the adoption of the "Islamic mode" of political, economic, and social development, including the use of terrorism and violence, to remedy what is perceived as national, regional, and global injustices. This is because national and international injustices are usually blamed for the populace's backwardness and violence (*Jihad*) is often recommended as the only alternative to overcome the national as well as the *ummat's* (Islamic community) problems worldwide.

The region of Southeast Asia may have foiled various terrorist plans with the arrest of key AJAI members. Yet, this is not to assume that the region is safe. The Bali and the Marriott Hotel bombings are stark reminders that the AJAI terror network is all but crippled. The capacity of the AJAI to regenerate and reorganize itself continues to challenge the security of the region. The key to fighting terrorism is to prevent it from happening in the first place. This necessitates a regional, if not a global, counterterrorism endeavor not only to fight the AJAI organization, but also to remedy the root causes of terrorism. While Australian Prime Minister John Howard's call for unilateral preemptive strikes against other neighboring countries is unfitting in a global community governed by international laws, cooperative actions (military strikes or otherwise) between countries in the region to prevent terrorist attacks are effective measures to combat terrorism. The key to successful counterterrorism in the region is thus cooperation.

When President George W. Bush declared the war on terror following the discovery of the AJAI network in Singapore in December 2001, slowly but steadily, almost the whole of Southeast Asia and other extraneous stakeholders from the Asia-Pacific region and beyond have similarly acted in concert to contain the threat posed by what has been described as the "*Al Qaeda* point in Southeast Asia." Countries in the region, unilaterally, regionally, and internationally have taken counterterrorism measures to stamp the threat. This has led to more than 300 arrests, including that of its leaders such as Hambali, as well as the death of key figures such as Fathur Rahman Al-Ghozi and Azahari Husin. All ASEAN countries have declared AJAI as a terrorist organization, and cooperative measures are being undertaken to stem the menace. Most countries have antiterrorist laws to deal with danger. Also, by most counts, the organizational structure of AJAI has been crippled with *Mantiqi* 1 and 2 in disarray. What has been a further blessing has been the intense divisions with the terrorist organization, especially between the pro-bombing and pro-preaching groups. Support for AJAI is also believed to be dwindling, mainly in reaction to the indiscriminate bombings that have resulted in the death of innocent people and massive destruction of property and economy of the country.

However, while the AJAI might appear to be down, it is certainly not out. If there is any lesson from the past, especially from the DI, internal divisions have never deterred *Jihadist* movements from continuing their operations. If anything, there is a danger that these might become even more dangerous and lethal. While AJAI is an important terrorist organization, having a head start in the region since the mid-1980s, what is even more frightening is the emergence of new groups around new *Jihadi*-based personalities (the super-empowered individual with a cause) who are even more militant and difficult to detect. New militant and extremist wings are sprouting and where intergroup collaboration is based not on organizational link but more on personal ties, ideological convergence, and through the concept of a "common enemy." As such, what Talibanization has achieved in Southeast Asia is that even if the tumor is removed from the head, this does not mean that the danger is over, as the cancer might have spread to other parts of the body.

In this regard, following the death of Azahari Husin in October 2005, one of the most dangerous AJAI leaders, Nordin Top Muhammad, is alleged to have started a new group, the *Tanzim Qoidatul Jihad.* Whether it is part of AJAI or not has become irrelevant, as what is dangerous and the real threat is mission of such an organization. Thus, what AJAI has done to Southeast Asia is exactly what *Al Qaeda* has done to the world, namely, to spread the ideology of terrorism. While *Al Qaeda* has spread *Al Qaedaism,* similarly, in Southeast Asia there is what can be called as *AJAIism.* What this means is that just like *Al Qaeda* and Osama are no longer needed for global Islamist terrorism, AJAI, Sungkar, Abu Bakar Ba'asyir, and Hambali are no longer needed for Southeast Asian terrorism, as it now has its own logic and *modus operandi,* and a unending supply of leaders and adherents who are prepared to pursue and die for the cause.

All this points to the fact that the "Southeast Asian Sea" has been increasingly accessible, receptive, and fertile for Islamist extremism and terrorism, and the balance of power is slowly shifting in favor of the latter. This is in line with the pro-preaching (*Dakwah*) faction of AJAI and the Islamist extremists that want to neutralize any opposition to them and eventually takeover the region from within through democratic means by 2025. This will mark their eventual triumph. While force is necessary, even more important is the "soft power" approach to victory, and inadvertently, the West and governments in the region have undertaken many policies that have abetted and assisted the eventual triumph of the extremists and terrorists. Thus, even though many AJAI members have been arrested and the organizational structured disabled, this has amounted only to the "partial draining of the pond," as there is a lack of willingness and capacity to deal with the threat due to the fear of an immediate Islamist backlash. Also, the Islamists have succeeded in socializing the society that a heavy-handed approach towards them is tantamount to being anti-Islamic. The continued presence of key charismatic AJAI leaders such as Nordin Top, Zulkarnaen, Abu Dujana, Dulmatin, Umar Patek, Asep, and Zulkifli means that the threat is far from over. How the region is going to deal with the fact that there are simply too many angry, highly motivated, and highly trained individuals who are prepared to make the ultimate sacrifice for their cause is one of the most difficult tasks facing counterterrorism strategists.

MANAGING AND TERMINATING THE AJAI THREAT IN SOUTHEAST ASIA—SOME POLICY PROPOSALS

While there is no denial that all Southeast Asian governments are committed to the war against terrorism, it is evidently clear that due to various constraints, this war is not being won. The fact that the AJAI had more than a decade head start before it was accidentally discovered, and that many of its regional associates and allies have been operating in various parts of the region for many years (even decades) and have successfully entrenched themselves, due mainly due to governmental failures, merely means that much more needs to be undertaken before the war is lost to the terrorists. Some of the actions and policies needed would include the following:

Need for Greater National Coordination of Policies

Nationally, there is a need for different agencies to collaborate more closely. Nationally, the different agencies, especially police, armed forces, antiterrorist units, customs and immigration, and intelligence need to work together and not compete with each other. Even the United States, recognizing this necessity, had appointed a single "intelligence czar" to coordinate the various intelligence agencies to ensure that another 9/11 type of incident does not happen.

Need for Greater Regional Coordination of Policies

Parallel to greater collaboration nationally, there is a dire need to coordinate policies regionally. ASEAN governments have signed many agreements, yet when it comes to the crux, there are serious difficulties, especially between Indonesia, Malaysia, and Singapore, the core ASEAN countries. All three countries, which are facing a heightened AJAI threat, need to do much more than what has already been undertaken. In addition to the existing policies, there is a need for a protocol on what to do when a terrorist or terrorist suspect is being pursued or caught. There is a need for a Standard Operational Procedure (SOP) as well as a Common Identification Code as far as the AJAI and other terrorists are concerned. Countries must agree who the terrorists are, and what acts constitute terrorism.

Understanding Political Islam, Islamic Extremism, and Potential Recruits for Terrorism

As long as governments in the region and elsewhere fail to understand the phenomenon of Islamist terrorism, no matter how many terrorists are caught or killed, the "flow" will not cease to swell the ranks of the AJAI, and the problem will simply not disappear. If anything, it might get worse. Understanding political Islam will assist in unraveling the AJAI's secrets of recruitment and how, despite multiple setbacks, the movement has continued to grow, and even more important, how it is never short of suicide bombers for its missions. Hence, the urgent need to understand political Islam, how *"lunak"* or moderate Muslims are metamorphosized into extremists and terrorists, and to undertake measures to win the hearts and minds of the Muslim populace.

Here, the keys to unraveling the puzzle would be to understand the importance of the individual and family. As elsewhere, the family is under increasing pressure, and it often fails in holding its members together. This leads to several of its members going astray. If this is the situation of the family, the community and nation is in an even more debilitating position. Hence, to save the individual, there is much that the family can still do, especially in developing countries that are found in Southeast Asia. The main reasons individuals are prepared to adopt and sanction the terrorist cause is due to their ideological beliefs, as was evident in the transformation of Imam Samudra from a grandson of an Indonesian nationalist to one championing the cause of terrorism. Individuals, due to various reasons, are confronted with a sense of vacuum, which enables terrorist entrepreneurs and mobilizers to exploit the situation by offering them a sense of fellowship, mission, and even paradise in afterlife. Thus, to prevent the individual from being lost to the cause of terrorism, the family as a unit must be strengthened. The importance of family values needs stressing so that it can act as an antidote to the "joys" of terrorism, even death, that is usually propagated by terrorist groups such as the AJAI.

Harden Resilience of Hard and Soft Targets

In the face of the AJAI threat, it has become axiomatic to hear that governments and counterterrorist agencies have busied themselves in hardening various hard and soft targets. Hence, government buildings that are of political, military, economic, and even symbolic importance have been secured through a whole array of measures to ensure that the terrorists are not able to attack and destroy them. Similarly, soft targets such as beaches, supermarkets, and other places where the masses gather, though much more difficult to secure, have been strengthened through greater presence of the security apparatus as well as various public education policies instituted to educate the citizenry about potential threats. These measures are important and have gone to some length to deny the AJAI simple targets of opportunities.

Yet, the single most important soft target that needs hardening is the individual. As long as the terrorists cannot attack and win over the individual, the terrorists' long-term plans and strategies are unlikely to succeed. Hence, everyone involved in the war against terrorism—the government and its various agencies—must concentrate on the single most important unit that exists in any society, the individual. As long as the individual is fortified from being won over by terrorism, the AJAI or any other terrorism group will not survive in the long run. This is where the main concentration must be emphasized and various comprehensive policies undertaken to win the war.

Conflicting Sphere of Operations between the Government and Terrorists

Why are people prepared to join the cause of terrorism? Why are they prepared to undertake the ultimate human sacrifice, to die for a cause, and joyfully, too? It is partly due to the fact that they believe the death of a martyr is a blissful one, in which all their afterlife wishes would be fulfilled. To that extent, terrorism involving sacrificing oneself is ideologically motivated, in this case, by religious ideology. If the ideology emanates from religion, then undertaking a terrorist act can be interpreted as a manifestation of a political statement. In a way, not only are religiously oriented terrorists prepared to die, they actually want to die! While governments may premised their counterterrorism policies on the basis that terrorists might want to live and hence, policies should be introduced that would induce them towards this cause, in reality it does not work, as the terrorists and governments are working on two different, divergent, and even conflicting planes.

The spheres in which the terrorists and governments are working might be totally opposite. If governments employ militaristic tools to contain terrorism, it is bound to backfire and prove counterproductive. If anything, by killing the terrorists, governments are strengthening and fulfilling the wishes of the terrorists, as they want to die joyfully as martyrs. This partly explains, in the case of Indonesia, why despite all the arrests made following the Bali, Marriott Hotel, and Kuningan bombings, the number of terrorists in the country has not decreased. It might just have the opposite effect. Also, one might find the behavior of the Bali bombers such as Ali Imron, Mukhlas, and Imam Samudra—who, being sentenced to death, joyfully welcome it —merely proves that they were looking forward to the death sentence. Anything less would have meant a "failure," for martyrdom would not have been achieved. Using the analogy of supply and demand of resources, governments cannot deplete terrorists by killing them; doing so actually helps in the replenishment, as more recruits are likely to be won over to the cause. Thus, the more nonrenewable resources one exploits, the more they become depleted; yet in the case of terrorism, the more terrorists are caught and killed, the more quickly it renews and replenishes themselves, as it will likely draw more recruits to the cause. It is thus vitally important to understand the psyche and psychology of the terrorists if one wants to effectively manage the scourge.

Silent Mainstream vs. Vocal, Proactive Minority Muslims

The majority of Muslims, especially in Southeast Asia, are moderates and law-abiding. They shun and oppose terrorism and deviant interpretation of Islam. Individuals and groups involved in terrorism are only a small fraction of the community at large and constitute a minority. In order for counterterrorism to be successful and to ensure that the Islamic community opposes terrorism, the radical minorities in the community must be sidelined, with the moderate majority taking leadership of the community. Otherwise, a vocal minority will hijack the community and make it appear as if the entire Islamic community is supporting a radical posture, when indeed it is nothing more than a political project of a militant minority within a particular community. In reality, there is a "world of moderates" and a "world of extremists," and the faster the former takes charge, the more quickly the war against terrorism will be won and the world's Islamic community given its rightful honored placed among the great religions of the world.

The Battle of Ideas

One of the fronts where the war against terrorism should be fought is not in the jungles or hideaways of terrorists, but on the intellectual front. In the end, it is the battle of ideas that will win this war. The ideology of hatred and violence that is being peddled by political Islamists must be countered. As the Islamic religion is being used as a cover to achieve a political goal, either a *Syariah*-oriented society or an Islamic state, there is a need for Islamic moderates and intellectuals to challenge the ideas put forward by extremists that have been winning adherents for terrorism and suicide bombings.

Challenge of Injustice

In any society, socioeconomic inequalities are normal and can be expected. In Southeast Asia, these are marked, as they would be in other regions of the world. When individuals or groups decide to exploit socioeconomic inequalities as injustices, then the issue is moved into the political plane. This can provide the potentials for terrorism to grow, and this is what governments and societies should be mindful of. In addition to doing the utmost through good and responsive governance to overcome the problems of socioeconomic inequalities, efforts must be made to neutralize the politicization of these issues by terrorist entrepreneurs and mobilizers.

Remove Global Reference Points That Assist Terrorist Recruitments

Increasingly, Western, especially American, policies have assisted the blossoming of terrorism worldwide. When the United States decided to support Islamic militancy and terrorism in its conflict with the USSR in Afghanistan from 1979–89,

Islamist terrorism, including Osama Bin Laden and the *Al Qaeda,* received their most important boost from Washington and the West. President Ronald Reagan described the likes of Osama and the *Mujahidin* as "freedom fighters," along the same line as American freedom fighters. When the Soviets "lost" and were forced to withdraw, the Islamists credited the victory for themselves, the self-styled *Mujahidin.* Since then and until 2001, Afghanistan, whether under the *Mujahidins* or Taliban rule, had become the single most important training ground for Islamist terrorists the world over and one of the most important success stories of Islamists.

What further aided the terrorist cause was the existence of various reference points that the Islamists could use to justify their version of *Jihad* and hence keep the flow of recruits to their ranks. Among others, the reference points include the continued Israeli brutal repression of the Palestinians; Washington's double standard of endorsing Tel Aviv's cruelties, while condemning those of the Palestinians; the United States' apparent anti-Islamic policies worldwide; the placement of American soldiers in what is dubbed as Islamic holy land, especially in Saudi Arabia; and, under Bush, its Afghan and Iraq invasions, which have come to be viewed as nothing more than "right-wing Christian crusades" against weak Islamic states. The Islamists have been adept in using Western labels and practices to win adherents, and this partly explains the neverending support for Islamist terrorism all over the world, including Southeast Asia. At the same time, the hypocrisy with which the West, especially the United States and its allies, champions democracy and human rights and yet tolerates "icons" of modern *gulags,* be they in Guantanamo, Bagram Airbase (Afghanistan), or Abu Ghraib,have merely benefited the cause of terrorism.

Appendix 1 ———————————————————————

General Guidelines on the Struggle of Jama'ah Islamiyyah (Excerpts)

FOREWORD

Islam prescribes that life on earth is a path that leads man to the Hereafter. Separating life and worldly affairs from acts of worship in its totality and the search for values before Allah marks the onset of calamity in man's life.

There are several divine stipulations governing man's life. First, man's life is only to worship Allah. Hence, all worldly possessions, be they time, energy and thoughts should be dedicated to the worship of Allah. Second, man in Islam is Allah's khalifah (vicegerent) on earth. Hence, his tasks include administering the world and ensuring that it thrives in accordance with Allah's laws. Third, the worldly life is a time of trial for man to identify who among them has dedicated the span of his life in virtuous deeds. Verily, virtuous deeds are deeds carried out for Allah's sake and in accordance with the prophetic traditions. Fourth, the Prophets are sent by Allah to uphold the religion, and the religion, according to the mufassirin (commentators on the Quran), is *Dienul Islam* (Islam) in every aspect, which according to "Abdullah bin Umar," in his explanation of the *Al-Fatihah* (the opening chapter of the Quran), encompasses *'aqidah* (faith), *ibadah* (acts of worship) and *manhajl-hayah* (way of life).

The *Pedoman Umum Perjuangan Al-Jamaah Al-Islamiyyah* provides the general guidelines on the Jama'ah's struggle. It gives a systematic picture of the principles and operational strategies of the Jama'ah.

The *Pedoman Umum Perjuangan* consists of:

1. *Ushulul-Manhaj Al-Harakiy Li Iqomatid-Dien;*
2. *Al-Manhaj Al-Harakiy Li Iqomatid-Dien;*

3. *Al-Manhaj Al'-Amaliy;* and

4. *An-Nidhomul-Asasiy*

The *Ushulul-Manhaj Al-Harakiy Li Iqomatid-Dien* are the ten principles on which all the other Manhaj (methods) created are based on. *Al-Manhaj Al-Harakiy Li Iqomatid Dien* are programmes based on the *Ushulul-Manhaj Al-Harakiy Li Iqomatid Dien,* and are carefully structured into systematic levels. *Al-Manhaj AI'-Amaliy,* meanwhile, are the general operational guidelines and *An-Nidhomul–Asasiy* are the set of rules and regulations for governing the Ja'maah's affairs.

Lastly, the Al-Jama'ah Al-Islamiyah strives to build up its strength for *izzul Islam wal-muslimin* (success of Islam and Muslims), restoring the *khilafah 'alaa Minhajin Nubuwwah* (The Prophet's style of leadership) and the sovereignty of Allah's laws on earth.

USHULUL MANHAJ AL-HARAKIY LI IQOMATID DIEN

I. Meaning

1. *Ushulul Manhaj Al-Harakiy Li Iqomatidien* refers to the main principles adopted for the struggle to uphold slam.

2. Uphold Islam refers to the establishment of a *Daulah Islamiyyah* (Islamic state) and followed by a *Khilafah Islamiyyah* (Islamic Governance).

3. The establishment of *Daulah* and *Khilafah Islamiyyah* is undertaken through the development of Muslim personnel, families and groups.

II. Function

Ushulul Manhaj Al-Harakiy Li Iqomatid Dien functions as the basis for *Al-Manhaj Al-Harakiy Li Iqomatid Dien* (Guidelines On Systematic Moves Towards Upholding Islam)

AL MANHAJ AL-HARAKIY LI IQOMATID DIEN (GUIDELINES ON THE STAGES OF UPHOLDING ISLAM)

I. Definition:

Al Manhaj Al-Harakiy Li Iqomatid Dien contains guidelines on the stages of upholding Islam.

II. Function:

It is built upon Ushulul Manhaj Al-Harakiy Li Iqomatid Dien and serves as the main guidelines for AI Manhaj AI Amaliy.

III. Stages:

The stages of Al Manhaj Al-Harakiy Li Iqomatid Dien are as follows:

A. Preparations to establish the Daulah (state)

1. Jama'ah-building through the:
  a. Formation of Qiyadah Ar-Rosyidah
  b. Formation of Qo'idah Solabah
  c. Implementation of Tanzim Sirri (secret organisation)
  d. Development of 1m an and as-sam'u wath thaatu
  e. Enjoinment of good and forbiddance of evil
  f. Hisbah

2. Strength-building through:
  a. Education
  b. Dakwah
  c. Hijrah (migration)
  d. Jihad
  e. Tajnid (military training)
  f. Qoidah Aminah (a safe base)
  g. Territorial establishment
  h. Diklat (education & training)
  i. Tamwil (financing)
  j. Jasus (spying)
  k. Co-operation with other groups

3. Use of Strength
  a. Dakwah (Indzar)
  b. Armed Jihad

B. Establishment of Daulah (state)

1. Daulah
  a. Tandhim (Hukumiy) (ruling system)
  b. Tajnid (military training)
  c. Jihad
  d. Tahkim (arbitration)
  e. Tamwil (fmancing)
  f. Establishing a Muslim community
  g. Tarbiyah (education)

2. Tatsbitud-Daulah (strengthening of the state)

3. Tansiq bainad-Duwal (co-operation with other countries)

C. Establishment of Khilafah (caliphate)

AL MANHAJ AL AMALIY LI IQOMATID DIEN
(GENERAL GUIDELINES ON OPERATIONS TO UPHOLD ISLAM)

I. General Definition

"Al Manhaj Al Amaliy Li Iqomatid Dien" means general guidelines on operations to uphold Islam.

1. Guidelines refer to the direction for achieving the objectives.
2. General means that:
   a. The guidelines serve only as a broad outline and members are welcome to use their initiatives.
   b. The guidelines are applicable to all and everyone in the Jama'ah.

II. Basis of Al Manhaj Al Amaliy:

1. It is built upon:
   a. Ushulul Manhaj Al-Harakiy and Al-Manhaj Al-Harakiy
   b. Characteristics and objectives of the Jama'ah
   c. Objective assessment of the Jama'ah's personnel, its enemies and surroundings
2. It shall remain in force indefinitely. Changes shall be made, but its main component shall not be changed or adulterated.
3. It may or may not be applied.

III. Its Scope

1. Al Manhaj Al Amaliy is divided into:
   a. Operations
   b. Administration
2. Operations and Administration shall complement each other.

IV. Strategy of Operations

1. Definition of Strategy:
   a. General method of gathering resources to achieve long-term objective.
   b. Tactics refers to deployment of resources to achieve a special short-term objective.
   c. Tactics is a small-scale strategy.
   d. Operations:

Military Terminology:

All endeavours, activities and actions that use the elements of strength to execute a guided plan at a certain time and location.

Elements of strength:

— Physical (mobility, use of arms, physical endurance)

— Non-physical (confidence, mental capacity, knowledge and management)

Plan: Operations must be carried out according to plan, but without ruling out other initiatives.

Guided: Operations' co-ordinator shall co-ordinate all tasks.

2. Procedure of the Operations Strategy (broad outline)

    a. To observe and analyse the Jama'ah, its enemies and surroundings.

    b. To choose from among the aspects of life that could serve as a potential strength.

    c. To develop potential strength for greater effectiveness.

3. Procedure of the Operations Strategy (detailed outline)

    a. To observe and analyse the Jama'ah, its enemies and surroundings.

    b. To make a frank assessments of the effectiveness of the Jama'ah's strength.

    c. To look for targets for attacks against the enemies.

    d. To make plan for programmes and operations.

    e. To discuss (c) with the leadership and the person to execute the plan.

    f. To conduct final testing.

    g. To decide on the operations strategy.

    h. To execute the plan.

4. How Operation Is Conducted

    — it should be based on the following cycle:

    — it should observe the following work mechanism:

       — centralise

- regulated decentralise, and
- non-regulated decentralise
- types of operations

i. Intelligence

ii. Development Strength

iii. Deployment of Strength

iv. Combat

DEVELOPMENT OF STRENGTH OPERATION

It involves a long process of developing potential into effective and ready for use strength.

- This operation shall include *diklat*(education & training) as well as personnel and territorial development
- This operation is best carried out before, during and after the establishment of *daulah* (state).

1. *Diklat* (education & training)

Definition:

a. It is the most important part in personnel development.

b. It is a process involving selection, recruitment, instruction, discipline building in the course to produce efficient and loyal personnel.

Scope of Work:

a. Physical preparedness and arms expertise.

b. Tactical thinking.

c. Strategic thinking.

d. Leadership vision.

Objectives:

- To produce skilful and loyal personnel who are able to work effectively and efficiently.
- To prepare reserve troops.

Basic Policies:

a. *Diklat*(education & training) is aimed at preparing personnel for all stages of work.

b. Staff of *Diklat*(education & training) are given full reign to carry out *diklat* but they shall observe closely the Ushulul Manhaj, Al-Manhaj Al-Harakiy and Al-Manhaj Al-Amaliy.

c. The curriculum shall be constantly reviewed and evaluated to maintain its relevancy.

d. The number of participants for *diklat* shall be determined by the size of the task and the situational needs.

Procedures:

a. The staff of *diklat*(education & training) shall be responsible in all affairs of *diklat* (education & training) as follows:

i. Overall planning including finding the location and accommodation.

ii. Deciding on the stages of *diklat* (education & training), selecting procedure and recruitment, drawing up curriculum and running the day-to-day affairs.

iii. Deployment of trainees shall be made with the consensus of the parties involved.

b. They shall make report of the participants' progress to parties concerned daily.

c. They shall make an evaluation report under the supervision of the central leadership.

d. They shall provide a complete report.

2. Development of Personnel

Definition: It refers to the development of members in the fields of:

a. Information/Recruitment

b. Education

c. Tajnid (military training)

d. Hisbah

3. Territorial Development

Definition:

a. Territorial development refers to the development of the territory's strength.

b. The area should include national territory or beyond.

c. Territorial development is best carried out before, during and after the establishment of *daulah*(state).

d. Territorial development shall be carried out by all members while the Qoidah Solabah shall serve as the main executor.

The development process will include a study on the territory's:

a. Geographical conditions

b. Demographical conditions

c. Social conditions

Areas of Work:

a. *Tarbiyyah Rasmiyah* (Education)

b. Da'wah

c. Administration

d. Support for the social conditions

4. Economic Development

5. Cooperation with other groups

NIDHOM ASASI
(BASIC RULES AND REGULATIONS)

Chapter I
Name, Characteristics and Area of Operation

Article 1

The jamaah (group) shall be called **"Al-Jamaah Al-Islamiyyah."**

Article 2

1. The Jama'ah is "Jama'atun minal Muslimin"
2. The Jama'ah is *'alamiy* (global) characteristically.

Article 3

Chapter II
Basis. Objects and Path of Struggle

Article 4

1. The Jamaah shall be based on the Quran and Sunnah which is consistent with the belief of the Salafus Solih
2. The object of the Jama'ah is to establish a *Daulah Islamiyah* (Islamic state) as a basis towards the restoration of Khilaafah Alaa Minhajin Nubuwwah.

Article 5

To achieve this objective, the Jama'ah shall undertake the following path of struggle: *dakwah, tarbiyah* (education), *amar m'ruf nahi munkar* (enjoining what is good and forbidding what is evil), *hijrah* (migration) and *jihadfi sabilillah* (jihad in the cause of Allah).

Chapter III
Tandhim

Article 6

1. The Jama'ah shall be led by an AMIR (leader).

2. In discharging his duties, the Amir shall be assisted by all the Majelis Qiyadah Leadership Council, Majelis Syuro (Consultative Council), Majelis Fatwa (Fatwa Council) and Majelis Hisbah (Hisbah Council).

3. The Majelis Qiyadah is made up of Majelis Qiyadah Markaziyah (Central Leadership Council), Majelis Qiyadah Mantiqiyah (Mantiqi Leadership Council) and Majelis Qiyadah Wakalah (Wakalah Leadership Council).

Chapter IV
Imaroh

Article 7

The Amir shall be nominated and appointed by the Majelis Syuro (Consultative Council).

Article 8

1. The Amir shall accept the *bai' ah*(oath of allegiance) of members;
2. The Amir shall appoint and expel members ofMajelis Syuro, Majelis Qiyadah Markaziyah, Majelis Fatwa and Majelis Hisbah;
3. The Amir shall conduct the meetings of the councils at Markaz level.
4. The Amir shall collect *infaq* (donations) from members, either on a routine or incidental basis;
5. The Amir shall mete out sanctions and punishments on members who violate the Jama'ah rules and regulations; and
6. The Amir shall establish relations with other parties that may benefit the Jama'ah.

Article 9

1. The Amir shall lead the administration of the Jama'ah;
2. In the course of administrating the Jama'ah, the Amir shall consult the Majelis Syuro, Majelis Qiyadah, Majelis Fatwa and Majelis Hisbah;
3. The Amir shall educate members on how to understand and practise Islamic teachings;
4. The Amir shall defend and protect members and look after their well-being;
5. The Amir shall enforce the implementation of Islamic law; and
6. The Amir shall delegate someone to represent him in his absence.

Article 10

An Amir shall cease to hold office when:

a) He dies;

b) He loses his personal capacity due to *uzur syar'i*(such as old age, ill health and other reasons that are permissible by Islam);

c) He is expelled by Majelis Syuro upon being found guilty of practising unIslamic acts; and

d) He is unable to run the Jama'ah according to the Islamic law due to external pressure.

Chapter 5
Majelis Qiyadah

Article 11

1. Members of Majelis Qiyadah Markaziyah shall be chosen and appointed by the Amir;
2. Qoid of Majelis Qiyadah Manthiqiyah shall be members of the Majelis Qiyadah Markaziyah;
3. Members of Majelis Qiyadah Manthiqiyah shall be nominated and appointed by Qoid of Majelis Qiyadah Manthiqiyah with the approval of the Amir.
4. Qoid of Majelis Qiyadah Wakalah shall be nominated and appointed by Qoid of Majelis Qiyadah Manthiqiah with the approval of the Amir;
5. Members of Majelis Qiyadah Wakalah shall be nominated and appointed by Qoid of Majelis Qiyadah Wakalah with the approval of Qoid of Majelis Qiyadah Manthiqiyah.

Article 12

1. All Majelis Qiyadah shall assist the Amir in administrating the Jama'ah in accordance to their level of authority and functions;
2. All Majelis Qiyadah under Qiyadah Markaziyah have the right to make decisions in accordance with their level of authority and functions;
3. Majlis Qiyadah Markaziyah shall set rules and regulations to ensure the smooth administration of the Jama'ah.

Article 13

1. A member of Majlis Qiyadah Markaziyah shall cease to hold office upon his death or being terminated by the Amir;
2. A member of Majlis Qiyadah Manthiqiyah shall cease to hold office upon his death or being terminated by the Qoid Majlis Qiyadah Manthiqiyah and with the approval of the Amir;
3. A Qoid of Majlis Qiyadah Wakalah shall cease to hold office upon his death or being terminated by the Qoid Majlis Qiyadah Manthiqiyah and with the approval of the Amir;
4. A member of Majlis Qiyadah Wakalah shall cease to hold office upon his death or being terminated by the Qoid of Majlis Qiyadah Wakalah with the approval of Qoid Majlis Qiyadah Manthiqiyah.

Article 14

The procedure of setting up the Majelis Qiyadah and associated organs that have not been incorporated will be regulated and organized through further information and regulations.

Chapter VI
Majelis Svuro

Article 15

1. Members of the Majelis Syuro shall comprise the *Dzu-Maalin*(people with wealth), *Dzu-Syaukatin* (people with influence) and members of the Jama'ah with certain expertise;

2. Members of the Majelis Syuro shall be appointed by the Amir;

3. Members of the Majelis Syuro shall be made up of 7 people:

a. 3 (three) to be appointed by the Amir, and

b. 4 (four) to be nominated by the Qoid of Mantiqiyah

4. Rais (leader) of the Majelis Syuro shall be appointed by the Amir upon the approval of members of the Majelis Syuro.

Article 16

1. The Majelis Syuro shall appoint and expel an Amir;

2. The Majelis Syuro shall introduce changes to the *Nidhom Asayiy*and make plans;

3. The Majelis Syuro shall have the right to put up proposals on the rules and regulations on pertaining to the administration of the Jama'ah; and

4. The Majelis Syuro shall make a global evaluation of the management of the Jama'ah.

Article 17

A member of Majelis Syuro shall cease to hold office upon his death, upon *uzur syar'i*or being terminated by the Amir.

Chapter VII
Majelis Fatwa

Article 18

1. Members of the Majelis Fatwa shall comprise the *Dzu'ilmin,*who also adhere strictly to the Quran and Sunnah;

2. Members of the Majelis Fatwa shall be appointed by the Amir; and

3. The Majelis Fatwa shall have a minimum of three members.

Article 19

1. The Majelis Fatwa shall reinforce the decisions of the Amir and correct him (Amir); and

2. The Majelis Fatwa shall be accountable to the Amir and shall have the right to make recommendations to the Amir.

Article 20

1. A member of Majelis Fatwa shall cease to hold office upon his death, upon *uzur syar'i* or being terminated by the Amir.

Article 21

2. The Majelis Fatwa shall have the right to consult other ulania outside the Jama'ah who are deemed to be credible and *'alim* (pious/knowledgeable)

Chapter VIII
Maielis Hisbah

Article 22

1. The Rais (leader) and members of the Majelis Hisbah shall be appointed by the Amir from among JI members; and

2. The Majelis Hisbah shall have a minimum of 3 members.

Article 23

1. Majelis Hisbah shall have control over the official and personal affairs of the Amir, his deputies and JI members on the whole;

2. Majelis Hisbah shall recommend to the Amir the sanctions and disciplines to be meted out to the Amir's deputies and all other members who violate, either officially or personally; and

3. Majelis Hisbah shall convene a court of justice in the event of violations by the Amir; and

4. In the event that the Amir has to be expelled for certain violations, the Majelis Hisbah shall call on the Majelis Syuro to convene a special meeting to discuss the Amir's expulsion.

Article 24

A member of Majelis Fatwa shall cease to hold office upon his death, upon *uzur sya-r'i* or upon being terminated by the Amir.

Chapter IX
Musyawarah (Meeting)

Article 25

1. The meeting of the Majelis Syuro, Majelis Qiyadah Markaziyah and Majelis Hisbah shall be convened at least once a year and shall be attended by the Amir or his representative;

2. The meeting of the Majelis Syuro or Majelis Hisbah shall be convened upon the request of one-third of the total members of each Majelis.

Article 26

The meeting of the Majelis Fatwa shall be convened at least once in three months and shall be attended by the Amir or his representative.

Article 27

The meeting of the Majelis Qiyadah under the Majelis Qiyadah Markaziyah shall be fixed by their respective Qoid.

Article 28

1. A meeting shall be considered valid upon the presence of two-thirds of the total membership of each Majelis;

2. In the event of there being no quorum, the meeting shall be adjourned for seven days later;

3. After the adjournment, if there is still no quorum, the meeting shall be convened with those present;

4. In the event of emergency, the Amir or members of the Majelis assisting him shall take the initiative to call for a meeting.

5. The decision of the meeting is considered valid by a majority vote.

6. With regard to the meeting of the Majelis Qiyadah Markaziyah, any decision made at the meeting shall be considered valid by a majority vote and an endorsement from the Amir; and

7. In the event of there being differences of opinion between the majority and the Amir, the Amir shall have the final say.

Article 29

The meeting shall be held as and when necessary and attended by the Amir and all the Majelis assisting him.

Chapter X
Membership

Article 30

An individual applying to join the Jama'ah shall:

a) *Be a Muslim who follows the aqidah (belief) of the salafus solih* and strives to ensure that his *ibadah* (acts of worship) are free from the elements of *bid'ah* (innovation) and *khurafat* (superstition);

b) Have knowledge of the teachings of Allah and His Messenger about the Jama'ah;

c) Have knowledge of the Usuhulul Manhaj al-Harakiy Ii Iqomatid Dien and be able to accept it;

d) Take the *bal'ah*(oath of allegiance) with the Amir of the Jama'ah, either directly, by proxy or in writing;

e) Have attained puberty; and

f) Have reached the *tamhiz* level.

Article 31

The responsibilities of a member shall be:

a) To hear and obey the Amir according to his ability in matters that do not involve vices;

b) To obey the rules and regulations of the Jama'ah;

c) To seek permission of the Amir and/or the Mas'ul if he is unable to discharge his duties;

d) To avoid actions that would bejeopardise the Jama'ah;

e) To assist the Amir if he is in the right and to correct him if he is in the wrong;

f) To defend and protect the Amir; and

g) To defend and protect fellow members.

Article 32

Members shall have the right:

a) To obtain guidance in understanding the teachings of Islam and in practising them;

b) To obtain care in social well-being cared for;

c) To offer views and suggestions as well as to correct the management of the Jama'ah at various levels;

d) To be nominated and appointed as Mas'ul and/or Mudabbir (functionaries); and

e) To get protection from the Jama'ah.

Article 33

Membership shall cease if a member fails to meet the membership criteria.

Chapter XI
Financial

Article 34

The financial source of the Jama'ah shall be derived from *infaq* (contribution), *shoda-qoh* (aim), *zakat* (tithe), other sources which are halal based on *ijtihad* (to exercise personal judgement based on the Quran and Sunnah or all the traditions and practices of Prophet Muhammad).

Article 35

The annual budget of the Jama'ah shall be fixed by the meeting of the Majelis Qiyadah Markaziyah and representatives ofMajelis Syuro, Majelis Fatwa and Majelis Hisbah.

Article 36

1. The procedure of allocating fmances to the Markaz and other levels under it shall be as stated in the rules and regulations.
2. Financial sources, assets and rules and regulations not available in any of the articles shall be taken into consideration.

Chapter XII
Economy

Article 37

Matters pertaining to economy shall be reflected in the rules and regulations.

Chapter XIII
Education

Article 38

Matters pertaining to education shall be reflected in the rules and regulations.

Chapter XIV
Communications

Article 39

1. Communications between the councils assising shall be made with the knowledge of the Amir;
2. Communications between the Majelis Qiyadah Manthiqiyah shall be made with the knowledge of the Amir;

3. Communicatons among the Majelis Qiyadah Wakalah shall be made with the knowledge of the Qoid of Majlis Qiyadah Manthiqiyah.

4. Communications between the various levels below the Majelis Qiyadah Wakalah can be arranged by the Majelis Qiyadah Wakalah.

5. Communications between members shall be made at the discretion of each Mas'ul.

Article 40

1. Communications between Majelis Qiyadah Manthiqiyah and the Amir or councils assisting the Amir shall be made through another party or with the knowledge of the Qoid of Majelis Qiyadah Manthiqiyah. Communications between the Qoid of Majelis Qiyadah Wakalah and the Amir or the councils assisting the Amir shall be made only with the consent of the Qoid of Majelis Qiyadah Manthiqiyah;

2. Communications between Majelis Qiyadah Wakalah and Qoid and/or members of the Majelis Qiyadah higher than the Majelis Qiyadah Wakalah shall be made through another party or with the knowledge of their respective Qoid.

Article 41

1. Relations with other Islamic organisations that share the JI principles and objectives, shall be based on the spirit of brotherhood and cooperation;

2. All Qoid shall establish relations with other organisations and institutions with the approval of the Arnir; approval of the respective Qoid;

3. Every n member shall establish relations with those outside the JI circles

4. Every member of the Jama'ah shall deliver talks to people outside the JI circles with the knowledge of the respective Qoid and should report it to his Qoid.

Chapter XV
Amendments and Additions

Article 42

1. A meeting to discuss a motion to introduce an amendment to the *Nidhom Asasiy* shall be attended by at least two-thirds of the total members of the Majelis Syuro.

2. A motion to introduce an amendment to the *Nidhom Asasiy* shall be considered valid for proposal to the Amir if agreed upon by more than half of the members of the Majelis Syuro.

3. An amendment to the *Nidhom Asasiy* shall be considered valid if approved by the Amir.

Article 43

This Nidhom Asasiy shall be carried out in stages

Clarifications

General Clarification:

1. This *Nidhom Asasiy*is created to serve as an administrative guideline in establishing a discipline towards upholding Islam;
2. This *Nidhom Asasiy*comprises a Foreword, Main Contents and Clarifications;
3. The Foreword comprises
4. The main contents ofNidhom Asasiy comprise 15 chapters and 43 articles on:

   — The identity and characteristics of the Jama'ah
   — Tandhim and lmaroh
   — Amendments and Additions

5. In the event there being differences of opinion in understanding this *Nidhom Asasiy,* the Indonesian version of the *Nidhom Asasiy validated on24 Rajab 1416H/17 December1995 shall be used as reference.*

THE FORMATION OF QO'IDAH SOLABAH

I. Definition

a. Literal meaning:
Al-qo'idah means base.
Solabah means solid.

b. Terminological meaning:
A core group of members with strong and solid characteristics that enable them to carry out the task of *"Iqomatid Dien"* (upholding of Islam).

c. The Formation of Qoidah Solabah:
It refers to planned and systematic efforts, activities and actions to use available resources.

II. ....

III. Functions of Qo'idah Solabah

1. To be the core leadership personnel.
2. To be the last bastions of the leadership.
3. To be a source of reference in matters involving the personnel
4. To be the main executor and defender of the Jama'ah mission.

IV. Criteria for Qo'idah Solabah

a. As an individual

— To be mentally, morally, ideologically and physically prepared for the struggle of the Jama'ah mission.

— To possess high mental, moral, ideological and physical endurance.

— To be highly disciplined.

b. As a group:

— To maintain close relationship among the personnel.

— To have a good teamwork.

— To have a high teamwork perseverance.

— To have a high teamwork discipline.

— To be a social prime mover.

c. Qo'idah Solabah As Potrayed in the Qu'ran:

1. As Party of Allah (Al-Maidah: 54-56), (Al-Mujadilah: 22)

2. As a small group (Al-Baqarah: 256)

3. As godly men (Ali-Imran: 146)

4. As the servants of Allah (Al-Furqon: 63-77)

5. As the men who are true to their covenant (An-Nur: 37); (At-Taubah: 108); (Al-Ahzab: 23)

6. As the vanguard of Islam (At-Taubah: 100)

7. As the foremost in good deeds (Fathir: 32)

8. As the nearest to Allah (Al-Waqi'ah: 10-26)

9. As Men of Understanding (Ali-Imran: 190-200)

10. As the Disciples/ Helpers of Jesus (Shof: 14), (Al-Maidah: 111)

11. As the true believers (Al-Anfal: 1-4 & 74)

12. As the successful believer (Al-Mu'min: 1-11)

13. As the best of people (Ali-Imran: 110)

14. As the helpers of Allah (Shaf: 14)

V. Methods of Forming Qo'idah Solabah

1. Selecting the personnel.

2. Introducing group specialisation.

3. Developing the right mentality, morals, ideology and physical strength.

4. Delegating tasks.

VI. Elements and Criteria of Tandzim Sirri:

— **Organisational Structure:**
Closed and simple (easy to implement)

— **Personnel:**
Disciplined and able to keep secret.

VII. Function of Tandzim Sirri:

— To keep the organisation safe and secure.

VIII. Methods of Implementing Tandzim Sirri:

— To be carried out by selected personnel.
— To be carried out covertly.
— To give periodic instructions and directives to members and leaders.

DEVELOPMENT OF JIHAD

I. Definition

a. Literal meaning:
To strive earnestly

b. Terminological meaning:
To fight in the cause of Allah with one's life, wealth, etc.

II. Definition of the development of Jihad

It constitutes efforts, activities and actions that are directed towards the carrying out of jihad.

FUNCTION OF THE DEVELOPMENT OF JIHAD

To prepare members to carry out *Jihad fie Sabilillah* or Jihad in the cause of Allah.

METHODS

1. **Personal**

a. Intellectual Development:

— To enlighten members on the justification to carry out jihad as well as on its laws and ethics.

b. Spiritual Development:

— To instil self-discipline, patience and trust in God.

c. Skills Development:

— To maintain *i'dad* (state of preparedness) and to pave the way for others to achieve that level of preparedness.

— To involve members in *jihad.*

2. **Development of Infrastructure**
3. **Development of Tanzim** (system)

TANSIQ BAINAL JAMA'AH

I. Definition

Literal meaning:
Tansiq means arrangement or coordination

Terminological meaning:
To cooperate with other groups so that the objectives of the Jama'ah can be achieved.

II. ....

III. The Criteria of Other Groups That We May Cooperate With

1. Groups whose *aqidah* (faith), objective and *wasilah* (way) are similar to ours.
2. Groups whose *aqidah* and objective are similar to ours but different *wasilah* yet still acceptable under Islamic teachings.

IV. Functions

1. To create *tafahum*(understanding), *ta'awun* (cooperation) and *takaful* (solidarity) among all Islamic groups with a view to share a common responsibility and objective of establishing a *Daulah Jslamiyah* (Islamic State) and *Khilafah* (Islamic system of governance).
2. To step up *I'dadul Quwwah* (physical/mental preparation).
3. To create a united Muslim community that will be able to counter its enemies.

AD-DA'WAH AL-INDZARIYAH

I. Preface

Before the launch of jihad, it is *wajib* (obligatory) to launch *Da'wah* (call to Islam) and issue firm *Indzar* (reminder).

II. Definition

1. Literal meaning:
Da'wah means: To call
Indzar means: To remind

2. Terminological meaning:
To urge the enemy to embrace Islam or surrender in peace before a war is waged on them.

III. Function

To offer the enemies of Islam, a last chance for them to accept Islam in total.

IV. Objective

To fulfil the obligation *of indzar.*

V. Target

To take note of the enemies attitude after issuing them with *indzar* so that a clear and accurate picture of them can be obtained.

VI. Method

a. Sending delegation to the enemies.

b. Announcing through the mass media

c. Delegating a third party to convey the message.

ARMED JIHAD

I. Definition

1. *Jihad Musallah* (Armed Jihad) means *Qital* (fight).

2. *Qital* is to fight the enemies of Allah such as non-Muslim authorities, the hypocrites, apostates, *zindiq* (atheists), *mustabdil* and their allies in the cause of Allah and His Messenger.

II. Functions

1. To destroy the influence of *toghut* (one who exceeds his legitimate limit; a transgressor) who has often prevented the setting up of an Islamic state according to the way of the Prophet. (Al-Anfal: 39)

2. To eradicate cruelty and uphold the truth so that destruction on earth could be prevented. (Al-Baqarah: 251- Al-Hajj: 39–40)

3. To safeguard the existence and dignity of Muslims and to assist those who are weak. (Al-Nisa: 75)

4. To humiliate and raise alarm among Allah's enemies and prevent them from creating mischief. (Al-Taubah: 29, Al-Anfal: 60, Al-Nisa': 84)

5. To separate the infidels/hypocrites from among the ranks of Muslims and to pave the way towards martyrdom. (Ali-Imron: 140–142)

6. To test one's faith (Muhammad: 4)

7. To maintain power on this earth to set up Allah's law Gustice) and live under Allah's *minhaj*. (39–41)

III. Target

To set up an Islamic state according to the Prophet's style of leadership. In the context of *manhaj harokiy, jihad bis silah* is targeted at the establishment of *Daulah Islamiyah* once again.

IV. Course of Action:

1. *I'dad* (To be prepared)
2. *Ribath* (To be alert and prepared)
3. *Qital* (To fight)

Appendix 2 ————————————————————————

ASEAN Agreements on Combating Terrorism

JOINT COMMUNIQUES

Joint Communique of the Fifth ASEAN Ministerial Meeting on Transnational Crime (AMMTC), Hanoi, Vietnam, 29 November 2005.

Joint Communique of the Second ASEAN Plus Three Ministerial Meeting on Transnational Crime (AMMTC+3), Hanoi, Vietnam, 30 November 2005.

Joint Communique of the 25th ASEAN Chiefs of Police Conference, Bali, Indonesia, 16-20 May 2005.

Joint Communique of the 24th ASEAN Chiefs of Police Conference, Chiang Mai, Thailand, 16-20 August 2004.

Joint Communique of the First ASEAN Plus Three Ministerial Meeting on Transnational Crime (AMMTC+3), Bangkok, Thailand, 10 January 2004.

Joint Communique of the Fourth ASEAN Ministerial Meeting on Transnational Crime (AMMTC), Bangkok, Thailand, 8 January 2004.

Joint Communique of the Special ASEAN Ministerial Meeting on Terrorism (AMMTC), Kuala Lumpur, 20-21 May 2002.

Joint Communique of the Third ASEAN Ministerial Meeting on Transnational Crime (AMMTC), Singapore, 11 October 2001.

Joint Communique of the Second ASEAN Ministerial Meeting on Transnational Crime (AMMTC), Yangon, 23 June 1999.

PRESS RELEASES

Joint Press Statement of the Informal ASEAN Ministerial Meeting on Transnational Crime Plus China Consultation, Hanoi, 30 November 2005

"ASEAN Strongly Condemns Terrorist Attacks in Bali, Indonesia," Statement by the 39th Chair of the ASC, Kuala Lumpur, 2 October 2005.

Statement by H. E. Somsavat Lengsavad, Deputy Prime Minister and Minister of Foreign Affairs of the Lao's People Democratic Republic, Chairman of the 38th ASEAN Standing Committee in connection to the terrorist bombing in Jakarta on 9th September 2004.

Co-Chairs' Statement of the Bali Regional Ministerial Meeting on Counter-Terrorism, Bali, Indonesia, 5 February 2004.

Statement by the Chairman of the ASEAN Regional Forum (ARF) on the Tragic Terrorist Bombing Attacks in Bali, Phnom Penh, 16 October 2002.

ARF Statement on Measures Against Terrorist Financing, Bandar Seri Begawan, 30 July 2002.

Statement by the Chairman of the ASEAN Regional Forum (ARF) on the Terrorist Acts of the 11th September 2001, Bandar Seri Begawan, 4 October 2001.

DECLARATIONS

ASEAN-India Joint Declaration for Cooperation To Combat International Terrorism, 8 October 2003, Bali, Indonesia.

Joint Declaration on Co-operation to Combat Terrorism, 14th ASEAN-EU Ministerial Meeting, Brussels, 27 January 2003.

Joint Declaration of ASEAN and China on Cooperation in the Field of Non-Traditional Security Issues, Phnom Penh, 4 November 2002.

Declaration on Terrorism by the 8th ASEAN Summit, Phnom Penh, 3 November 2002.

2001 ASEAN Declaration on Joint Action to Counter Terrorism, Bandar Seri Begawan, 5 November 2001.

Manila Declaration on the Prevention and Control of Transnational Crime, 1998.

ASEAN Declaration on Transnational Crime, Manila, 20 December 1997.

OTHER DOCUMENTS

ASEAN Convention on Counter-Terrorism, Cebu, Philippines, 13 January 2007.

Treaty on Mutual Legal Assistance in Criminal Matters, Kuala Lumpur, 29 November 2004.

Agreement on Information Exchange and Establishment of Communication Procedures.

Work Programme to Implement the ASEAN Plan of Action to Combat Transnational Crime, Kuala Lumpur, 17 May 2002.

Memorandum of Understanding between the Governments of the Member Countries of the Association of Southeast Asian Nations (ASEAN) and the Government of the People's Republic of China on Cooperation in the Field of Non-traditional Security Issues. ASEAN-United States of America Joint Declaration for Cooperation to Combat International Terrorism, Bandar Seri Begawan, 1 August 2002.

ASEAN Standing Committees Chairman's Letter to US Secretary of State Colin Powell on Terrorists Attack, Bandar Seri Begawan, 13 September 2001.

ASEAN Plan OF Action To Combat Transnational Crime, 1999, Manila.

Source: ASEAN Secretariat (Jakarta, 2006).

Appendix 3 ────────────────────────────

ASEAN's AJAI Operatives Who Have Been Detained, Released, or Killed (as of June 2007)

SINGAPORE

1. Abdul Majid, son of Niaz Mohamed
2. Abdul Wahab Bin Ahmad
3. Adnan Bin Musa
4. Andrew Gerard alias Ali Ridhaa Bin Abdullah
5. Azman Bin Jalani
6. Faiz Abdullah Ashiblie
7. Faiz Bin Abu Bakar Bafana
8. Fathi Abu Bakar Bafana
9. Fauzi Bin Abu Bakar Bafana
10. Habibullah, son of Hameed
11. Haji Ibrahim Bin Haji Maidin,
12. Halim Bin Hussain
13. Hashim Bin Abas
14. Husin Bin Ab Aziz
15. Ja'afar Bin Mistooki
16. Mahfuh Bin Haji Halimi
17. Mohamad Anuar Bin Margono
18. Mohamed Ellias, son of Mohamed Khan
19. Mohamed Khalim Bin Jaffar
20. Mohamed Nazir Bin Mohmmed Uthman

21. Mohamed Noor Bin Sulaimi
22. Mohammad Hisham Bin Hairi
23. Mohd Jauhari Bin Abdullah
24. Munain Bin Turru
25. Naharudin Bin Sabtu
26. Nordin Bin Parman
27. Othman Bin Mohamed
28. Said Bin Ismai
29. Sajahan Bin Abdul Rahman
30. Salim Bin Marwan
31. Sanin Bin Riffin
32. Simon Bin Sabtu
33. Syed Ibrahim
34. Zulkifli Bin Mohamed Jaffar

MALAYSIA

1. Abd Nasir Anuwarul
2. Abd Razak Baharuddin
3. Abdul Hanif Mansor
4. Abdul Manaf Kasmuri
5. Abdul Murad Sudin
6. Abdul Rashid Bin Anwarul
7. Abdul Razak Abd Hamid
8. Abdul Samad Shukri Mohd
9. Abdullah Minyak Silam
10. Abdullah Mohamad Nor
11. Abi Dzar Jaafar
12. Abu Bakar Che Doi
13. Agang Biyadi Ahmad Bunyamin
14. Ahmad Pozi Darman
15. Ahmad Sajuli Abd Rahman alias Fadlul Ahmad
16. Ahmad Tajuddin Abu Bakar
17. Ahmad Yani Ismail
18. Ahmadi Asab
19. Alias Ngah
20. Alias Othman

21. Alias Sani
22. Al-Bakry Mohamed Alias
23. Asfawani Abdullah
24. Ashraf Barretto Kunting
25. Azman Hashim
26. Azmi Khan Mahmood
27. Bakkery Mahamud
28. Dr Abdullah Daud
29. Eddy Erman Shahime
30. F Muchlis Abdul Halim alias Ferry
31. Idris Salim
32. Jafar Saidin alias Jaafar
33. Khaider Khadran
34. Khairuddin Saad
35. Masran Arshad
36. Mat Shah Mohd Satray
37. Mazlan Ishak
38. Mohamad Amin Musa
39. Mohamad Faiq Hafidh
40. Mohamamad Nasir Bin Abas alias Khairudin
41. Mohamed Lothfi Ariffin
42. Mohammed Kadar
43. Mohd Akil Abdul Raof
44. Mohd Azmi Abdul Rahim
45. Mohd Fadhali Abdul Raof
46. Mohd Ikhwan Abdullah
47. Mohd Kamrudzaman Samsudin
48. Mohd Nasri Ismail
49. Mohd Rashid Ismail
50. Mohd Salleh Said
51. Mohd Sha Sarijan
52. Mohd. Rafi Bin Udin alias Ferdiansyah
53. Mohidin Shaari
54. Muhamad Ismail Anuwarul
55. Muhamad Zulkepli Mohamad Isa
56. Muhamad Zulkifli Mohamad Zakaria
57. Muhammad Azian Abdul Rahman

58. Muhammad Radzi Abdul Razak
59. Murad Halimmuddin Hassan
60. Nasaruddin Nasir
61. Nik Abdul Rahman Mustapha Afifi
62. Nik Adli Nik Abdul Aziz
63. Noralwizah Lee Abdullah
64. Nordin Ahmad
65. Othman Mohd Ali
66. Rezzal Shah Jamal Shah
67. Roshelmy Md Sharif
68. Sabri Jaafar
69. Shahime Remli
70. Shahrial Sirin alias Syahrial Sirin
71. Shahril Hat
72. Shakom Shahid
73. Shamsuddin Sulaiman
74. Shamsul Bahri alias Farhan
75. Shukry Omar Talib alias Shukry B. Omar
76. Solehan Abdul Ghafar
77. Suhaimi Mokhtar
78. Sulaiman Suramin
79. Syed Ali Syed Abdullah
80. Wan Amin Wan Hamat alias Wan Min Wan Mat
81. Yazid Sufaat
82. Yusrin Haiti
83. Zaini Zakaria
84. Zainon Rashid
85. Zainun Ismail alias Cikgu Nan
86. Zamzuri Sukirman
87. Zid Sharani Bin Mohamad Isa

INDONESIA

1. Aan alias Ramses
2. Aang Hasanuddin
3. Abdul Azis alias Abu Umar alias Imam Samudra alias Fais Yunshar alias Heri alias Henri alias Kudama

4. Abdul Hamid

5. Abdul Rauf alias Sam

6. Abdullah Slam

7. Abu Bakar Baasyir

8. Abu Dzar alias Harris Fadillah (Deceased)

9. Abu Fatih

10. Abu Jibril alias Fihirudin alias Mohamed Ibal Bin Abudrrahman

11. Abu Rusdan alias Thoriqudin

12. Abu Yasar alias Dani Sitorus alias Dani

13. Agus Dwikarna

14. Ahmad Budi Wibowo

15. Ahmad Sofyan alias Tamim

16. Ali Imron alias Alik

17. Amin Bin Sukastopo

18. Amrozi alias M. Rozi alias Khoirul Anam

19. Andi Hidayat alias Agus

20. . Andri Octavia alias Yudi

21. Ari alias Mushofa alias Samuri alias Farich

22. Arkam alias Arqom alias Haris

23. Arnasan (Acong) alias Jimmy alias Iqbal1

24. Asmar Latin Sani

25. Azhari Dipo Kusumo

26. Bambang Tutuko alias Abu Umar

27. Basyir alias Abu Mukhilsun

28. Bima alias Karyo

29. Chotib

30. . Dadang Suratman alias Abu Yusof

31. Dr Azahari Husin (Deceased)

32. Dul Matin alias Ahmad Noval alias Joko Pitono alias Amar Usman

33. Dzulkarnain alias Arif Sunarso alias Uztad Daud

34. Edi Indra alias Ra'is

35. Edi Suprapto alias Yasir alias Tsalabah

36. Fadli Sadama

37. Fajri alias Yusuf

38. Fathur Rahman al-Ghozi (Deceased)

39. Fauzan Arif alias Heri

40. . Fer alias Isa alias Iqbal2

41. Firmansyah alias Iskandar
42. Gogon alias Agus
43. Hambali alias Ridwan Isamudin alias Encep Nurjaman
44. Hamim Tohari
45. Hamzah Baya alias Soleh
46. Heri Hafidin alias Mubarok
47. Herlambang Bin Zaidun alias Lambang
48. Hernianto Bin Zaidun
49. Heru Setyanto
50. . Idris alias Gebrot alias Jhoni Hendrawan
51. Ihsan Miarso
52. Ikhwanudin alias Hasyim
53. Ilham alias Didik
54. Iman Susanto alias Eko Suparman
55. Joko Ardianto alias Lulu Sumaryono
56. Joko Santoso
57. Junaedi alias Edi alias Amin
58. Luthfi Fadillah alias Zubair
59. Mahmudi Haryono alias Yusuf
60. . Malikul
61. Masykur alias Abul Abdul Kadir
62. Mochtar Sutrisno
63. Moh Yunus
64. Mohamad Qital
65. Mohd Rafi Bin Udin alias Ferdiansyah alias Ilham al. Basir
66. Muhaimin Yahya alias Ziad
67. Muhajir alias Idris
68. Mujarod
69. Mukhlas alias Ali Gufron
70. . Muri alias Mahmuri
71. Mustakim alias Mustaqim
72. Mustofa alias Abu Tholut alias Pranata Yudha alias Herman alias Hafid Ibrahim
73. Mustofa alias Endra
74. Nabirin
75. Najib alias Muh Nawawi
76. Nano Maryono
77. Nizam Kaleb

78. Noor Din Mohd Top
79. Nuim alias Zuhroni
80. . Nurmindah
81. Nurwismali alias Ibrohim alias Nurdin alias Firman alias Adriyansyah alias Dicky
82. Pepen alias Urwah alias Slamet Widodo
83. Purwadi
84. Puryanto alias Hartono
85. Qamar
86. Ramli
87. Rudy Hermawan alias Ali
88. Saad alias Achmad Roichan alias Ucang alias Arkam
89. Saeful alias Bambang Setiono alias Suroso
90. . Samian alias Zaid
91. Sardono Siliwangi
92. Sawad alias Sarjiyo
93. Sirojulmunir
94. Siswanto
95. Sofyan Hadi
96. Solahudin
97. Solichin
98. Solihin alias Rofi'
99. Solihin alias Soleh
100. Sugeng
101. Sukastopo Bin Kartomiharjo
102. Sumarno
103. Suprapto
104. Suradi alias Abu Usman
105. Surono alias Fadli
106. Sutikno
107. Suyatno alias Yatno alias Heru Setiawan
108. Toni Togar alias Indrawarman
109. Tono alias Regar
110. 10. Tulus Raharjo
111. Umar (Besar) alias Wayan alias Suranto alias Abdul Ghani
112. Usman
113. Utomo alias Abu Faruq
114. Utomo Pamungkas alias Mubarok

115. Uztaz Afif Abdul Mazid
116. Yono alias Moh. Aryo
117. Yovri Yosarmen alias Datuk Rajo Ame
118. Yudi
119. Zahri
120. Zulkifli bin Hir
121. Wiwin Kalahe
122. Agus Suryanto (deceased)
123. Sarwo Edi Nugroho
124. Akhyas alias Sutarjo
125. Sikas
126. Amir Ahmadi
127. Maulana Yusuf Wibisono
128. Achmad Yahrul alias Holis alias Cholis
129. Abu Dujana alias Ainul Bahri
130. Abu Irsyad alias Zarkasih alias Nuaim
131. Nur Afiffudin alias Suharto alias Haryanto
132. Azis alias Mustafa alias Ari
133. Tri alias Aris Widodo
134. Arif Syarifuddin alias Firdaus alias Fito

Notes

INTRODUCTION

1. This figure is taken from "An Analysis of the World Muslim Population by Country." See http://www.factbook.net/muslim_pop.php. According to another source, "Muslim Population Worldwide," the total Muslim population in Southeast Asia in 2005 was 226,656,000. See http://www.islamicpopuation.com/asia_general.html

2. According to latest statistics, after Indonesia, which has an Islamic population of 196.28 million, India and China have probably the second- and third-largest Islamic nations in the world, with an Islamic populace of 133.29 million and 133.10 million, respectively. While much has been written about the role of the Middle East and India in the spread of Islam in Southeast Asia, what is little known is that China played a crucial role in the spread of Islam to Indonesia, especially Java. Six out of the nine *Walisongos* (the nine saints) were of Chinese origin. See http://www.islamicweb.com/begin/population.htm.

3. See Zachary Abuza, *Militant Islam in Southeast Asia: Crucible of Terror* (Boulder, London: Lynne Rienner Pub., 2003), 1–5.

4. See Dana Robert Dillon, "Evolving Counterterrorism Strategy," The Heritage Foundation, September 29, 2005, 5–6.

5. See Iqbal Hussain, *Terrorism in Action—Why Blame Islam?* (Lahore: Humanity International, 2003), 89–90.

6. Opening Remarks by Dr. Rohan Gunaratna at a workshop on "Transnational Islamist Movements in Asia: Networks, Structure, Threat Assessment," organized by the Hudson Institute and The Institute of Defence and Strategic Studies, September 19–20, 2006, Singapore.

7. See Joe Cochrane and Julia Yeow, "Radical Islamists in Southeast Asia Make Gains Since 9/11," Deutsche Presse Agentur, September 4, 2006. See http://rawstory.com/news/2006/Radical_Islamists_in_South_East_Asi_09042006.html

8. See Martha Crenshaw, "Theories of Terrorism: Instrumental and Organizational Approaches" in *Inside Terrorist Organizations,* ed. David C. Rappoport (London: Frank Cass, 2001); Alex P. Schmid, *Political Terrorism* (New Brunswick, NJ: Transaction Books, 1983).

9. See *Al-Baqarah* 2, p. 256. Cited in http://en.wikipedia.org/wiki/Al-Baqara

CHAPTER 1

1. See Fred Halliday, *Islam and the Myth of Confrontation: Religion and Politics in the Middle East* (New York: I. B. Tauris, 2003), x–xi.

2. Samir Amin, "Political Islam," in http://www.loompanics.com/cgi-local/SoftCart.exe/Articles/PoliticalIslam.html?L+scstore+qjcs2889ffa55ca5+1088353573.

3. See Leonard Weinburg and Ami Pedahzur, *Religious Fundamentalism and Political Extremism* (London: Frank Cass, 2004), 57.

4. Mahathir Mohamad, "The Need to Identify Terrorists and Remove the Causes of Terrorism," in *Terrorism and the Real Issues,* ed. Hashim Makaruddin (Petaling Jaya, Malaysia: Pelanduk Publications, 2003), 29–41.

5. Nazih Ayubi, *Political Islam: Religion and Politics in the Arab World* (London: Routledge, 1991).

6. For an extensive account, see Ahmed Rashid, *Taliban: Militant Islam, Oil and Fundamentalism in Central Asia* (New Haven, CT: Yale University Press, 2001).

7. Halliday, *Islam and the Myth of Confrontation,* x–xi.

8. Edward Said, "The Necessity of Skepticism: Backlash and Backtrack," *Counterpunch,* September 28, 2003. See http://www.humanities.psydeshow.org/political/said-column.htm. Said notes how the demonic religion of the Middle Ages and early Renaissance was represented to have hit back in the 1970s, threatening welfare and, through issues such as oil, reminding the West of the greater danger the Orient, which was supposed to have been subdued, was posing.

9. For Armando Salvatore's critique, see *Islam and the Political Discourse of Modernity* (Reading, Berkshire: Ithaca Press, 1997), 169.

10. Gilles Kepel, *The Revenge of God: The Resurgence of Islam, Christianity and Judaism in the Modern World* (London: Polity Press, 1994).

11. Samuel Huntington, *The Clash of Civilizations and the Remaking of World Order* (New York: Simon and Schuster, 1996).

12. Francis Fukuyama, "The End of History," *National Interest* 16 (1989), 4–18.

13. Daniel Pipes, "The Muslims Are Coming! The Muslims Are Coming!" *National Review,* November 19, 1990. See http://www.danielpipes.org/article/198.

14. Barry Rubin and Judith Colp Rubin, "The Radical Critique of Islam," in *Anti-American Terrorism and the Middle East,* ed. Rubin and Rubin (Oxford: Oxford University Press, 2002), 6.

15. See Samir Amin, "Political Islam."

16. Bernard Lewis, "The Revolt of Islam," *New Yorker,* November 19, 2001, 1.

17. Emmanuel Sivan, *Radical Islam: Medieval Theology and Modern Politics* (New Haven, CT: Yale University Press, 1985), x.

18. Abdelwahab Meddeb, *Islam and Its Discontents* (London: Willian Heinemann, 2002), 95–100.

19. Halliday, *Islam and the Myth of Confrontation.*

20. Ayubi, *Political Islam: Religion and Politics in the Arab World,* 158–59.

21. Ibid, 177.

22. Edward Said, "The Clash of Ignorance," *Nation,* October 4, 2001. Said noted Eqbal's five motivations for terrorism, namely state, religion, protest or revolution, crime, and pathology.

23. Kouser J. Azam, "Political Islam and Terrorism in Contemporary Times," in *Terrorism in South Asia: Views from India,* ed. Adluri Subramanyam Raju (New Delhi: India Research Press, 2004), 84–85.

24. Majid Khadduri, *War and Peace in the Law of Islam* (Baltimore: Johns Hopkins Press, 1955), 60–61.

25. Ibid.

26. See Iqbal Hussain, *Terrorism In Action: Why Blame Islam?* (Lahore: Humanity International, 2003), p. 80.

27. Ibid.

28. According to the *al-Ikhwan,* "Allah is our objective. The Prophet is our leader. Koran is our law. Jihad is our way. Dying in the way of Allah is our highest hope." Cited in "al-Ikhwan al-Muslimin," FAS Intelligence Resource Program in http://www.fas.org/irp/world/para/mb.htm; "Muslim Brotherhood," in http://en.wikipedia.org/wiki/Muslim_Brotherhood.

29. Hussain, *Terrorism In Action,* 81.

30. See Ibid., 82–84.

31. Cited in Ibid, 87.

32. Sayyid Qutb, *Milestones* (Indianapolis: American Trust Publications, 1990).

33. Ibid.

34. William Shepard, *Sayyid Qutb and Islamic Activism* (Leiden, NY: E.J. Brill, 1996).

35. Qutb, *Milestones.*

36. Halliday, *Islam and the Myth of Confrontation: Religion and Politics in the Middle East,* 3.

37. Qutb, *Milestones.*

38. Ibid., 37.

39. Michael Youssef, *Revolt Against Modernity* (Leiden : E.J. Brill, 1985).

40. Ibid, 11.

41. Ibid, 56.

42. Ibid., 74.

43. http://www.globalsecurity.org/military/world/afghanistan/sayyaf.htm

44. M.J. Gohari, *Taliban: Ascent to Power* (Karachi: Oxford University Press, 2000).

45. "Former bin Laden mentor warns the West," *Telegraph,* December 3, 2001

46. http://www.globalsecurity.org/military/world/afghanistan/sayyaf.htm

47. Gohari, *Taliban: Ascent to Power,* 26.

48. Ibid.

49. http://www.uscirf.gov/mediaroom/press/2003/november/11042003_afghanistan.html

50. Ibid.

51. See Nasir Abbas, *Membongkar Jamaah Islamiyah: Pengakuan Mantan Anggota JI* (Jakarta: Grafindo Khazanah Ilmu, 2005), 67–73.

52. Abdullah Bin Umar, "Abdullah Azzam, the Struggling Sheik (July 1996)," in *Anti-American Terrorism and the Middle East: A Documentary Reader,* ed. Barry Rubin and Judith Colp Rubin (Oxford: Oxford University Press, 2002), 62–64.

53. http://www.ict.org.il/articles/articledet.cfm?articleid=388

54. Ibid.

55. Ayubi, *Political Islam: Religion and Politics in the Arab World.*

56. See Yoram Schweitzer and Shaul Shay, *The Globalization of Terror: The Challenge of Al-Qaida and the Response of the International Community* (New Delhi: Viva Books, 2004), 23.

57. Ibid, 24.

58. Kepel, *The Revenge of God,* 79.

CHAPTER 2

1. Prior to April 1975, North and South Vietnam existed as two separate countries. In 1999, East Timor seceded from Indonesia to form a separate state. Whether it is part of Southeast Asia or the South Pacific is a question that is yet to be settled, even though East Timorese leaders have been attending the Association of Southeast Asian Nations (ASEAN) meetings as observers.

2. See "Background Note: Indonesia" (Washington, DC: U.S. Department of State, Bureau of East Asian and Pacific Affairs, January 2007). See http://www.state.gov/r/pa/ei/bng/2748.htm

3. Al Chaidar, however, has argued, "the origins of Darul Islam emerged firstly in the year 1905 with the appearance of the *Sarikat Dagang Islam,* the United Islamic Merchants, which was pioneered by H. Samahudi. Following this organization came the birth of Sarikat Islam, United Islam, in the year 1912, which was pioneered by H.O.S. Cokrominoto, and during the development of this organization, there arose the PSII, the United Islamic Party of Indonesia. The movement was oriented towards the various aspects of life—political ideology, economy and social. By means of a long exhaustive process, in the year 1949, the Islamic State of Indonesia or *Darul Islam/Tentara Islam Indonesia* was formed under the leadership of Imam Sekarmadaji Maridjan Kartosuwiryo until he was arrested by the Soekarno regime of the Indonesian Republic." See Al Chaidar, "Terrorism and Islamic Fundamentalism: The Darul Islam's Responses towards Indonesian Democracy, 1949–1982," paper presented at a regional workshop on "Contemporary Islamic Movements in Southeast Asia: Militancy, Separatism, Terrorism and Democratisation Process," Bogor, October 28–31, 2002, organized by the RIDEP Institute and the Friedrich-Ebert-Stiftung, Indonesia.

4. For a biographic reference, see Irfan S. Awwas, *Menelusuri Perjalanan Jihad S.M. Kartosoewirjo* (Jogjakarta: Wihdah Press, 1999), and Al Chaidar, *Pemikiran Politik Proklamator Negara Islam Indonesia S.M. Kartosoewirjo* (Jakarta: Darul Falah, 1999).

5. Cited in Adam Schwarz, *A Nation in Waiting: Indonesia's Search for Stability* (St. Leonards, NSW, Australia: Allen and Unwin, 1999), 169.

6. For details, see C. Van Dijk, *Rebellion under the Banner of Islam: the Darul Islam in Indonesia* (The Hague: Martinus Nijhoff, 1981); for a more recent update, see *Recycling Militants in Indonesia: Darul Islam and the Australian Embassy Bombing,* Asia Report No. 92 (Jakarta, Brussels: International Crisis Group, Feb. 22, 2005), p. 2.

7. For details, see Ibid.

8. See Michael R.J. Vatikiotis, *Indonesian Politics Under Suharto: Order, Development and Pressure For Change* (London: Routledge, 1993), 184.

9. See Nazaruddin Sjamsuddin, "Issues and Politics of Regionalism in Indonesia: Evaluating the Achenese Experience," in *Armed Separatism in Southeast Asia,* ed. Lim Joo-Jock and Vani S. (Singapore: Institute of Southeast Asian Studies, 1984), 111–28.

10. Rabasa Angel and Peter Chalk, *Indonesia's Transformation and the Stability of Southeast Asia* (Santa Monica , CA: RAND Corporation, 2001), 85.

11. For a history of this conflict, see Omi Eliseo R. Mercado, "Culture, Economics and Revolt in Mindanao: The Origins of the MNLF and the Politics of Moro Separatism," in *Armed Separatism in Southeast Asia,* 151–75.

12. Moro is a generic term referring to 13 ethnolinguistic groups of people residing in southern Philippines and who share a common bond of Islam and a history of struggle against the largely Christian "colonisers," be they the Spanish, Americans, or Catholic Filipinos. These groups include Maranaos, Maguindanos, Tausugs, Samals, Yakans, Iranus, Jama-Mapuns, Badjaos, Kalibugans, Kalangans, Molbogs, Palawanis, and Sanglis. Of these, the most important are the Maguindanaos, Maranaos, and Tausugs, See Ibid, 152.

13. According to the independence declaration, "the Muslim inhabitants of Mindanao, Sulu and Palawan...desire (d) to secede from the Republic of the Philippines, in order to establish an Islamic state." See Ibid, 156.

14. Ibid, 155–56.

15. Cited from Angel and Chalk, *Indonesia's Transformation and the Stability of Southeast Asia.* For further details, it was recommended by the author to see Mark Turner, "Terrorism and Secession in the Southern Philippines: The Rise of the Abu Sayyaf," *Contemporary Southeast Asia* 17, no. 1 (1995): 10; P.B. Sinha, "Muslim Insurgency in the Philippines," *Strategic Analysis* 18, no. 5 (1995): 638; and A. Misra, "Guerrillas in the Mist," *Pioneer,* July 11, 1994.

16. Larry Niksch, *Abu Sayyaf: Target of Philippine-U.S. Anti-Terrorism Cooperation* (Washington, DC: Congressional Research Service, Library of Congress, 2003).

17. Hashim Salamat, a Cairo-trained scholar, accused Nur Misuari and the MNLF leadership of "being manipulated away from Islamic basis, methodologies and objectives and fast evolving towards Marxist-Maoist orientations." See Taha M. Basman, "MILF and Abu Sayyaf Group: Roots, Prospects and Linkages," paper presented at a conference on "Contemporary Islamic Movements in Southeast Asia: Militancy, Separatism, Terrorism and Democratisation Process," Bogor, October 28–31, 2002, organized by the RIDEP Institute and the Fredrich-Ebert-Stiftung, Indonesia.

18. Peter Chalk, "Muslim Separatist Movements in Philippines and Thailand", in Angel and Chalk, *Indonesia's Transformation and the Stability of Southeast Asia,* 87.

19. C.S. Kuppuswamy, "Thailand: Troubled by Terrorists," *South Asia Analysis Group,* paper no. 925, February 16, 2004.

20. *Muslim Separatism in Southern Thailand* (Virtual Information Center, United States Pacific Command), July 23, 2002.

21. Associate Professor Perayot Rahimmula, Prince of Songkhla University, Pattani, Thailand, interview with author, March 2004.

22. 22. See "Sejarah Ringkas Perubahan PULO," Pataninews.net, May 13, 2005 at http://www.pataninews.net/ReadReport.asp?ID=5

23. See Andrew Tan, *Armed Rebellions in the ASEAN States: Persistence and Implications,* Canberra Papers on Strategy and Defence, No. 135 (Canberra: Strategic and Defence Studies Centre, Australian National University, 2000), 46–49.

24. See "Sejarah Ringkas Perubahan PULO," Pataninews.net, May 13, 2005, at http://www.pataninews.net/ReadReport.asp?ID=5

25. Chalk, "Muslim Separatist Movements in the Philippines and Thailand."

26. Ibid.

27. Kuppuswamy, "Thailand: Troubled by Terrorists."

28. *Nation,* February 25, 2007.

29. Ibid.

30. Andrew Selth, "Burma's Muslims: Caught in the Crossfire," *The Irrawaddy* 11, no. 7 (August–September 2003).

31. Ibid.

32. Nelson Rand, "Setback Fails to deter Karen Guerillas," *Burma Update,* October 22, 2003.

33. Ibid.

34. Ibid.

35. Ibid.

36. Ibid.

37. Andrew Perrin, "Weakness in Numbers," *Time,* October 3, 2003

38. "Rohingya Politics—The Advancement of the Rohingya People," ARNO Web site, http://www.rohingya.org.

39. Ibid.

40. Ibid.

41. Ibid.

42. Ibid.

43. Ibid.

44. Ibid.

45. Ibid.

46. See Audrey R. Kahin and George McT. Kahin, *Subversion as Foreign Policy: The Secret Eisenhower and Dulles Debacle in Indonesia* (New York: The New Press, 1995).

47. See M. Imadadun Rahmat, *Arus Baru Islam Radikal: Transmisi Revivalisme Islam Timur Tengah Ke Indonesia* (Jakarta: Penerbit Erlangga, 2005), 80.

48. See Martin van Bruinessen, "Genealogies of Islamic Radicalism in Post-Suharto Indonesia," in http://www.let.uu.nl/~martin.vanbruinessen/personal/publications/genealogies_islamic_radicalism.htm

49. Ibid.

50. Khamami Zada, *Islam Radikal: Pengulatan Ormas-Ormas Islam Garis Kera di Indonesia* (Jakarta: Penerbit Teraju, 2002), 159.

51. *Indonesia: Violence and Radical Muslims* (Jakarta, Brussels: International Crisis Group, 2001), 9.

52. For details on this section, see Zachary Abuza, "A Breakdown of Southern Thailand's Insurgent Groups," *Terrorism Monitor* 4, issue 17 (September 8, 2006): 3–6.

CHAPTER 3

1. See *White Paper: The Jemaah Islamiyah Arrests and The Threat of Terrorism* (Singapore: Ministry of Home Affairs, 2003), 1.

2. According to Australian Attorney General Philip Ruddock, that *Jemaah Islamiyah* is also "known as: *Jema'ah Islamiyah, Jemaah Islamiya, Jemaah Islamiyah, Jemaah Islamiah, Jamaah Islamiyah, Jama'ah Islamiyah, Jeemah Islamiyah, Jemaa Islamiya, Jema'a Islamiya, Jemaa Islamiyah, Jema'a Islamiyya, Jemaa Islamiyya, Jemaa Islamiyah,* and *Jema'ah Islamiyah.*"

3. See "Menteri Said Agil: Jangan Gunakan Istilah Jemaah Islamiyah," http://www.tempo interaktif.com/news/2003/8/30/1,1,6,id.html

4. See Abdullah Sungkar, interview in *Nida'ul Islam* magazine, February–March 1997, http://www.islam.org.au.

5. For details, see A. Maftuh Abegebriel and A. Yani Abeverio, *Negara Tuhan: The Thematic Encyclopaedia* (Jakarta: SR-Ins Publishing, 2004), 825–27.

6. Singapore security officials have indeed described it as a "deep clandestine terrorist organization."

7. In this connection, the admission by Al Chaidar, one of the more prominent leaders of the DI today, is interesting. He argued that against the backdrop of Suharto's persecution of Islamic forces, those grouped under the DI umbrella reacted in various ways: "the real Islamic forces grouped in DI who tends to a fundamentalistic reaction than a radical one are those which consistently oppose militarism with militarism. The Islamic groups in Aceh, Lampung, Tanjung Priok and other places have held lots of demonstrations to protest the massacre of their community by the military....But the remnants of the DI who tend to and had been influenced by the fundamentalistic tendencies planned retaliation in the form of terror attacks, crimes against law and order, and other violent way. *Jama'ah Islamiyah* which has the purpose of establishing *Dawlah Islamiyah* by applying the strategies of *iman* (belief), *hijrah* (migrating) and *jihad* (war). [This is to] realise an Islamic Community (*Jama'ah Islamiyah*) by the mobilization of the three strengths: *quwwatul aqidah* (faith), *quwwatul ukhuwwah* (brotherhood) and *quwwatul musallahah* (military)" Al Chaidar argued that "the three elements of strengths are essential in order to establish *Dawlah Islamiyah*, especially by means of *jihad*." See Al Chaidar, "Terrorism and Islamic Fundamentalism: The Darul Islam's Response towards Indonesian Democracy, 1949–1982."

8. Angel Rabasa, "Radical Islamist Ideologies in Southeast Asia." Cited in http://www.futureofmuslimworld.com/research/publD.31/pub_detail.asp

9. For details of the conflict in DI, see *Recyling Militants in Indonesia: Darul Islam and the Australian Embassy Bombing*, Asia Report No. 92 (Jakarta, Brussels: International Crisis Group, February 22, 2005), 2–26.

10. Ibid, 20.

11. See *Al-Qaeda in Southeast Asia: The Case of the 'Ngruki Network' in Indonesia* (Jakarta, Brussels: International Crisis Group, August 8, 2002), 5.

12. Ibid.

13. Professor Eqbal Ahmad's recount of this is most instructive: "In 1985, President Ronald Reagan received a group of bearded men. These bearded men I was writing about in those days in The *New Yorker*, actually did. They were very ferocious-looking bearded men with turbans looking like they came from another century. President Reagan received them in the White House. After receiving them, he spoke to the press. He pointed towards them, I'm sure some of you will recall that moment, and said, "These are the moral equivalent of America's founding fathers". These were the Afghan *Mujahdin*. These were at the time, guns in hand, battling the Evil Empire. They were the moral equivalent of our founding fathers! In August 1998, another American President ordered missile strikes...to kill Osama Bin Laden and his men in the camps in Afghanistan. I do not wish to embarrass you with the reminder that Mr Bin Laden...was only a few years ago the moral equivalent of George Washington and Thomas Jefferson! He got angry over the fact that he has been demoted from 'Moral Equivalent' of your 'Founding Fathers.' So he is taking out his anger in different ways." See Ahmad, "Terrorism: Theirs and Ours," in http://www.sangam.org/ANALYSIS/Ahmad.htm

14. Nasir Abbas, *Membongkar Jamaah Islamiyah: Pengakuan Mantan Anggota JI* (Jakarta: Penerbit Grafindo Khazanah Ilmu, 2005).

15. Abu Bakar Ba'asyir, interview with author in Solo, Indonesia, November 2006.

16. Ibid.

17. Ibid. The same argument was forwarded by Irfan Awwas, the leader of the MMI, whom the author interviewed in Yogjakarta, Indonesia, in November 2006.

18. See Akh. Muzakki, "Islamic Radicalism in Southeast Asia: With Special Reference to the Alleged Terrorist Organization, Jama'ah Islamiyah," *Al-Jami'ah Journal of Islamic Studies* 42, no. 1 (2004): 76.

19. Alfitra Salamm, "Peniliti LIPI: JI Organisasi Maya Buatan Malaysia dan Singapura," *Detikcom,* October 30, 2002. Cited in Muzakki, "Islamic Radicalism in Southeast Asia," 76.

20. In this regard, the Centre for Democracy and Social Justice Studies in Jakarta has undertaken an excellent survey on this issue and identified not only the history of Indonesian radicalism since 1948, but more important, identified the linkages between the Indonesian military and Islamic radicalism.

21. According to former chief of the Indonesian State Intelligence Coordinating Board, A.C. Manulang, "Al-Faruq is a CIA-recruited agent and if this is correct, the US government funded the growth of Jemaah Islamiyah." He "was assigned to infiltrate Indonesia's Islamic radical groups. He entered the country as a refugee and married locally." Following his arrest on June 5, 2002, he was whisked away on CIA Gulfstream V aircraft number N379P to Afghanistan. See Kerry B. Collison, Crescent Moon Rising, in http://sidharta.com/book/extra/crescentmoonrising.jsp; On another occasion, Manulang accused Omar Faruk of being "a CIA-recruited agent." According to him, Omar was assigned to infiltrate Islamic radical groups and recruit local agents within these groups. "When al Faruk finished his assignments, the CIA created a scenario that he had been arrested." Manulang argued that this was common of the CIA and in intelligence operations because once "the CIA obtained complete data on this matter, they them made al-Faruk disappear." Manulang argued that the lack of involvement of the National Police in Faruk's arrest and the lack of official documents of Faruk's handing over to the United States created suspicions. The former intelligence chief argued, "in the handing over of a detainee to other country, there should be an announcement or deportation document. Al Faruq's case indicated a lack of coordination between the Indonesian Police and intelligence agencies."

22. A senior retired police officer in Jakarta, Indonesia, interview with author, July 2005.

23. A senior military intelligence officer in Jakarta, Indonesia, interview with author, March 2005.

24. See Damien Kingsbury and Clinton Fernandes, "Terrorism in Archipelagic Southeast Asia," in *Violence in Between: Conflict and Security in Archipelagic Southeast Asia,* ed. Kingsbury (Melbourne: Monash University Press, and Singapore: Institute of Southeast Asian Studies, 2005), 20–21.

25. See "Inside Indonesia's War on Terror," SBS Dateline, October 12, 2005, http://www.rebelwarez.com/rebelblog/2006/10/06/former-president-of-indonesia-abd.

26. See "Police 'had role in' in Bali blasts," *Australian,* October 12, 2005.

27. See "Inside Indonesia's War on Terror," SBS Dateline, October 12, 2005. See http://www.rebelwarez.com/rebelblog/2006/10/06/former-president-of-indonesia-abd

28. Ibid.

29. Ibid.

30. Ibid.

31. Ibid.

32. Ibid.

33. See "Terror War Is Capitalism, Islam Feud: Raw ex-Chief," *Asian Age* (New Delhi), June 26, 2006.

34. When the Soviets invaded Afghanistan, an indigenous Islamic resistance movement arose against the Soviets but had no chance of succeeding on its own. The United States, for its own strategic reasons, though it had no common bond with the resistance fighters, developed a common link with the *Mujahidin* through the use of religion. From the Islamic point of view, the world is essentially bipolar in nature, divided between the *Darul Islam* (abode of the faithful) and *Darul Harb* (abode of the infidels). The United States, by establishing a common cause of reversing the Soviet invasion, became a full partner in *jihad* against the USSR. For 10 years, 1979–89, the U.S. government through the CIA funneled billions of dollars in close collaboration with Pakistan to equip the Afghan *Mujahidin* and thousands of *jihadis* from the Muslim world to fight the Soviet "infidels." In the end, not only was the USSR defeated and forced to withdraw, the country was devastated, with Islamic fundamentalism heavily embedded in its society. Global terrorism that has spread worldwide was one of its long-lasting consequences that the world has to live with it, especially the United States, which has now declared "war against terrorism."

35. The launch of "Operation Cyclone" symbolized the nexus between the Pakistani and United States' governments, between the CIA and ISI and the multitude of *jihadi* groups. See "CIA's Cyclone Spawned Pak Madrasas," The Pioneer, in http://www.meadev.nic.in/news/clippings/20030331/pio.htm

36. According to Professor Fred Halliday, "In 1979, the United States launched the largest covert operation in the history of the CIA in response to the Soviet invasion of Afghanistan." See Halliday, "The Un-great Game: The Country that Lost the Cold War," *New Republic,* March 25, 1996.

37. "According to the official version of history, CIA aid to the *Mujahidin* began during 1980, that is to say, after the Soviet army invaded Afghanistan in December 1979. But the reality, secretly guarded until now, is completely otherwise: indeed, it was July 3 1979 that President Carter signed the first directive for secret aid to the opponents of the pro-Soviet regime in Kabul. And that very day, I wrote a note to the President which I explained to him that in my opinion this aid was going to induce a Soviet military intervention...We didn't push the Russians to intervene, but we knowingly increased the probability that they would do so. That secret operation was an excellent idea. It had the effect of drawing the Russians into the Afghan trap...The day the Soviets officially crossed the border, I wrote to President Carter: We now have the opportunity of giving to the USSR its Vietnam War." Cited in http://emperors-clothes.com/interviews/brz.htm.

38. According to Dr. Farrukh Saleem, "in 1980, Prince Turki al-Faisal, the then head of Istakhbarat, Saudi Arabia's secret service, handpicked Osama bin Laden to provide engineering and organizational help to the fighting Mujahidin in Afghanistan." See Saleem, "Quetta and Surplus *Jihadis,*" *News International* (Pakistan), July 15, 2003, http://www.countercurrents.org/ipk-saleem150703.htm.

39. According to Dilip Hiro, Zbigniew Brezinski hoped "not just to drive the Russians out of Afghanistan but to ferment unrest within the Soviet Union. His plan was to export a composite ideology of nationalism and Islam to the Muslim-majority Central Asia states and Soviet Republics with a view to destroying the Soviet order." See Dilip Hiro, *War Without End: The Rise of Islamist Terrorism and the Global Response* (New York: Routledge, 2002), 42–44.

40. According to Hiro, "Predominant themes were that Islam was a complete socio-political ideology, that holy Islam was being violated by the atheistic Soviet troops, and that

the Islamic people of Afghanistan should reassert their independence by overthrowing the left-ist Afghan regime propped up by Moscow." Ibid., 44–45.

41. Obsessed with the long-term strategic goals of the United States, Zbigniew Brezinski was quoted as saying, "What was more important in the world view of history? The Taliban or the fall of the Soviet Empire? A few stirred-up Muslims or the liberation of Central Europe and the end of the Cold War?" See Olivier Roy, *Afghanistan: From Holy War to Civil War* (Princeton, NJ: Princeton University Press, 1995).

42. See Ahmed Rashid, *Taliban: The Story of the Afghan Warlords* (Basingstoke and Oxford: Pan Books, 2001), 130.

43. *Washington Post,* July 19, 1992.

44. See http://www.satp.org/satportp/nsa/Al-Qaeda.htm.

45. In this connection, Selig Harrison, a longtime observer of American foreign policy, argued, "the CIA made a historic mistake in encouraging Islamic groups from all over the world to come to Afghanistan. They (the CIA) told me that these people were fanatical, and the fiercer they were, the more fiercely they would fight the Soviets. I warned them that we were creating a monster." Cited in "CIA worked in tandem with Pak to create Taliban," *Times of India,* March 7, 2001.

46. As was argued by a security analyst, "Over the past 10 years, the Afghani network has been linked to terrorist attacks...everywhere. This is an insane instance of the chicken coming home to roost. You can't plug billions of dollars into an anti-communist Jihad, accept partici-pation from all over the world and ignore the consequences. But we did." Similarly, another expert opined, "The point is that we created a whole cadre of trained and motivated people who turned against us. It is a classic Frankenstein's monster situation." Ibid.

47. Jagmohan Meher, *America's Afghanistan War: The Success That Failed* (Delhi: Kalpaz Publications, 2004), 200.

48. Singapore security officials have indeed described it as a "deep clandestine terrorist organization." See *White Paper: The Jemaah Islamiyah Arrests and The Threat of Terrorism* (Singapore: Ministry of Home Affairs, 2003).

49. See Sungkar, interview in *Nida'ul Islam* magazine, February–March 1997, http://www.islam.org.au.

50. See *White Paper: The Jemaah Islamiyah Arrests and The Threat of Terrorism,* 6.

51. There are many versions of Sungkar and Ba'asyir's past. This version is adopted from the International Crisis Group. See *Al-Qaeda in Southeast Asia: The Case of the "Ngruki Network" in Indonesia* (Jakarta: International Crisis Group, 2002).

52. See *Al-Qaeda in Southeast Asia: The Case of the Ngruki Network in Indonesia,* Indone-sian Briefing, August 8, 2002, 11.

53. Ba'asyir, interview with author, November 2006.

54. Ibid.

55. For additional details, see Marc Erikson, "Southeast Asia: The Osama bin Laden and al-Qaeda of Southeast Asia," in *Asia Times Online,* http://www.atimes.com/se-asia/DB06Ae01.html

56. See *Risalah Kongres Mujahidin 1 Dan Penegakan Syari'ah Islam* (Yogjakarta: Wihdah Press, 2001).

57. See Lee Hudson Teslik, "Profile: Abu Bakar Bashir (a.k.a Ba'syir)," *Backgrounder,* June 14, 2006. Cited in http://www.cfr.org/publication/10219/profile.html.

58. In their interviews with the author, both Abu Bakar Ba'asyir and Irfan Awwas denied having any knowledge of the PUPJI.

59. According to a *Newsweek* report, the head of the *Al Qaeda* organization is Osama Bin Laden. He is supported by a Consultative Council. In turn, there are four main committees responsible for various aspects of the terrorist network. This includes the Finance Committee that controls the financial aspects of *Al Qaeda* that sustains the network. Next is the Religious/Legal Committee. This functions to justify the terrorist attacks based on extremist interpretations of Islam. The Media Committee disseminates information in support of the organization's activities. Finally, the Military Committee recruits and trains Islamic fighters, allocates weapons to assist in terror campaigns and coordinates attacks. Below these main committees are support cells, groups of four to five people who lay the groundwork for various terrorist operations. See "The Nuts and Bolts of Terror," *Newsweek,* October 15, 2001, 36.

60. According to Internet sources, Asian intelligence officers believe that the AJAI has branched out of Southeast Asia with a cell being established in Australia. According to intelligence sources, the AJAI now has four main cells, the first covering Malaysia, Singapore, and Thailand; the second covering Sumatra and Java in Indonesia; the third covering Indonesia's Sulawesi Island, Kalimantan, Brunei, and southern Philippines; and the fourth covering Australia and Indonesia's province of Papua. See *Straits Times* (Singapore), October 23, 2002.

61. Following the arrest of the second batch of AJAI operatives in Singapore, it was announced that by 1999, a regional network of Islamic militant groups bent on using, among others, terrorism, to pursue their political objectives, had already been set up. The AJAI is said to have initiated an alliance called *Rabitatul Mujahidin,* involving among others, the MILF, the *Abu Sayyaf, Gerakan Mujahidin Islamic Pattani,* and possibly the *Gerakan Aceh Merdeka,* which has been fighting for an Islamic state in northern Sumatra and where the *Al Qaeda* leadership had paid a visit to facilitate cooperation. See "AJAI spreading to southern Thailand," *Straits Times* (Singapore), September 18, 2002. According to a media report, the *Rabitatul Mujahidin* unites at least nine homegrown Muslim militant groups in the region. See *Foreign Broadcast Monitor* (Singapore), No.218/02, September 20, 2002, 3.

62. See "Terror in Asia: The region is still on the danger list," *Time,* December 2, 2002, 48.

63. According to Sidney Jones, the director of the International Crisis Group in Jakarta, "The AJAI, which shared the same philosophy (as the DI), however, dreamt bigger and wanted to establish an Islamic Republic unifying Malaysia, Indonesia, Mindanao in the Philippines, Singapore, southern Thailand and Brunei." *Indonesia Backgrounder: How the Jemaah Islamiyah Terrorist Network Operates* (Jakarta: International Crisis Group), Asia Report No. 43, December 11, 2002, p. 1. Also see Kumar Ramakrishna, *Constructing the Jemaah Islamiyah Terrorist: A Preliminary Inquiry,* Working Paper No. 71 (Singapore: Institute of Defence and Strategic Studies, October 2004), p. 1.

64. See Sungkar, interview in *Nida'ul Islam* magazine, February–March 1997, http://www.islam.org.au.

65. See Nasir Abas, *Membongkar Jamaah Islamiyah: Pengakuan Mantan Anggota JI* (Jakarta: Penerbit Grafindo Khazanah Ilmu, 2005), 81–86.

66. Ba'asyir, interview with author, November 2006.

67. Ibid.

68. Ibid.

69. Kumar Ramakrishna, p.11.

70. Cited in Malise Ruthven, *A Fury for God: The Islamist Attack on America,* London and New York: Granta, 2002), p. 203. Cited in Kumar Ramakrishna, p. 17.

71. See Behrend, "Reading Past the Myth."

72. See *Kompas,* October 6, 2003.

73. A senior member of the Task Force on Counter-Terrorism, interview with author in Jakarta, Indonesia, November 2006.

74. See talk by Dr. Sidney Jones, "The Latest Bombing in Jakarta—Facts and Perceptions on Terrorism in Indonesia," presented at the Institute of Southeast Asian Studies, Singapore, September 27, 2004.

75. See Wong Chun Wai and Lourdes Charles, "More than 100 Marriages Involve Key JI Members," *The Star,* September 7, 2004.

76. Ibid.

77. "One Big Terrorist Family," *Straits Times* (Singapore), September 8, 2004.

78. Noor Huda Ismail, "The Role of Kinship in Indonesia's *Jemaah Islamiyah,*" *Global Terrorism Analysis* 4, no. 11 (June 2, 2006).

79. A good example of this was the involvement of four different cells in the second Bali bombing in October 2005. See "A Four-Cell Network," *Tempo,* September 18, 2006, 20–21.

80. For instance, see "Asian groups among those banned," *Bangkok Post,* November 5, 2001.

81. Cited in "BG Lee calls for help to fight SE Asia terror," *Straits Times* (Singapore), February 3, 2002.

82. See "KL militant 'played key role,'" *Straits Times* (Singapore), January 29, 2002.

83. Ibid.

84. Senior member of the Task Force on Counter Terrorism, interview with author at the Police Headquarters in Jakarta, Indonesia, November 2006.

85. See "Analysis: Indonesia's Islamic Radicals," BBC News, November 15, 2001. Cited in http://news.bbc.co.uk/2/hi/asia-pacific/1657514.stm

86. Ibid.

87. Nasir Abas, *Membongkar Jamaah Islamiyah: Pengakuan Mantan Anggota JI* (Jakarta; Penerbit Grafindo Khazanah Ilmu, 2005), 81–87.

88. See *Indonesia Backgrounder: How the Jemaah Islamiyah Terrorist Network Operates,* ICG Asia Report No. 43 (Jakarta and Brussels: International Crisis Group, December 11, 2002), 5.

89. When President Suharto enforced the "asas tunggal policy" of Pancasila-only, the group that broke away from the main HMI body formed the HMI-MPO, with Agus and Tamsil part of this group. For details of components of the LJ, see Ibid., 21.

90. Ibid, 19.

91. Ibid., 3.

92. Ibid, 4.

93. Ibid. 5.

94. Cited in Carlos L. Augustin, "State of Radicalization in Muslim Communities in the Philippines," paper presented at a regional conference on "The Radicalization of Moslem Communities in Southeast Asia," Manila, Philippines, December 1, 2005.

95. Cited in Ibid.

96. See Augustin, "State of Radicalization in Muslim Communities in the Philippines"; and *Philippines Terrorism: The Role of Militant Islamic Converts,* Asia Report No. 110 (Jakarta, Brussels: International Crisis Group, December 19, 2005).

97. See *Utusan Malaysia,* July 8, 2001

98. See Phann Ana and Kevin Doyle, "Putting Down Roots: Radicals Try to Strengthen Ties in Cambodia," *Cambodia Daily,* September 13, 2003.

99. This was popularized by President George W. Bush in the aftermath of the terrorist attacks.

100. See "Al Qaeda's Southeast Asian Reach: Group Operating in 4 Nations Believed Tied to Sept. 11 Hijackers," *Washington Post,* February 3, 2002.

101. Cited in *Straits Times* (Singapore), February 3, 2002

102. According to the ISD (Singapore), following the arrest of AJAI operatives in August 2002, "a significant finding is that the regional AJAI did not operate alone, but formed the *Rabitatul Mujahidin* regional alliance of "AJAIhads"/militant groups. The *Rabitatul Mujahidin* comprised a central committee made up of leaders from the militant groups in the region, which included: a. Moro Islamic Liberation Front (MILF); and b. a south Thailand *"Jihadist"* group (based in Narathiwat). The AJAI's role was to set up and coordinate meetings of the alliance partners. Secrecy was very strictly maintained and only the invited senior members of these groups were allowed to participate in *Rabitatul Mujahidin* meetings. Apparently, three meetings have been held so far between late 1999 and mid-2000.

103. See "Profile: Abu Bakar Ba'asyir," http://news.bbc.co.uk/2/hi/asia-pacific/2339693.stm

104. See "Bin Laden Funded Christian Haters," http://www.mailarchive.com/eskol@mitra.net.id/msg00006.html

105. See "Terrorism's New Front: Minds of Singaporeans," *Straits Times* (Singapore), May 22, 2002.

106. See "Government News Release on the ISA Arrests—The Link of the Yishun Video," http://www2.mha.gov.sg/mha/detailed.jsp?artid=41&type=4&root=0&parent=0&cat=0

107. See B. Raman, "Thailand and International Islamic Front," South Asia Analysis Group, Paper No. 890, January 9, 2004, 1–6; http://www.saag.org/papers9/paper890.html

108. Ibid.

109. Described as "sleeper cells of AJAI," Pakistani officials later claimed that "this is the first time Pakistani authorities have found imprints of the AJAI, a Southeast Asian extremist group linked to Al Qaeda on Pakistani soil." See B. Raman, *Hambali's Brother: Another Tell-Tale Arrest,* (South Asia Analysis Group), Paper No. 794, September 23, 2003.

110. In addition to Hambali's brother, three of the five Malaysians were sons of AJAI members and one was a brother of an AJAI suspect. According to a Singapore government statement, "two of the Singaporean arrested was among several students who were talent-spotted by the AJAI leadership to be groomed to become the next generation of key operatives and leaders in the organization." Ibid.

111. See B. Raman, "Thailand and International Islamic Front," 1–6; http://www.saag.org/papers9/paper890.html

CHAPTER 4

1. This list of church targets is taken from *Indonesia Backgrounder: How the Jemaah Islamiyah Terrorist Network Operates,* 27–29

2. The Bali bombing was particularly important as it signalled the JI's threat to Australia rather than simply to Southeast Asia. That *Mantiqi* 4 covers Australia is not surprising, all the more, as Abu Bakar Ba'asyir and other senior JI leaders are believed to have made a number of visits to Australia to establish the JI network in Australia. See "Australia Probes Jemaah Islamiyah Money Trail," http://asia.news.yahoo.com/.021103/reuters/asia-1321447.html

3. For details, see "The Family behind the Bombings," *Time,* November 25, 2002, 16–22; "Where will they strike next?" *Time,* November 25, 2002, 44–53.

4. For details, see Rohan Gunaratna, "The Singapore Connection," *Jane Intelligence Review* 14, no. 3 (March 2002): 8–11.

5. In a number of organizational charts, the *Dakwah* and Educational groups are often combined as one unit even though the religious and propagandistic wings tend to undertake clearly differentiated functions. For instance, Rohan Gunaratna combines the two units under "Mission Unit" with the educational one totally ignored. See Rohan Gunaratna, "The Singapore Connection," 8.

6. See Ibid., 9.

7. From the arrests made by the Singapore government under the Internal Security Act, five have been served with Restriction Orders and not detained. Two persons, Faizal Khan bin Gulam Sarwar, 34, and Mohd Agus bin Ahmad Selani, 34, were among the 15 arrested in December 2001. They were released on January 6, 2002, and served with Restriction Orders under Section 8(1) (b) of the ISA with conditions prohibiting them to have any contact with any terrorist organization, to prevent them from deeper and further involvement with the Moro Islamic Liberation Front (MILF). The Restriction Order, which is for a period of two years, will be reviewed annually. Even though they were not members of JI, they supported the MILF. From the second batch of arrests of 21 persons in August 2002, three—Fauzi bin Abu Bakar Bafana (Fauzi), Mohamad Hisham bin Hairi (Hisham), and Sajahan bin Abdul Rahman (Sajahan)—were served with ROs on September 14, 2002. Fauzi and Hisham are JI members, while Sajahan had visited the MILF training camp in 1999. However, like the earlier two, they were released, as they did not participate in terrorism-related activities.

8. "Fiah" refers to a cell within the local JI structure. A "fiah" usually receives directives from the JI "shura" (consultative council) via the "fiah" leader. A local JI group will typically have several "fiahs," each with a specified function, e.g., "dakwah" (missionary work), fund-raising, and operations. Each "fiah" usually comprises an average of four JI members, including the leader. The composition of the "fiah" is often fluid and members may be switched between "fiahs" or undertake jobs in more than one "fiah" at the same time. Around 1999–2000, there appeared to have been a reorganization of resources at the direction of the Indonesian JI leadership so that more JI members were directed to join the operations "fiahs." In the investigations, which led to the first arrests of JI members in December 2001, ISD uncovered the existence of three operations "fiahs" (*fiah ayub, fiah musa,* and *fiah ismail*). Following the second batch of arrests in August 2002, an additional four operations "fiahs" were uncovered (*fiah yakub, fiah syuib, fiah daud,* and *fiah nuh*). Most of the details about the organization and tasks of the JI *fiahs* in Singapore have come from the ISD.

9. See "Singapore bomb plot mastermind 'held in Oman,'" *Straits Times* (Singapore), July 13, 2002.

10. See Lee Hsien Loong, speech in Munich, Germany, February 2, 2002.

11. See *Indonesia Backgrounder: How the Jemaah Islamiyah Terrorist Network Operates,* 3–4.

12. See Martin van Bruinessen, "Genealogies of Islamic Radicalism in Post-Suharto Indonesia," ISIM and Utrecht University, 2002, p. 3; http://www.let.uu.nl/~martin.vanbruinessen/personal/publications/genealogies_islamic

13. Zachary Abuza, "Tentacles of Terror: Al Qaeda's Southeast Asian Network," excerpt from unpublished book (Boulder, CO: Lynne Rienner Publishers, March 2003), 1.

14. Refer to a five-part report titled "Asia's Own Osama," in http://www.time.com/time/asia/features/malay_terror/hambali.html

15. Ibid.

16. See "JI suicide squad on the loose," *Straits Times* (Singapore), August 13, 2003.

17. See "Indonesian bombing trial begins," http://news.bbc.co.uk/2/hi/asia-pacific/43564507.stm

18. See "Bali bomber Ali Imron gets life term," *Straits Times* (Singapore), September 19, 2003.

19. See transcript of interview with DPM BG Lee Hsien Loong by Hwee Goh, Channel News Asia on September 28, 2001 (Singapore Government Press Release, Media Division, Ministry of Information and the Arts).

20. Cited in *Straits Times* (Singapore), September 23, 2001.

21. See Statement by Prof. S. Jayakumar, Minister for Foreign Affairs at the United Nations Security Council Ministerial Meeting on November 12, 2001, (Singapore Government Press Release, Media Division, Ministry of Information and the Arts).

22. See "US-ASEAN Anti-Terrorism Pact May Threaten Human Rights: Watchdog," http://www.islamonline.net/english/news/2002–08/03/article19.shtml

23. According to one report, Osama's second in command, Ayman Al Zawahiri, together with the then *Al Qaeda*'s military chief, Mohammed Atef, visited Aceh in 2000 and were "impressed by the lack of security, the support and extent of Muslim population." See "Osama's Men Visited Aceh: Report," *Today,* July 11, 2002.

24. See *Straits Times* (Singapore), November 6, 2001; and http://www.aseansec.org

25. See Mohd Huzsaire Bin Jantan, *ASEAN Combating Terrorism: A Comparative Study* (Bangi, Kuala Lumpur: Faculty of Social Sciences and Humanities, University Kebangsaan Malaysia, 2005), 72.

26. See "Thailand is latest to sign on to anti-terror pact," *Straits Times* (Singapore), November 6, 2002.

27. The alleged hijacking was supposed to be led by Mas Selamat Kastari. However, before they could be arrested, they are believed to have fled to Malaysia, following which they are believed to have gone into Thailand and from there to Medan in Indonesia via Langkawi (Malaysia). Their whereabouts have been unknown since then. However, Mas Selamat was arrested in February 2003 in Tanjung Pinang. For details, see "PM reveals plans to crash jet into Changi," *Straits Times* (Singapore), April 6, 2002; and "Militants fled to Medan via Malaysia," *Straits Times* (Singapore), April 7, 2002.

28. According to investigations, a group of 20 people, organized in four cells, were planning to set off seven simultaneous explosions in Singapore. The Singapore group had already obtained access to 4 tons of ammonia nitrate that was stored in Muar, Johor, in Malaysia, and had been given money to buy an additional 17 tons of chemicals and seven trucks. The trucks were each to contain three tons of nitrate and were to be used as bombs, creating seven simultaneous explosions. See *Straits Times* (Singapore), February 10, 2002.

29. The seriousness with which this effort is being made is mainly to ensure that the JI operatives do not succeed in their endeavors, as this can have very serious repercussions for national and regional security. Unlike the first batch of detainees, according to the Singapore government, the second batch of detainees were bent on undertaking activities that could have severely harmed Singapore's all-round interests. The Singapore government believed that this time, the JI operatives "planned to generate animosity between Singapore and Malaysia and make Malaysia an Islamic state. By turning 'Chinese Singapore' against Malay/Muslim

Malaysia, they hoped to turn the two countries into another Ambon, racked by ethnic strife and religious clashes." See *Straits Times* (Singapore), September 20, 2002.

30. See "12 JI members dispersed and hiding in the region," *Sunday Times,* September 22, 2002.

31. To date, more than 100 suspected terrorists have been detained in various ASEAN countries, especially Malaysia, Singapore, and the Philippines.

32. According to Dr. Tony Tan, the Coordinating Minister for Security and Defense, this was needed as "Singapore was facing a new type of international terrorism, which was strategic in outlook, and much more dangerous and sustained than the one-off terrorist attacks carried out in the past by disparate groups. It is not possible for us to deal with these new threats with the same type of structure and capabilities we had in the past." Cited in *Straits Times* (Singapore), January 7, 2002.

33. See Bill Guerin, "Indonesia's Terror Dilemma," *Asia Times,* October 8, 2005, in http://articles.ibonweb.com/webarticles.asp?num=1536.

34. A senior police officer, interview with author at the police headquarters in Jakarta, Indonesia, November 2006.

35. A senior officer from the Task Force on Counter-Terrorism, inteview with author in Jakarta, Indonesia, November 2006.

36. See Rommel C. Banlaoi, *War on Terrorism in Southeast Asia* (Manila: Rex Books, 2004), 50.

37. Ibid, 50–51.

38. Ibid, 54.

39. Following the collapse of the *Taliban* regime in Afghanistan, the next major country the United States concentrated in its war of terrorism was the Philippines. It dispatched nearly 1,200 military advisors to Mindanao (southern Philippines) to assist the Philippines Armed Forces in its war against the *Abu Sayyaf.* Under the cover of "Exercise Balikatan 02–1," American troops were deployed in southern Philippines, especially in Basilan Island. Following the end of the "exercise," another one started, this time with more American troops being deployed in the country. It was mainly due to this that the U.S. Secretary of State Colin Powell praised the Philippines as being "in the forefront of leadership in Southeast Asia in respect to the global war against terrorism." See "US-ASEAN Anti-Terrorism Pact May Threaten Human Rights: Watchdog," cited in http://www.islamonline.net/English/2002–08/03/article19.shtml; also see "MSLA not on agenda in Gloria-Powell Meeting," http://www.inq 7.net/nat/2002/aug/03/text/nat_1–1p.htm

40. See *CSIS Pacnet Newsletter,* Issue 1, January 4, 2002.

41. Walter Laqueur, *The New Terrorism: Fanaticism and the Arms of Mass Destruction* (New York: Oxford University Press, 1999).

42. "It is a national problem affecting everyone," *Straits Times* (Singapore), September 21, 2002.

43. Admiral Dennis Blair, the former commander-in-chief of U.S. forces in the Pacific, for instance, stated on February 5, 2002, that despite the Congressional ban, some cooperation was being undertaken with the Indonesian military. However, he made it clear that "the U.S. could not resume a full military relationship with Indonesia until its armed forces completed reforms that bring the standards of conduct and accountability to what we expect of advanced armed forces." Cited in *Sydney Morning Herald,* February 6, 2002.

44. As was argued by Singapore's Deputy Prime Minister Lee Hsien Loong, Indonesia has thus far acted circumspectly in dealing with extremist religious groups and their leaders due

to four main reasons: "First, it has had to watch its flanks, to avoid being attacked by political opponents for acting too harshly against fellow Muslims. Second, elections are due in 2004, and potential contenders are wary of souring the Muslim ground, which form 90 percent of the population. Third, the slackening of law and order in Indonesia post-Suharto has made it harder for any government to enforce its will in this country of 13,000 islands. Finally, the armed forces are the strongest institution, which can safeguard the unity of the country. But the armed forces are wary of being accused of human rights violations, if they act against the militants as they had done in the past." See Lee Hsien Loong's speech in Munich, Germany, on February 2, 2002.

45. Even though the Malaysian and Singaporean authorities believed that Ba'asyir was the "Emir" behind the *Jemaah Islamiyah* and its terrorism in the region, due to various legal loopholes and fears of a backlash from Muslim hardliners, Justice Minister Yusril Ihza Mahendra recommended a presidential pardon on grounds that the country's subversion laws had already been repealed in 1999. Similarly, due to political pressures and the close association of Tamsil and Abdul Jamal with Amien Rais, the Speaker of the People's Consultative Assembly, the Indonesian government pressured the Philippines to release the two even though the third accused, Agus, remains in Philippines' detention. See *Straits Times* (Singapore), April 27, 2002.

46. See "US 'using terror claims to control Indonesia,'" *Straits Times* (Singapore), May 27, 2002.

CONCLUSION

1. This claim was made by Australian Foreign Minister Alexander Downer in March 2004. See *Straits Times* (Singapore), March 19, 2004.

2. According to a senior police officer who was involved in a number of AJAI's bombings, since the second Bali bombings in 2005, the terrorist organization is still in possession of more than 1.5 tons of explosives hidden away in Indonesia. Interview with author, Jakarta, Indonesia, November 2005.

3. See http://www.foxnews.com/printer-friendly-story/0,3566.128052,00.html.

4. Cited in *Taipei Times,* January 16, 2004. See http://www.taipeitimes.com/News/world/archives/2004/01/16/2003091596

5. See Rini Hindryati, "Officials Warn of More Attacks by Terror Group," *Asian Wall Street Journal,* September 13, 2004.

6. See *Jihad in Central Sulawesi* (Jakarta and Brussels: International Crisis Group, February 3, 2004), 2.

7. See http://www.foxnews.com/printer-friendly-story/0,3566.128052,00.html.

8. See "Sejumlah Pesantren di Jateng jadi taget binaan Jemaah Islamiyah," *Suara Pembaruan,* July 18, 2003.

9. See "Self-Confessed AJAI leader say hardliners behind bombings," ClariNews, September 26, 2003. See http://www.quickstart.clari.net/qs_se/webnews/wed/cm/Qindonesia-attacks-AJAI.Rkx8-DSQ.html.

10. Ibid.

11. Ibid.

12. See "Marriott bombers wrong, say radical cleric Baasyir," *Today,* February 2, 2005.

13. Ibid.

14. Ba'asyir, interview with author, November 2006.

15. See *Jihad in Central Sulawesi* (Jakarta and Brussels: International Crisis Group, February 3, 2004), 2–3.

16. Ibid, 2.

17. Ibid, 3.

18. Ibid.

19. Ibid.

20. *The Age,* September 21, 2004.

21. See Ibid.

22. *Koran Tempo,* December 17, 2004.

23. See *Indonesian Daily,* December 18, 2004.

24. Cited in Ibid.

25. Ibid.

26. Ibid.

27. Ibid.

28. Quoted in *Investor Daily,* December 20, 2004.

29. Cited in *Jakarta Post,* December 17, 2004.

30. See *The Age,* September 20, 2004.

31. See *Straits Times* (Singapore), March 10, 2004.

32. The Indonesian Police has tried to argue that various witnesses have linked Abu Bakar Ba'asyir to various acts of terrorism, even though this has not been proven in court. If anything, most witnessed have denied this. For instance, in December 2004, three key witnesses withdrew their earlier statements, arguing that confessions were extracted under torture. For instance, Sutikno and Imron Baihaki, both of whom have been convicted of earlier terror attacks, retracted their earlier confessions that Abu Bakar was the head of the *Jemaah Islamiyah* and that he once visited the rebel training camp in southern Philippines. Imron stated under oath, "I was told by a person—Nasir Abbas that Baasyir had replaced Abdullah Sungkar as the Head of the Jemaah Islamiyah. Later, I discovered that Baasyir was not but was actually Head of the MMI." Another witness, Muhaimin Yahya alias Ziad also denied seeing the cleric in southern Philippines. See Ibid.

33. For details, see Catherine Zara Raymond, "Reviewing Maritime Security Code," *Jakarta Post,* December 16, 2004.

34. See "State Department Updates Terrorist List, Adds Jemaah Islamiya," cited in http://www.islamonline.net/English/News/2002–10/25/article81.shtml.

35. Ibid.

36. See *Straits Times* (Singapore), September 15, 2004.

37. See "ASEAN must set itself a terrorism free-zone," http://scoop.bangkpost.co.th/bkpost/2001/october2001/bp20011030/news/30Oct2001_opin...4/14/02

38. Muhammad Nafik, "Radicalism extends roots, becoming institutionalized," *Jakarta Post,* December 26, 2005.

39. Ibid.

40. Ibid.

41. Cited in Ibid.

42. See Maria Ressa, "Jihad rules in Islamic Schools," CNN Asia, February 26, 2004, cited in http://edition.cnn.com/2003/World/asiapf/southeast/09/04/indonesia.school.index.h....

43. See Amy Chew, "Starting Young: JI targets schools," CNN.com, February 26, 2004, cited in http://edition.cnn.com/2003/WORLD/asiapcf/southeast/08/11/indonesia.schools/.

44. Muhammad Nafik, "Radicalism extends roots, becoming institutionalized," *Jakarta Post,* December 26, 2005.

45. Cited in Ibid.

46. See Azyumardi Azra, *The Origins of Islamist Reformism in Southeast Asia* (Crownest, Australia: AAAS; Allen & Unwin; Honolulu: University of Hawaii Press; and Leiden: KITLV Press, 2004).

47. Ba'asyir, interview with author, November 2006.

48. Ibid.

49. Ibid.

50. Ibid.

51. Ibid

52. See "Aussie raids may hamper anti-terror fight: Jakarta," *Straits Times* (Singapore), November 1, 2002.

53. See "Outcry and the SM Factor," *Today* (Singapore), February 22, 2002.

54. John Howard argued that "it stands to reason that if you believe that somebody was going to launch an attack on your country, either of a conventional kind or a terrorist kind, and you had a capacity to stop it and there was no alternative other than to use that capacity, then, of course, you would have to use it." On taking preemptive action against terrorists in neighboring countries, Howard said, "Oh yes. I think any Australian prime minister would." See "Aussie 'act against terror' remark riles neighbours," *Straits Times* (Singapore), December 2, 2002.

55. In reaction, an Indonesian government spokesperson commented that "Australia cannot 'willy-nilly' flout international law" and the Malaysian defense minister warned that his country "will not allow any foreign military action in the country." See Ibid.

Bibliography

BOOKS

Abuza, Zachary. *Tentacles of Terror: Al-Qaeda's Southeast Asian Network.* Boulder, CO: Lynne Rienner Publishers, 2003.

———. *Political Islam and Violence in Indonesia.* New York: Routledge, 2006.

Al-Qaeda in Southeast Asia: The Case of the Ngruki Network in Indonesia. Jakarta and Brussels: International Crisis Group, 2002.

Alagappa, Muthiah. "Regionalism and Security: A Conceptual Investigation." In *Pacific Co-operation: Building Economic and Security Regimes in the Asia-Pacific Region,* edited by Andrew Mack and John Ravenhill. St. Leonards, NSW: Allen & Unwin, 1994.

Al-Anshari, Fauzan. *Saya Teroris? (Sebuah Pleidoi).* Jakarta: Penerbit Republika, 2002.

Armstrong, Karen. "Was It Inevitable?: Islam Through History." In *How Did This Happen?: Terrorism and the New War,* edited by James F. Hoge Jr. and Gideon Rose. New York: Public Affairs, 2001.

Ayubi, Nazih. *Political Islam: Religion and Politics in the Arab World.* London: Routledge, 1991.

Barber, Benjamin. *Jihad vs. McWorld.* New York: Times Books, 1995.

Barton, Greg. *Jemaah Islamiyah: Radical Islamism in Indonesia.* Singapore: Ridge Books, 2005.

Batley, Brek. *The Complexities of Dealing With Radical Islam in Southeast Asia: A Case Study of Jemaah Islamiyah.* Canberra Papers on Strategy and Defence, no. 149. Canberra, Australia: Strategic and Defence Studies Centre, Research School of Pacific and Asian Studies, Australian National University, 2003.

Bodansky, Yossef. *Bin Laden: The Man Who Declared War on America.* Rocklin, CA: Prima, 2001.

Brunn, Stanley. *11 September and Its Aftermath: The Geopolitics of Terror.* Portland, OR: Frank Cass, 2004.

Cady, L. C., and S. W. Simon, eds. *Religion and Conflict in South and Southeast Asia: Disrupting Violence.* London and New York: Routledge, 2007.

Chalk, Peter. *Non-Military Security and Global Order.* New York: St. Martin's Press, 2000.

Clutterbuck, Richard. *Terrorism in an Unstable World.* London and New York: Routledge, 1994.

Collins, Alan. *The Security Dilemmas of Southeast Asia.* Basingstoke, Hants.: Macmillan, 2000.

Combs, Cindy, and Martin Slann. "US & International Reaction to September 11, 2002, Day By Day." In *Encyclopedia of Terrorism,* edited by Cindy Combs and Martin Slann. New York: Facts on File, 2002.

Combs, Cindy C. *Terrorism in the Twenty-first Century.* 3rd edition. Upper Saddle River, NJ: Prentice Hall, 2003.

Conboy, Kenneth J. *The Second Front: Inside Asia's Most Dangerous Terrorist Network.* Jakarta: Equinox Pub., 2006.

Crouch, Harold A. *The Politics of Islam in Southeast Asia.* Bedford Park, S.A.: Flinders University, 1987.

Effendy, B. *Islam and the State in Indonesia.* Singapore: Institute of Southeast Asian Studies, 2003.

Esposito, John L. *Unholy War: Terror in the Name of Islam.* New York: Oxford University Press, 2002.

The Fight Against Terror: Singapore's National Security Strategy. Singapore: National Security Coordination Centre, 2004.

Forest, James J. F., ed. *Teaching Terror: Strategic and Tactical Learning in the Terrorist World.* Lanham, MD: Rowman & Littlefield, 2006.

————. *Global Terror: Unearthing the Support Networks that Allow Terrorism to Survive and Succeed.* New York: New York University Press, 2002.

————. *Terrorism in the Asia-Pacific: Threat and Response.* Singapore: Eastern University Press, 2003.

Hakim, Syed Shahid. "Islamic Terrorism: Reality or Myth?" In *Encyclopaedia of International Terrorism,* edited by Verinder Grover, vol. 2. New Delhi: Deep & Deep Publications, 2002.

Hefner, R. W. "The Sword Against the Crescent: religion and violence in Muslim Southeast Asia." In *Religion and Conflict in South and Southeast Asia: Disrupting Violence,* edited by L. C. Cady and S. W. Simon. London and New York: Routledge, 2007.

Hoffman, Bruce. *Inside Terrorism.* London: Victor Gollancz, 1998.

Huntington, Samuel P. *The Clash of Civilizations and the Remaking of World Order.* New York: Simon & Schuster, 1996.

Isaacson, Jason F., and Colin Rubenstein, eds. *Islam in Asia: Changing Political Realities.* New Brunswick, NJ: Transaction Publishers, 2002.

The Jemaah Islamiyah Arrests and the Threat of Terrorism. Singapore: Ministry of Home Affairs, 2003.

Jenkins, Brian. "International Terrorism." In *The Use of Force,* edited by Robert Art and Kenneth Waltz. 5th edition. Lanham, MD: Rowman & Littlefield, 1999.

————. *International Terrorism: A New Kind of Warfare.* Santa Monica, CA: Rand Corporation, 1974.

Johannen, Uwe, Alan Smith, and James Gomez, eds. *September 11 & Political Freedom: Asian Perspectives.* Singapore: Select Publishing in association with Friedrich Naumann Foundation, 2003.

Juergensmeyer, Mark. *Terror in the Mind of God.* Berkeley: University of California Press, 2000.

Kartha, Tara. "Transnational Terrorism and Radical Extremism." In *Encyclopaedia of International Terrorism,* edited by Verinder Grover, vol. 2. New Delhi: Deep & Deep Publications, 2002.

Kepel, Gilles. *The Revenge of God: The Resurgence of Islam, Christianity and Judaism in the Modern World.* London: Polity Press, 1994.

Kushner, Harvey. *Terrorism in America.* Springfield, IL: Charles C. Thomas, 1998.

Laqueur, Walter. *The New Terrorism: Fanaticism and the Arms of Mass Destruction.* New York: Oxford University Press, 1999.

Lesser, Ian O., Bruce Hoffman, John Arquilla, David F. Ronfeldt, Michele Zanini, and Brian Michael Jenkins. *Countering the New Terrorism.* Santa Monica, CA: Rand Corporation, 1999.

Malik, S.K. *The Quranic Concept of War.* Delhi: Adam Publishers, 1992.

McDonald, George R. *Political Terrorism in Southeast Asia and US Policy Issues: Case Studies of Thailand and Indonesia.* Monterey, CA: Naval Postgraduate School, 1998.

Morgenthau, Hans. *Scientific Man.* Chicago: University of Chicago Press, 1946.

Murphy, John. *State Support of International Terrorism.* London: Mansell Pub., 1989.

Neighbour, Sally. *In the Shadow of Swords: On the Trail of Terrorism from Afghanistan to Australia.* Sydney: HarperCollins Publishers, 2004.

Netanyahu, Benjamin. *Fighting Terrorism.* New York: Farrar Straus Giroux, 1995.

Onwudiwe, Ihekwoaba. *The Globalisation of Terrorism.* Aldershot, Hants.: Ashgate, 2001.

Ramakrishna, Kumar, *"Constructing" the Jemaah Islamiyah Terrorist: A Preliminary Inquiry.* IDSS Working Paper no. 71. Singapore: Institute of Defence and Strategic Studies, 2004.

Rashid, Ahmed. *Taliban: Militant Islam, Oil, and Fundamentalism in Central Asia.* New Haven, CT: Yale University Press, 2001.

Reeve, Simon. *The New Jackals: Ramzi Yousef, Osama bin Laden and the Future of Terrorism.* Boston, MA: Northeastern University Press, 1999.

Reich, Walter, ed. *Origins of Terrorism.* The Woodrow Wilson Center Press, 1998

Schmid, Alex. *Political Terrorism.* New Brunswick, NJ: Distributors, Transaction Books, 1983.

Simon, Sheldon. "Southeast Asia: Back to the Future." In *Confronting Terrorism in the Pursuit of Power, Strategic Asia 2004–05,* edited by Ashley J. Tellis and Michael Wills. Seattle, WA, and Washington, DC: National Bureau of Asian Research, 2004.

Singh, B. *ASEAN, Australia and the Management of the Jemaah Islamiyah Threat.* Canberra: Strategic and Defence Studies Centre, Australian National University, 2003.

Tapol, *Muslims on Trial.* London: Tapol, 1987.

Vas, Luis S.R. *Osama bin Laden: King of Terror or Saviour of Islam?* New Delhi: Pustak Mahal, 2001.

White, Jonathan. *Terrorism: An Introduction.* Pacific Grove, CA: Brooks/Cole Pub. Co., 1991.

Yunanto, S., et. al. *Militant Islamic Movements in Indonesia and Southeast Asia.* Jakarta: Friedrich-Ebert-Stiftung, Ridep Institute, 2003.

JOURNAL AND MAGAZINE ARTICLES

Balakrishnan, K.S. "Terrorism in the ASEAN Region." *Asian Defence and Diplomacy* 8, no. 6 (June 2001).

Banlaoi, Rommel C. "Maritime Terrorism in Southeast Asia." *Naval War College Review* 58, no. 4 (October 1, 2005).

Brimley, Shawn. "Tentacles of *Jihad*: Transnational Support Networks." *Parameters* 36, no. 2 (July 1, 2006).

Buzan, Barry. "The Southeast Asian Security Complex." *Contemporary Southeast Asia* 10, no. 1 (June 1988).

Capie, David. "Between a Hegemon and a Hard Place: The 'War on Terror' and Southeast Asian-US Relations." *Pacific Review* 17, no. 2 (June 2004): 223–48.

"Confessions of an *Al-Qaeda* Terrorist." *Time,* September 23, 2002.

Cotton, James. "Southeast Asia after 11 September." *Terrorism and Political Violence* 15, no. 1 (Spring 2003): 148–70.

Dalpino, Catharin E. "Second Front, Second Time Counter-Terrorism and US Policy toward Southeast Asia." *Cambridge Review of International Affairs* 15, no. 2 (2002).

Davies, Philip. "United We Stand." *Asian Defence and Diplomacy* 8, no. 12 (December 2001).

Desker, Barry. "Islam and Society in Southeast Asia After September 11." Singapore: Institute of Defence and Strategic Studies, 33 (September 2002).

———. "Islam in Southeast Asia: The Challenge of Radical Interpretations." *Cambridge Review of International Affairs* 16, no. 3 (October 2003).

Desker, Barry, and Kumar Ramakrishna. "Forging an Indirect Strategy in Southeast Asia." *Washington Quarterly* 25, no. 2 (2002).

Dhume, Sadanand. "Terror's Web." *Far Eastern Economic Review,* December 19, 2002.

Emmerson, Donald. "Southeast Asia: What's in a Name?" *Journal of Southeast Asian Studies* 15, no. 1 (March 1984).

Gershman, John. "Is Southeast Asia the Second Front?" *Foreign Affairs* 81, no. 4 (July–August 2002).

Hamilton-Hart, Natasha. "Terrorism in Southeast Asia: Expert Analysis, Myopia and Fantasy." *Pacific Review* 18, no. 3 (September 2005): 303–25.

"Indonesian Security and Countering Terrorism in Southeast Asia." *Strategic Survey* 103, no. 1 (May 2003): 219–36.

"Interview: Lee Kuan Yew—What Went Wrong?" *Far Eastern Economic Review,* December 12, 2002.

International Crisis Group. "Indonesia Backgrounder: How the *Jemaah Islamiyah* Terrorist Network Operates." ICG Asia Report No. 43, December 11, 2002.

"Islam Mengutuk Islam Dituduh," *Majalah Islam Sabili* 28, no. 3 (August 28, 2003).

Jones, David Martin, Michael L. R. Smith, and Mark Weeding. "Looking for the Pattern: Al Qaeda in Southeast Asia—The Genealogy of a Terror Network." *Studies in Conflict and Terrorism* 26, no. 6 (November–December 2003): 443–57.

Jones, Sidney. "The Changing Nature of Jemaah Islamiyah." *Australian Journal of International Affairs.* 59, no. 2 (June 2005): 169–78.

Kadir, Suzaina. "Mapping Muslim Politics in Southeast Asia after September 11." *Pacific Review* 17, no. 2 (June 2004): 199–222.

Karniol, Robert. "A Total Defence." *Jane's Defence Weekly* 38, no. 9 (August 28, 2002).

Koschade, Stuart. "A Social Network Analysis of Jemaah Islamiyah: The Applications to Counterterrorism and Intelligence." *Studies in Conflict and Terrorism* 29, no. 6 (September 2006): 559–75.

Krueger, Alan, and Jitka Maleckova. "Education, Poverty, Political Violence and Terrorism: Is There a Causal Connection?" National Bureau of Economic Research, Working Paper 9074, July 2002.

Leheny, David. "Terrorism, Social Movements, and International Security: How Al Qaeda Affects Southeast Asia." *Japanese Journal of Political Science* 6, no. 1 (2005): 87–109.

Mancall, Mark. "The Roots and Societal Impact of Islam in Southeast Asia." *Stanford Journal of East Asian Affairs* 2 (Spring 2002).

Ogilvie-White, Tanya. "Non-Proliferation and Counter-Terrorism Cooperation in Southeast Asia Meeting: Global Obligations through Regional Security Architectures." *Contemporary Southeast Asia* 28, no. 1 (April 1, 2006).

PoKempner, Dinah. "The New Non-State Actors in International Humanitarian Law." *George Washington International Law Review* 38, no. 3 (May 30, 2006).

Rabasa, Angel. "Moderates, Radicals and Terrorists," unpublished paper, RANDRand Corporation, October 2002.

———. "Chapter 5: Terrorist Networks in Southeast Asia." *Adelphi Papers* 43, no. 358 (July 20, 2003): 59–66.

Ramakrishna, Kumar. "911, American Praetorian Unilateralism and the Impact on State-Society Relations in Southeast Asia." Singapore: Institute of Defence and Strategic Studies 26 (June 2002).

Raymond, Catherine Zara. "Maritime Terrorism in Southeast Asia: A Risk Assessment." *Terrorism and Political Violence* 18, no. 2 (Summer 2006): 239–57.

Rosand, Eric. "The Security Council's Efforts to Monitor the Implementation of Al Qaeda Taliban Sanctions." *American Journal of International Law* 98, no. 4 (October 2004): 745–63.

Singh, Bilveer. "The Challenge of Militant Islam and Terrorism in Indonesia." *Australian Journal of International Affairs* 58, no. 1 (March 2004): 47–68.

Singh, Daljit. "The Post–September 11 Geostrategic Landscape and Southeast Asian Response to the Threat of Terrorism." *Trends in Southeast Asia,* no. 9. Singapore: Institute of Southeast Asian Studies, September 2002.

Smith, Anthony. "What the Recent Terror Attacks Mean for Indonesia." *Trends in Southeast Asia,* No.14. Singapore: Institute of Southeast Asian Studies, November 2001.

———. "The Politics of Negotiating the Terrorist Problem in Indonesia." *Studies in Conflict and Terrorism* 28, no. 1 (January–February 2005): 33–44.

Swanstrom, Niklas, and Emma Bjornehed. "Conflict Resolution of Terrorists Conflicts in Southeast Asia." *Terrorism and Political Violence* 16, no. 2 (Summer 2004): 328–49.

Tan, Andrew. "The Emergence of Postmodern Terrorism and Its Implications for Southeast Asia." Singapore: Institute of Defence and Strategic Studies, November 2001.

———. "Terrorism in Singapore Threat and Implications." *Contemporary Security Policy* 23, no. 3 (December 2002): 1–18.

———. "Southeast Asia as the 'Second Front' in the War Against Terrorism: Evaluating the Threat and Responses." *Terrorism and Political Violence* 15, no. 2 (Summer 2003): 112–38.

Ungerer, Carl. "Australia's Policy Response to Terrorism in Southeast Asia." *Global Change, Peace & Security* 18, no. 3 (October 2006).

Van Bruinessen, Martin. "Genealogies of Islamic Radicalism in post-Suharto Indonesia." *South East Asia Research* 10, no. 2 (2002).

Väyrynen, Raimo. "Regional Conflict Formations." *Journal of Peace Research* 21 (April 1984).

Wain, Barry. "One Year On—Unfriendly Fire." *Far Eastern Economic Review,* September 12, 2002.

Wanandi, Jusuf. "A Global Coalition against International Terrorism." *International Security* 26, no. 4 (Spring 2002).

"Weak Regionalism in Southeast Asia." *Strategic Survey* 104, no. 1 (May 2004): 254–67.

Wright-Neville, David. "Dangerous Dynamics: Activists, Militants and Terrorists in Southeast Asia." *Pacific Review* 17, no. 1 (March 2004): 27–46.

NEWSPAPER ARTICLES

"Abu Sayyaf Chief, Jemaah Islamiyah Militants Avoid Philippine Military." *BBC Monitoring Asia Pacific,* August 29, 2006.

Abuza, Zachary. "Killer Network Spreads." *Australian,* October 9, 2006.

"AFPs Hunt vs Elusive Janjalani, JI Terrorist Bombers Continues." *Philippines News Agency,* October 29, 2006.

"Al Qaeda Type Attacks Are Biggest Worry of World's Police Interpol." *Agence France Presse,* March 16, 2004.

"Allegations of Terror Targets in Singapore Rattle Region." *Asian Wall Street Journal,* January 8, 2002.

"Analysis—Lack of Funds, Red Tape Hurt Manila's Terror Fight." *Reuters News,* March 3, 2005.

"Analysis/Terrorism in Southeast Asia: Bounty Turns Up Heat on JI Mystery Man." *Bangkok Post,* October 10, 2005.

"Anger Over Early Release of Bali Bomb Prisoners." *Guardian Unlimited,* October 24, 2006.

"AP ENTERPRISE: Threat of International Terrorism Looms as 1,000 Die in Thailand's Muslim Insurgency." *Associated Press Newswires,* September 19, 2005.

"ASEAN Pledges Cooperation Against Terrorism." *Asian Wall Street Journal,* November 5, 2001.

"ASEAN Talks Focus on Anti-Terror Measures." *Straits Times* (Singapore), February 22, 2002.

"Asia-Pacific Making 'Significant Progress' in Fighting Terrorism—Southeast Asia Still 'A Majorfront,' State Department Report Says." *State Department Press Releases And Documents,* April 28, 2006.

"Asian Meeting to Boost Anti-Terror Fight." *Agence France Presse,* April 19, 2006.

"Australia Announces Across-The-Board Tax Cuts in Big Surplus Budget." *Agence France Presse,* May 9, 2006.

"Australia, Philippines Say Jemaah Islamiyah Remains Biggest Regional Terror Threat." *Associated Press Newswires,* June 28, 2006.

"Australian Intelligence Hunts Jemaah Islamiyah Sleeper Cells." *Kyodo News,* February 11, 2003.

"Authorities Heighten Pursuit Operation vs ASG, JI." *Philippines News Agency,* October 26, 2006.

"Avoid Indonesia, Malaysians Urged." *Straits Times* (Singapore), October 2, 2001.

"Ba'asyir Blessed Bali Bombing—Da'i." *Jakarta Post,* January 29, 2003.

"Bali Blasts—Bomber's Show and Tell." *Straits Times* (Singapore), February 12, 2003.

"Bali Bombings Wake-up Call for Indonesian Muslims." *Jakarta Post,* December 11, 2002.

Baudrillard, Jean. "The Spirit of Terrorism." *Le Monde,* November 2, 2001.

"Behind the Riots in Phnom Penh." *Nation,* February 1, 2003.

"Bilateral Issues not Zero-sum Game." *Business Times,* March 15, 2002.

Boey, David. "Motive Behind Misreading of Book on SAF." *Straits Times* (Singapore), February 14, 2003.

"Bomb Blasts Blamed on JI." *Philippine Daily Inquirer,* October 19, 2006.

"Bomb Victims Despair as Terrorists Freed." *Advertiser,* November 17, 2006.

Borsuk, Richard. "Even Safe Haven Singapore Isn't Immune from Terrorism." *Asian Wall Street Journal,* January 28, 2002.

"Brunei Safe from Jemaah Islamiyah Threat—Analyst." *BBC Monitoring Asia Pacific,* May 5, 2005.

"Bush Faces Rising Anti-U.S. Sentiment in Predominantly Muslim Indonesia." *Associated Press Newswires,* November 17, 2006.

"Call for Meeting of ASEAN Five on Anti-Terror Plans." *Straits Times* (Singapore), November 14, 2001.

"The Chilling Jemaah Islamiyah Goal." *New Sunday Times (New Straits Times),* January 19, 2003.

"Comment/Fighting Islamic Terrorism: In Southeast Asia, Moderation Is the Key." *Bangkok Post,* October 4, 2005.

"Cooperation Vital for Security Now." *Straits Times* (Singapore), February 25, 2002.

"Davao City Mayor Tags Jemaah Islamiyah for Sasa Wharf Blast." *BBC Monitoring Asia Pacific,* April 7, 2003.

Desker, Barry. "After Bali, Will Indonesia Act?" *Straits Times* (Singapore), October 31, 2002.

Dillon, Dana, and Paolo Pasicolan. "Security Matters: Fighting Terror in Southeast Asia." *Asian Wall Street Journal,* January 16, 2002.

———. "Southeast Asia and the War Against Terrorism." Washington, DC: The Heritage Foundation Backgrounder, No. 1496, October 23, 2001.

"DJ Philippine Arroyo: Asean May Adopt Anti-Terror Convention." *Dow Jones Commodities Service,* October 26, 2006.

"Don't Let the Race and Religion Derail Malaysia-Singapore Ties." *Straits Times* (Singapore), February 11, 2002.

"Dulmatin's Wife Says Jemaah Has RP in Crosshairs." *Manila Times,* October 8, 2006.

"Even Safe Haven Singapore Isn't Immune from Terrorism." *Asian Wall Street Journal,* January 16, 2002.

"5,700 US Marines, Sailors Arriving for Bilateral Exercises—Thousands of Japan-Based United States Marines and Sailors Will Arrive in Manila This Month to Begin the Two-Week Bilateral Exercise with the Armed Forces of the Philippines (AFP) from Oct. 16–31, the US Embassy Bared Yesterday." *Manila Bulletin,* October 4, 2006.

"Focus/Religion: A Gentler Islam in a Globalised World." *Bangkok Post,* August 30, 2006.

From Nice Boys to Terrorists; How Western Youths Are Recruited and Trained in Terrorism." *Today,* February 10, 2006.

"GIs Target Muslim Youth for Anti-Terror PR Drive." *Philippine Daily Inquirer,* October 28, 2006.

"Group Linked to Jemaah Islamiyah Planning Terror Attack in Indonesia." *Associated Press Newswires,* March 23, 2003.

"Gulf News: Army Captures Abu Sayyaf Leader." *Gulf News,* October 28, 2006.

"Gulf News: Jemaah-Trained Militant Arrested in the South." *Gulf News,* November 14, 2006.

Gunaratna, Rohan. "Jane's Intelligence Review." *Straits Times* (Singapore), January 4, 2002.

"Hambali 'No Longer Useful' to Indonesia." *Australian,* October 10, 2006.

Hoong, Chua Lee. "US Fears of Terror Here Exaggerated." *Straits Times* (Singapore), January 10, 2002.

"Indonesia Attacks US Refusal to Grant Access to Terror Suspect." *Agence France Presse,* September 29, 2006.

"Indonesia Charges Jemaah Islamiyah Suspect with Immigration Violations." *BBC Monitoring Asia Pacific,* February 10, 2003.

"Indonesia Makes Progress Against Terrorism, but Threat Remains." *Voice of America Press Releases and Documents,* October 11, 2006.

"Indonesia Marks 2002 Bali Bombing Anniversary." *Agence France Presse,* October 12, 2006.

"Indonesia Militant Jailed for 2002 Bali Bombings Freed." *Dow Jones International News,* August 17, 2006.

"Indonesia Nabs Suspected Couriers for Top Terrorist Fugitive: Report." *Agence France Presse,* November 1, 2006.

"Indonesia Suspect Not Linked to Al-Qaida." *Associated Press Newswires,* November 13, 2006.

"Indonesia Winning Plaudits in Post-9/11 Terrorism Battle." *Agence France Presse,* September 5, 2006.

"Indonesian Jailed for Eight Years Over 2005 Bali Bombings." *Agence France Presse,* September 5, 2006.

"Indonesian Police Arrest Jemaah Islamiyah's Singapore Leader." *Asian Political News,* February 3, 2003.

"Indonesian Police: Restaurant Bomber Had Mental Disorder." *Dow Jones International News,* November 15, 2006.

"Indonesian Prosecutors Seek 20-year Sentence for Suspected Islamic Militant." *Associated Press Newswires,* November 1, 2006.

"Indonesia Risk: Political Stability Risk." *Economist Intelligence Unit,* January 12, 2006.

"An Iraq in the Making in Southern Philippines." *Business Times,* September 26, 2006.

"Islamic Militants Still on the Run In Sulu, Says AFP." *Manila Times,* November 1, 2006.

"Jakarta Helping Anti-Terrorism Fight." *Straits Times* (Singapore), January 9, 2002.

"Jakarta Raps KL Plan to Axe Workers." *Straits Times* (Singapore), January 29, 2002.

"Jakarta—Singapore Is Too Authoritarian to Understand Us." *Straits Times* (Singapore), February 25, 2002.

"Japan, Asean Set Up Fund to Fight Terror, Aid Development." *Dow Jones International News,* March 27, 2006.

"Japan, ASEAN to Hold Antiterror Talks Next Week." *Jiji Press English News Service,* June 23, 2006.

"Jemaah Islamiyah: Al-Qaeda's Southeast Asian Branch?" *Agence France Presse,* April 23, 2003.

"Jemaah Islamiyah—Bali and Beyond." *Guardian,* April 24, 2003.

"Jemaah Islamiyah Created as Al-Qaeda's Pan-Asian Outfit." *Straits Times* (Singapore), January 25, 2002.

"Jemaah Islamiyah Planning Assassinations." *Associated Press Newswires,* August 5, 2004.

"Jemaah Islamiyah Said Grooming Malaysian, Singaporean Militants in Pakistan." *BBC Monitoring Asia Pacific,* February 2, 2006.

"JI White Paper's Suggestion on Self-Policing Raises Concerns." *Channelnewsasia,* January 10, 2003.

"Little Room for Error in the War Against Terror." *Straits Times* (Singapore), November 30, 2002.

"A Long and Incremental Struggle Against Islamic Terrorists." *Australian,* May 12, 2006.

"Malaysia Says Jemaah Islamiyah Threat 'Under Control'." *Agence France Presse,* March 21, 2003.

"Malaysia Seizes Suspected Jemaah Islamiyah Arms—Report." *Dow Jones International News,* March 17, 2003.

"Malaysian Expert Says US Hindering Regional Counter-Terror Effort." *BBC Monitoring Asia Pacific,* February 22, 2005.

"Manila: Jemaah Islamiyah-Local Militants Nexus Largely Cut." *Dow Jones International News,* September 14, 2004.

"Media-Indonesia: Journalism as Jihad Against Terrorism." *Inter Press Service,* September 26, 2006.

"Megawati in the Middle." *Washington Post,* December 12, 2002.

Meo, Nick. "Freed Bashir Fans the Flames of Terror Bali Bombing Victims Struggle to Come to Terms with Release of the Suspected Mastermind." *South China Morning Post,* June 17, 2006.

"Military Insiders Cold-Shoulder Terrorist Agency." *Jakarta Post,* October 1, 2001.

"New Picture Emerges of Militant Network in Southeast Asia—Jemaah Islamiyah Aided Al Qaeda, But Has Own Agenda: Islamic State—Area Frictions Hurt Antiterror Steps." *Asian Wall Street Journal,* August 9, 2002.

"The New Strategic Base of Jemaah Islamiyah." *Newsbreak,* April 13, 2005.

"No Let-up in Fight Against Terrorism." *Straits Times* (Singapore), January 30, 2002.

"Non-Partisan Think Tank Releases New Study: Beyond the Campaign: The Future of Countering Terrorism." *U.S. Newswire,* March 4, 2004.

"Norian Receives Distinguished Service Award." *Bernama,* January 24, 2003.

"Officials: Al-Qaida, Jemaah Islamiyah Funded Terror Operations in Philippines." *Associated Press Newswires,* May 6, 2004.

"One Killed, 4 Wounded in Army, Abu Sayyaf Clashes in Sulu." *Philippines News Agency,* August 24, 2006.

"Palace Seeks Legislators' Help on Terror Bill." *Manila Standard,* November 4, 2006.

"PAS Should Openly Condemn Terrorism—Najib." *Bernama Daily Malaysian News,* February 10, 2003.

"Philippine Bombing Suspicions Fall on Indonesian Militant." *Dow Jones International News,* October 12, 2006.

"Philippine Daily Views Statement on MILF-Jemaah Islamiyah Links." *BBC Monitoring Asia Pacific,* September 29, 2004.

"Philippine Islamic Convert Group Should Be Banned: Expert." *Agence France Presse,* September 28, 2006.

"Philippine Military Braces for Post-Ramadan Attacks." *BBC Monitoring Asia Pacific,* October 11, 2006.

"Philippine Paper Says Over 300 Jemaah Islamiyah Members in Country." *BBC Monitoring Asia Pacific,* April 11, 2003.

"Philippine Police Hold Suspected Terrorist-Trained Bomber." *Dow Jones International News,* November 13, 2006.

"Philippines Authorizes Civilian Militia; Rights Activists Warn of a Return to the Violence of the Marcos Era." *International Herald Tribune,* October 30, 2006.

"Philippines Deploys More Troops in Hunt for Bali Bomb Suspects." *Agence France Presse,* October 20, 2006.

"Philippines Fears Lebanon War Could Revive Terrorism in Southeast Asia." *Agence France Presse,* August 11, 2006.

"PNP Eyes Volunteers to Help Fight Terrorists." *Manila Times,* October 14, 2006.

"Police Capture Alleged Jemaah Islamiyah Bomb Expert in Southern Philippines." *BBC Monitoring Asia Pacific,* November 14, 2006.

"Police Hunt Militants in Southern Philippines." *Agence France Presse,* November 14, 2006.

"Politics—Al Faruq's Death Does Not Lessen Terrorist Threat, Says Offcial." *LKBN ANTARA,* September 27, 2006.

"Powerful Explosion Rocks Philippine Police Camp Injuring Three." *Agence France Presse,* October 15, 2006.

Ramakrishna, Kumar. "Win Hearts and Minds of Muslims to Fight Terror." *Straits Times* (Singapore), October 4, 2001.

"Reinventing ASEAN." *Jakarta Post,* November 5, 2001.

"Renewed Pressure on Indonesia to Outlaw Jemaah Islamiyah." *Dow Jones International News,* October 4, 2005.

"Research Council Hits Back at Critics." *Australian,* September 16, 2006.

"Responding Effectively to Terrorism." *New Straits Times* (Singapore), August 5, 2006.

"RI Slams Lee over Terrorist Remarks." *Jakarta Post,* February 21, 2002.

"Portrait of a Radical Network in Asia—Jemaah Islamiyah Looms as Cohesive Islamic Group Dedicated to Violence." *Wall Street Journal,* August 13, 2002.

"Regional Perspective—The Thai Jemaah Islamiyah Is Unlike Others." *Nation,* January 6, 2003.

"Region's War on Terrorism Suffers from Lack of Trust." *South China Morning Post,* January 22, 2003.

"Report Cites Emergence of New Islamic Militia in Indonesia." *New York Times,* February 4, 2004.

"Report: Jemaah Islamiyah Has Territorial Cells Across Much of Southeast Asia." *Associated Press Newswires,* November 8, 2002.

"SE Asian Muslims Turn to Radicals." *Australian,* September 29, 2005.

"Send Holy Warriors to Israel, Says Bashir." *Today,* July 4, 2006.

"Singapore at a Turning Point, with Formidable Challenges." *Straits Times* (Singapore), March 26, 2002.

"Singapore a Free Port But Will Give No Quarter to Terrorism." *Straits Times* (Singapore), October 12, 2001.

"Singapore Brings JI Terror Suspect Back from Afghanistan: Report." *Agence France Presse,* January 26, 2003.

"Singapore Details Anti-terrorism Actions to UN." *Straits Times* (Singapore), January 9, 2002.

"Singapore Govt: Jemaah Islamiyah Targeted American School." *Dow Jones International News,* January 9, 2003.

"Singapore Govt. Publishes Report on Jemaah Islamiyah." *Dow Jones International News,* January 10, 2003.

"Singapore, Jakarta Can Move on Fighting Terror." *Straits Times* (Singapore), February 28, 2002.

"Singapore, Malaysia Turn Away More Than 300 Indonesians." *Asian Wall Street Journal,* February 25, 2002.

"Singapore Mosque Urges Support for White Paper on Jemaah Islamiyah." *BBC Monitoring Asia Pacific,* January 14, 2003.

"Singapore Releases 5 Linked to Jemaah Islamiyah Militant Group." *Associated Press Newswires,* July 1, 2006.

"Singapore's Slyness in Exploiting the Agreement." *Berita Harian Malaysia,* February 7, 2003.

"Singapore Stresses Biometric Passport's Role." *Xinhua News Agency,* April 12, 2006.

"Singaporean Jemaah Islamiyah Leader Detained Under Internal Security Act." *BBC Monitoring Asia Pacific,* February 7, 2006.

"6 Suspected Bombers on the Run with Dulmatin—The Detained Wife of a Top Indonesian Terror Suspect Hiding in the Southern Philippines Has Identified Six Other Asian Militants Allegedly on the Run with Her Husband, a Police Official Said on Tuesday." *Manila Bulletin,* November 16, 2006.

"SM Says Terrorist Penetration of Singapore Inevitable." *Straits Times* (Singapore), February 10, 2002.

"Soldiers in Western Mindanao to Get Training from Australians." *BusinessWorld,* September 15, 2006.

"Southeast Asia Prefers Low Profile Military Cooperation with US." *Agence France Presse,* June 13, 2006.

"Special Report." *Observer,* November 12, 2006.

"S'pore's Anti-Terror Strategy: A Network to Fight a Network." *Straits Times* (Singapore), November 25, 2002.

"Spotlight Turns on Radical Cleric." *BBC,* October 15, 2002

"Survey Shows Filipinos More Positive Towards Muslims." *Agence France Presse,* October 25, 2006.

"Terror May Shadow Us 'For a Generation'." *Australian,* May 12, 2006.

"Terror Suspect's Wife Names Others Hiding in Philippines." *Dow Jones International News,* November 14, 2006.

"Terror Warning: Govt 'Blind to JI Link'." *Nation,* March 7, 2005.

"Terrorism Debate and Mahathir's Battle." *Straits Times* (Singapore), October 22, 2001.

"Terrorism Scorecard: Five Years After 9/11 the Terror Networks Have Not Been Eliminated and Although Key Figures Have Been Captured or Killed a New Generation Has Taken Their Place." *Middle East,* October 1, 2006.

"Terrorism Shakes Southeast Asia, But Strengthens ASEAN." *Jakarta Post,* December 27, 2002.

"A Terrorist Strike in Bali, Choreographed for the Bombers on a Plotter's Computer." *New York Times,* July 3, 2006.

Teo, Eric. "The Elusive Handshake." *Today,* February 14, 2003.

"Threat of Terrorism Remains Strong in SE Asia." *Voice of America Press Releases and Documents,* December 20, 2003.

"Thai Experts Warn of Foreign Terror Links in S Thailand." *Dow Jones International News,* March 7, 2005.

"Thailand: Malay-Muslim Insurgency Gaining Ground." *Inter Press Service,* August 3, 2006.

"Thailand: Talks Set with Rebel Leaders—But From Which Decade?" *Inter Press Service,* October 13, 2006.

"Thinking Anti-Terrorism." *Asia Inc,* April 1, 2004.

"Top UN Counterterrorism Official Urges South East Asia to Cut Terrorist Funds." *BBC Monitoring Asia Pacific,* April 21, 2006.

"Trial Starts of Alleged Terror Group Leader Bashir." *Agence France Presse,* April 23, 2003.

"200 Kilos of Bomb-Making Component Seized in Zambo Wharf." *Philippines News Agency,* October 18, 2006.

"Two Members of Jemaah Islamiyah in Malaysia Detained." *Associated Press Newswires,* January 25, 2003.

"2 Militants Jailed for 2002 Bali Bombing Freed as Indonesians Mark Islamic Holiday." *Associated Press Newswires,* October 24, 2006.

"UN Panel Urges S.E. Asia to Choke Terrorist Funds." *Reuters News,* April 20, 2006.

"Unilateral Actions Not Effective in Fighting Terrorism." *Jakarta Post,* December 12, 2002.

"The United States and Southeast Asia: Developments, Trends, and Policy Choices." *States News Service,* September 21, 2005.

"UK Warns RP: Terror Plot in Final Stages." *Philippine Daily Inquirer,* October 18, 2006.

"US, Asian Leaders Hail Hambali Arrest as Breakthrough in War on Terror." *Agence France Presse,* August 15, 2003.

"U.S. Expanding Outreach to Islamic Publics, State's Huhtala Says - Deputy Assistant Secretary Discusses Islam in Southeast Asia." *State Department Press Releases And Documents,* February 15, 2005.

"U.S. Fights Terror on Humanitarian Front." *International Herald Tribune,* July 6, 2006.

"US Intelligence Guides Hunters of Abu Sayyaf." *Manila Times,* August 4, 2006.

"U.S. Intelligence: Jemaah Islamiyah Could Expand Beyond Southeast Asia." *Associated Press Newswires,* September 28, 2006.

Wanandi, Jusuf. "Jakarta Needs to Be More Hands-on on Terrorism Issue." *Straits Times* (Singapore), December 11, 2001.

Wanandi, Jusuf, and Simon Tay. "Indonesia and Singapore—Reaching Across the Divide." *Straits Times* (Singapore), October 22, 2001.

"We Must Remind Ourselves We are Singaporeans." *Straits Times* (Singapore), October 1, 2001.

Wechsler, Maxmilian. "An Invisible Army: The Few 'Successes' in the War on Terror Haven't Done Anything to Thin the Ranks of Terrorist Organisations; In Fact They Are Growing Stronger Everyday." *Bangkok Post,* August 6, 2006.

———. "Closing the Net on Terror: Security Specialists Believe the Thai Intelligence Community Is Catching Up with the Leaders of the Southern Insurgency and Their Current Operations Are Driven Partly by Desperation." *Bangkok Post,* May 28, 2006.

———. "Threat Is Evolving: The Consensus of Security Analysts and Other Experts Is that Unless the US and Its Allies Leave Iraq, Terrorist Activities Will Continue and Perhaps Even Increase This Year All Over the World." *Bangkok Post,* May 21, 2006.

"White Paper Sheds Light on Singapore JI Indoctrination Process." *Channelnewsasia,* January 9, 2003.

CONFERENCE PAPERS

Azra, Azyumardi. "The Megawati Presidency: Challenge of Political Islam." Paper delivered at the "Joint Public Forum on Indonesia: The First 100 Days of President Megawati."

organized by the Institute of Southeast Asian Studies (ISEAS) and the Centre for Strategic and International Studies (CSIS), November 1, 2001, Singapore.

Chaidar, Al. "Terrorism and Islamic Fundamentalism: The *Darul Islam*'s Responses Towards Indonesian Democracy, 1949–1982." Paper presented at a conference on regional workshop on "Contemporary Islamic Movements in Southeast Asia: Militancy, Separatism, Terrorism and Democratisation Process," organized by The RIDEP Institute/ FES, Bogor, Indonesia, October 28–31, 2002.

Singh, Bilveer. "Singapore's Policy Towards Islamic Militant Groups: A Perspective." Paper presented at a conference on regional workshop on "Contemporary Islamic Movements in Southeast Asia: Militancy, Separatism, Terrorism and Democratisation Process," organised by The RIDEP Institute/FES, Bogor, Indonesia, October 28–31, 2002.

PRIMARY SOURCES

2001 ASEAN Declaration on Joint Action to Counter Terrorism. http://www.mfa.gov.sg/unsc/ AnnexF.doc.

ASEAN Secretariat. http://www.aseansec.org.

ASEAN Secretariat. "ASEAN Police to Set Up Anti-Terrorism Task Force." January 22, 2003.

ASEAN Bangkok Declaration. http://www.aseansec.org/history/leader67.htm.

Badawi, Abdullah Ahmad. Keynote address at the 13th Asia-Pacific Roundtable, May 30, 1999.

Blair, Dennis. "Taking Back Our World from Osama bin Laden." Editorial released by the Office of the U.S. Commander-in-Chief, Pacific Command (CINCPAC), October 23, 2001.

Bush, George W. Address to a Joint Session of Congress and the American People, September 20, 2001.

Clamor, Ma. Concepcion B., Assistant Director General of the Philippines' National Intelligence Coordinating Agency. "Terrorism and Southeast Asia: A Philippine Perspective." Paper presented at a conference in Honolulu in May 2002.

Committee on House International Relations Subcommittee on International Terrorism, Nonproliferation and Human Rights. *Terrorism in Asia and the Pacific—Dr. Zachary Abuza.*

Government of Singapore. White Paper, "The Jemaah Islamiyah Arrests and the Threat of Terrorism." Singapore: Ministry of Home Affairs, 2003.

Human Rights Watch. "Indonesia: The Violence in Ambon." March 1999.

Jayakumar, S. Statement in Parliament of Singapore, January 25, 2003.

Laskar Jihad. (http://www.laskarjihad.or.id).

Lee Kuan Yew. "The East Asian Strategic Balance After 9/11." Address at the 1st International Institute for Strategic Studies Asia Security Conference, May 31, 2002.

Ministry of Home Affairs. *The Jemaah Islamiyah Arrests and the Threat of Terrorism: White Paper.* Singapore: Ministry of Home Affairs, 2003.

Ministry of Foreign Affairs, Indonesia. http://www.dfa-deplu.go.id.

Ministry of Foreign Affairs, Singapore. Letter to the United Nations Security Council, "Request for the Addition of *Jemaah Islamiyah* to the List of Terrorists Maintained by the United Nations."

Mohamad, Mahathir. "Islam, Terrorism and Malaysia's Response." Address at the Asia Society, New York, February 4, 2002.

Partai Persatuan Pembangunan (PPP). http://www.ppp.or.id.

Parti Islam SeMalaysia (PAS). http://www.parti-pas.org.

United Nations, Policy Working Group on the United Nations and Terrorism. "Report of the Policy Working Group on the United Nations and Terrorism." http://www.un.org/terrorism/a57273.doc.

U.S. Department of State, Bureau of Consular Affairs. "Southeast Public Announcement." http://travel.state.gov/seasia_announce.html.

Wilson, Chris. Australia's Foreign Affairs, Defence and Trade Group, "Indonesia and Transnational Terrorism." *Parliament of Australia,* October 11, 2001.

Wong Kan Seng, BBC Interview, "Extent of Threat by JI to Singapore Security." British Broadcasting Corporation, 24 September 2002.

Index